The Song of the Sirens

Greek Studies: Interdisciplinary Approaches
General Editor: Gregory Nagy, Harvard University
Assistant Editor: Timothy Power, Harvard University

On the front cover: A calendar frieze representing the Athenian months, reused in the Byzantine Church of the Little Metropolis in Athens. The cross is superimposed, obliterating Taurus of the Zodiac. The choice of this frieze for books in *Greek Studies: Interdisciplinary Approaches* reflects this series' emphasis on the blending of the diverse heritages—Near Eastern, Classical, and Christian—in the Greek tradition. Drawing by Laurie Kain Hart, based on a photograph. Recent titles in the series are:

The Shield of Achilles and the Poetics of Ekphrasis, Andrew Sprague Becker,
  Virginia Polytechnic Institute
The Blinded Eye: Thucydides and the New Written Word, Gregory Crane, Tufts
  University
The Wrath of Athena: Gods and Men in the Odyssey, Jenny Strauss Clay,
  University of Virginia
Talking Trojan: Speech and Community in the Iliad, Hilary Mackie, Rice
  University
Poet and Audience in the Argonautica *of Apollonius*, Robert V. Albis,
  The Hotchkiss School
Theatrical Space and Historical Place in Sophocles' Oedipus at Colonus,
  Lowell Edmunds, Rutgers University
*Choruses of Young Women in Ancient Greece: Their Morphology,
  Religious Role, and Social Function*, Claude Calame, University of
  Lausanne, Switzerland; translated by Derek Collins and Jane Orion
Eurykleia and Her Successors: Female Figures of Authority in Greek Poetics,
  Helen Pournara Karydas, Boston Latin School and Harvard University
Speech in Speech: Studies in Incorporated Oratio Recta *in Attic Drama and
  Oratory*, Victor Bers, Yale University
*Aegean Strategies: Studies of Culture and Environment on the European
  Fringe*, P. Nick Kardulias, College of Wooster and Mark T. Shutes,
  Youngstown State University
Aglaia: The poetry of Alcman, Sappho, Pindar, Bacchylides, and Corinna,
  Charles Segal, Harvard University

The Song of the Sirens

Essays on Homer

PIETRO PUCCI

ROWMAN & LITTLEFIELD PUBLISHERS, INC.
Lanham • Boulder • New York • Oxford

ROWMAN & LITTLEFIELD PUBLISHERS, INC.

Published in the United States of America
by Rowman & Littlefield Publishers, Inc.
4720 Boston Way, Lanham, Maryland 20706

12 Hid's Copse Road
Cummor Hill, Oxford OX2 9JJ, England

British Library Cataloguing in Publication Information Available

Library of Congress Cataloging-in-Publication Data

Pucci, Pietro
    The song of the sirens : essays on Homer / Pietro
Pucci.
        p.   cm.
    Includes bibliographical references and index.
    ISBN 0-8226-3058-3 (cloth : alk. paper).—ISBN 0-8226-3059-1
(paper : alk. paper)
        1. Homer—Criticism and interpretation. 2. Epic poetry, Greek—History and
    criticism. 3. Odysseus (Greek mythology) in literature. 4. Achilles (Greek
    mythology) in literature. 5. Trojan War—Literature and the war. I. Title
    PA4037.P86   1998
    883—dc21   97-39863
                                                                    CIP
ISBN 0-8226-3058-3 (cloth : alk. paper)
ISBN 0-8226-3059-1 (pbk. : alk. paper)

Printed in the United States of America

⊖™ The paper used in this publication meets the minimum requirements of American
National Standard for Information Sciences—Permanence of Paper for Printed Library
Materials, ANSI Z39.48–1984.

Contents

Editor's Foreword   vii

Preface   ix

The Song of the Sirens   1

The Proem of the *Odyssey*   11

The Language of the Muses   31

Banter and Banquets for Heroic Death   49

    The Frame: The Mane in the Royal Figure 51; The Banter 53;
    What the Lycians Think of the King's Image 55; Iliadic Writing
    62; The Structure of Supplementarity 65; The Text's Reading of
    Itself 66

Textual Epiphanies in the *Iliad*   69

Epiphanic Strategy and Intertextuality   81

Antiphonal Lament Between Achilles and Briseis   97

The I and the Other in Odysseus's Story of the Cyclopes   113

Odysseus Narrator: The End of the Heroic Race   131

The Narrator 135; Odysseus's I-Narrative and Odyssean Poetics 140; Between fairy tales and true experience 143; Practical Functions of Odysseus's Narrative 145; Discontinuity Between Narrator and Character 147; The Stories 149; The Cicones 150; The Goats' Island 154; Circe 159; Agamemnon and Achilles 163; The End of the Heroic Race and Tradition 171; The Sirens 175.

Honor and Glory in the *Iliad*   179

Two Voices 182; The Word that Gathers Acquiescence 187; The Marginalization of Achilles 194; Existential Rhetoric 199; Illustriousness of *Kudos* 204; Monumental Glory (*Kleos*) 208; The Urging of the Heart: Heroic Death 214; *Kleos* and the Poetry of the *Iliad* 224;

Reference List   231

Index   242

Editor's Foreword

Building on the foundations of scholarship within the disciplines of philology, philosophy, history, and archaeology, this series spans the continuum of Greek traditions extending from the second millennium BC to the present, not just the Archaic and Classical periods. The aim is to enhance perspectives by applying various disciplines to problems that have in the past been treated as the exclusive concern of a single given discipline. Besides combining the strengths of older disciplines, as in the case of historical and literary studies, the series encourages the application of such newer ones as linguistics, sociology, anthropology, and comparative literature. It also encourages encounters with current trends in methodology, especially in the realm of literary theory.

The Song of the Sirens: Essays on Homer, by Pietro Pucci, is both a theoretical and a practical approach to the reading of Homer as text. It explores questions of intertextuality and cross-reference within the Homeric tradition, with a focus on the relationship of the *Odyssey* to the *Iliad*. The author is a distinguished literary critic and Classicist endowed with a special gift for subtle literary interpretation. His interpretations show a deep appreciation for the artistry and monumentality of the Homeric tradition. Experts and non-experts alike will find this book an essential companion to Pucci's other major work on Homer, *Odysseus Polytropos: Intertextual Readings in the Odyssey and the Iliad* (Cornell University Press 1987).

Preface

I thank Gregory Nagy for his inviting me to bring out a collection of my essays on Homer. Of the ten I have chosen, eight are previously published, and two appear here for the first time. After some reflection I decided not to revise the eight articles being reprinted here other than to correct errors of fact, clarify and enlarge some passages, standardize my references, and in "Epiphanic Strategy and Intertextuality," to delete some passages intended for the original Italian audience unfamiliar with my work. Occasionally I have added a reference to a recent work. The translator of the three originally Italian essays is Gregory Hays. I thank Naomi Rood and Phillip Kennedy who have been the final editors of the work and have prepared the camera-ready copy.

I decided to leave the essays as they were conceived and to present my revisions, my comments, and my additions in the two new papers, "Odysseus Narrator" and "Honor and Glory in the *Iliad*."

The critical concerns and ideas that have guided me have not changed since I began teaching Homer in the sixties. I have always attended to Homer's language, and I have always tried to tie my critical discourse to the linguistic and rhetorical features that I was gradually uncovering and elaborating.

Essentially my work has always questioned what the meaning is that the text produces. This is not an easy proposition. Meaning is a hypothesis one arrives at using the codes of grammar and syntax, but these codes are not closed sets of rules. They are rather always in the making, always inventing meaning.

As De Man emphasized, grammar is not an isotope of logic, as it was conceived in the long classical tradition of the *trivium*, nor is logic that mental process that allows for the passage to the real world. Furthermore, no utterance, for all its grammatical and syntactical correctness, is conceivable outside its rhetorical dimension. Rhetoric has become, in the recent deconstructive criticism (or textualist criticism as Richard Rorty calls it), the spearhead of the attack against the cognitive dimension of literary language. Accordingly, meaning emerges, to say it with the greatest simplicity, from the tension that organizes the linguistic artifact: a tension between the constructive and the unsettling features of language. For the sign is both referential and unmotivated—and when the signifier produces sense it unsettles the referentiality of the signified; grammar and syntax are conventional sturctures in constant becoming; rhetoric undermines the cognitive force of language; and the creative authorial project is always somehow undercut by the passivity of the linguistic and stylistic conventions in which this project is performed. It is not that authorial activity is absent—as many unfavorable critics of deconstruction imply; on the contrary, the activity and the energy of great authors is powerfully exercised in the *agôn* of this tension, since they are perfectly aware of the unsettling features of their language. In this battle their powerful personalities and texts emerge, but to imprint in the language the authorial *pragma* so as to make it mirror their intentions remains an utopian attempt, for the unsettling thrust of language complicates the picture of the signs on the surface of that mirror.

The ancient rhetoricians considered rhetoric an ornament of and an adjunct to grammar: rhetoric so conceived cannot contest grammar's rule over the production of sense. But rhetoric has epistemological effects: that this is so shatters the master position of grammar and renders untenable the very concept of univocal meaning with its logic and cognitive power.

In the essays that follow, I focus especially on two features of Homer's rhetoric. The first concerns the repetition of expressions (formulas) and its effects on meaning. The crux of the matter, of course, is identifying and defining the protocols of these repetitions. The notion that such repetitions are merely mechanical has been refuted by many studies in the last thirty years. Still, we cannot claim that they are not mechanical at all: even the most carefully composed language is mechanical to some extent, although the measure and the effects of this with respect to Homer's language are still a matter of debate for theorists of oral style. The second is the issue of intertextuality. It has been disputed whether intertextuality belongs to rhetoric, but, leaving the theoretical question aside, I analyze how its effects affect deeply the rhetoric of the text, its power of evocation. The first two essays of this collection begin a line of research that resulted in my book *Odysseus Polutropos* (1987).

As I read the Homeric texts I am not digging out precious relics of the past ensconced in them, or anthropological themes we can compare with those of other cultures. I am focusing on the protocols of their composition and on their reading of themselves. For both the *Iliad* and the *Odyssey* speak about the function of the poetry they recycle; they are aware of the modes of their composition (of their textuality), of their construction—through privileged repeated expressions—and of their effects. The first duty of a critical reading is to uncover that awareness and its claims. The Homeric and the Hesiodic texts read each other and react to each other. Reading the glances they throw askance at each other, interpreting the dialogue they install among themselves and the shades of the variations they obtain by the most sophisticated game of repetition, brings us close to an appreciation of their formidable artistry, of their meaning and poetic value.

The way this dialogue is reconstructed and the direction it takes are the critical issues that open up and promise the most exciting and rewarding discoveries. This book is also about the dialogue between the two poetics and presents some of the possible discoveries ensuing from the reading of that dialogue.

The *Odyssey*'s poetics of pleasure and enchantment and the *Iliad*'s austere one in which the song of glory coincides with the funeral *thrênos* clash in many jarring notes. They seem aware of their relative strengths and weaknesses. In the end, the *Iliad*'s bold auto-sufficiency ensconces the terrible frailty of its poetic extolling of heroic death.

This approach should also be considered as the closest possible thing to a historical reading of the texts. However, since this reading is grounded in the rhetorical phenomena, the effects of reading they produce are often multiple, contradictory, and undesirable. The reader must be patient and recognize a certain necessity in this state of affairs. To channel all these effects toward a unique direction of meaning could really be the project of a modern metaphysical attitude. To avoid even the temptation to force on my past interpretations the straitjacket of a unifying, synthesizing reading, I am publishing them as I wrote them.

The effect of reading that I am discussing in the repetitions, in the conscious textuality of the poems, could appear to be produced by modern attitudes about literature and by modern expectations from literary texts. It is difficult to deny that risk and that necessity.

A sure answer to this criticism depends on the enigmatic question of what is implied in historical interpretation. For the practice of a historical interpretation is an impossible ideal. The historical and grammatical method of interpretation, as Peter Szondi has argued, can be true in its intention, but never true in its practice, because the parameters of interpretation are historically determined. Accordingly, the interpreter's own standpoint will participate in determining whether a text is comprehensible or not, whether it needs a correction or not, and if the necessity of a correction is recognized, the historical standpoint of the interpreter will contribute to the elaboration of the conjecture. These arguments are ostensibly clear for classical philologists who see new editions of the same classical texts conceived either by conservative criteria or liberal ones depending on the philosophical temper and general culture of each editor and of each historical epoch. If the unavoidability of relativity must not be used as a pretext to ignore historical precaution and shirk historical responsibility, one must, however, not misjudge the conundrum of meaning: it is historically grounded and yet passes through history; it is original and also translatable; it often claims to be univocal and yet is polysemic.

Furthermore, it is not known how the *Iliad* and the *Odyssey* were understood by their original audiences. What is clear is that some of the fifth-century interpretations of Homer we are familiar with are as bold and penetrating as any modern one. The *polytropy* of Odysseus, for instance, was understood as a rhetorical characteristic, while some philological interpretations of recent years still deny metaphorical value to this notion and interpret the *polutropos* of the opening line of the *Odyssey* exclusively as "much wandered." Can't this denial be traced back to a certain historical prejudice about Homer as "naive" or "simple"?

My reading focusing on the poetics of the two poems aims also at producing the complex protocols of each one of the two poetics. The Iliadic song, close to the Muses' inspiration, focuses on heroic death with insistent aberration, both showing the limitless brutality of numberless deaths, and lovingly collecting, like gems of terrible light, the words of heroes who accept or even choose death. Awareness of death and choosing one's own death shine as "authentic" modes of being, death itself being an essential part of man that can be objectified as other than the self only by provoking it in a sort of gallant dalliance with it, as Sarpedon and Hector do. But Achilles lets himself be the carrier of his own and of others' deaths.

In the following pages I also uncover in the text the ensconced signs that reveal the frailty of this sublime rhetoric and deconstruct its tremendous compactness and force by showing also its perversity, destructiveness, and errancy.

In my 1987 *Odysseus Polutropos* I examined at length the poetic protocols of the *Odyssey*, aiming at producing the pleasure and the enchantment that the Sirens and Odysseus himself produce in their audiences, through their knowledge, *mêtis*, and rhetoric. Here I am returning to some of these aspects as I analyze Odysseus's rhetoric as the narrator of Books ix-xii, and I focus on the powerful critical glance that the *Odyssey* casts at the *Iliad*. Odysseus, the outcast, is not simply a shipwrecked sailor, but is also the lonely survivor of the heroic age whose splendor and destructiveness he does not cease remembering with burning nostalgia and rejecting as something irremediably past. The way the *Odyssey* reads the Iliadic *kleos* opens up our path in examining the frailty of that poetics.

I thank the following editors and journals for the permission to publish the articles that appeared in their publications:

"The Song of the Sirens" *Arethusa* 12 1979.
"The Language of the Muses" *Classical Mythology in 20th Century Thought and Literature*. Texas Tech. University 1980.
"The Proem of the Odyssey" *Arethusa* 15 1982.
"Epifanie testuali nell'*Iliade*" *SIFC* Terza Serie vol. III 1985.
"Banter and Banquets for Heroic Death." in *Post-structuralist Classics*. Edited by Andrew Benjamin. London and New York: Routledge 1988.
"Strategia epifanica e intertestualità nel secondo libro dell'*Iliade*" *SIFC* Terza Serie vol VI 1988.
"Antiphonal Lament Between Achilles and Briseis" *Colby Quarterly* xxix 1993.
"L'io e l'altro nel racconto di Ulisse sui Ciclopi" *SIFC*. Terza Serie. vol. 11 1993.

I quote the Greek text from *Homeri Opera*, edited by David B. Monro and Thomas W. Allen, Oxford Classical Texts (1920).

I have transliterated most Greek words into Latin characters for Anglophone readers, and I have used the Latinate forms of the familiar proper names, Achilles and not Akhilleus, and so on, for my readers who do not know Greek. To them, I apologize for the technical aspects of the first essay. When Roman numerals are used to indicate books in Homer, the lower case numbers designate books of the *Odyssey,* the capital numbers the books of the *Iliad.*

CHAPTER 1

The Song of the Sirens*

δεῦρ᾽ ἄγ᾽ ἰών, πολύαιν᾽ Ὀδυσεῦ, μέγα κῦδος Ἀχαιῶν,
νῆα κατάστησον, ἵνα νωϊτέρην ὄπ᾽ ἀκούσῃς.
οὐ γάρ πώ τις τῇδε παρήλασε νηῒ μελαίνῃ,
πρίν γ᾽ ἡμέων μελίγηρυν ἀπὸ στομάτων ὄπ᾽ ἀκοῦσαι,
ἀλλ᾽ ὅ γε τερψάμενος νεῖται καὶ πλείονα εἰδώς.
ἴδμεν γάρ τοι πάνθ᾽, ὅσ᾽ ἐνὶ Τροίῃ εὐρείῃ
Ἀργεῖοι Τρῶές τε θεῶν ἰότητι μόγησαν·
ἴδμεν δ᾽ ὅσσα γένηται ἐπὶ χθονὶ πουλυβοτείρῃ.
(*Odyssey* xii.184–91)

[Come hither, Odysseus, skillful in telling stories, great glory of the Achaeans. Stop your ship, listen to our voices. Never has any man passed by in his black ship without hearing the honey-sweet voice from our lips, but he has taken his pleasure and has gone on with greater wisdom. For we know all the pains Argives and Trojans suffered in the wide land of Troy because of the gods' will, and we know whatever happens on the bountiful earth.]

The Sirens invite Odysseus to stop his ship and to listen to their voice so that he may enjoy their song and return wiser. For they know the god-sent toils the Argives and the Trojans suffered in war and they know each time whatever has happened in the world (*Od.* xii.184–91).

The most remarkable feature of this text is that its diction "reproduces"—so to speak—the diction of the *Iliad* in such a way that it should be recognized as

---

* I presented an earlier draft of this essay at Johns Hopkins, Stanford, and USC, where I reaped interesting contributions from the discussion with colleagues and students. It was first published in *Arethusa* 12 (1979).

different from that of the *Odyssey*. The first noun-epithet that the Sirens address to Odysseus (184), πολύαιν᾽ Ὀδυσεῦ, μέγα κῦδος Ἀχαιῶν [skillful in telling stories, great glory of the Achaeans] is found only here in the *Odyssey*, while it occurs twice in the *Iliad* in passages that narrate important deeds of Odysseus: the Embassy (IX.673) and the Doloneia (X.544). It is indeed customary to consider both these parts as late, but recent critics have forcefully argued that often what is labeled as late or interpolated contains on the contrary the key for interpreting "older" passages.[1] Even the first part of the whole noun-epithet phrase, πολύαιν᾽ Ὀδυσεῦ, occurs only in the *Iliad* and in a reversed order, in a passage in which Odysseus is momentarily the center of the action (XI.430). The compound adjective πολύαινος is a fixed, exclusive epithet for Odysseus and characterizes him as the one who uses stories for his success and survival.[2] Yet, oddly enough, this epithet appears only here in the *Odyssey* while in the *Iliad* it occurs in three important occasions for the hero. The Sirens' purpose in choosing this epithet cannot leave any doubt: they identify Odysseus as the warrior at Troy rather than the hero of the *Odyssey*. They call him also μέγα κῦδος Ἀχαιῶν, which, though not exclusively an epithet for Odysseus, is never used in the *Odyssey* to refer to Odysseus except in this passage. The Sirens make their purpose clearer as they continue to speak. In line 187, πρίν γ᾽ ἡμέων μελίγηρυν ἀπὸ στομάτων ὄπ᾽ ἀκοῦσαι, two remarkable features attract our attention. First the traditional phrase, ὄπ᾽ ἀκοῦσαι, occurs in the *Odyssey* only to indicate listening to the Sirens' voice (*Od.* xii.52, 160, 185, 187), while in the *Iliad* it refers to the voice of different people (gods VII.53, Agamemnon XI.137, and Achilles XXI.98). As concerns the digamma of ὄπα only in *Od.* xii.52 and 160, among the examples quoted above, is it metrically guaranteed.

Coming to the second feature, we note the extraordinary precision of the expression ἀπὸ στομάτων. For στόμα in Homer is rarely connected with the production of the voice, *glôssa* being used to denote the source of the voice (see, for instance, *Il.* I.249: ἀπὸ γλώσσης μέλιτος γλυκίων ῥέεν αὐδή). Yet στόμα is connected with the voice 4 times: 3 times in the *Iliad* and only once in the *Odyssey*, in the song of the Sirens. The analysis of the Iliadic passages is rewarding, for in *Il.* II.489, στόμα is used by the poet to indicate his own mouth as producing the song, while in *Il.* II.250 and XIV.91 this word is used by Odysseus. The Sirens, then, while inviting Odysseus to listen to their song, pick a usage that in the *Iliad* characterizes only the poet's and Odysseus's diction.

Line 188 offers surprising new evidence that the diction of the Sirens has been poetically edited in order to show its Iliadic marks used to characterize Odysseus as one of the important heroes of the *Iliad*. For the phrase of line 188

---

1. See the whole argument in Nagy 1979.
2. On the meaning of πολύαινος "having many *ainoi* (fables)," see Meuli 1975, 2:742, where it is translated as "fabelreich." Meuli (2:742–43) accounts for the two possible meanings of the word "storyteller" and "object of many praises" on which modern scholars are still disagreeing, and he makes the important point that the epithet implies neither "Sagenkundig" nor "Causeur," but rather that Odysseus's *ainoi* are means for fighting and rescue, just like *mêkhanai*.
On *ainos* and its connection, in Homer, with gifts, see Pucci 1977, 76 n. 3.

καὶ πλείονα εἰδώς ("with greater wisdom") is a *hapax* in the *Odyssey* (and yet what appeal could be more alluring for the Odysseus of the *Odyssey* than that of πλείονα εἰδώς), while the same phrase is repeated four times in the *Iliad*. This phrase (καὶ πλείονα οἶδα, ἤδη...) is used by the poet to single out Zeus as stronger and wiser than Poseidon (*Il.* XIII.355), and later it is used by Poseidon himself to exhibit the grounds of his superiority over Apollo (XXI.440). In both cases the phrase is part of a larger expression which says "I" or "he" was born first and know(s) more:

	γεγόνει	ἤδη.
πρότερος	καὶ πλείονα	
	γενόμην οἶδα	

Now in *Il.* XIX.219, when Odysseus begins to advise Achilles, he recognizes Achilles' military superiority, but he asserts that he surpasses Achilles in counsel, since "I was born first and know more": πρότερος γενόμην καὶ πλείονα οἶδα. The Sirens know their hero well: they pick up this bold expression used by Odysseus to emphasize that he is superior to Achilles in wisdom just as Zeus is superior to Poseidon and Poseidon to Apollo.[3]

Line 188 is also crucial to the Sirens' message, for they utter two promises of great significance in this context. First they promise joy to their listener, and then they specify that he will return home. As we know, Circe had warned Odysseus that the Sirens' listener fails to return home, but the Sirens deny that claim. However, I shall comment on this point later.

Lines 189–190 are also most surprising because the obvious Odyssean color exposes more forcefully the Iliadic mark, once it is perceived. The phrase, ὅσ᾽ ἐνὶ Τροίῃ εὐρείῃ Ἀργεῖοι Τρῶές τε θεῶν ἰότητι μόγησαν, at first looks typically Odyssean, since the expression θεῶν ἰότητι μόγησαν at the end of the line occurs exclusively in the *Odyssey*; vii.214 and xvii.119 (= xii.190). But this impression must be corrected by noting that here the Sirens use the word ἰότητι in accordance with the exclusive usage or grammar of the *Iliad*. It has been noticed by P. Krarup (1948, 12) that this word appears exclusively in dialogue both in the *Iliad* and in the *Odyssey;* but what attracted no attention is that, in the *Iliad*, only gods use that expression (V.874, XV.41, XVIII.396, XIX.9), while in the *Odyssey* (where the word occurs seven times) only mortals use it with the single exception of the Sirens. They, therefore, follow the grammar of the *Iliad*.

Even the common phrase ἐπὶ χθονὶ πουλυβοτείρῃ by which the Sirens close their song is Iliadic: six times in the *Iliad* and only here in the *Odyssey*! One should nevertheless add that a slight modification of that phrase, ποτὶ χ. π., occurs in *Od.* viii.378 and that the simple dative is found four more times in the *Iliad*.

---

3. The last example of the expression καὶ πλείονα οἶδα in the *Iliad* occurs in XXIII.312: it is somehow different from the other examples we have reviewed, for it is used negatively (*oude*), with the plural *isasi* and, therefore, also in a different place in the line. Finally, it concerns the superiority of horse racers.

So far, I have analyzed only large phrases, formulaic expressions, the dictional material, so to speak, of which the Homeric mosaic is composed. But it is possible to argue that the Sirens obey the grammar of the *Iliad*, even in the minutiae: νωϊτέρην in line 185 is a *hapax* in the *Odyssey*, though it is a *hapax* in the *Iliad* too (XV.39);[4] οὐ γάρ πώ in the opening of line 186 is essentially Iliadic, for in that poem these words open the line six times out of seven occurrences, while in the *Odyssey* the same words most often occupy the middle part of the line.[5] There is, finally, not one line in the Sirens' utterance that does not contain conspicuous formulae or expressions which are, for us, exclusively or almost exclusively Iliadic.

The Sirens' conspicuous use of Iliadic traditional phrases can hardly be an accident; on the contrary, it forces upon the listener the realization that they mean to define Odysseus as the Odysseus of the *Iliad*. A certain degree of uniqueness in the composition of the text and the cumulative evidence I have gathered discourage the sort of explanation that would justify the Iliadic color of the text on mechanical grounds. It would be possible to argue, for instance, that line 184, δεῦρ' ἄγ' ἰών, πολύαιν' 'Οδυσεῦ, μέγα κῦδος 'Αχαιῶν, owes its composition to the fact that the only vocative formula that the poet has at hand to cover the part of the line after δεῦρ' ἄγ' ἰών is precisely this one; but to argue in this way would imply that the poet chooses a traditional, fixed beginning, δεῦρ' ἄγ' ἰών, and then attaches to it the only possible noun-epithet. But δεῦρ' ἄγ' ἰών itself is not traditional in our epic unless in the limited forms of δεῦρ' ἴθι or δεῦρ' ἴτω that may begin the line. It is therefore created uniquely for this occasion. It looks, then, as if the only fixed part of the line is the noun-epithet and that therefore, even on the grounds of the Parryan principle of economy, this is the part on behalf of which the first part of the line has been composed.[6] In other terms, given the uniqueness of the beginning of this line, and of the next one, the poet could have arranged the expressions in many different ways had he wanted the Sirens to address Odysseus by a different noun-epithet phrase.

This argument indicates that the poet used a certain degree of compositional freedom in order to choose the noun-epithet phrase and confirms therefore the results of the cumulative evidence. No doubts should remain about the intention of the passage: its diction points insistently at Iliadic phrases, selecting them in such a way that, while they are common and repeated in the *Iliad*, they are *hapax legomena* in the *Odyssey*. This intention is consonant with a series of facts and implications that we are now able to look at in their full significance. First of all the Iliadic color with which the Sirens portray Odysseus agrees with their

---

4. Risch 1974, 34b shows the formation of νωϊτέρην from the dual νωΐ.

5. More precisely, οὐ γάρ πώ occurs five times in the *Odyssey* and seven in the *Iliad*. Out of the seven examples in the *Iliad* only once (IV.331) does οὐ γάρ πώ occur in the second part of the verse whereas out of the five examples in the *Odyssey* only in xii.186 and xix.365 does the expression occur at the beginning of the verse.

6. Notice also that the beginning of the next line (186) νῆα κατάστησον is not traditional: in fact it is a *hapax* and confirms the large freedom of composition in these two lines of the Sirens' song. Had the poet wanted the Sirens to address Odysseus with an Odyssean noun-epithet phrase he had many choices.

claim to be able to sing the deeds of the Trojan war. The toils Odysseus suffered at Troy—and that the Sirens are ready to sing about—must be identified with the themes of that epic tradition that for us is represented by the *Iliad*. The Sirens' stylistic and formulaic appropriation of that tradition entails that the epic songs about the Trojan war were already fixed in closed-up, immutable forms or compositions, namely in what we call "texts." For without the existence of these fixed compositions, the sort of allusions we have discovered would not be thinkable. Of all those texts, we possess only the *Iliad*, and the argument that the *Iliad* must have been already a fixed text operates also in this case. We may speculate whether the typical Iliadic features of the Sirens' song are common characteristics of the whole tradition of which the *Iliad* is part; it remains however clear and certain that the Sirens' song alludes also to the *Iliad*, to the text of the *Iliad*. The deeds that the Sirens are ready to sing are *also* part of the Iliadic themes.[7]

It is therefore correct to say that Odysseus can be appealed to as a "literary" character of the *Iliad* and that Odysseus is indeed seduced by this idea and longs to listen to this song that presents him as an important character. The Sirens expose Odysseus's awareness of being such a character and consequently their invitation to listen to their song means in reality an urging—to put it bluntly— to stop the ship, to disembark from the ship that takes him on the Odyssean wanderings, and to remain with them; in other words, they invite him to change poet and poem, and to return to be the character of the *Iliad*. The poet of the *Odyssey* ironically exposes Odysseus's readiness to leave the wandering of the *Odyssey* in favor of the splendid toils of the *Iliad*. But he preempts Odysseus's longing by making sure, with the help of Circe, that Odysseus will not be able to stop the ship, and by warning him (and explaining to us) that this longing means death. The text of the *Odyssey* has already presented to us various examples of the possible truth of this. Odysseus asks the bard Demodocus to sing about Odysseus's last glorious deed and the final assault against Troy (viii.499ff.), and in response Odysseus weeps and cries just as one of the captive women whose husband the conquering soldiers have killed (*Od.* viii.521ff.). The "reverse simile" indicates a specific intention in the Odyssean text, namely to show that the song about glory or glorious deeds (*kleos* and *klea*) elicits an irresistible cry, a sort of funereal weeping rather than boasting and confidence. Odysseus, the sacker of Troy weeps just like one of the victims of his victorious action.[8] Menelaus's inability to turn his mind from the past proves the same point. A sort of self-destructive nostalgia compels these old heroes to dwell in

---

7. In accordance with Nagy's view, the tradition may have already been fixed into two (or more) "genres," each of them endowed with specific scenes and therefore with specific language and formulas. We face what we could call a chain of tightly related events (texts), each with some fixity and uniqueness.

8. On the "reverse similes," see Foley 1978. Diano (1968) interprets Odysseus's crying as moved by pity (206): "Certo è il poeta che piange su Troia, e quella 'pietà' è innanzitutto la sua, ma è anche Ulisse, perchè il cuore del poeta è il cuore stesso di Ulisse." The analysis which follows shows a depth in Diano's thought that is not made visible by this short quotation and cannot be reproduced without long argument.

the memory of their splendid and grievous past. The Sirens with their specific
Iliadic diction appeal both to Odysseus's literary complacency and to his
nostalgia for his glorious deeds: that is why the Sirens' song would bring
Odysseus out of the *Odyssey* to rot on their island.

But the poet of the *Odyssey* watches over his Odysseus and does not allow
him to leave the ship, clever though he is. He even arranges for Odysseus to
listen to the Sirens' song but he has doctored the hero (and us) to such an extent
that neither he nor we can listen to it impartially. An extraordinary dialogue
between the poet of the *Odyssey* and that of the *Iliad* takes place in this scene.
The Sirens look like Muses and speak with the diction of the *Iliad*: the
implication is obviously that the poet of the *Odyssey* considers the divine
inspirers of the *Iliad* to possess the attributes of the Sirens rather than the
attributes generally granted to the Muses. The poet of the *Odyssey* presses the
point that the inspirers of the *Iliad* are turned toward an irretrievable and remote
kleos and grief, whose song indeed fascinates the listeners; yet the memory of
that *kleos* and grief spells only death.[9] In this way, by incorporating their Iliadic
song into the poem, the *Odyssey* appropriates the *Iliad* with a gesture of
disavowal.

We do not need to refer to the brilliant assumptions and arguments formulated
by E. Buschor in his book *Die Musen des Jenseits* (1944) to realize that in their
song to Odysseus, the Sirens ascribe to themselves the attributes of Muses. The
Sirens define themselves as melodious singers, as bestowers of pleasurable song,
and as being omniscient. These traits indeed identify the Muses as we know
them from the epic texts and in particular from II.484ff., viii.63, 73ff.,
xxiv.60ff., Hes. *Theog.* 97ff., and so on. The Sirens emphasize their omniscience and, to some extent, rightly so, for they recognize Odysseus at *sight*,
whereas other goddesses or divine beings, such as Circe and Polyphemus, for
instance, fail to do so. The Sirens must really know what happened in Troy, if
they know personally and recognize at sight who is who. They therefore have the
same power of presence as the Muses or Apollo who inspire Demodocus when
he sings the truth about Troy (viii.488–91):

η σέ γε Μοῦσ' ἐδίδαξε, Διὸς πάϊς, ἤ σέ γ' Ἀπόλλων·
λίην γὰρ κατὰ κόσμον Ἀχαιῶν οἶτον ἀείδεις,
ὅσσ' ἔρξαν τ' ἔπαθόν τε καὶ ὅσσ' ἐμόγησαν Ἀχαιοί,
ὡς τέ που ἤ αὐτὸς παρεὼν ἤ ἄλλου ἀκούσας.

---

9. Notice, however, that the Sirens do not speak of *kleos* or *klea*, but use the verb
mogeô (πάνθ', ὅσ'...μόγησαν). One might be tempted to give relevance to the
exclusion of *kleos*, but we must remember that in the *Iliad* itself *kleos* can be a very
ambivalent notion (see for instance II.486). On *kleos* in the *Odyssey*, see Segal
1983.

The interpretation that I am suggesting would help to explain that strange epithet
that Odysseus uses in xxiii.326 to describe the Sirens: ἠδ' ὡς Σειρήνων ἀδινάων
φθόγγον ἄκουσεν. *Hadinos*, which has baffled interpreters, is a common epithet for
funeral lamentations in the *Iliad*: *hadinou gooio* (XXII.430, XVIII.366, etc., and see
iv.721, xxiv.317, etc.). As singers of deeds that spell death, the epithet is
appropriate to the Sirens.

[Either the Muse, daughter of Zeus, taught you, or Apollo taught you, for you sing the doom of the Achaeans so accurately, and what the Achaeans did and suffered and what they endured, as though either you yourself were present there or you heard it from another.]

Furthermore the Sirens "know each time all things that [ἴδμεν δ' ὅσσα] have happened on the bountiful earth," or "things that shall happen on the bountiful earth."[10] Their omniscience equates the Sirens with the Muses of II.484ff., who know all things (πάντα) since they are ever present: ὑμεῖς γὰρ θεαί ἐστε πάρεστέ τε ἴστέ τε πάντα. The repetition of the verb ἴδμεν at the beginning of the two lines, 189 and 191, reminds us of the repeated ἴδμεν that the Muses utter in Hes. *Theog.* 27 and 28.

As concerns the pleasure, the *terpsis* that the Sirens bestow—a fixed element in the epic description of the song, or of the Muses—the Sirens are explicit: ἀλλ' ὅ γε τερψάμενος νεῖται καὶ πλείονα εἰδώς [He shall return home, as he has gotten his pleasure and with greater knowledge].

Finally they are outspoken about the beauty of their song: they term their voice μελίγηρυν, "sweetly singing," a *hapax* in the *Iliad, Odyssey,* and all of Hesiod. The word is picked up by *Hymn to Apollo* 519 to define the *aoidê,* the song that the Muse inspires.[11]

All these connotations prove that the Sirens present themselves to Odysseus as melodious, sweet singers who possess the same attributes (power of memory,omniscience, and pleasure) that the epic Muses possess. But, as I have already suggested, the Sirens' subjective view of themselves is framed by the ruse of the poet. For, at the time in which we listen to their song, Odysseus has already been warned by Circe about the danger that the Sirens present for him (xii.39–54) and we, the listeners, have received the additional warning that Odysseus utters to his companions (xii.158–64). A synchronic analysis of these three scenes (to which one should add the quick but revealing mention in xxiii.326) would be rewarding, but it is too long to be presented here.[12]

---

10. The interpretation of the aorist subjunctive γένηται in line 191 is not certain. Ameis and Hentze (1886) take it to be an *iterative* subjunctive and translate "alles was jedesmal geschieht." But Ruijgh (1971, 561 n. 10) remarks that it could represent a permanent fact with a distributive-iterative subjunctive ("we know each time all that has happened") or a subjunctive with a future meaning ("that which shall happen").

The distributive-iterative subjunctive is rare with these relatives: one case with ὅσσα in III.66 (with κεν), one case with οἷον in xviii.137, without τε as in our passage.

11. The word μελίγηρυς is composed of μέλι, "honey," and it is the theme of γηρύω, a word of high tone, used by the Muses themselves in Hes. *Theog.* 28, where they say: ἴδμεν δ' εὖτ' ἐθέλωμεν ἀληθέα γηρύσασθαι.

12. This synchronic analysis should take into account both the personality of the narrators and the strategy of the narrative. For we cannot neglect the fact that the song of the Sirens is related and termed a ruinous "enchantment" by three masters of incantation and magic. First Circe, the magician, expert in spells that transform men into pigs, second Odysseus, who here casts his spells on the Phaeacians (xi.334 =

By an amusing stroke the poet has Circe interpreting and framing the Sirens for Odysseus and for us. Circe, the sensual magician, who possesses the same destructive power of *thelgein* (*Od.* x.213, 291, 318, 326) that she attributes to the Sirens, emerges as a savior of Odysseus against powers who are so similar to herself. The irony, of course, is manifold: not the least because the Sirens are so unaware of the plot that frames and preempts their success. These omniscient singers fail to see what happens before their eyes, for it escapes them that Odysseus is bound fast to the ship's mast and they do not know that his companions hear neither him nor their song. The Sirens, who claim to know each time everything that has happened on the surface of this world, show a pathetic blindness to what is present and so visible.

At any rate Circe has already characterized the Sirens' pleasing song as a powerful incantation, which creates confusion and paralyzes the will (*thelgein*): no one, she says, returns home from their island, and a huge heap of bones proves her claim.[13] Yet the Sirens themselves assert that their listener will return home, and no mention of bones occurs when Odysseus sees their meadow. Who is right? We, of course, will never know.

If the Sirens, however, are really the polemical embodiment of what for the poet of the *Odyssey* is wrong in the *Iliad*, then we know the reason for this ruse and irony. The Sirens must sound like Muses, inspirers of the *Iliad*, in order to be truthful singers of Odysseus's past toils: therefore they establish the genuine identification of the Odyssean hero with the *Iliad* by enhancing his glorious literary pedigree; but since Odysseus must not abandon the ship that the Singer of the *Odyssey* leads through his poetic wanderings, then the Sirens must be

---

xiii.2) with his stories, and third the poet of the Odyssey, who knows that the poet always enchants (i.337, xvii.518–21).

13. The narrative strategy is complex: in the three narratives in which the Sirens are described (xii.38ff., 158ff., 181ff.) some details are new and some are left aside, probably in order to enhance the mystery of the Sirens and to make the narrative and the narrator, Odysseus, more appealing. Some of these changes are easy to understand. It is reasonable that Odysseus fails to describe the huge pile of bones as he sees the Sirens on their meadow. The mention of bones and death would have emptied part of the charm Odysseus felt and wanted to describe. Yet the question remains: did a huge pile of bones in fact lie around the Sirens?

Concerning the etymology of *"seirēn"* there is no agreement among scholars. Chantraine with his characteristic self-restraint refers to various hypotheses without being convinced by any one. Within Greek itself the word *seirēn* has been connected with *seira*, "rope" (in which case the *Seirēnes* would be those who "tie up") or with *seirios*, the Dog Star (in which case the Sirens would be daimons of the South and of the sea stillness: Solmsen 1909, 126ff., Latte 1968, 106–121). W. Brandestein 1961, 169, V. Pisani 1957, 391; 1968, 377, and M. Durante 1971, 158 opt for a Thracian origin of the word: *Zeirēnê*, as Hesychius testifies, means "Aphrodite" in Macedonian and can be connected with Greek *khairô*. The Sirens therefore would be the "desiring" ones.

Both Chantraine and Frisk are silent on the possibility that *Seirēn* may be connected with Semitic *sir*, "song," on which see Marót 1960 and Gresseth 1970, 204 and note 5.

made to appear destructive and a little bit pathetic, in that their innocence is so adroitly questioned by the poet of the *Odyssey*.

Finally the Sirens prove to be blind to that which occurs before their eyes: these singers that have the same knowledge as the Muses of the *Iliad* are really turned to the past, live in a spatial and temporal remoteness which is frightening, since their musean memory becomes forgetfulness of the present, and spells only grief, pity, and death. Against this Iliadic song, the *Odyssey* asserts a memory that fulfills the present, grants successful knowledge, and insures earthly, though controlled, pleasures.

CHAPTER 2

The Proem of the *Odyssey**

More than a century ago, Immanuel Bekker asserted that the proemial lines of the *Odyssey* were strikingly similar to the corresponding lines of the *Iliad*, that they might even be called an imitation of the Iliadic proem. Yet Bekker (1863, 99ff.) also identified the sharp difference between the two texts in what he called the "unhomeric indefiniteness (or vagueness) of the expression" and in the "obscurity of meaning" of the *Odyssey* proem. By these labels, Bekker referred to such facts as the anonymity of the hero (this "man" returning home from Troy could be anyone, he argued, Menelaus, for instance, or Agamemnon, or Diomedes), the imprecision of the epithet *polutropos*, which could mean "much wandering" or "wily," the lack of any distinctiveness in the expressions that should rigorously identify the nameless hero, that is, "he saw the cities of many people," "he suffered many pains in his heart," etc. In his view, the composer of those vague, obscure, Odyssean lines could not have been Homer. Bekker's seminal paper initiated a long, ponderous controversy that continues even today,[1] though the terms of the controversy no longer concern literary excellence or success of the *Odyssey* proem nor aim specifically at the question of authorship. In fact, especially in the last twenty years, scholars from all points on the methodological spectrum have been able to explain and justify the features of the *Odyssey* proem that most struck Bekker and to integrate them with the poetics of the *Odyssey*. The striking similarity between the two proems, however, has drawn little new commentary. Nevertheless, a certain consensus exists among

---

* "The Proem of the *Odyssey*" was first published in *Arethusa* 15 (1982).
1. The most recent complete survey of the literature on the *Odyssey* proem is Rüter 1969, 13ff.

scholars in interpreting the formal similarity of the initial lines of the two proems.

It has been clear since ancient times that the first words of the two proems, *mênin* and *andra*, define a vast opposition of content and ethos, and it is clear today that this contrast is articulated through the whole fabric of the two poems.[2] The opposition refers first to the subject matter: the object of the *Iliad* is Achilles' wrath, a fatal event in his warrior destiny, while that of the *Odyssey* is a man, a character, a *bios* (Rüter 1969, 47). However, since the wrath is a conventional, even professional feature of the heroic warrior,[3] and since Achilles' wrath becomes the turning point in his warrior destiny, it is clear that *mênin* and *andra* contrast two different sorts of heroes.

On the Odyssean *ennepe* instead of the Iliadic *aeide*, we may agree with A. Pagliaro that the expression *enepein* indicates simply a focusing of the poet's attention on the content of the narrative, rather than a change from song to recitation, as Wilamowitz seemed to imply.[4] Pagliaro goes on to emphasize the subjective moment implicit in the prayer to the Muse: tell "me" (*moi*). This *moi* puts in the foreground the person of the poet as a recipient of the Muse's tale and emphasizes, among other features, the fact that these words are not inspired by the Muse but are words of the poet himself. J. Strauss Clay has recently called attention to this neglected feature. The poet's subjectivity and his speaking his own words could be connected with his obvious intention to defend his hero, to proclaim his innocence: "From the very outset . . . Homer shows a pro-Odyssean bias, a desire to show Odysseus in a favorable light."[5] While the subjectivity and the personal authorship of the proemial lines constitute difficult critical problems we cannot discuss here, it is correct in my view to emphasize the apologetic force of his proem. For, as will become evident in the course of this paper, the proem initiates not only the epilogue of the *Iliad*—as the *De Sublimitate* defines the *Odyssey*—but also the apology of Odysseus in contrast to Achilles. Directly after the two imperatives *ennepe* and *aeide*, however, the formal similarity between the first lines of the two poems is suddenly highlighted by a violent disruption on which we will comment later: to the ponderous presence of Achilles' name with his patronymic corresponds the anonymity of the hero in the *Odyssey*.

In the next lines, the formal parallelism remains striking. In both texts, the adjectival forms *oulomenên* and *polutropon*, in agreement with the main objects *mênin* and *andra* and followed by a relative clause, open up the description of the

---

2. See, for instance, Eustathius's commentary and the distinction traced in *De sublimitate* between the dramatic force of the *Iliad* and the *ethopoiia* of the *Odyssey*. For modern authors, see Rüter, and add to his list Pasquali 1951, 35–38, and Codino 1965.

3. On the professional features of the Homeric heroes, see Codino 1965, 136ff.

4. A. Pagliaro 1953, 15–16; Wilamowitz-Moellendorff 1920, 354ff.

5. Strauss Clay 1976, 313–16, and especially 317. See also Stewart 1976, 188ff. Of course, the subjectivity of the poet has triggered other speculations, especially on the lateness of the *Odyssey* proem in relation to that of the *Iliad*. See Marzullo 1952, 484, note 2.

essential features of the subject. In both texts, the relative clauses are emphasized by the anaphora of a form of *polus*: in the *Iliad pollas d'* (3) picks up anaphorically *muria* (2), while in the *Odyssey mala polla* (1)—which seems a *variatio* of *muria*—is followed by *pollôn d'* (3) and *polla d'* (4) in what might seem an exercise of *auxesis* upon the Iliadic pattern. This formal symmetry or parallelism emphasizes a contrast between Achilles' wrath and Odysseus's behavior. Since the wrath of Achilles is termed *oulomenên* ("ruinous" or better "accursed") and the cause of countless griefs (*algea*) for the Achaeans, Achilles appears in the Iliadic proem as the source of ruin for his own compatriots. Contrast Odysseus's behavior in the proem of the *Odyssey*: through all sorts of hardships and griefs (*algea*) wily Odysseus tries to save his own men. The opposition pits the morose hero who disregards the life of his own people to satisfy his high destiny against the resourceful hero who is paternally attentive to the welfare of his own men.

At this point, we realize that the contrasts created by the first words of the two proems have developed into a large and direct confrontation of the two heroes, their behavior, their heroic *pragma*. In order to pursue this confrontation, we must take into consideration passages that occur outside the proem. Yet, in fact, we will not abandon the proem of the *Odyssey*. For the formulaic diction of this proem encourages us to pursue this confrontation. Indeed, it asks us to be alert to its profound and unmistakable echoes in other parts of the two poems.

When we turn our attention to i.4–5, we realize the pathetic force of the expression πολλά...πάθεν ἄλγεα ὃν κατὰ θυμόν [he suffered many griefs in his heart]. This specific way of representing the grief of a hero is rare: very few heroes in either the *Iliad* or the *Odyssey* are characterized so pathetically. The expression πάθεν/ον ἄλγεα ὃν κατὰ θυμόν occurs only four times in the *Iliad*, once for Hephaestus (XVIII.397), once for Euchenor (XIII.670), and twice for Achilles in two of his most uncontrolled outbursts of anguish and despair (IX.321, XVI.55). (In fact, the expression is used three times for Achilles if we include XXIV.7 where καὶ πάθεν ἄλγεα, notwithstanding its metrical oddity and its formulaic incompleteness, still achieves the pathos of the whole formula.)[6] In the *Odyssey*, πάθεν ἄλγεα θυμῷ is used twice, by Odysseus to describe his own griefs in xiii.267 and by Odysseus of Eumaeus in xv.487. The fuller expression, πολλά...πάθεν/ον ἄλγεα ὃν κατὰ θυμόν,[7] occurs twice, in line 4 of the proem and in xiii.90, again to describe Odysseus's griefs with the intention certainly of referring to the usage in the proem.[8] There is no doubt, therefore, that this

---

6. In the *Odyssey*, too, we have variations of the full expression. See ix.53, x.457, and xiv.32.

7. I take πάθεν/ον ἄλγεα θυμῷ and πάθεν ἄλγεα ὃν κατὰ θυμόν as connotatively identical. The expression ὃν κατὰ θυμόν in all passages of the *Iliad* and *Odyssey* shows the respect of the digamma. The first "corruption" of the formula appears in Hes. *Op.* 358 καὶ τέρπεται ὃν κατὰ θυμόν, where the digamma is no longer operative. See Hoekstra 1957, 207.

8. As will become clearer later, Book 13 constitutes a sort of sacred proemial book of the *Odyssey*. The limitation of my analysis of the patterns πάθεν/ον ἄλγεα θυμῷ and πάθεν ἄλγεα ὃν κατὰ θυμόν is justified by the fact that this formula is unique, having no variants, for instance, with other forms of *paskho*. Indeed, *algea*

pathetic expression characterizes Achilles in the *Iliad* and Odysseus in the *Odyssey*. We have here another stylistic feature that, like the epithets "the best of the Achaeans" (*aristos Achaiôn*) and "city sacker" (*ptoliporthos*) describes exclusively or almost exclusively the two heroes.⁹

This sharing of formulas by the two heroes establishes a parallelism within which individual features acquire a tremendous rhetorical power: for example, those that emerge from a close comparison of IX.321f.: ἐπεὶ πάθον ἄλγεα θυμῷ / αἰεὶ ἐμὴν ψυχὴν παραβαλλόμενος πολεμίζειν [after I suffered griefs in my heart / risking continuously my life in battle] and i.4–5: πολλὰ δῷ ὅ γῷ ἐν πόντῳ πάθεν ἄλγεα ὃν κατὰ θυμόν, / ἀρνύμενος ἥν τε ψυχὴν καὶ νόστον ἑταίρων ("and on the sea, he suffered many griefs in his heart / trying to preserve his life and insure the return of the companions"¹⁰ The comparison of IX.322 and i.5 is legitimated by several stylistic particularities. The most decisive one is the whole context (grief in the heart in the process of preserving or risking life) with its parallel formulaic expressions. In particular, in both passages *psykhê* is used with the abstract meaning of "life," that is, without the usual connotations of shade-ghost (as for instance in phrases like "the *psykhê* flies to Hades") and,

---

and the present forms of *paskho* create completely different clusters: for instance, ἀλώμενος ἄλγεα πάσχων (II.667, xiii.418, etc.) and κρατέρ' ἄλγεα πάσχων (II.721, v.13, etc.). With *thumôi* we have different clusters of words: for instance, ἔχοντά περ ἄλγεα θυμῷ (xvii.13).

9. On these epithets, see Nagy 1979. It is remarkable that in all the examples referring to Achilles and Odysseus, the text connects their suffering (*algea*) with specific occasions and events, yet the listener of the poems gets the impression that this *pathos* is not only distinctive, since it distinguishes them from the other heroes, but is also an almost permanent feature of their lives. For Achilles connects this suffering with his constant risk in battle (IX.322), while his mother later laments that his life is full of sorrows (*akhnutai*) "as long as he lives and sees the light of the sun" (XVIII.61f.). Odysseus's whole life before his return to Ithaca is summarized by the expression μάλα πολλὰ πάθ' ἄλγεα ὃν κατὰ θυμόν (xiii.90), and obviously the proposed etymology of his name could be interpreted in accordance with this *pathos*: Odysseus = "he who is pained," "the Hated." On the name of Odysseus, see Austin 1972, 1–19, with bibliography.

Finally, it is noteworthy that at least two of the passages of the *Iliad* where we find the expression πάθον ἄλγεα θυμῷ contain other expressions that mark in analogous ways specific features of the two heroes in the *Iliad* and in the *Odyssey*. In IX.321ff. we find another pathetic and hyperbolic expression, ὡς καὶ ἐγὼ πολλὰς μὲν ἀύπνους νύκτας ἴαυον, whose last part, ἀύπνους νύκτας ἴαυον, while unique in the *Iliad*, is uniquely repeated for Odysseus in xix.340. The case of *Il*. XXIV.7ff. is more complex, since the formulaic diction of line 8 is again unique for Achilles in the *Iliad* and for Odysseus in the *Odyssey*; but suspicion has arisen that the Iliadic passage may be an adaptation of the Odyssean one. See Leaf, ad loc.

10. Bekker (1863) was not wrong in pointing out the oddity of the expression: the implication that Odysseus did not have to save his companion's lives, too, in order to ensure their return. But Bekker was wrong in attributing the anomaly to the poet's lack of skill, for the oddity of the expression derives from a diction that seems, as I am suggesting, to allude to IX.321f.

therefore, without any of the concrete or personified aspects of its meaning.[11] Such an abstract meaning is very rare in both poems: in the *Odyssey*, for instance, we find only three examples of it, iii.73f., ix.254f. and i.5.[12] Finally, in both passages the word *psykhê* refers to the life of a specific hero and is preceded by the pronoun, both features being unique among the usages of the word in the *Odyssey*. It seems, therefore, possible that the oddity of the expression in i.5 depends on the intention to employ a variation of the construction in IX.322 (see note 10).

This structure of references between the proem of the *Odyssey* and IX.321ff. corrects any simplistic view of Achilles' destructiveness of his own people. As we have noticed, if we compare directly the proem of the *Odyssey* with that of the *Iliad*, we see that while Achilles' wrath is destructive of his people, Odysseus strives to save his companions. But since lines 4–5 of the *Odyssey* proem recall IX.321ff., we have to readjust that reading. The contrast between Achilles' anguish as he puts his life "always" at stake and Odysseus's anguish in saving his life constitutes the existential difference between the two poems and needs no comment. The *Iliad* is the poem of total expenditure of life and the *Odyssey* is the poem of a controlled economy of life. Achilles speaks of himself as constantly risking his life for his people, just like a mother bird who brings morsels to her little ones still wingless, and herself fares badly. This simile reveals Achilles' tendency to compare himself, in his private and emotional outbursts, to feminine figures, and exemplifies the uncontrollable excitability of his rhetoric. Achilles' hyperbolic, oversensitive simile evokes the spiritual anxiety (the mother bird) and the physical defenselessness (the wingless little birds) of the human condition that he tries vainly to resist by constantly risking his life. Yet any listener will also remember Achilles' failure to save Patroclus, and the anguish and sleepless torment of the hero for the death of his companion. Viewed in this way, the text of the *Odyssey* proem acquires a hypertrophic excess of signification, an overdetermination of contrasting elements. Through it we may glance not only at the difference between Odysseus and Achilles but also at the whole spiritual adventure of the Iliadic hero. To this extent, the comparison would even efface the distinctiveness and vividness of Odysseus's portrayal, and would create an overlapping of existential modes.

This excess of connotational significance parallels a certain poverty of denotation. The denotation in our texts of the word *algea*, for instance, is drifting

---

11. See Vivante 1956; Warden 1971, 95ff.; Marcus 1979, 33; and Vermeule 1979, 212 n. 12 for the meaning of *psykhê* as "life" in its abstract force.

12. iii.73f. = ix.254f.: οἷά τε ληιστῆρες ᾧ ψυχὰς παρθέμενοι. Here it is a question of pirates who risk their lives. Notice the plural and the absence of the pronoun. Moreover, ψυχὰς παρθέμενοι has a variant in ii.237: σφὰς γὰρ παρθέμενοι κεφαλὰς κατέδουσι βιαίως / οἶκον Ὀδυσσῆος, which shows the same equivalence between *kephalas* and *psykhas* that we find implicit in I.3 and XI.550.

The exact connotation of *psykhê* as either "life" in the abstract or in the concrete, personified sense is not always absolutely clear: see, e.g., IX.401–8, where in a few lines we have a more abstract and more concrete use of *psykhê*. Yet even in IX.401, where *psykhê* is used with the general meaning of "life," a shade of concreteness is introduced by the comparison between *psykhê* and the riches a man may own.

and unstable, besides being vague and imprecise. In the *Odyssey* proem *algea* must imply, in an uncomfortable simultaneity, physical hardships and spiritual pains.[13] In IX.321 *algea* seems to refer to Achilles' inner torment at constantly risking his life without any adequate compensation; in XVI.55 *algea* may simply refer to Achilles' humiliation at having been deprived of his *timê* (as Leaf takes it), but the notion of "hardships in war" cannot absolutely be ruled out. In short, the denotation of various usages in each text *may* be different, besides being so imprecise as to be ungraspable, notwithstanding the qualifying phrase "in his heart." The identity of the formula does not guarantee any identity of denotation; iteration by implying difference can just as well enlarge the spectrum of denotational meanings, but it also enlarges their vagueness and their poverty in each case.

If we recognize the self-referentiality of the formulas, we add an *allusive* connotation to each of these passages. This allusive connotation opens an endless self-mirroring or self-echoing of the texts and leads us to a hypertrophic signification. When we read in accordance with this excess, we recover a sort of sublime pathos: Odysseus's suffering many griefs in his heart opens up a vast horizon of heroic pathos, and our minds are befuddled by the vastness and discordance of the notes that are resonating here. Yet the sublime richness of this tonal excess also becomes blurred and undistinguished and goes along with the poverty, the imprecision, and the deficiency of the very expressions which create such sublime pathos. Before we elaborate on this point, we need to analyse another certain example of reference and allusion in line 2 of the *Odyssey* proem: ἐπεὶ Τροίης ἱερὸν πτολίεθρον ἔπερσε [after he sacked the holy city of Troy]. This temporal clause breaks the syntactical and stylistical parallelism between the initial lines of the two proems. Moreover, the attribution of such a glorious deed exclusively to Odysseus betrays the poet's bias in favor of Odysseus. It seems inappropriate, even though he shares with Achilles the epithet of "sacker of cities" (*ptoliporthos*),[14] for many other heroes—and gods, as we will soon see— share the glory of having destroyed Troy. Indeed, Odysseus himself attributes

---

13. The phrasing in i.4–5 is odd indeed: πολλὰ δ᾽ ὅ γ᾽ ἐν πόντῳ πάθεν ἄλγεα ὃν κατὰ θυμόν, / ἀρνύμενος ἥν τε ψυχὴν καὶ νόστον ἑταίρων. Besides the infelicity of line 5 to which Bekker already called our attention (see note 10), we must recognize a certain strain or tension in line 4, since *algea* is somehow forced to mean at once physical and spiritual pain. In fact, because of the locative ἐν πόντῳ, the expression πάθεν ἄλγεα seems to imply the hardships of seafaring, but because of the other locative "in his heart," the same expression would more likely take a spiritual connotation. The strain is not catastrophic, but it is clearly there: the scholiast, evidently trying to resolve the strain, suggests punctuating at *algea* and thus connecting the locative ὃν κατὰ θυμόν with ἀρνύμενος. But this is a foolish solution. The strain remains.

14. The epithet *ptoliporthos* is shared in the *Iliad* and the *Odyssey* by Odysseus (ten times), by Achilles (four times), by Ares (once), Enyo (once), Oeleus (once), and Otrynteus (once). Among all the major heroes, therefore, only Odysseus and Achilles are characterized as "sackers of cities." More specifically, the *Iliad* defines Achilles as *ptoliporthos* four times, Odysseus two times, while in the *Odyssey* only Odysseus gets this epithet.

such a glory to Agamemnon in ix.263–65: "We proudly declare we are the people of Agamemnon, son of Atreus, whose immense glory reaches the heavens, such a great city did he sack and a large army did he destroy." In the thirteenth book of the *Odyssey*—a book of great significance for our purpose because it functions as a proem to the second part of the *Odyssey*—Odysseus courteously ascribes to Athena as well the glory of having sacked Troy. As he speaks to her and plans the new strategy, he mentions Athena's assistance in the old days of Troy and asks her same assistance now (xiii.388): οἷον ὅτε Τροίης λύομεν λιπαρὰ κρήδεμνα [just as when we pulled down the shining battlements/veils of Troy].

The line produces powerful effects and a dissemination of motivations and purposes, since it repeats with a slight but purposeful variation a line of Achilles. In book XVI, a few lines after Achilles has lamented the suffering of *algea* in his heart, he has a sort of vision or desire. Speaking to Patroclus he envisions a utopia of savagery and love (XVI.97–100): "O father Zeus, Athena and Apollo, would that no one of the Trojans, as many as they are, might escape death and not even one of the Achaeans, but that we might avoid destruction so that we alone could pull down the holy battlements/veils (*krêdemna*) of Troy." The Iliadic passage obviously suggests a rape of the city (Nagler 1974, 53ff.) and lets us see, therefore, the two heroes united in the same violent action, in a warriors' camaraderie of extreme force and exclusion. The *Odyssey* obviously understands the erotic force of the Iliadic expression and marks this understanding by making it explicit, even glaring or offensive. The Iliadic epithet for *krêdemna* "battlements, veils" is *hiera*, "holy," which is conventional for the name of some cities:[15] in this way the *Iliad* combines a metaphorical use of the noun with a "literal" epithet. The *Odyssey* replaces the epithet *hiera*, "holy," with *lipara*, "shining," which is the conventional epithet for a woman's "veil." The *Odyssey* therefore retrieves the whole erotic force of the expression and forces both noun and epithet to take on a difficult, unstable metaphorical stance.

The dissemination of connotations in the Odyssean line, however, is not limited to these effects. No one can miss the point that Odysseus with his line substitutes his and Athena's friendship for Achilles and Patroclus and their warriors' camaraderie. The effect of this substitution must have been held to be worth the risk of an infelicitous side effect. For the couple Athena-Odysseus fits less properly than Achilles-Patroclus in the rape scenario: obviously Odysseus must have acted alone in carrying out whatever literal meaning is still present in the not fully metaphorical rape of the city. Because of this unfitness, the text turns the subdued erotic image of the *Iliad* into an obvious and offensive one, with the purpose of calling attention to the Iliadic model and to rape. Put otherwise, the *Odyssey* seems to replace the pathos and savagery of the Iliadic image with a sort of literal and literary shrewdness and lurid mockery. By this smooth adaptation of the Iliadic line, the *Odyssey* is able to indict with the greatest economy Achilles' foolish vanity and unaccomplished glory, while simultaneously building upon the energy of the Iliadic text the assertion that the

---

15. See I.266, IV.378, VII.20, XXI.108.

real sacker of Troy has been Odysseus, the tricky man of many ways, the survivor in all situations.

Accordingly, we find this same set of assertions and innuendoes in the second line of the *Odyssey* proem: ἐπεὶ Τροίης ἱερὸν πτολίεθρον ἔπερσε [after he sacked the holy city of Troy]. The metrical features and the diction of this expression unmistakably recall XVI.100 and xiii.388. In all these examples, the phrases Τροίης...ἔπερσε (i.2), Τροίης...λύωμεν (XVI.100), Τροίης...κρήδεμνα (xiii.388) occupy the same metrical position. The genitive of *Troiê* occurs in the *Iliad* 5 times: only in XVI.100 does it function as a possessive genitive (the battlements or veils *of Troy*), and only here does it occupy the position after the first foot and a half; in all the other four examples we find ἐκ Τροίης at the beginning of the line.[16] In the *Odyssey* the frequency of *Troiês* is higher, but *Troiês* as a genitive possessive occurs only once, namely, in the expected passage xiii.388.[17] In i.2 *Troiês* functions as a genitive after the noun "city" just as in English "the city *of* Troy" or in French "la ville de Troie." This genitive with the name of Troy is unique: the common way to say "the city of Troy" in epic diction would be either Τρώων... πτολίεθρον (I.164, etc.) or Ἰλίου...πτολίεθρον (II.133, and elsewhere), since *Ilios* is the proper name for the city while *Troiê* indicates more commonly the region of Troy. Notice, furthermore, that *Trôôn* in place of *Troiê* in our line would have been perfectly metrical. These considerations suggest that the composition of this line has developed from a substitution of *ptoliethron* "city" for *krêdemna* "battlements, veils" of XVI.100. By this substitution, that which in the Iliadic line is a possessive genitive, "the battlements *of* Troy," becomes in the *Odyssey* line a different genitive, "the city *of* Troy." This peculiarity distinguishes i.2 from the only other example in all of Homer in which *hieron* is used as an epithet of *ptoliethron*.[18] Accordingly, *hieron* might have come into the Odyssean line: Τροίης ἱερὸν πτολίεθρον from the Iliadic line Τροίης ἱερὰ κρήδεμνα.

Assuming that all these arguments are cogent, the text invites us to read in the second line of the *Odyssey* a most complex intertwining of themes, personalities, and tones. The *polutropos* "man," not the quick-footed Achilles, son of Peleus, sacked the city of Troy. Through the metrical parallelism and the consonance of the expressions, we glance at Achilles' mad prayer in the episode in which his destiny is decided forever and where we remember him as the hero who "suffers griefs in his heart" as he constantly risks his life. Because of the substitution of *ptoliethron* for *krêdemna*, we have here a moralized version of

---

16. None of these unique features is at the origin of the old athetization of the passage: as we might expect, Alexandrian scholars rejected lines 97–100 on moral grounds. When more recent critics bracketed the passage, they did so because of the *crux* in line 99 (ἐκδῦμεν). See Leaf, ad loc.

17. With the names of other cities, note the possessive genitive in IV.378, 406, and so on.

18. The *Iliad* does not offer any example of *hieron* as epithet of *ptoliethron*, but the *Odyssey*, besides i.2, offers the example of ix.165: Κικόνων ἱερὸν πτολίεθρον ἑλόντες. Notice the plural possessive genitive *Kikonôn* in accordance with the common epic practice.

Odysseus's deed, yet this touch might trigger the recollection of xiii.388, where Odysseus heavily emphasizes the sexual connotation of the Iliadic metaphor. We find again an overdetermination of signification: the overlapping of references creates a sublime embroidery whose outline cannot really be contained, but spreads indefinitely through the references that the formulaic diction incessantly weaves anew with its repetitions through both texts.

It is possible to expand this analysis of allusive passages to lines 7–9 of the *Odyssey* proem, to retrieve the echoes and the contrasts that resonate in the formula of line seven[19] and to outline the different theology that informs the proem of the *Iliad* (line 5) and the proem of the *Odyssey*,[20] but I think that the

---

19. The formula (σφετέρῃσιν) ἀτασθαλίῃσιν ὄλοντο occurs in IV.409, i.7 and x.437. While in the *Iliad* the formula seems to point to something that is "incidental," in the *Odyssey* the formula indicates something "consequential" (Rüter 1969, 50). The essential importance of the *atasthaliai* theme in the Odyssey can be easily illustrated by the fact that Odysseus, too, is accused of having caused the ruin of his companions because of his own *atasthaliai* (x.437), and that *atasthaliai* is the term by which the moral flaw of the suitors is indicted (xxii.317 = 416; xxiii.67, see xxiv.282).

In i.7 the pro-Odyssean bias of the poet is at work (see Strauss Clay 1976, 315–17), and it seems intended to counter the charge by Odysseus's companions in x.437 that they were ruined by his *atasthaliai*. As J. Strauss Clay demonstrates, the proem stresses the wantonness of the companions and Odysseus's innocence in order to preempt this indictment. This apology is strengthened by its theological implications. For while the poet "exculpates Odysseus from the destruction of his companions" (316–17), he simultaneously implies that *he* knows of no divine *boulê* which would determine the companions' destruction. On the contrary, had they observed Odysseus's warning and spared the cattle of the Sun, they too might have returned home. The passage, therefore, implies two directions of thought. In exculpating Odysseus, the poet stresses that his companions perished through their fault, and *not through his*. On the other hand, he strengthens his point by a gesture that enhances his personality—notice his intervention in the patronizing apostrophe, "fools!"—and displays his knowledge of the gods. The companions perished, the poet says, through no fault *of the gods* either, for gods do not plan the destruction of men unless they disregard the divine word. In this way the poet anticipates Zeus's statement beginning in line 34. This interpretation is consonant with the Homeric use of *atasthaliai*, for this wantonness or recklessness consists almost always in transgressing either divine order or sound human advice (whose source may often be divine). Here the companions transgress both.

20. Modern scholarship has long investigated the different theological stances that emerge from the two proems. In the Iliadic proem the accursed wrath of Achilles, cause of countless ruins and deaths for the Greeks, is problematically connected with the plan or will (*boulê*) of Zeus (I.5). Human responsibility for ruin and disaster is suspended in a problematic parallelism or confusion between human and divine realms. A clear, consistent answer to the question of the origin of evil is never given in the *Iliad*. (On the connection of the *Dios boulê* "the will of Zeus" with line 6 of the Iliadic proem, see Pagliaro 1956, 13ff., 17ff. The proem of the *Odyssey*, on the contrary, outlines immediately the problem of human responsibility: Odysseus's companions died because of their wantonness, the fools! who ate the cattle of the Sun

evidence we have already presented sufficiently establishes the thoroughly
allusive quality of the proem and its consistent anti-Iliadic point of view, within
which the opposition between Achilles and Odysseus, in particular, emerges
with great clarity. Despite the importance of this last point and the evidence that
every day accumulates on the question (see also Chapter One), the problem is
too large and complex to be treated here. I confine myself to some remarks on
the effects of the formulaic allusion and repetition.

As I have noted, if, on the one hand, we activate all the references that the
formulaic diction suggests, even through most rigorous and selective procedures,
we find a hypertrophic accumulation of meanings, a dissemination of
significations and tones so uncontrollable that the word "irony" even in its most
extended literary sense cannot contain it. On the other hand, if we refuse to deal
with the overdetermination of meanings and connotations and if we stick to the
notion of a mechanical, economical repetition, then we face the known
traditional questions, namely, the epic indifference to the signified, the
monotonous connotation of "heroism" as the only "literary" legitimation of the
repetition. The hypertrophy or the mutilation of meaning seem to be two
inescapable risks the critic faces. The reason for this either/or situation depends
on the very iterability of the formula. Iterability determines the status of the
formula as something whose meaning depends on the fact of being repeated. Yet,
as Derrida puts it:

> Intention or attention directed towards something iterable which in turn
> determines it as being iterable will strive or tend in vain to actualize or fulfill
> itself, for it cannot by virtue of its very structure ever achieve this goal. In no
> case will it be fulfilled, actualized, totally present to its object and to itself. It
> is divided and deported in advance, by its iterability, towards others, removed
> [écartée] in advance from itself. (Derrida 1977, 194)

This split or removal of intention in the very act of being actualized provokes
a certain either/or situation, so that the deficiency of intention and excess of
intention simultaneously drift and mar any text.

The epic diction is determined by repetition of phrases that we call formulaic:
at one level this repetition does not differ from the general condition of
iterability that makes language a language, namely, understandable; on another
level, this iterability is conscious and purposeful, insofar as it constitutes a
technical device and mode of composition. This double level explains the
complexity of the problem of intention and purpose of the formula. For on the
former level, the formula reveals the partially mechanical function of iterability,

---

(i.7–9). Compare Nagy 1979, 113 n. 3, "the narrative convention of the *Dios boulê*
'will of Zeus' as at *Iliad* I.5 is treated as a foil by *Odyssey* i.7," and Maehler 1963, 23.

On the different theology of the two poems the bibliography is immense. I like to
quote Pasquali's too often forgotten "Pagine meno stravaganti" (1968) and, among
more recent writings, with different shading on the question of theological difference,
Jaeger 1960, 1314–37; Lesky 1961; Finley 1978, 52–53; Rüter 1969, 38; *LFGE*,
s.v. *"aitios"*; and Schwabl 1978.

which in all languages is the condition of its producing meaning, while on the latter level the formula clearly announces some purpose for its being a repetition. But since iterability makes intention removed and split, the formulaic diction never reveals to the listener the fullness of its purposes: the mechanical force of repetition is never fully passive and the purpose in repetition is never fully active, present and activated. Accordingly, deficiency and excess of meaning must constantly appear to the critic as the *ostensible* and not merely *unavoidable* characteristic of this diction.

The removal or split of intention—however relative—in the process of repetition of the formulas deprives them of their full and present signification. Yet another feature occurs in the movement of repetition, namely, the interplay between the sameness of the signifier and the differences of the signified. Since it is inevitable that different contexts affect the meaning of the formula, the repetition of the signifier precludes the full meaning of the formula. We know that many Homeric formulas are used with no consideration for the context and that, therefore, while their denotation may be still the same, they make no sense in the actual occurrence. In our examples, the context is rather similar (a hero in pain trying to obtain something against great difficulties), but even here the meaning of the formulas is flattened into a generic signification within which the grief (*algea*) Achilles and Odysseus suffer may be physical or spiritual or both. This difference belies the identity of the signifier. This happens because repetition is made possible by the differential structure of language, by its lack of any origin, for were language a re-presentation of things, it would not be repeatable but the enactment of sameness. Consequently, the repetition of formulas always involves difference in the sameness, lack of origin, and gaps and articulations that make possible the extrapolation of a segment for its repeatability: the meaning of such repeated segments must drift into generic signification or into multiplicity of significations. Repetitions, in other words, preclude the full identity of meaning.

The formulaic style, therefore, both enhances the metaphysical intentionality of epic language and debunks it. For on the one hand, the formulaic style by repeating exactly the forms which seem to adhere perfectly to a certain heroic and divine content reproduces or invents that specific content, *sub specie aeternitatis*, as unchanging presence. The manifold aspects of grief mingle together under the veneer of identity in each instance of Achilles' and Odysseus's grieving: such mingling in identity creates a hypertrophic sense of pathos, of sublime vastness or excess in evoking pain, that startles our imagination. But, of course, such sublime sense is baffled by the difference between signifier and signified, for the iterability of the signifier writes off the full presence of meaning and triggers the proliferation of meanings and differences under and above the veneer of identity. At this point, the identity of the signifier simply emphasizes the inadequacy, the deficiency, the mutilation of meaning. We are left with the sense that the repetition of the formula is, after all, only a mechanical process, and that such a process, by anticipating and framing all actual and present intentions, is rhetorically purposeless. Because repetition both makes possible the rhetorical, purposeful, and creative use of iterability and simultaneously enhances its mechanical, drifting, and mutilating movement, repetition itself seems to justify only the critical stance that takes simultaneously into account all its effects. The text shows awareness of the daedalic, uncheckable force of its formulaic diction. In a paper on *kleos* in II.484ff., I have suggested that the poets both felt exhilarating confidence in the truth of their repeated tradition and deep anxiety about the drifting and scattering of meaning that ensue from this repetition (see Chapter Three). The *Odyssey* proem allows us to see an analogous awareness, though this awareness does not concern specifically the formulaic repetition but the rhetorical use of its epithets. More precisely, the *Odyssey* proem displays a textual awareness that any identity in repetition is always marred by the proliferating force of the text, inasmuch as the text is enacted and made both consistent and unstable by a figural supplementarity.

I open up this point in analyzing an aspect of the *Odyssey* proem that I have not yet discussed but is, nevertheless, most exciting and revealing. I am referring to the last part of line 1 of the *Odyssey*: πολύτροπον, ὃς μάλα πολλὰ / πλάγχθη [(the man) of many ways who wandered widely].

This line is very important both for what it does not say and for what it says. The line, of course, is silent about the name of Odysseus, a silence already commented upon in antiquity[21] and discussed frequently today. In Fenik's long chapter on "the nameless stranger," for instance, we find subtle observations on the systematic strategy of ironies that surround the frequent withdrawal of Odysseus's name in several episodes of the *Odyssey*, though the author inexplicably fails to mention the anonymity of the hero in the proem (Fenik 1976). Rüter, in his painstaking analysis of the whole proem, correctly notes that the name of Odysseus is "replaced by a definition of the man," a remark that hints at the *Odyssey's* concern for the characterization, the ethos of its hero (Rüter 1969, 47). More suggestively, Austin (1972) refers to the magic and apotropaic force of the name and explains that in the proem "the *Odyssey* introduces Odysseus obliquely because that is the way in which sympathetic characters consistently introduce or talk about Odysseus: the *andra* (man) of v. 1 is virtually a formulaic periphrasis for Odysseus through the proem" (also see Stewart 1976, 188–89). The problematic status of the name in the *Odyssey* is the point made by Mattes, who argues that Odysseus withdraws his name in scenes in which, given his actual unheroic, wretched conditions, he feels unable to identify himself with that which the name Odysseus—already steeped, we may add, in a heroic, literary pedigree—means to himself (Mattes 1958, 129ff.). All these observations testify to the acute sense that scholars have of the problem of Odysseus's name in general and of its absence in the proem. Let us only add that such a silence suddenly becomes obliquely and perversely telling, if we interpret it as a foil to the ponderously sounding name of Achilles, son of Peleus, in the corresponding first line of the *Iliad*.

I hope to move toward a more circumscribed and more forceful analysis of the absence of Odysseus's name by bringing into discussion the epithet that we find

---

21. Eustathius, *Commentarii ad Od.* vol. 1, 1381, 20, notices the absence of Odysseus's name and remarks that the poet extols the hero by noble epithets and keeps the listener in suspense.

at the place of Odysseus's name, *polutropos*. There are four aspects of this word worth considering.

(1) *Polutropos* occurs only one other time in Homer, again applied to Odysseus (*Od.* x.330) and twice for Hermes (*h. Merc.* 13 and 439). Possibly, *polutropos* ascribes some divine, Hermes-like power to Odysseus, since the epithet is used exclusively for them. Accordingly, the expression ἄνδρα...πολύτροπον may suggest the notion of a human being who possesses a peculiarly divine power. On the other hand, the word for "wrath" in the first line of the *Iliad* will be used in the poem only for gods' and Achilles' wrath.[22] Consequently, a sort of divine attitude is ascribed to Achilles, while the text simultaneously mentions his and his *human* father's name. The first lines of the two poems, therefore, form an antithesis and a chiasmus: the divine wrath of a man and a man possessing divine powers.[23]

Besides being used exclusively of Odysseus in the *Odyssey, polutropos* evokes what is characteristic of Odysseus's other distinctive epithets, namely, their notion of versatility, of many-sidedness—or as I shall call it with a rare but useful English word—of manyness. Stanford has quoted the distinctive epithets of Odysseus: *poluainos* "of many stories," *polukerdês* "of many crafts," *polukêdês* "of many cares," *polumêkhanos* "of many devices," *polutlas* "much suffering," to which one should add epithets which are almost exclusively his own, such as *polumêtis* "of many plans," which is used also for Hermes, *polutlêmon* "much enduring," and *poluphrôn* "much wise."[24] Such an array of *polu-* compounds among Odysseus's *distinctive* epithets confers on the hero a chief characteristic: versatility and manyness of travels, devices, resources, tricks, stories, and so on. A forceful understanding of this manyness leads us to a deeper understanding of the character and of his tortuous, contradictory life. These several *polu-* compounds imply not simply that Odysseus knows a variety of tricks and devices, but also that he confronts situations by offering the *same* response, a wily one. Accordingly, Odysseus's manyness outlines not only a horizontal structure, but also a vertical one, a structure of repetition. The opening lines of the proem emphasize just this point by repeating four times the adjective *polus*: the man of *many* turns, who wandered in *many* travels, saw the cities of *many* men, and suffered *many* griefs. The notion of repetition, of a certain accumulation of the same, seems here inescapable.

Such manyness as repetition of the same or of the similar leads to the notion of constant accumulation and hoarding. As I give an economic connotation to Odysseus's manyness, I wish to describe a certain economy in Odysseus's project, an economy of hoarding, conservation, and survival that sharply contrasts with Achilles' gesture of total self-expenditure: "May I die *at once* . . . ." Yet, can we really speak of a project of Odysseus and of a self-same character, once we have immersed both of them in the movement of repetition?

---

22. While *mênis* is used only for Achilles and for the gods, *mêniô* and its compounds are used also for other heroes—Agamemnon, Aeneas, Telemachus and Odysseus.

23. I owe these specific remarks to H. Foley.

24. On these epithets, see Stanford 1950 and Finley 1978, 34–35.

It is clear that the structure of iterability implies both a repetition of the same and a difference from the same. Odysseus confronts all situations repeatedly with the same wily, disguised mind, but his devices sometimes vary. As a result, the character, Odysseus, inasmuch as he is fully contained and distinct in his manyness, emerges in the accumulating and in the exploitation of having accumulated the same and the different from the same. Such a structure implies that Odysseus, while repeating himself, is also constantly on the track of otherness. This condition is the cause and/or effect that makes Odysseus resourceful, devious, and wily. For his manyness as repetition means that he is always removed in advance from himself, always split: he is always himself and other than himself. By being removed from and ahead of himself, he is always to some extent positioned after the events and therefore able to turn around them and to turn them around. The fact that Odysseus is constantly in disguise, other than himself, is not alien to this structure.

Furthermore, as the accumulation of manyness implies repetition, i.e., the contradictory movements of sameness and difference, it must create an odd capital and unstable hoarding. Such hoarding, such piling up of sameness and difference, must simultaneously and constantly dissolve into loss and scattering. The evidence from this point is glaring: Odysseus gains and endlessly loses all that which he aims at, riches, honor, friends, house, wife, and life. Odysseus's *nostos* is a return from hiding places—Calypso's island, Hades—which are figuratively emblems of his death. Odysseus's survival, therefore, alternates with his constant disappearing, hiding, and leaving. And, in fact, he is told that after his arrival in Ithaca, he will have to abandon house and wife and to put out to sea again.

These few remarks are intended only to open the problem of Odysseus's manyness, not to elaborate it. We must only add that, of course, the text tries to control the daedalic force of his hoarding and disseminating repetition. For there would be literally no progress in the plot or in the character, but only a constant drifting, were this manyness not controlled. That is why the text suggests that a sort of completeness, a sum and a fullness, emerges from Odysseus's manyness in the form of wisdom—*boulê, noêma, mêtis*—and in the form of a fulfilled return and victory. Even in precise texts, it is easy to see how the notion of manyness slips into that of totality. Thus, for instance, as Athena praises Odysseus's trickery and crafts, she says (xiii.291ff.): "He would be a cunning knave, the man who would surpass you in all tricks" (ἐν πάντεσσι δόλοισι). Analogously, as Odysseus introduces himself to the Phaeacians, he says, according to one interpretation of the text (ix.19f.):[25] "I am Odysseus, son of Laertes, and I am a concern to men for all (my) tricks" [ὃς πᾶσι δόλοισιν ἀνθρώποισι μέλω]. The totality of the tricks that Odysseus knows may still be only "many," but the whole of those "many" is such an absolute that he is insuperable by men and gods: his manyness becomes a model of full and absolute value. It is not otiose at this juncture to note that the etymology of *polus* connects the word with *pimplêmi*, i.e., with the notion of "filling" and

---

25. On the ambivalence of ix.19–20 and on its peculiarities, see Segal: forthcoming.

"full." This totality of Odysseus's trickiness and resourcefulness is expressed by the words of Finley, as he comments on these *polu-* epithets: "They relate . . . to his *whole power* of successful survival" (Finley 1978, 36; emphasis mine). And indeed, in the scene in xiii.291ff., Odysseus's whole power reaches a sort of sublime measure and sum.

Here we see how the process of manyness reproduces the process of repetition of the formulas. Here, too, the sublime sum is achieved by shutting out the loss and dissemination that at each moment threaten the hoarding and the sum. We have already suggested how this loss and dissemination operate in the large frame of the poem, but we can now see how they operate in a specific example. For Odysseus's manyness in the first line of the *Odyssey* refers specifically to his *tropoi,* his "turns," and this word already suggests the zigzagging movement of repetition and manyness.

(2) The first question that arises is, of course, whether *polutropos* should be taken in a literal, "proper" sense, i.e., with the meaning "of many journeys" or in the metaphorical, figural meaning, "of many turns of mind." Today scholars tend to accept that here the text is purposefully ambivalent: "il y a peut-être une ambivalence voulue," writes Chantraine (1974, 927).

This ambivalence is neither simple nor innocent. On the one hand, the phrase that follows *polutropos,* "who wandered widely," seems added in order to explain the epithet and to limit the meaning of *polutropos* to its literal sense. On the other hand, we should not miss the point that the word *polutropos,* by calling our attention to *tropos,* invites us to recognize in this *tropos* the *tropos par excellence,* that is, the metaphor. We are invited to recognize the *polutropia* of the text that installs the tantalizing possibility of a metaphor in the very word which may also mean "of the many turns of language."

The possibility of this meaning in Homeric times is unfortunately not absolutely ascertainable. Antisthenes in the fifth century B.C. understood Odysseus's *polutropia* exactly in this sense, and he even provided something like evidence for it.[26] And Plato's Hippias agrees with him in accepting the rhetorical meaning of the word.[27] Of course, the fact that *tropoi* could indicate the "turns" or "modulations" of the voice, as Antisthenes saw in xix.521, does not absolutely prove that *tropoi* in Homeric diction did indicate the "turns," i.e., the "figures" of speech. Yet it shows at least that *tropos* was open to other metaphorical possibilities than "turns of mind." The best textual evidence that,

---

26. See Decleva Caizzi 1966, frag. 51 = schol. *ad Od.* i.1. On xix.521 commentators emphasize the musical meaning of θαμὰ τρωπῶσα. For example, see Ameis, Hentze, and Cauer ad loc.: "'häufig wechselnd,' von den mannigfachen Modulationen und Tonarten." Also see Stanford 1959, ad loc.: "*Trôpôsa* is a form . . . of *trepô* . . . apparently referring to the many turns and trills in the nightingale's very complex song." Neither editor notices here the connection between *trôpôsa* and *poluêchea* "many-toned," a connection which to some extent could be taken as a matrix of *polutropos.*

27. Plato, *Hippias Minor,* 365a–b: when Hippias defines *polutropos* as "liar," Socrates says that he understands what Hippias means, but invites Hippias to leave Homer aside, because "it is impossible to ask him what he had in his mind when he composed these lines" (365c).

among these possibilities, we must also consider the notion of "turns of speech" remains the fact that *polutropos* contains in itself a metaphor: since the *tropoi* of Odysseus are metaphorical, we are invited to understand *tropoi* also as figures of speech.

Several features indirectly support this interpretation: (a) Odysseus himself is a unique master of puns and figures of speech; (b) his grandfather Autolycus was famous for his double-talking;[28] (c) the epithet *polutropos* is typical of Hermes.[29] In the *Iliad* Odysseus is not only famous for his eloquence, but he is also shown using unique puns and metaphors. In IV.353–55 he defines himself as "father of Telemachus" only to pun with *promakhoisi* and to suggest, therefore, that the father of "Far-fighting" will, on the contrary, fight in "the first line" (Risch 1947, 87). In the same passage he uses the celebrated expression ἕρκος ὀδόντων, a formula that in connection with "words" fleeing from the "fence of the teeth" is used in the *Iliad only by* Odysseus (IV.350 and XIV.83). Today we tend to take this expression as a kenning to indicate the "lips" (Humbach 1967, 21–31). But it would be impossible here to follow all of Odysseus's figures of speech. Be it sufficient to quote in addition the celebrated pun by which he calls himself *Outis* (Nobody) and befuddles the Cyclops. Let us note also that the poet adds his own pun by troping on *outis* in *mêtis* in *Od.* ix.410 and *métis* "ruse" in 415. It

---

28. *Od.* xix.364ff.: "Autolycus . . . who surpassed men in theft and oath. And the god Hermes gave him this preeminence." On ὅρκοι τε, Stanford writes, ad loc.: "Presumably this does not mean by positive perjury, for which the most terrible punishment was prescribed (see on v.184–85), but by cleverly framing his oaths so as to leave loopholes for advantageous evasions later—a form of trickery that many Greeks would commend (van Leeuwen cites Herodotus 4.201 and Thuc. 3.34.3). Odysseus himself exploits this ruse in X.382ff. when without making any positive promises he encourages Dolon to hope for mercy and then lets Diomedes, his companion, kill him. Notice that the connection between Autolycus and Hermes repeats that between Odysseus and Hermes as revealed by the epithet *polutropos*. Autolycus also uses a figure of speech, when he confers an eponymon upon Odysseus: he names his grandson "Odysseus," a significant name, because he himself is *odussamenos* (*Od.* xix.406ff.)

29. Hermes is *polutropos* in *Hymn to Hermes* 13 and 439. I derive from Kahn 1978 some points that have bearing on my own, although the author concentrates on epithets other than *polutropos*. To begin with, Hermes, like Autolycus, is a master of perjury by playing on words, and the source of Pandora's *epiklopon êthos, pseudea*, and *haimulíous logous* (Hes. *Op.* 67f., 78); see Kahn 1978, 51, 78ff., 140ff. Furthermore, in the same Hesiodic text, Hermes invents the name Pandora and its playful etymology (see Pucci 1977, 97–98). Hermes' mastery in using language, puns and double meanings could be seen as one aspect of his *polutropia*. Kahn's close comparison between Hermes' and the Sophists' rhetorical skills (146ff.) adds weight to my point, but the author prefers to limit the power of Hermes' (and his myth's) words within the "magic" or religious rather than the rhetorical frame of reference (162f.). Finally, the "mediating" features of Hermes' *mêtis*, ambivalence, turning (*strephein*), position at the borders or thresholds, passage from one stance to another, permutation, exchange, reversal, parody, *poikilia* and polysemy that Kahn describes so eloquently (165ff.) could felicitously be summarized by and contained within the word *polutropos* in all its possible meanings.

seems to me impossible, therefore, to resist the intimation offered by *polutropos.*

We have reached now three possible and all present meanings of *polutropos*: the man of many journeys, of many turns of mind, of many turns of language. The drifting, turning manyness of these *tropoi* reproduces in one word alone that excess of meanings that we have discovered before, when we activated the self-referentiality of rigorously and pointedly repeated formulas.

(3) It would now be necessary to follow all these three notions of Odysseus's *polutropia* and investigate their inner relations, overlappings, and contrasts. Unfortunately, I can here follow only the suggestion that emerges from the textual event that replaces the name of Odysseus with his *polutropia.* I shall connect the perverse silence of his anonymity with the excessive meaning of *polutropia.*

The drifting, turning meanings of the *tropoi* of *polutropos* hang together in an instability that prevents a univocal, "proper" sense from emerging. Moreover, the rhetorical meaning itself has no intrinsic consistency: Plato's Hippias read in this *polutropia* Odysseus's lies, Antisthenes his wisdom. Finally, the fact that *polutropos* may even imply "of many figures of speech" and constitutes itself one of them, questions the status of the expression *polutropia*: can this *polutropia*, in whatever sense we may take it, be anything other than a figure of speech? To put it otherwise, we have a metaphor in the word for metaphor. Accordingly, *polutropia* indicates the metaphor of the metaphor, the figural supplementarity that inscribes the possibility for any bit of language to become a *tropos* and for any *tropos* to be always part of an uncontrollable multiplicity and repetition, a manyness of *tropoi.* The literality of language—should we assume that something like that exists—is certainly taken in and absorbed by its figurativity or tropicality, so that language appears as a figural supplementarity. As I mention supplementarity, I hark back to Derrida's notion of *supplement,* its differential relationship to presence/absence, its retroactivation of meaning.

Now, this notion of supplement, the tropicality of the *tropos,* the aftereffect of the figural, all this defines in the first line of the *Odyssey* the very nature and essence of the hero. Consequently, the hero cannot appear with his "proper" name, which would indicate the individuality and exclusivity of his personality, the precise literary pedigree already formed through another tradition. It is curious and indicative that the epithet *polutropos* and the name Odysseus occur together only in x.330, when Circe addresses Odysseus. But there Odysseus has just enacted a trick that Hermes taught him: Odysseus's *polutropia* is connected with Hermes; and this connection perhaps reduces the semantic power of the word to indicate a single, "proper" source of Odysseus's trickery. In the proem, however, the word *polutropos* defines Odysseus's identity and self-sameness in a way that shuts out that identity and self-sameness, since *polutropos* defines them by the dissemination of meaning that is implicit in the very process of becoming the figure of the figure. We have here a double process of repetition: through *polu-*, repetition appears, so to speak, vertically, as manyness and accumulation, and through *tropoi,* repetition appears as the expansive movement that places meaning always at several removes from a putative origin. Accordingly, the identity of Odysseus must run forever in the tracks of displacement and must be enacted by figures of speech, disguises, and riddling turnings of turns. His name is here coherently excluded.

The vanishing of the name "Odysseus" in the folds of many *tropoi* implies also the figurative death of the hero, inasmuch as his life, *qua* hero, depends on his being known and famous. For the vanishing of the name "Odysseus" implies the vanishing of his *kleos*, of his being heard by name through the song of the poets, since name and *kleos* are necessarily connected (see xxiv.93f.). We can confirm this figurative death of the hero *qua* hero with the arguments that Nagy has elaborated around the notion of *kleos*. As Nagy shows, the *Iliad* attributes *kleos* (fame and renown) to the hero who encounters a glorious death. The *Iliad* would refuse glory to the warrior who goes back home to live in peace in his old age. Accordingly, the *Iliad* would deny fame and name to a man who, like Odysseus, "suffers many griefs in his heart trying to preserve his life" and to ensure his return home. The *Odyssey*, then, at its crucial beginning, seems to grant obliquely a point to the principle of the *Iliad*, to agree to some extent with the Iliadic prescription for obtaining *kleos*. But, in fact, the manyness of Odysseus's *tropoi* constitutes the very weapon of his survival: these *tropoi*— voyages, turns of mind, of language, shrewd wisdom, blatant lies—are the zigzagging structure of behavior that keeps him alive. These *tropoi* condemn his *kleos* to vanish, his name to be absent. Yet the silence of death, the silence of Odysseus's *kleos* in the folds of his *tropoi*, is also what insures his new life. The very gesture by which the *Odyssey* represses the name of Odysseus in its first line is at once a foil for *Il.* 1, a bowing to the principle of the *Iliad*, and an intrinsic product of the *Odyssey*'s own *polutropia*. The silence of Odysseus's name now speaks too much, and it questions or contests the simplicity of notions such as model and foil.

(4) We have already mentioned the *polutropia* of the text. The text places its own fullness and integrity in the very manyness of its *tropoi*. While momentarily and obliquely honoring the Iliadic principle of *kleos*, the text puts in motion a new *tropos* that will make Odysseus famous and recognizable by name, despite his anonymity. The text turns the form of the proem into a sort of *ainigma*, a riddle. The riddling structure of the proem is obvious. It starts with a generic object, "the man," and follows with qualifications that limit successively the generality of man "of many *tropoi*," "who traveled widely after he sacked Troy," etc., until the last qualification leads to the recognition of the hero. For the fact that "the man's" companions ate the cattle of the Sun is an "individual feature" (Bekker 1863, 101) and should make the identification sure. Yet the identification depends on the audience's knowledge of this feature and its ability to connect it with the other qualifications as elements of an *ainigma*. The text accordingly connects Odysseus's name with something outside the text, that is, to the precise knowledge and "reading" of the audience.

This mode of identification, therefore, does not restore the name in the text. It simply puts the name in the audience's mind or "on the tip of the tongue." The restoration occurs outside the text, through a successful appropriation of the text by the audience. Thus, as the *polutropia* of the text causes the vanishing of the name of Odysseus, so also it causes the vanishing of the text's integrity and self-containedness. For the success of the *tropos* of the riddle entails a certain mutilation of the text. We find here again hypertrophy and mutilation of the text as inseparable features. The repetition of the formula, the accumulation of the same, the figural supplementarity, all lead to the same structure, since in all of them difference is the necessary element that makes them possible. They all simultaneously add to and subtract from the putative origin of the repetition, from the wishful sameness of the accumulation, from what is only an aftereffect, the presence of things.[30]

---

30. I wish to thank Ann Bergren for her careful and sympathetic editing of this chapter.

CHAPTER 3

The Language of the Muses*

Pindar narrated the origin of the Muses, divine daughters of Zeus, in his *Hymn to Zeus,* but unfortunately we know it only through the summary by Aristides (second century A.D.): "Pindar went so far that in his 'Marriage of Zeus,' upon Zeus asking the gods whether they felt the want of anything, the gods demanded that he create for himself some gods, who, by means of words and music, would set in order [*katakosmêsousi*] this great work and his whole creation [of the world]."[1]

As the divine family wonders at the creation that Zeus has just finished,[2] they feel that something is still missing from the created order. What is missing is the musical voice of the Muses. Aristides describes this deficiency (*ei tou deointo*) as the need for divinities who *katakosmêsousi* the whole world. I translate the verb *katakosmeô* as "I set in order" rather than as "I praise"—as do other translators and commentators[3]—in order to emphasize the primary meaning

---

* "The Language of the Muses" was first published in *Classical Mythology in 20th-Century Thought and Literature,* Texas Tech. University 1980.

1. *Aristides,* ed. W. Dindorf 1964, 2.142; translation mine.

2. Another late source, Choricus of Gaza (see Snell/Maehler 1975, part 2, frag. 31) makes clear that Zeus questions the gods when he had just finished "ordering the whole" (*to pan arti kosmêsanta*).

3. See, for instance, among the translators C. A. Behr (1973, 1:535), who says: "Gods who would honor in words and music these great deeds." And see, among commentators, Barmeyer 1968, 65, who says "preisend ausschmückten."

of the verb in this passage. Both the philological arguments and the context of Pindar's works favor the meaning "set in order,"[4] for Pindar sees the poet as the "wise" person who does not simply celebrate but interprets and gives meaning to great deeds.[5] Although the above argument can be made, it is nevertheless true that the meaning "to praise" is not absent from the verb, since the term "setting in order and adorning by means of music and logic" can easily be taken metaphorically to mean "to praise." Finally, the problem of understanding precisely the meaning of this verb goes beyond mere philology. For the ancients did not easily distinguish "praise," "interpretation," and "saying the truth about someone." When the poet celebrates something or somebody he also gives a "meaning" to the object he celebrates; the *kosmos,* that is, the "order" he attributes to the object, becomes constitutive and functions as a principle of interpretation. This ambivalence concerns also—as we will see—the epic poets who "celebrate" the deeds of men, in the wake of the truthful song of the Muses. This ambivalence is still felt at the beginning of the fourth century, as we realize from Plato's *Symposium.* Here, the participants in the banquet agree to praise (*kosmêsai* 177c) and celebrate (*enkômion* 177e, etc.) the god Eros. Now each of the speakers who celebrates and praises Eros thinks that he is also saying the truth about Eros's origin, parents, and benefits. Finally Socrates exposes the problem of this ambivalence: "For my part," he says, "because of my simplicity I thought that one should say the truth about each person to be praised, and that this should be the groundwork, and that one should choose the most beautiful truths and set them down in the comeliest way. And indeed I was quite confident of speaking well since I knew the truth of praising each thing." Socrates then ends his point by stating that he will not praise the god but will speak the truth about him (198d–199a). The entire passage shows that the notions of encomium and of interpretation and truth can be hopelessly entangled[6] even at a time well

---

On the *Hymn to Zeus,* see Snell 1953, 71ff. and especially 77ff., where Snell also translates the verb *katakosmeô* as "praise," and implies that the world is already beautiful and ordered and that the Muses simply celebrate it: "On the day when the world attained its perfect shape, he [i.e., Pindar] affirms that all beauty is incomplete unless someone is present to celebrate it" (78). Walter F. Otto also translates this word as "praise," but he admits a large meaning to this praise (see Barmeyer 1968).

4. The examples collected in the *LSJ* show only the meanings "to set in order" and occasionally "to adorn." It is easy to see how the verb *kosmeô* acquires from the idea of "adorning" the metaphorical meaning "to celebrate," especially in a context which clearly indicates that this adorning occurs by means of *logoi* and music.

5. See Snell 1960, 78: "Pindar frequently says that the great deeds stand in need of a singer so as not to lapse into oblivion and to perish . . . But he deepens the thought by implying that a great deed requires a 'wise' poet who will lay bare its special significance. The beauty and the order of the world . . . depend on the wise singer to have their meaning made clear to men."

6. The problem in the *Symposium* remains a complex one, and one that I cannot discuss here. It involves various aspects: Socrates' first statement about the fact that praising somehow means to harmonize truths and encomium means a careful choice of the most beautiful truths; Socrates' later commitment to simply speak the truth about

beyond the archaic period, and that, therefore, it is vain to try to separate these notions by mere philological debate in the passage from Pindar. As the above discussion indicates, what Pindar actually said was that the Muses attribute order and meaning to the world created by Zeus, and that accordingly the Muses praise Zeus's creation.

As the gods are all gathered before Zeus's creation, they want a song interpreting and celebrating the creation. We cannot, unfortunately, submit Aristides' brief outline of the myth to a more thorough test and ask, for instance whether the order and the beauty the Muses will create by means of words and music does or does not correspond to that intended by Zeus in his act of creation. But what is clearly apparent, nevertheless, from the myth is that Zeus's creation does not by itself assure the beauty and sense he intends; it may have such beauty and sense but these qualities are not evident to the gods. For the gods request an addition, a supplementary force able to make that creation orderly, full of sense and beauty. We may therefore argue that Zeus did not intend any of these qualities to mark his creation, or that, if he did, these qualities are not clear to the gods.

Walter F. Otto, in *Die Musen,* stresses the difference between the Psalmist, for whom "the heavens tell the glory of God," and this Greek myth that separates the voice of the creation from the creator (Barmeyer 1968, 26). But, more radically, in my view, the Greek myth implies that God's creation, to the extent that it cannot manifest by itself its own order and beauty, is unaware of these qualities, and furthermore that the *creator himself* is blind to the *needs* of his own creation. Zeus asks the other gods what they feel is missing and wanting, as if he himself were not quite satisfied with what he had done and yet is unable to understand why he is dissatisfied. The result of this consultation is the creation of new divinities, the Muses, who will provide the missing order by means of words and music.

The blindness of the creator may appear odd but it is understandable. He is so fully identified with his own creation that he cannot see how strange his creation is for the other gods. In other words, Zeus cannot understand that, whatever he intended his work and arrangement of things to be, his real intentions remain latent. Therefore the gods need an interpreter, a seer as it were, who will bring to light the order, the *kosmos,* of things.

The myth, therefore, demands interpretation; the meaning and the order of the work are possibly there, but they can become manifest only through the work of the interpreter, for a meaning and an order emerge only *after* the Muses' song. The myth would then also suggest that the "meaning" could always be an aftereffect of interpretation and not a fixed structure, a closed-up entity residing in the work and constituting its essence or its informative principle.

The need that the gods feel for the Muses also indicates the unique and privileged relationship that language enjoys in the world of Being. As Otto writes: "The song and the words [*Sagen*] are a divine business [*Geschäft*] to be

---

Eros, while in fact his long discourse is *also* a praise of Eros; Pausanias's reflections on the necessity of praising all gods even those who are less desirable, and so on.

performed originally and authentically only by a divinity. These songs and words are so connected to the nature [*Wesen*] of things and to the divine profundity, that Being becomes manifest in these and only in them" (Barmeyer 1968, 28). This privileged relationship of language and Being is the assumption of all Western philosophy and is also the most specific metaphysical gesture of this philosophy.

This privileged relationship implies that Being becomes known, is appropriated and present through the power of the logos. The Pindaric myth is only another instance of this belief; the absolute silence and otherness of the world of Being becomes intelligible and communicable through the order that the Muses' logos attributes to it.

Yet recently we have become critical of this metaphysical assumption; no world of Being can emerge in its immediacy and presence since it emerges only through the grid of language, through the gaps and lags of the logos. When the text or the discourse seems to retrieve the very presence of Being, a mark retraces the oblivion of the difference. This mark retraces the *différence*, the supplementarity, the *pharmakon*, the ontological difference (see Derrida 1972). It is within these structures that Being itself is encompassed and inscribed and that the name for the ontological difference continues to vanish from our grasp.

Accordingly, the Pindaric myth, as we have already begun to see, shows the troubling power of the logos. For the Muses' logos emerges as an addition that does not trace any specific relationship with the world of Being. As far as we know, the Muses' song of the world will recreate it. In addition, the Muses' logos defines its own operation and function as *katakosmêsai*: "order" and "praise" are at once implied as unstable terms that already mark a difference, a gap, a gulf of some sort.

We cannot see how Pindar resolves this unstable tension in his myth, but we can see how the problem emerges in Homer, and how he confronts it. In Homer the celebrating encomiastic function of the poetic logos is defined by words like *kleos* (glory), while the truth of the poetic discourse is assured by the inspiration of the Muses.

Accordingly, when entering Homeric territory, we try to let the various facts of this poetic discourse emerge. The Muses are thought of as the goddesses who inspire the poet in celebrating the deeds of gods and heroes. The celebratory form of the Muses' song acquires some emphasis in Homer and Hesiod, for whom the task of setting an order, interpreting the world (as we saw in Pindar) is not so explicit as is the task of celebrating the world of the gods and men.

The terms of this task of celebration are various; to the Homeric *kleos* (glory), *kleiô* (glorify), and *humnos* (song), Hesiod adds *humnein* (sing of, celebrate). In this conception, logos and music would seem to be purely ornamental manifestations, pleasing additions, in order to edify the listeners. Furthermore, the world of beings, their history and life, would have a sense by themselves and in themselves, and the Muses would not introduce any *kosmos* in this world, but simply cosmetics.

Yet for the reasons that we have already mentioned, the Muses' song is not merely cosmetic. For these "cosmetics," far from being accidental additions, appear to be a human rendition of a divine song, that of the Muses. The song of the Muses in Homer is, just as in Pindar, necessary and not a mere caprice of sophisticated gods. Moreover, the Muses enjoy a wide view of the world; their words therefore correspond to the things they see, to the things as they were, are, and will be. It follows that the encomiastic song of the epic poet is marked by the same connotations as that of the divine song. In particular the epic is truthful. Before we discuss this latter point, we must show how Homer also makes use of the Muses' song as a necessary element in the life of the gods.

In the first book of the *Iliad* (601ff.) Homer equates the need for food and songs at the gods' banquet:

Thus thereafter the whole day long until the sun went under
they feasted, nor was anyone's hunger denied a fair portion [*oude ti thumos edeuto*],
nor denied the beautifully wrought lyre in the hands of Apollo
nor the antiphonal sweet sound of the Muses' singing.

(Lattimore 1951, 75)

The paratactic negative construction implies that the gods, by eating and by listening, satisfy their need for food just as they do their desire for song and music (Barmeyer 1968, 67). Indeed the lyre is a conventional accompaniment of human and divine banquets as we read in the *Odyssey* (viii.99, xvii.272), but the gods *must be* surrounded by beauty.

The poet does not tell us what the Muses are singing about, and to guess would be vain: probably the fact that their song is alternating excludes epic song. Yet, whatever its theme, the Muses' song in this instance defines the distance of gods from men. After the quarrel between Zeus and Hera, and after Hephaestus's intervention, the gods laugh and turn to the banquet and song. The Muses' song therefore indicates that the immortals have complete access to beauty and serenity; it also shows that their concern for human affairs is only superficial and fitful. But if the Muses' song bestows a *kosmos* to whatever they sing about, the song also signifies the truth. The song, then, points out essential traits of immortality, and also necessary features of that which is divine. To this extent, the fact that the gods need songs means that beauty and knowledge are traits that mortals necessarily attribute to the gods. Accordingly, since the song is a divine attribute, it will always be only "lent" to man.

To mortals, the divine song of the Muses constitutes a link to the gods, but this link, though necessary for singing, does not establish any durable connection and does not carry any divine fullness or blessedness. On the occasion of Achilles' funeral, the Muses come to sing a *thrênos,* again singing alternately with their beautiful voices,[7] but they excite only tears. The song of the Muses comforts mortals about the inevitability of death, but this comfort consists in a merely reflected glory.

The song is not a necessary feature of the human condition, though when man sings, the link with the Muses becomes necessary. As we learn from the

---

7. *Odyssey* xxiv.60. It is curious that *hopi kalêi* ("with the beautiful voice") also characterizes Circe in *Odyssey* x.221.

experience of Thamyris the Muses may strike the poet who challenges them, and make him unable to sing. He who can speak about the world, about the gods, and about the past and the future possesses a special language, memory, inspiration, and power. All these possessions can be summarized in one word: presence. For, thanks to the Muses, the poet gains access to the *things themselves* in their totality. The *locus classicus* occurs in the second book of the *Iliad*.

> Tell me now, you Muses who have your homes on Olympus—
> For you are [este] goddesses, you are there [pareste], and you know [iste] all
>   things [panta],
> but we [the poets] hear only the rumor [kleos] and know nothing—
> Who then were the chief men and the lords of the Danaans?8

The Sirens, different and strange Muses of the Iliadic song, invite Odysseus to stop and listen to their song.

> For we know all the things that in broad Troy
> The Argives and the Trojans suffered at the will of the gods.
> We know each time all that has happened on the much nourishing earth.9

In both cases we hear the same claim. The Muses know and control all things past, present, and future, both far and near; their song accordingly manifests things as they are, in their truth.

The epic song celebrates gods and heroes while recounting the absolute truth about them. Though neither in the *Iliad* nor in the *Odyssey* do we find any explicit statement that the song of the Muses is true, no one can doubt the song of the Muses who see and know everything. In our epic texts, only Hesiod questions the truth of the Muses' song. As I have shown in my book, *Hesiod and the Language of Poetry*, the text of the *Theogony* suggests that poetic language is capable of inventing, to some extent, an unreal similarity/identity with the world of Being. By this recognition the *Theogony* reveals what is problematic concerning imitation, difference, and the self-referential nature of language.

In Homer, on the contrary, the identity of Being and poetic language is never doubted, but there other uncontrollable aspects of language contest that comfortable presumption of identity. In the passage from the *Iliad* (II.484–87) quoted above, the poet stresses his lack of knowledge and vision by making the specific point that poets only hear rumors (*kleos*).10 The etymology of *kleos* connects the voice to *kluô* (to hear), to the Latin *inclutus*, to the Sanskrit *śravas*

---

8. Translation mine. This passage in the *Iliad* (II.484–93) has not received the critical attention it deserves. It is marked by several ambivalences and is couched in an uncommon language which I cannot hope to sufficiently explore in this chapter.

9. *Odyssey* xii.189–91, translation mine. See Chapter One, and in particular no. 10, p. 7 for the translation of line 191.

10. On the opposition between the Muses who see everything and the poet who only hears, cf. Luther 1966, and Luciano Canfora 1972, 15.

(glory) and to the Slavic *slovo* (word). In Homeric language the word carries the neutral, "zero-degree" meaning of "that which is heard," "rumors," and the marked meaning of "fame, reputation, glory." Thus, for instance, in xvi.461, *kleos* simply means "what the people" in town "speak about," but in IX.413, Achilles speaks about the possibility of this imperishable *kleos* (glory) if he remains in Troy: "My returning," he says, "is lost, but my fame [*kleos*] shall be imperishable." In the same book we find Achilles singing to himself and to Patroclus about the *klea andrôn*, "the famous deeds of men" (IX.189). If the subject matter of his song is identical to that of the epic song, then *klea* also means the content itself of the epic poetry. Nagy, from whom I derive this analysis, has forcefully stressed this last point (1976, 246ff.). *Kleos*, then, implies (1) mere hearsay—sources of ignorance; (2) repeated talk about a person or an event, source of fame, and then, glory; and (3) in the plural, the deeds of the epic song.

If we now reread the invocation to the Muses in the *Iliad* (II.484–87) cited above, these facts cause difficulties.

Tell me now, you Muses who have your homes on Olympus—
For you are [*este*] goddesses, you are there [*pareste*], and you know [*iste*] all
    things [*panta*],
but we [the poets] hear only the rumor [*kleos*] and know nothing—
Who then were the chief men and the lords of the Danaans?

One interpretation of these same lines might read: "but we [the poets] hear only reputation [from hearsay or tradition] and we do not know anything." Another might read: "but we [the poets] hear only the reputation [or fame] [that the Muses tell us] and we do not know anything."

All the possible meanings in the spectrum of the *kleos* are here valid in principle, but the text introduces indicators that support, contradictorily, both the meanings of *kleos* as mere human rumor and that of *kleos*, the divinely inspired "reputation and fame." Let us review these indicators. On the one hand, the singular form of the word *kleos*, the lack of a genitive (see on the contrary *klea andrôn* "Famous deeds of men"),[11] and finally the connection of *kleos* with a verb of hearing imply the meaning "mere rumor."[12] In fact, in this context, the connection of *kleos* (that which is heard) with *akouomen* (we hear) emphasizes

---

11. With the exception of *klea andrôn*, Homer does not use *kleos* to indicate the poet's song itself. A note of cautiousness on the technical designation of this word in M. Durante 2.51.

12. Achilles (IX.198) and the poet himself (viii.73) *sing* the *klea andrôn*. And in the *Odyssey* and Hesiod the action of celebrating and praising (*kleiô*) is explicitly connected with an expression that indicates the song: i.338–39, *Theog.* 31–32, 44, 67, 104–05, *Erga* 1 (and see also Ibykus 282.47P).

On the other hand, any connection of *kleos* with a verb of hearing seems to indicate human fame or mere rumors, i.298 (cf. XX.204), xvi.241, xvii.126 (cf. iii.83), *Hymn to Hermes*, 1.277 (which rephrases *Iliad* II.486).

In *Odyssey* i.283 (repeated in ii.217), Zeus's voice or *ossa* (see Clay 1974, 135–36) is the source of *kleos* among men; it becomes rumor, fame.

the process of repeating rumors, the repetition of something that is already a repetition insofar as it is a rumor. The text therefore introduces conspicuous elements that indicate what specific meaning of *kleos* is intended. Clearly we are invited to understand that the poets know nothing because they only hear rumors, and they are therefore only able to repeat indiscriminately what are already mere repetitions. On the other hand, if we read the whole invocation, we realize that the Muses are invited to tell the name of the leaders and the lords of the Danaans.[13] Muses will confer also reputation and fame on the heroes, namely what is called *kleos*.

The text, accordingly, contains an ambivalence. While the textual indicators imply that *kleos* is not divinely inspired, the context suggests that heroes will receive a *kleos* that is divinely inspired. Yet, by identifying *kleos* with ignorance and knowledge with the Muses' vision and memory (II.492), the text raises conceptual oppositions (words against vision, repetition against memory) that may block the ambivalence of *kleos*. But how is it possible to distinguish between the rumors and the renown the poets hear about heroes (*kleos*-ignorance) and the renown that the poets sing about the heroes (the *kleos* that the Muses confer on them by their tale, vision, and memory)?

It is now clear that the polysemic force of *kleos* reveals the play and the movement of the *différence* that marks the text. It maintains the difference, for *kleos* is not merely the point of contact of polysemic and opposite directions, but what "precedes" them and, so to speak, produces and sustains them. *Kleos* (that which is heard) implies *at once* both irresponsible and truthful modes of repetition in such a way that this "at once" is unresolvable, and accordingly the meaning of *kleos* can only be shifted obliquely or deferred. *Kleos* thus sustains and contains the differences while displacing them through oblique movements, and holds them back (deferral) so that, as we have seen, at each moment of the spectrum of *kleos* differences emerge in the same signifier.

It is, therefore, understandable that the text at this point should connect the unfavorable connotation of *kleos* with ignorance and, therefore, discriminate against *kleos*. Yet the work and play of *différence* emerge here with all their power and create a strategy which is itself contradictory. To the extent that the discrimination jettisons the unfavorable connotation of *kleos,* it also exposes the intriguing and uncheckable force of *kleos.*

The opposition between the merely wordy *kleos* and the direct vision that the Muses have of the *panta* is strongly emphasized by the text. The line that refers to the Muses' presence and vision (*"humeis gar theai este, pareste te iste te*

---

13. As will later become evident by my translation, I take lines 488ff. to mean: "But I would not say or name the multitude [of the common people], not if I had ten tongues . . . unless the Muses of Olympus . . . recalled all those who came to Ilion." The frequent opposition between *plêthus* and the leaders may support this translation but nothing prevents us from reading: "And I would not say or name all the multitude [of the leaders], not if I had ten tongues . . . unless the Muses of Olympus . . . mentioned all those who came to Ilion." As I will later indicate, the former interpretation creates a logical inconsistency that the latter avoids.

panta") repeats the sound *este* to support the conceptual identity of their several attributes: their being goddesses, their being present, and their knowledge. The text sustains the notion of a privileged access to the divine world by several devices. The most common device is that of exhibiting an intimate knowledge of the divine world. The poet knows at every moment the precise activity of gods and goddesses, and he lets us know that none of his characters have his knowledge. Even Odysseus, for instance, knows about the gods only if they appear to him and reveal themselves to him; otherwise he is blind to their disguises.

Another literary technique used by Homer involves quoting the names or nouns that belong to the divine vocabulary; the poet proves in this way his intimacy with the arcane source of his song. Yet, by doing so, the poet leaves room for our assessment of the distance that may exist between the original song and that which he adapts to the mortal language.[14]

The poet does repeat. In this invocation he says that the poets hear only that which is heard: here the reason why the Muses should tell the poet the names of the heroes is unmistakably clear. The *kleos* of each hero, of each family and clan exists in the form of traditional tales that men have long repeated.

Glaukos, Achilles, Aeneas, to mention only a few, know the *kleos* about their family. Thus Aeneas says to Achilles:

> We know each other's family, we both know our parents
> Since we hear the fame of old from mortal men;
> Only you have never with your eyes seen my parents, nor have I seen yours.
> For you, they say, are the son of blameless Peleus.
>
> (*Iliad* XX.203–6)

Then, as Aeneas relates the story of his family's more remote past, of his ancestors from Zeus to Dardanos, he introduces his story with the following words: "If you wish to learn this too and be certain / Of my genealogy: there are plenty of men who know it" (XX.213–14). These last words also introduce Glaukos's story about his family (VI.145ff.). The indicators that we have already gathered about the word *kleos* are here the same. Aeneas has heard the *proklut(a)* . . . *epea* ("words" that have been "heard of olden time"). The text therefore stresses, by the etymological *figura*, the passive repetition of rumors or words just as it had done in the invocation to the Muses. In fact, this repetition helps to create the saga, the famous story. Neither hero ever doubts the truth or better the "reality" of these *proklut(a)* . . . *epea*; Aeneas seem to believe that the mere repetition of their family stories—"words" that have been "heard of olden time"—assures their legitimacy, their reality. Notice also that Aeneas—the son of a goddess—does not attribute these repeated stories to any special sources, but

---

14. Concerning divine naming in Homer, Güntert 1921 thinks that Homer chooses more polysemic, suggestive, and allusive words for the language of the gods. He shows that divine naming is often a poetic periphrasis. Clay observes that "the presence of these peculiarly divine names points to the existence of a sphere of knowledge accessible solely to the gods" (1972, 131).

significantly only to the olden time and to the plurality of *human* voices that repeated them.[15]

Each time the poet begins to sing, the Muses tell him or teach him, or finally liberate his song just as other gods release the hero's *menos* (might or passion) in the heat of the battle.[16] Accordingly, our picture is correct; whenever the poet sings, he repeats the present tale of the Muses. "Tell me *now* . . ." the poet asks the Muses; he does not repeat what the Muses taught him some time ago, or even yesterday. In each performance he feels linked with the Muses; in each song he relies on them, reducing his repetition to immediacy or almost simultaneity, avoiding intermissions, the risk of forgetting, the risk of adding by himself.

Yet nothing is straightforward and simple in this invocation, for, while in line 484 the demand for the Muses' tale is indicated by the verb *espete* (tell), in line 492 the poet's word *mnêsaiath'* from *mimnêskomai* introduces a more complex notion. This verb means that the Muses' tale is a "recalling," "reminding," though it is not clear whether the Muses simply recall to themselves what they see, whether they recall to the poet (or simply mention to him) what they see, or finally whether they remind the poet of what he has already sung about on other occasions.[17] This question is probably insoluble, and we must be satisfied with the fact that the Muses' tale is itself a "recalling," a *mnêmê*. Obviously this "recalling" implies a repetition, but we must assume that it is a direct and immediate repetition of that which the Muses have seen or see.

The text of the invocation also suggests that the tale of the Muses resounds within the poet: "*Espete nun moi*" [Tell *me* now], the poet asks the Muses. "*Me*" does not idly qualify the person to whom the Muses will speak, but it points out the directness of the relationship. Probably within the poet, as Hesiod suggests (*enepneusan de moi audên /thespin*, "They breathed the song in me," *Theogony* 1.31), the Muses sing their song. While the *kleos* spreads outside the poet, in the towns, everywhere, by a repetition no one controls, the Muses' *kleos* enters the poet directly, without turning, meandering, going astray.

The poet attempts to minimize and almost to eliminate temporal and spatial dimensions; his rendition of the Muses' tale and memory would in fact eliminate, were it possible, temporality, deferral—the condition of repetition—and the distance which marks the territory of difference.

As we consider the ambivalence of *kleos*, the movement of repetition, and the textual attempt to intercept the dangerous aspect of repetition, we recognize a situation and a strategy analogous to that of Plato's distinction between memory (*mnêmê*) and "reminding" (*hypomnêsis*). Jacques Derrida, in "La Pharmacie de

---

15. We must consider the possibility that *proklut(a) epea* may indicate the epic verses that were already archaic in the eyes of Aeneas.

16. See, for instance, *Iliad* V.3 and 792–93.

17. The *LSJ* translation appears as *mimnêskô* 5.2; "make mention of" is too weak to render the connotation of *mnêmê*. We also note here that the Muses, in Hesiod's *Theogony*, are daughters of Zeus and Mnemosyne, that is, Memory. Detienne emphasizes the connotation of memory by the verb "rappeler" (1973, 10).

Platon," has studied the articulation of "memory" and "reminding" within the ambivalent "notion" of *pharmakon* in Plato's *Phaedrus*. This distinction points out "a subtle opposition between knowledge as 'memory' and non-knowledge as 'reminding,' between two modes and moments of the repetition. One, the repetition of truth (*alêtheia*), shows and reveals the *eidos*; the other, the repetition of death and oblivion (*lêthê*), conceals and leads astray, since it does not reveal the *eidos*, but represents its presentation, repeats the repetition" (Derrida 1972, 155).

The reader of that essay need not gather all the other aspects of these two different modes of repetition that Derrida has uncovered: the repetition of the *eidos*, by the discourse of dialectic, developing in the soul, moves legitimately to another soul, eschewing the dangerous meandering and fatherless anonymity of writing. These few hints sufficiently illustrate how the strategy implicit in Homeric *kleos* corresponds to that of the Platonic *pharmakon*, including the two modes of repetitions. Just as the repetition by memory repeats the *eidos*, so the Muses' tale (*mnêmê*) about the heroes' deeds and glory (*kleos*) would repeat the *panta* that they see (notice that *iste* and *eidos* are etymologically connected); on the other hand, the Platonic "reminding" would correspond to the *kleos* that Homer jettisons in the invocation to the Muses, because it is a source of ignorance. In fact, the poet merely "hears that which is heard" (*kleos akouomen*) and therefore can only *repeat*, literally repeat a repetition. The categories of inside and outside, of directness and obliqueness, equally characterize the two modes of repetition within *kleos*. Both Homer and Plato attempt to control the structure of repetition by means of the discriminating value of truth. To paraphrase and adapt from Derrida's analysis (194ff.), we may repeat that, for Homer, the opposition between truth and falsehood is contained wholly in the structure of repetition and does not exceed it.

This structure is "primary" and necessary; without repetition there would be no truth, since truth uncovers that which can be repeated in intelligible form from the *panta* (everything) that the Muses see. Derrida writes: "But on the other side, repetition is the movement itself of non-truth: the presence of Being gets lost, scattered and multiplied by mimens, icons, phantoms, copies, *etc*."

Both modes of repetition operate in this *kleos* that implies *at once* the uncontrolled spreading of rumors and the direct repetition of the *panta*, the hearsay without sources and the Muses' voice-*mnêmê*, rumors from the outside and the careful reception of precious words inside the poet's mind, the poet's distance from the events and the presence of the Muses before the whole. Truthful knowledge intervenes to intercept and block the movement that "produces" and holds in its grip this "at once" and even denies that the song of the Muses has anything to do with *kleos* and repetition. But the song suggests many times that the Muses' tale produces *kleos* and repetition; the discriminating value of truth does not take control of the structure of repetition, but is contained in it. Finally the movement of repetition hides the fact that the "model," or the "source" of the repetition, far from being at the start of the repetition itself, is simply "implied" by the repetition. In fact the "model," the "source," is thought of and postulated, so to speak *post eventum*. Accordingly, the divine source of the Muses' song and truth are only one side or one track of the movement of the repetition and we will show later in what way this track gains the status of being a divine source.

But at this point we might pause and think about the intriguing similarities between Homer's *muthos* and Plato's *logos*. I am well aware that, in Plato, *muthos* is still alive and operating along with *logos,* but the question about these similarities is still interesting, for Homer and Plato nevertheless differ so much in this respect, and not least in the avowed intention of the philosopher.

The *muthos* and the *logos* orchestrate the same structure of repetition, the same attempt at domination. Both are ostensibly marked by an intriguing, ambivalent notion, *kleos* on the one hand and *pharmakon* on the other; both *muthos* and *logos* trace a blurred line upon which a complex strategy of concealment is acted out.

What, then, does distinguish *muthos* from *logos?* The question is a sort of trap because it demands that *logos,* which first discriminated against *muthos,* rehearse its old and successful performance. We should not, therefore, follow the wake of this discrimination; and if I use momentarily these two notions, *logos* and *muthos,* it is only for the sake of questioning the sense and the legitimacy of their distinction. Let us compare the series of oppositions in Homer and Plato in the structure of repetition. In Homer, there is the *kleos-mnêmê* of the Muses, daughters of Zeus, who live on Olympus, and, on the other hand, there is the human, unaccountable *kleos;* in Plato there is dialectic and, on the other hand, writing/rhetoric. The difference between the two structures seems now immense; Plato does not operate such a neat separation and does not build such a rampart between truth and falsehood as does Homer. Myth, then, reassures by promising a safer control of the difference and deferral. Myth puts on stage characters who face presence itself and whose language is thought to be identical to that presence. It believes, therefore, that it has completely overstepped the gulf of difference by speaking a "special" language that does not counterfeit or mime things but simply names and repeats them. The fixity of the epic expressions and their traditional continuity in the same rhythmical and musical pattern implies a repetition that has nothing to do with the repetition of common language; the myth's repetition repeats things as they are through the medium of the divine song.

The language of *logos,* on the contrary, recognizes and takes into account the gulf of difference, the traps of re-presentation and imitation. Few philosophers are as aware as Plato of the corrupting force of the discourse because of its mimetic or representational functions.[18] But Derrida's reading of the *Phaedrus* shows that Plato aims at effacing the difference by a series of metaphysical moves and decisions such as that of exempting the spoken discourse of the soul from the predicaments (errance, sourcelessness, etc.) that threaten the truth of the written discourse. Moreover, Plato's discourse of truth tries to demonstrate the immortality of the soul and the *anamnêsis.* When we recall Plato, we realize that the divine vision that Homer attributes to the Muses' song reappears, notwithstanding dialectics, and, notwithstanding Plato's objections to Homer's myths, as the capability of the human soul-*logos* to retrieve a vision of Being.

---

18. See Lacoue-Labarthe 1975 for a discussion of mimesis in Plato's *Republic.*

These few hints show the pertinence of our comparison, the correspondences existing between *muthos* and *logos*, together with the difficulty of assessing precisely the divergences and the similarities. It seems safe to say that *muthos* and *logos* are facets of the *logos* which the *logos* polarizes in its own interest, in its battle against *muthos* in order to acquire the stronger claims to truth it boasts of possessing. But under the veneer of the polarization that the *logos* has effected, we uncover a subtle set of similarities and divergences that contests that polarization. Finally, the question of repetition and representation remains insurmountable for the *logos* that aims at truth.

And the question is insurmountable for the language of myth. For the poet's rendition of the divine tale-*mnêmê*, the source of truth and knowledge, remains indeed a repetition. It is a repetition not only because the poet would at any rate repeat the tale of the Muses, were they really speaking from within him, but especially because the Muses' tale is itself already a repetition, since it is a recalling, a *mnêmê*. Their vision of the *panta* becomes a tale (*espete*), and the tale is itself a *mnêmê*. But are the Muses really speaking within the poet? Just as we contested all the distinctions and discriminations that occur in the text, we are led to the conclusion that the tale-*mnêmê* of the Muses and the poet's rendition of it are finally only one. But in order to introduce this point, we must read the whole invocation to the Muses and become aware of the emphasis on the pronouns and of the force of the "voice" that is contained in it.

> Tell me now, you Muses who have your homes on Olympus—
> For you are goddesses, you are there, and you know all things,
> But we [poets] hear only the *kleos* and know nothing—
> Who then were the chief men and the lords of the Danaans?
> I could not tell over the multitude nor name them,
> Not if I had ten tongues and ten mouths,
> Not if I had an unbreakable voice and a breast of bronze within me,
> Not unless the Muses of Olympus, daughters of Zeus of the aegis,
> Recalled all those who came beneath Ilion. / But I will tell the lords of the
>   ships, and the ships' numbers.

It is not absolutely clear how to take the two conditional clauses: "not *if* I had ten tongues" (see note 13) and "unless the Muses . . . recalled," especially in view of the ambivalence of lines 488ff. The poet might simply mean that no matter how powerful his voice was, even if it were divine, he would be unable to sing about the heroes without the Muses' *mnêmê* memory and tale. Or alternatively, the poet may suggest that the two conditional clauses are not correlative; if the Muses were asked by the poet to sing about the common people they would probably comply. In this case would the poet have sufficient breath and voice? The hyperbole ("ten tongues and ten mouths") would be intended to stress the extraordinary number of the people who came to Troy, but it might also imply that the poet is afraid of not having sufficient breath. Accordingly, the impossibility of recording the names and the stories of the multitude would depend on the weakness of the poet's voice (*phônê*), on the limited power of his voice. His voice might cease functioning,[19] since—as *phônê* itself makes clear—it is human, the poet's own, and apparently, from the context of the passage, it cannot be strengthened by the Muses.

These two interpretations emphasize the following points: the poet identifies his activity with the power of his voice, and this voice reproduces the Muses' *mnêmê*. Yet the degree of importance and necessity of the poet's voice in relation to the Muses' *mnêmê* would vary in accordance with the different interpretations. In the light of the former interpretation, the importance of the poet's voice is diminished in comparison to the Muses' *mnêmê*, while in the latter interpretation, the poet's vocal powers function as necessary assets, as an unavoidable condition, though insufficient by itself.

I follow the second interpretation because it more clearly emphasizes the unique power of the voice, but my argument would still hold with the other interpretation.

The weak point, the human deficiency, is identified in the poet's mouth, tongue, chest, and voice; and significantly, it is just in connection with this identification that the pronoun *ego* (I) becomes an active subject (*Il.* II.488). Until this point, the poet had asked the Muses to tell him (*moi* II.484) or he had dissolved his "ego" in the phrase "we" (*hêmeis* II.486) covering the whole class of the poets. Now the ignorance of the poets can be obviated by the Muses' willingness to share their vision of the *panta* and their *mnêmê* with the poets; but the weakness of the voice qualifies, without ambiguity, the poet who sings the song, this invocation to the Muses.

The whole passage (II.488–92) might mean nothing more than "it would be too long to record and name all those who came to Troy," but the way in which this point is made is important. For the poet's "subjectivity" depends upon both his reception of the Muses' memory and tale and upon his own voice, that is to say simply upon his physical capability at reproducing their sounds. And, to some extent, these limitations reveal the true picture: of course, the poet's only task seems to be that of repeating, with his own voice, word for word what the Muses tell him.[20]

---

19. *Arrêktos* ("unbreakable") has some curious features in this passage. First, the adjective almost always refers to divine objects or attributes (the only exception being XIV.56-68 where *arrêktos* refers to the Argives' wall); secondly, in no other case does the adjective modify such an impalpable object as the word "voice."

The word for mouth, *stoma*, is very rarely connected to the "voice" in Homer. In about twenty-eight examples of the word only three times in the *Iliad* does the word have such a connection (II.489, II.250, where Odysseus addresses Thersites; XIV.91, where Odysseus addresses Agamemnon), and only once in the *Odyssey* (xii.87, which refers to the Sirens' mouths).

20. It is not easy to define the extent to which the author is conscious of his authorship and the mode of his consciousness. Insofar as he is a mouthpiece of the Muses' song, a reproducer of that song, he correctly identifies himself with his receptivity and his voice—whose power, force, effects, and so on, are exclusively his own. Yet the poet's perception of himself is far from simple. Even in the first line of the *Iliad* the goddess is asked to sing the "wrath" (*mênis*) of Achilles, a story, in other words; in the *Odyssey* (i.1), the Muse is asked to speak about or to tell of the "man"

Moreover, in comparison with *kleos*, which means the pure passivity of a sound's "being heard," *phônê* (voice) involves the active notion of *producing*, emitting a meaningful sound. As Ernout-Meillet write: "the meanings 'to narrate,' 'to state,' 'to declare' are conspicuous in this root."[21] In this context the poet's *phônê* is the voice that sings (*aeidein*) and that, therefore, does not simply *produce* sounds, but also enchanting sounds (*Odyssey* i.337, xvii.514–21, etc.) and exciting, charming words (*Odyssey* xvii.519: *epe'himeroenta*). Accordingly, the *phônê* is the force that reproduces the Muses' *mnêmê*. By this repetition the voice sings about the heroes' fame (*kleos*) and replaces the heroes' fame (*kleos*) that the poet hears from human sources and that he considers mere ignorance. Simultaneously, this alliance of the Muses' *mnêmê* and poet's voice, though itself a repetition of a memory, replaces the repetition of repetitions (*kleos*) that again marks the poet's ignorance. This is indeed the poet's willful interpretation of his song.

We must now understand what occurs in the utterance of the voice. The poet may not possess ten tongues, ten mouths, an unbreakable voice, and a bronze chest, but the conditional evocation of this powerful vocal system already suggests where the relative degree of the poet's *own* power and subjectivity lies. Not surprisingly, then, he ends his invocation to the Muses with this proud assertion: "But *I'll* tell the lords of the ships."[22] Obviously something intriguing occurs in the realm of the voice, something like the establishment of the poet's subjectivity. We must imagine an effect by which the resounding of the poet's voice inside himself creates the illusion of the poet's freedom and autonomy from the world of *kleos* (i.e., from the condition of repeating repetitions), from the outside world.

Such an effect, as Jacques Derrida has often shown, lies in the process through which the speaker affects himself by his own voice (*autoaffection*). In this process the speaker listens to himself speaking and is impressed and affected by the sound, the signifier that he produces. The speaker "does not have to pass forth beyond himself to be immediately affected by his expressive activity" (Derrida 1973, 76). As a result of this production of *autoaffection* the signifier

---

(*andra*): it is therefore clear that the poet chooses the theme of the song. In viii.73ff. and 481, the Muse teaches *oimai*, and in the second instance the poet chooses the theme that Odysseus suggests.

In the Iliadic passage of the invocation the term *espete* is pointed: the aorist form of the imperative implies the atemporal, instantaneous aspect of the action; the choice of the verb may have been prompted by some affinity of sound with *epos* (though no etymological connection exists).

21. *Dictionnaire étymologique de la langue latine* (1932). Benveniste (1969) also shows the religious connotations of this root and the impersonal act of speech in some specific forms: *phêmis*, *fama*, and so on.

22. Scholars have already noticed the emergence of subjectivity or of the individual personality in this passage. Benedetto Marzullo, for instance, ascribes the singer's anonymity to the earlier stages of the epic tradition and attributes the emphasis on the personality of the poet (*Odyssey* i.1, *Iliad* II.484, Hesiod, etc.) to later stages (Marzullo 1952, 482, no. 2).

seems to vanish as something involving the exteriority, otherness, physical articulation, and temporality of language. By this effacement of the signifier—or by its becoming, so to speak, not perceived—the voice produces a pure, inner "signified" (meaning, idea, etc.) that seems to share nothing with the established contingent and external aspects of language, nothing with the articulations of language. What is signified resounds fully in the speaker as meaning that is present, immutable, and ideal, just as an abstract idea, notion, or presence can be.

No doubt that through this process, the "notions" of what is interior, subjective, conscious, etc., emerge as pitted against the opposite terms. As a result the voice fosters upon the speaker the impression that his voice gains control of that which lies outside, without sharing in itself anything of the outside.

This process is universal and applies to the structure of the "voice" in general. But for the ancient poet who relies on the power of his voice, this process must have been very effective and most self-serving. As the voice creates in the poet the illusion of its freedom and autonomy from the outside world, an essential separation between inside and outside is drawn. The voice, then, appears as a meaning, a force that puts in order and makes present the world itself; because it does not share anything with the world and makes the world alive, it must come from outside the world, which means from the gods. For only the Muses, as Pindar teaches us, put an order and a meaning in the world of Being.

The poet's rendition of the Muses' words means, finally, that the poet listens to his voice as this same voice sounds to him to be constituted by the characteristics we have mentioned—its autonomy from the world, as it were, its beyondness: the fullness and the presence of what it signifies or of the meaning seems to eschew the world of contingency and articulations while ordering and signifying the world. Such an effect is made possible by the repression of difference and deferral that seems to take place in the process of *autoaffection* by the voice. For the whole articulating and differential operation of the signifier seems to vanish in favor of a "full" signified.

Thus the poet in this invocation to the Muses mentions *kleos* only as a negative notion. For against this *kleos*, mere sound, repetition of signifiers that signify no knowledge, mere meandering rumor, he puts the active, meaningful utterance of this voice repeating the *mnêmê* of the Muses, the words that set in order the *panta*.

But the poet cannot, even here, hide all traces of the repression of the difference. The indirect mention of the weakness of the human voice points at the physical, toiling, articulatory (ten tongues and mouths) process of the voice, without whose articulated sound no Muses' truth would appear. Therefore, the conditional clauses that make the poet's naming of the common people depend on his vocal power and/or on the Muses' assistance is the place of a significant indecision. There the articulating, physical, temporal structure of the voice is *at once* subordinated to the Muses' voice—and, therefore, made unimportant—*and* enhanced as its hyperbolic, unreal quality becomes the distinctive difference between the two conditions.

Therefore, we end this analysis with a double set of results. On the one hand, the ambivalent meaning of *kleos* and the conspicuous connotation of *kleos* in the invocation has allowed us to show the attempt that is waged here to block the dangerous ambivalence of repetition. On the other hand, we have seen a new attempt to block the difference and deferral in the process itself of the voice.

The complex interplay of strategic moves that organize and control the text of the invocation to the Muses should help us to formulate accurately the historical and literary categories within which Homeric scholarship comprehends the description and the interpretation of the poems. The phenomenon of repetition and its thorough ambivalence are constantly referred to by scholars to explain, often empirically, the "composition" of the poems. It is perhaps instructive that our distinction between two modes of *kleos* finds some analogy in the double "concept of song" that Albert B. Lord (1976, 100) has found in the Yugoslav epic:

> We can say, then, that a song is the story about a given hero, but its expressed forms are multiple, and each of these expressed forms or tellings of the story is itself a separate song, in its own *right, authentic* and *valid* as a song unto itself.
>
> We must distinguish then two concepts of song in oral poetry. One is the general idea of the story, which we use when we speak in larger terms, for example, of the song of the wedding of Smailagic Meho, which actually includes all singings of it. The other concept of song is that of a particular performance or text, such as Avdo Mededovic's song, "The Wedding of Smailagic Meho," dictated during the month of July, 1955. (Italics mine)

Or, alternatively, we could evoke here the Saussurian distinction between *langue* and *parole*, or the political and cultural tension between the poet and the demands that his society imposes on him.[23] Yet in any of these analogies we should be aware that the distinction so drawn is wishful just as the distinction drawn by the poet is self-serving. The two modes of repetition suit the poet's

---

23. As I introduce the terms "langue" and "parole," I imply, of course, the basic distinctions of structural linguistics as Pino Paioni suggested to me during a reading of this paper at the University of Urbino (21 July 1978). It is clear, for instance, that the Muses have a paradigmatic form of knowledge, for their *kleos* (*mnêmê*-voice) embraces at once all alternatives, the whole crowd of soldiers included, and can be qualified as "parole." The poet's form of knowledge, on the contrary, is syntagmatic, that is, sequential and transmissive, and his *kleos* can be qualified as "langue."

Finally, I emphasize that the attempt to attribute a concrete historical identification to the Muses is a common project among scholars. Indeed, it is a most sensible assumption that, for some poets and at some moments of the tradition, the Muses may have functioned as comfortable pretextual entities behind whom the poet could hide, either to justify his neglect of traditional and political demands or, alternatively, to justify his compliance with those demands. A recent attempt to explain the Muses in this way was made by Jesper Svenbro (1976) who maintains that the Muses are the embodiment and the personification of sociopolitical control without the approval of which the poet could not aspire to any success or fame.

ideological gesture as he tries to preempt the other poet's criticisms and his own anxiety that he may be merely repeating uncontrollable stories.

In concrete terms, the text denounces the inescapable risk of repetition, that is at once deadly and vital, effacing truth and revealing truth; the text suggests both the anxiety of being forced to accept the pattern of repetition and the assurance that repetition does not prevent a special, even somehow subjective voice. But the text, by failing to support the distinctions, intimates that both modes of *kleos*, that is to say *kleos* (rumor-ignorance) and *kleos* (voice-*mnêmê*), resound and echo together at each moment, while the whole rhetoric of the poet tries to separate this combined echo in order to isolate and exalt the note of a pure, living voice.[24]

24. I want to thank Ann Bergren for her criticism and suggestions. She has raised some important points in the interpretation of the Homeric passages, and this study has been enriched by her contributions.

CHAPTER 4

Banter and Banquets for Heroic Death*

Pulchrumque mori succurrit in armis.
—Virgil, Aeneid 2.317

Among the many passages in the *Iliad* that represent a hero's decision and a motivation in favor of a glorious course of action, those which state the hero's reasons for accepting his death are memorable and exemplary. They are also psychologically difficult and morally enigmatic. First, all subjective motivation in Homer raises the thorny questions of the subject, of its will, and of its autonomy from the theological forces—with which the text is identified—under whose laws the hero operates. But in the specific case of an heroic *prohairesis*, when the king decides to take his stand and to stake his life, his motivations reflect more than ever the text's *raison d'être*, and therefore its theological and edifying purposes. In those passages the metaphysics of the *Iliad* rises to its most sublime, as it upholds the glamorous portrait of the king, his inflexible will to obtain imperishable glory (*aphthiton kleos*), and it develops the great consolatory themes that make death acceptable and even freely chosen.[1] The monumental funeral oration that the *Iliad* utters through its doomed heroes contains many of these edifying passages.[2] I choose Sarpedon's speech in *Il.*

---

* "Banter and Banquets for Heroic Death" was first published in *Post-Structuralist Classics,* edited by Andrew Benjamin. London and New York: Routledge 1988.

1. On the theme of the beautiful and glamorous death of the hero see the important papers: Vernant 1979, 1367–74; "La belle mort et le cadavre outragé," in Gnoli and Vernant 1982, 45–76; Loraux 1982, 27–46; and Vidal-Naquet 1984, 23 and 51ff.

2. Among these, one cannot omit Achilles' statement on the choice he faces between a long joyful life and an immediate but immortally glorious death (*Il.* IX.410–16); Achilles' desperate knowledge that, godlike though he is, he is doomed

XII.310–28 in which he impresses on himself the necessity of staking his life. It is exemplary in many ways: the king has no private reasons to fight in Troy and therefore he grounds his decision on general arguments that evoke his exalted position, his royal portrait, and his human mortal destiny.[3] The text therefore exposes here in the most vivid fashion its large concerns and its most far-reaching consolatory themes: it erects what for us is the first edifying oration that affected generations of readers and still has a tremendous power. For these very reasons, however, the passage also unveils the paradoxical aspects of the metaphysics of the *Iliad*, and it displays what it is my goal here to demonstrate, the desultory discontinuities of the text, the occasional opacities in the reading that it offers of itself.

> Glaukos, why in fact are we honored [*tetimêmestha*] so greatly
> by a (distinctive) seat *(hedrêi)* and meat and full cups,
> in Lycia, and all people look at us as at gods?
> And why are we granted a domain [*temenos*] by the bank of Xanthos,
> a fair domain with orchard and wheat bearing arable land?
> Therefore now we must stand among the foremost
> and face the fiery battle
> so that some of the well-corseleted Lycians may say:
> "Truly our kings are not without glory [*ou . . . akleees*] as they rule
> over Lycia
> and eat fat sheep and choice wine sweet like honey,
> but they have also excellent might,
> since they fight in the foremost ranks of the Lycians."
> O friend! If we could escape from this war
> and if we would live forever ageless and immortal,
> then I myself would not fight in the front rank
> nor would I send you into the battle that gives glory to men [*machên
> es kudianeiran*];
> but now—for all the same countless fates of death stand upon us
> and it is not possible for a mortal to escape or to avoid them—
> let us go: either we shall give the boast [*eukhos*] to others or others
> to us.
>
> (*Il.* XII.310–28)

This passage has always been admired,[4] but as far as I know, never extensively commented on,[5] though as my analysis shows, it requires attention and

---

to die like everybody else (*Il.* XXI.106–13); Odysseus's short but moving speech in *Il.* XI.404–10 where he asserts his will to be an *aristos*, a hero, and to take a stand alone against the Trojans, and so on.

3. Sarpedon is Lycian and not Trojan; he has no revenge to take; finally, no divine compulsion induces him to run in the front rank of the battle.

4. I recall here Epictetus (*Diatribai* 1.27–28), who quotes the final part of this passage as an argument which can calm the fear of death. An even more noble use of Sarpedon's words is illustrated by Lord Granville (Carteret) at the end of the Seven Years War (1763): he fixes his attention on the last part of Sarpedon's speech (322–

explanations. The first part of Sarpedon's speech (310–20) is unanimously considered today as a statement of *noblesse oblige*, and the second (322–28) as a paradoxical and moving argument of existential order.[6] And yet there is much more and much less in Sarpedon's episode than the sober and coherent line of thought critics describe. Much more: the "portrait" of the king is huge and has a supernatural glow, a divine and bestial beyondness; his decision to stake his life is sublime since it is almost gratuitous; in fact, he accepts immediate death in order to uphold the truth of his (supernatural) portrait . . . . Much less: his royal portrait crumbles in ruin and the image of his frailty takes its place; the truth of his epic portrait is doubtful; the gain of an imperishable glory, uncertain.

The superimposition of these features endows the text with the desultory, discontinuous movement I shall analyze as the trace of Iliadic "writing."

The Frame: The Mane in the Royal Figure

Sarpedon begins to speak *suddenly* (*autika*, 309). Before this moment he is described as a lion in one of the longest and most elaborate lion similes in the *Iliad* (XII.299–308).[7] The suddenness of his words corresponds to the suddenness

---

28), as R. Wood relates: "he insisted that I should stay, saying, it could not prolong his life, to neglect his duty; and, repeating the following passage out of Sarpedon's speech, he dwelt with particular emphasis on the third line (324)" (Leaf 1960, 1:548). William E. Gladstone calls Sarpedon's speech "incomparable" and comments on it with admiration (1858, 3:58).

5. The most recent commentary is by Griffin (1980), who touches upon this passage with short notes on 14, 73 and 92–93.

6. I derive these interpretations from Willcock 1976, 142, Hogan 1979, 192–93; and from Griffin 1980, 73: "Sarpedon utters the fullest and most explicit statement of *noblesse oblige*: 'We are noble and wealthy, therefore we must fight in the front rank' and then goes on to say that 'If by avoiding death today we could make ourselves immortal, then I should not fight; but we must die some day, so let us go, to win glory ourselves or to serve the glory of others.'"

7. The image of the lion to represent the fierce force of kings is conventional and could be described as a fixed piece of the "portrait" of the king. There are about forty occurrences of lion similes in the *Iliad* alone. Of the extensive bibliography on the lion in Homer, I quote here only a few recent essays: Gourbeilloun 1981; Wolff 1979; Frederick 1982, 120–37.

As the reader will see, I am identifying the "portrait of the king" with the "glorious renown" (*kleos*) that epic poetry celebrates. In this sense *kleos* is used also for a living hero, as for instance in *Il.* VI.446, etc. On the question whether the *"Basileus"* is a king and whether all *"Basileis"* are kings and what sort of king they are, cf. Drews (1983), who agrees that the word defines different types of monarchs and leaders, and Carlier (1984), who argues that "Basileus" always designates a king but "Basileis" also names various types of counselors. I call "king" the great leader who is designated as "Basileus" or who is mentioned among the *basileis* or among the *boulêphoroi*.

of his return to humanity. For, as a lion, he was fighting, of course without a word just like Sarpedon, the king; even in the details he was engaged in the same sort of attack that he launches as a hero. For as a lion, a "valiant heart" (*thumos agênôr* 300) incited him to attack a well-built stable (*pukinon domon* 301) just as the king's heart excites him to attack the Achaean wall; as a lion, he was willing to be wounded in the front ranks (*en prôtoisi* 306), just as he is ready to do now (*meta prôtoisi(n)* 315, 321, 324); as a lion, he was needing meat, just as he, as a king, consumes abundant meat (*kreiôn* 300, *kreasin* 311). Though the lion and the king have different sources of provision, they have the same requirement of rich, bloody food for their meals.[8]

Because of this thorough assimilation, the simile confuses the identification of the comparing entity and of the compared one, so that it is no longer clear who is compared to whom. The mere ornamental function of the simile should be seriously doubted, and the leonine features of Sarpedon's portrait should be seriously considered.

The king's portrait, however, while showing some fierce traits of the lion, encompasses a larger set of features. He is represented as being human and godlike. The text combines the animal traits with the human and the godlike ones in the concluding lines of the simile (XII.307–10): "So then his heart incited the God-like (*antitheon*) Sarpedon to attack the wall and to break through the parapet. And suddenly he spoke to Glaukos son of Hipplokhos; 'Glaukos, why in fact are we honored . . .'" The portrait of the king is now complete. By turning suddenly to Glaukos and asking, "Why . . .," its human traits emerge and take prominence. Unlike the lion whose noble heart and need of meat constitute the unique sources of motivation, Sarpedon needs to know "why . . .'" and for eighteen lines he analyses his motivations. For unlike a God, the king is also mortal.

To introduce the lion features among the divine and human traits that the *Iliad* is outlining and ascribing to the *kleos* of Sarpedon is not critically otiose, or erratic. Readers so eager to appreciate the aesthetic values of the *Iliad* should not miss the extravagant complexity of this portrait which exhibits savage brushes, sublime tones, violent and untamed contrasts. Our Sarpedon is not a modern gentleman.

My critical reasons for insisting on this portrait, however, are more specific. Sarpedon ultimately considers it his duty to uphold his *kleos,* his glorious portrait, and to substantiate it in the eyes of his subjects, the Lycians, with an heroic gesture, by which he stakes his life. It will not be otiose therefore to ask which sort of portrait he wishes to live up to and which (epic) portrait the *Iliad* wants him to uphold and to support. One of the most troubling critical questions the *Iliad* raises for its readers is in fact the consistency of the theological

---

8. Gods, kings, and even lions feast in *daites,* the princely banquets which, without the kings' presence, are off limits to commoners. Occasionally the meal of a lion is also named *dais,* see *Il.* XXIV.43. The *dais* is a ceremonial meal: it has social and religious importance because the eating of meat implies the sacrifice, see Nagy 1977, 277ff.

premises and underpinnings of its narrative, and when once we ask such a concrete question, we begin to unravel it.

The Banter

The ferocious banquet (*dais*) of the lion in which he feasts on meat is a sort of mirror image of the tamer banquets of the kings. Sarpedon mentions them, listing accurately all the features of this gala, the place of honor, the meat, the wine, the respectful attitude of the Lycians (XII.310–12). This list is conventional and traditional, and it occurs, complete or partial, when the privileges of the kings are described. Food is a serious matter in Homer,[9] even if it also serves jocular purposes. The jocular purpose occurs in the type of mockery that the kings like to level at each other, when they compare their greed for these privileges (*timê*) with their poltroonery. Typical of this mockery is the insult Agamemnon hurls at Odysseus:

> . . . you master of evil tricks, greedy of gain[10] why are you recoiling and standing apart and waiting for the others? It benefits you to stand among the foremost, (*meta prôtoisin*) and to face the fiery battle, [11] for you are the first to be heard at my banquet for the Elders. There you love to eat roast meat and drink your cups of honey-sweet wine, as long as you like. (IV.338–46)

This mockery intimates the kings' awareness that their exalted position (*timê*) creates expectations of heroic behavior and that those expectations are not infrequently frustrated by their cowardice. At the gala of the banquets there are not always gallant kings.

The text therefore plots with its characters to attach suspicion to the truth of kings' *kleos* (warrior's glory), and even if it does so only in these scenes of a bantering mood and even if generally it unveils this suspicion only in order to assert, with greater assurance, the truth of the kings' *kleos*, nevertheless, to attach doubt and suspicion to their heroic portrait is a sore business for epic poetry. Since this poetry is the source of the kings' *kleos*, the text exhibits itself and its own fabrications.[12]

By raising the intimation that the *kleos* of the king may be exaggerated or contain mere flatteries, the text of the *Iliad* is perverse, for it reverses,

---

9. See Griffin 1980, 13ff., and Codino 1965.

10. *Kakoisi doloisi kekasmene, kerdaleophron. Kerdaleophrôn* is also used by Achilles to insult Agamemnon in *Il.* I.149. This word is never used in the *Odyssey*. On *kekasmene* see Durante (1976, 11, 41), who rightly considers *kekastai* a "literary" expression of the *Epos*. Notice the heavy, expressive alliteration of *k*, which of course emphasizes and repeats the consonant sound of *kakoisi* and *kerdos*.

11. These two lines occur in Sarpedon's passage *Il.* XII.315–16. The antithesis between the rear and front line of battle is almost formulaic, and occurs many times, see *Il.* XI.596, XII.35, XIII.330, 668, XVII.253, etc.

12. I analyse the unstable meaning of *kleos* in Chapters Three and Ten.

amusingly, its normal function, which is that of edifying a real, well-deserved renown for the kings, what I call in this chapter the "glorious portrait" of the king.[13] The *Iliad* allows Odysseus to reconfirm his excellence with a noble response. Yet, perhaps because it is a question of Odysseus, the *Iliad* speaks tongue in cheek. For indeed, Odysseus has no great reputation as a *promakhos* (a fighter among the front ranks), but a splendid one—in the *Odyssey*—for his shrewdness (*mêtis Od.* ix.19–20; xiii.287–95, etc.).[14] Besides, it is certainly true that an Odyssean trait of Odysseus represents him as indulging in the pleasures of the belly (*gastêr*),[15] and the *Iliad* seems to recall this tendency here and in another passage.[16] Be that as it may, Odysseus's answer, for all its apparent nobility, does not entirely refute Agamemnon's reproach.

> Atreides, what word has escaped from the barrier of your teeth? How can you say that we are slack in battle? When we Achaeans excite sharp Ares against the horse-taming Trojans, you shall see, if you wish and if you care, the dear father of Telemachus mingling among the front ranks (*promakhoisi*) of the horsetaming Trojans. What you say is empty air. (*Il.* IV.350–55)

Formally Odysseus's answer is noble and enhances the warrior's excellence. On the surface, at any rate, Agamemnon's reproach seems to have served only as a foil in order to spell out with greater energy the excellence of Odysseus. But in fact, even if Agamemnon now praises Odysseus (358–63), the reproach does not function simply as a foil. The rest is interesting. I follow Risch in interpreting the line "you shall see . . . the dear father of Telemachus mingling among the front ranks" as a pun.[17] The name "Telemachus" etymologically means "fighting from afar" and therefore Odysseus is made to say: "You will see the father of 'fighting from afar' mingling among the front ranks." Since by epic convention the children often are named from some characteristics, accidents or events in the

---

13. In all epochs, the king or queen of every monarchy is known through a specific "portrait." Such a portrait is inevitable because being a king means, basically, to respond to a set of representations and prescriptions. The sheer fact that the king has authority over others entails a series of images, that of the father, of the god, and so on; the king's role to represent and defend his people confirms and enlarges that set of images and includes his being a lion, close to gods, and so on. It would be preposterous to try in a note to open up all the aspects and the articulations of the image or portrait of the king. I simply state here that this portrait is unavoidable, that all sorts of politicians and artists work at this portrait, and that the *Iliad* is for us a gallery of such portraits, a gallery of kings' *klea*. See Marin 1981: he analyses the general features of the royal portrait in the specific one of Louis XIV.
14. As a hero of *mêtis*, Odysseus's military excellence appears mainly in the activity of the *lokhos* (ambush). It is by virtue of this skill that he is involved in the plans concerning the Trojan Horse. See Edwards 1985 and Pucci 1986, 7–28.
15. See *Od.* vii.215–21; xvii.284–90, etc.
16. On this theme, see Pucci 1987, 157ff.
17. Risch 1947, 72–91. Odysseus probably puns on his name in v.423: this linguistic gusto could therefore be attributed to him in the *Iliad*.

life of the father,[18] the *Iliad* humorously forces Odysseus to say that though he is known as a man of the rear lines (that is, a man of the bow, or the ambush, and so on) he will be seen fighting as a *promakhos*.[19] When the *Iliad* is humorous it is splendidly so. Here the text takes its pleasure in tantalizingly suspending and keeping undecided the "Iliadic" excellence of Odysseus, and, at the end the text gives it back to him, at least partially, in the form of his heroic determination to fight as *promakhos*, that is, to become, against his tradition and *kleos*, an Iliadic hero. Just as Odysseus is made to respond with an heroic decision to the legitimate suspicion that his son's name Telemachus attaches to his claim to be *promakhos*, so Sarpedon will feel his duty to prove his force and thus to dispel the suspicion the Lycians attach to his *kleos*. In both cases the text initially presents a contested and dubious portrait; apparently the text uses this initial move as a foil in order to produce unquestionable evidence for the truth of the kings' excellence. Yet in the case of Odysseus the text seems unwilling to re-establish his heroic portrait without a humorous touch; in the case of Sarpedon the text unquestionably aims at substantiating the truth of Sarpedon's *kleos*. Sarpedon's speech is no joke: its sublime pathos makes more emotional for the reader the textual incapacity to demonstrate fully the truth of the portrait for which he is determined to die.[20]

What the Lycians Think of the King's Image

When Sarpedon, the lion, turns to address Glaukos, like him a king of Lycia, he questions his peer and himself as to why they are honored as they are. He begins to speak, therefore, as a king, conscious of the prerogatives a king enjoys and aware of the questioning, admiring glances the subjects bestow on their king:

> Glaukos, why in fact are we honored [*tetimêmestha*] so greatly
> by a distinctive seat [*hedrêi*] and meat and full cups
> in Lycia and all people look at us as at gods?
> And why are we granted a domain [*temenos*] by the bank of Xanthos,

---

18. Sulzberger 1926, 383ff. The classical example of this convention is the name Odysseus itself: as we learn from *Od.* xix.406ff., Odysseus is named in this way by his grandfather's immediate concerns.

19. On the opposition between Achilles, the *promakhos* and Odysseus, the man of the *lokhos*, see Edwards 1985. See also Latacz 1977, 159, who, summarizing his long analysis of *promakhoi*, writes that the substance of the notion *promakhos* does not lie either in the social aspect or in the ethics. The substance lies in the fact that the *promakhos* fights in the front ranks. The *Odyssey* picks up line IV.354 (characterized also by the unicity of *migenta*) in xviii.379: Odysseus boasts, just as in IV.354, that he will be seen "mingling among the front ranks" but he does not—and in fact he cannot at this point—call himself "the father of Telemachus."

20. Perhaps the reader feels uneasy about the comparison I have established between the passage IV.338–55 and XII.310–21. I recall however that two lines recur in both passages (IV.341–42; XII.315–16), evidence that the passages echo each other.

a fair domain with orchard and wheat-bearing arable land?
Therefore now we must [khrê] stand among the front ranks
and face the fiery battle
so that some of the well-corseleted Lycians may say:
"Truly our kings are not without glory [ou . . . akleees] as they rule
over Lycia
and eat fat sheep and choice wine, sweet like honey,
but they have also excellent might (is)
since they fight in the front ranks of the Lycians."

(XII.310–21)

There is no doubt that the introductory question: "Why are we honored . . ."
constitutes, so to speak, the framing of Sarpedon's speech as far as line 321, and
therefore intimates that the duty (khrê 315) Sarpedon feels is somehow attached
to his being a king and receiving the timê he so effectively evokes (tetimêmestha
310). And yet the precise logical connection between the timê and his awareness
of duty is lacking: the text deviates from timê and evokes the glances the
Lycians bestow on the king. It is in relation to those glances that Sarpedon
conceives his duty to take a stand.

As a consequence, critics vary in their appreciation of the specific connection
between the king's timê and his duty to stake valiantly his life. Some consider
that Sarpedon embraces this duty idealistically as the commitment that alone
justifies his royal prerogatives;[21] others, denying that in Homer moral decisions
are autonomous and self-grounded, reverse the order of priorities and read the
passage as a statement of noblesse oblige (Finsler 1914, 163). Thus for instance
Jasper Griffin (1980, 73) paraphrases it as follows: "We are noble and wealthy,
therefore we must fight in the front rank."[22]

The difficulty in this matter is that the question, "Why are we honored so
greatly . . . ," is not answered in Sarpedon's words, by the direct suggestion
that royal honors entail the duty to fight, but the question is transformed in the
evocation of the Lycians' expectations; and the Lycians do not expect the king to
behave valiantly on the ground of his timê, but on the ground of his kleos, that
is of his royal heroic image: "Therefore, now, we must stand among the front
ranks . . . so that (ophra) some of the Lycians may say: 'Truly our kings are

---

21. See Gladstone 1858, 3:58: "So entirely is the idea of dignity and privilege in
the Homeric king founded upon the sure ground of duty, of responsibility, and of
toil."

22. "Dans son exhortation à Glaukos, après avoir rappelé les privilèges materiels
dont jouissent les rois lyciens, Sarpedon ajoute qu'en contrepartie, il est de leur
devoir de se battre 'en premier rang des Lyciens.' (12.315) Tous les rois homériques
n'ont pas de leur devoir une idée aussi exigeante" (Carlier 1984, 172). This
interpretation is canonical. Already Plato in Rep. 468d–e, when he thinks of which
compensations and prizes will honor the valiant warriors, does not find anything
better than to quote our passage and suggest the compensation of song, seat or honor,
meat, and cups of wine.

not without glory ... but they have also excellent might.'"[23] Sarpedon considers it his duty (*khrê* 315) to give his Lycians some evidence, a demonstration of the qualities that are written in his royal image. But the syntax and the style of 318–21 deserve more careful analysis, and the disruptive force of *kleos* must also be considered within that frame: "Truly our kings are not without glory (*a-kleees*) ... but (*alla*) they have also (*kai*) excellent might." This adversative *alla* and the adverb *kai* add a new idea to the previous one, either with opposition or without opposition.[24] I do not see any way to determine the exact extent of the adversative clause. Sarpedon may only wish that his Lycians witness something besides his *kleos*, its truth for instance, or something different from his *kleos*, something that his *kleos*, his royal image of warlike glory, does not say or says falsely.

In both cases Sarpedon's full identity with his royal portrait turns out to be fractured in the eyes of the Lycians, but the measure of their disbelief, or of their mistrust, varies in accordance with the reading we offer of this remarkable passage. For, on the one hand, we could read the Lycians' attitude as sarcastic and as cynical, like the attitude we encounter in the mockery by Agamemnon or Achilles. The instability of the meaning of *kleos*, the ironical mention of the banquets, the adversative clause and the possibly sarcastic litotes ("not without glory" or "not inglorious"), the concrete, almost physical meaning of *is* (force) would allow us to paraphrase the Lycians' thinking as follows:

> Yes, during the rich banquets we prepare for the kings in Lycia, they of course are not without a glorious renown; indeed, they are extravagantly praised by all sort of divine epithets; they are vaingloriously described in incredible adventures,[25] but as we see them now in the front rank, we must say that they have, flatteries aside, also excellent force as well.[26] There is something true in all that old flattery.

Sarpedon would prove, by taking a valiant stand, that, really, the royal portrait is not all boasts, only part of it. Alternatively the Lycians' thinking may be represented less ironically and less sarcastically: "Our kings do not only

---

23. *Tô* (*therefore*) of line 315 is proleptic of *ophra* (317) so that the previous question ("why are we honored ... ?") merely introduces the frame of the royal honors (*timê*) among which there is also that of a royal image of warlike glory (*kleos*).

24. LFGE (1, p. 531 col. 1, 1ff.) takes this *alla*-clause as introducing a stress on a new idea without opposition. Accordingly the previous clause, "they are not without glory," turns out to be incomplete and partially negative even if we take this *alla* as introducing no opposition. But how to determine that this adversative adverb here has no oppositional force? On the other hand the new idea is stressed also by *kai* (also), not only by *alla*.

25. Among the extraordinary adventures that are sometimes attributed to the kings, see for instance Diomedes' fight with the Gods in book V of the *Iliad*. The Lycians would be sarcastic in using litotes and speaking of *kleos* as "mere rumors."

26. *Is* names the physical force of men or of natural phenomena like the wind or the sun.

enjoy their due honors and their proper reputation, but as we see them now in the front rank, we must say that they also live up to that reputation."[27]

Therefore Sarpedon feels that he must substantiate or validate the truth of his royal portrait by giving evidence through his action. He feels that fighting as a *promakhos* provides the Lycians with the ultimate test of his might.

Should we say that the former reading of the Lycians' sarcastic disbelief in the royal portrait is inappropriate to Epic poetry? The scenes of flyting and bantering are built on this very disbelief and prove that the answer is no. Nor is this interpretation at odds with our passage, which begins with the mention of concrete privileges before turning to the ascetic views of 322–28.

It remains also undecidable what Sarpedon thinks of the Lycians' suspicion, whether he would agree with them that his *kleos* is exaggeratedly flattering, or a correct representation of what he is. Accordingly it remains uncertain whether he means to substantiate some of the reasonable and still heroic features of his flattering portrait, or to live up to his full *kleos*. If he thinks that his portrait, however flattering, is nevertheless a correct representation of himself, he considers it a duty to show that he is as good a king as his image says he is. The *Iliad's* premises would encourage us to uphold this interpretation. Sarpedon considers it a duty to prove that he is as good a king as his *kleos* says he is because he is afraid of the criticism or of the mockery that the discrepancy between his portrait and his deeds would allow the Lycians to level at him. He would then respond to a sense of fear and reverence that the Homeric Greek calls *aidôs* and which induces kings to act valiantly on other occasions as well.[28] As a result, Sarpedon would consider it a duty to substantiate *a posteriori* the portrait which the Lycians have of him. He would grant the evidence of truth to his portrait by a gesture that logically and morally should lie at the origin of his *kleos*.[29] Therefore while his response to the Lycians' criticism or suspension of

---

27. In this case the mention of the banquets (319–20) would simply function as a textual reference to Sarpedon's first lines, when he evokes the royal privileges, and would harmonize the two passages. The litotes, instead of being ironic, would stress the relative modesty of the king's portrait, and *kleos* would name the proper, deserved, truthful representation of the kings.

28. Cf. Hector in XXII.99–110 when he decides to wait for Achilles because he feels *aidôs*, that is he fears the criticism of the Trojan men and women: he had resisted Polydamas's proposal of withdrawing the troops within the walls, and now after heavy losses, the Trojans would reproach him for having presumed too much of his force. Another interesting example is found in XX.83–85, where Apollo provokes Aeneas by recalling his previous boasts and menaces against the Achaeans.

Historically speaking, I do not believe that a king such as Sarpedon would feel the duty because his subjects expect him to act as a hero in response to the royal privileges they grant him. First I suspect that the Lycians, in Sarpedon's view, would under no circumstances imagine ceasing to grant honors to the king and to listen to his splendid reputation; and moreover, the statement of *noblesse oblige* must come from the king, not from his subjects.

29. Sarpedon's decision would be marked by a modern sense of ethics if he were considering it a duty to substantiate an ideal, noble reputation (*kleos*) that he, himself, has built in the course of this life through a consistent noble behavior. But

belief can be considered a moral decision, the specific goal of behaving *a posteriori* just as his portrait—which he did not compose—prescribes, is gratuitous. Or, even if we assume that Sarpedon agrees with the moral prescriptions that are contained in that image, that goal remains unmotivated, since he produces no argument to uphold those moral prescriptions. Consequently his acceptance of the prescriptive, authoritative force of his portrait is unconditional, gratuitous, and it is fully accounted for only by the ideological premises of Epic poetry. Such lack of motivation characterizes some of the greatest Homeric heroes at the moments of their entry in the epic story. A sort of reckless and seigneurial gratuitousness must lie also at the source of Achilles' decision to come to Troy in order to win imperishable glory (*aphthiton kleos*). He, like Sarpedon in the passage I have commented upon, must put his life in jeopardy to serve, so to speak, the creative purposes of Epic poetry.

Sarpedon has argued until now that he must live up to his splendid *kleos*. The question that Sarpedon leaves open to the reader is why does he—like the other great heroes—treasure this glory so much? The last words of Sarpedon try to give us the answer to this question:

O friend! If we could escape from this war[30]
and if we could live forever ageless and immortal
then I myself would not fight in the front rank
nor would I send you into the battle that gives glory to men (*makhên es kudianeiran*);
but now—for all the same countless fates of death stand upon us
and it is not possible for a mortal to escape or to avoid them—
let us go: either we shall give the boast (*eukhos*) to others or others to us.

(*Il.* XII.322–28)

The passage contains one of the strongest statements in Homer. The huge portrait of the king with its epic paraphernalia and rhetorical embellishments shrinks to the frail image of a mortal man, even more, to the image of a man who knows that he is besieged at each moment by the menace of death. Homer spells out the recognition that the awareness of death is the quintessence of man, and by defining man uniquely in all of nature, among beasts and gods, by this awareness, he founds, for us, a notion that will reappear insistently in the history of western metaphysics.[31]

---

his royal reputation exists, in part at least, independently from his behavior—as the Lycians' suspicions prove—since it is to some extent traditional and conventional.

30. The phrase could also be translated as a wish: "Would that we could escape . . . and that we could live for ever ageless and immortal! Then. . . ." Pierre Chantraine (1963, 219) considers the phrase potential rather than a wish; I follow him.

31. See Derrida (1980, 376ff.), where he, analyzing Freud's speculations on the death instinct in *Beyond the Pleasure Principle* and Heidegger's notion of authenticity, writes pages that could be read as an inspiring commentary on our Iliadic passage.

The consoling aspects of this conception reside in the implication that what is "proper" and "essential" to man is stronger than or as strong as the insuperable force of death. For man is somehow made able to take up death and to administer, through his awareness, the economy that makes death simultaneously a menace and a resource, other and self.

Accordingly Sarpedon too lets himself be affected by this economy, when he describes the countless fates of death constantly standing over him as an inevitable menace, and yet also as a resource for an heroic decision that somehow anticipates and therefore masters those countless fates. One should not miss, in this powerful text, the astuteness of its formulation: Sarpedon impresses upon himself the inevitable presence of countless *Kêres* "destinies," "fates of death," and he opposes them with the energy and vitality of the imperative, "let us go" (*iomen*), and the force of his will to take a gamble, a hopeful chance.

As a master and accomplice of his own death, Sarpedon would also free himself from the haphazardness, anonymity, facelessness of death. And here there is probably another strong consoling element implicit in his words. His willingness to go to face a hero and gamble his life acquires the specific implication of protesting against the necessity of death and its anonymity.[32] He capitalizes on the distinction of his gesture, on the public splendor of his attitude. For all these reasons his gesture names his desire to battle death.[33] And of course he is sure of outwitting death as he knows that the splendor of his gesture will survive. Accordingly the *eukhos* he speaks of in line 328 must also name—though improperly as we shall see—the "glory" and the "fame" that the epic song celebrates. If Sarpedon should die he would substantiate, or found, the truth of his heroic image (*kleos*).

These views are powerful and deeply affect the reader. The Epic text produces motivations for gallantly accepting death that seem capable of reducing the power of death, and accordingly have the force of the greatest power of all. By gaining some mastery over death the hero shows how his acceptance of death also makes fuller sense of his life, how in fact, through glory he—on a different level—immortalizes himself.[34] And yet this comforting vision of man's mortality seems simultaneously to domesticate the issues which it faces with such force. First of all this comforting vision presupposes that the consciousness of death and its controlling economy parallel the economy of real death. But this is not the case. Consciousness of death implies life, but death extinguishes all consciousness.[35] Consciousness of death involves a discourse

---

32. In analogous terms, W. Thomas McCary explains this sort of death wish that Sarpedon utters here by the Hegelian notion that life-and-death struggle is essential to self-definition (1982, 197).

33. In view of Sarpedon's desire for real immortality, we may also understand J. Griffin's comment: "It is not unreflective or unconscious heroism that drives these men on. Facing death they see both the obligation and the terror and their speech reflects the totality of their situation and response" (1980, 73).

34. On the awareness of mortality as a source of morality for the Homeric hero, see Griffin 1980, 93.

35. One is reminded of the criticism which has been addressed for instance by George Bataille to Hegel's analysis of the encounter of consciousness that results

that in Sarpedon's experience survives, as epic song, the death of the kings, and develops—as indeed it does also in the case of Achilles for instance XXI.106–13—the themes of the equality of all men before death, of the shortness of life, of the inevitability of death.

Furthermore, to appropriate death as what is proper, close, essential to man looks like an unstable, paradoxical appropriation since death is other than he is.[36] Indeed, in our passage, it is paradoxical that Sarpedon's awareness that death menaces him at each moment should persuade him actually to stake his life, now, immediately (cf. *nun* 315 and 326).

In fact, it is undecidable whether Sarpedon suspends his heroic decision totally on his existential awareness that death is inevitable or also on the edifying advantage that *kudos* and *eukhos* finally would bring to him. The answer to this question remains uncertain, for the text could be construed so as to satisfy both meanings. To begin with, we do not know exactly what *kudos* and *eukhos* meant for the epic poets; furthermore the last line (328), "let us go: either we shall give *eukhos* to others or others to us," presents an odd gamble which could end with no *eukhos* for Sarpedon. Finally, the whole train of thought, as we shall see, is unclear.

Let us start from *eukhos*. I incline with Emile Benveniste (1969, 2:242) to attribute to this word the meaning of "*vœu de victoire*" and then "*victoire*," though it is possible to reach the same result by postulating "scream or boast of triumph" and then "triumph," "victory." This meaning appears in the only other example of the formula (XII.328: XIII.327), where *eukhos* does not imply death of one hero, or his glory, but the victory of a wing of the army.[37] As concerns *kudos* in Sarpedon's *makhên es kudianeiran* of line 325, not even here would there be specific mention of glory.[38] On the ground of these elements we could sustain the pure existential inflection of the passage: defeat (death) in battle is only one of the countless fates that threaten men, and the hero gambles whether god will give power (*kudos*) and victory (*eukhos*) to him or to his adversary.[39]

There are passages, however, in which *eukhos* seems to mean the boast and glory of victory (see, for instance, VII.203, and especially VII.81–91), and we

---

with a master and a slave. Because Hegel visualizes an encounter of consciousness he cannot confront the actual death of one of the parties.

36. Derrida (1980, 379) develops this point.

37. Here Idomeneus says: "Let us see whether we will give *eukhos* to others or others to us"; the context and the governing verb "let us see (know) *eidomen*" imply that Idomeneus speculates whether the Achaeans or the Trojans will have victory as the enemies are pressing on the left side of the battlefield.

38. Benveniste (1969, 57–69) maintains that *kudos* names "the magical power" the god grants to a victorious hero.

39. "A hero," Odysseus says, "either is wounded or he wounds another one" (XI.410). But of course, *balein* may mean a fatal wound. It is noteworthy that the lion in the simile with Sarpedon (XII.299–308) is willing to undergo the same: *eblet'en prôtoisi* (306).

cannot confidently exclude this sense from our passage.[40] Accordingly the
gamble that Sarpedon raises in line 328 could still look at death in the battlefield
as a privileged death, one that would be marked off from the countless fates of
death. The *eukhos* in the battlefield might be prolonged in the *kleos* that
immortalizes the hero.[41]

The decision between a pure existential interpretation and an edifying reading
of Sarpedon's willingness to embrace death remains difficult to make. It is
easier, on the contrary, to perceive and to appreciate the vocal connotation of
eukhos. For this speech act certainly designates a "marked utterance," and
therefore its meaning is contained within the semantic field of *kleos, logos,
muthos*.[42] It is with a view to this special utterance—whether or not connected
with *kleos*—that Sarpedon raises his gamble with death, or his dalliance with
epic glory: accordingly his speech—the one we are commenting upon—
anticipates and rehearses that cry of boasting (*eukhos*) he hopes to scream in the
battlefield. Then the awareness that death is close and proper to man emerges as a
voice and an utterance which are even closer than that consciousness, because
they are prior to it. They affect the character while being produced by the
character himself.[43]

Iliadic Writing

With the last turn of argument I have begun a deconstructive reading that
exposes the comforting and/or edifying force of the voice (*eukhos, kleos*) in

---

40. Often *eukhos* seems to be used as a full synonym of *kudos* and *kleos*; but in
some passages differences appear. In VII.81–90 the difference between *eukhos* and
kleos is evident: *kleos* is attached to a *sêma* and accordingly becomes permanent and
personalized glory, so much so that Hector can say "my *kleos* will never die."
Eukhos, on the contrary, points to the actual (scream of) triumph the god will grant
Hector at the moment of the fight. In fact, most often *eukhos* indicates the victory the
hero is hoping for (VII.203, XI.290, VII.81, XV.462, XVI.725, XXI.297, V.654 =
XI.445 = XVI.65). In VII.200–205, the difference between *eukhos* and *kudos* lies in
the fact that *eukhos* goes along with the verb *eukhonto* (200) while *kudos* repeats
kudiste, epithet of Zeus.

41. Hector, sensing his defeat, boasts of his future glory: "May I die," he says,
"not without struggle and glory (*a-kleiôs*) but with the accomplishment of a great
deed to be known to future generations" (XXII.304–5). The last line not only
explains what *kleos* is, and why a *kleos* is to some extent always permanent, but also
calls attention shamelessly to the textual self-referentiality. The negative form *a-
kleiôs* occurs, though not adverbially, in Sarpedon's passage (XII.318) and
elsewhere, in VII.100; i.241 = xiv.371.

42. *Eukhos*, in fact, is connected to *eukhomai* whose usages, as Pierre Chantraine
writes, refer to "une déclaration insistante et solennelle" (1970, 389). See also
Müllner 1976, 108ff.

43. I allude here to the phenomenon of "autoaffection" and its interference in the
production of "consciousness," see Derrida 1967.

Sarpedon's speech and accordingly in the Iliadic "writing" in general.[44] This reading continues in the analysis of textual reflexivity. For it is clear that when Sarpedon speaks of his duty to perform the originary act that logically and morally starts the edification of his *kleos* or when he urges himself to rush into the battle in order to obtain *eukhos*, he reflects the textual premises of the *Iliad*, its *raison d'etre* and even the effects that the poem, as an oral one, creates. For there is no reason to doubt that the poem knows the power of the voice, and that it develops in its "writing" the situations and the structures in which the power of the voice obtains more powerful effects: dialogue, prayers, self-exhortations, invocations, and so on.[45]

Now to start from the critical view that merely shows the reflexive consciousness a work has of itself is not yet a deconstructive move; the business of deconstruction is to unravel the process of signification, to expose the metaphysical premises that found all texts, the complicity of the readers with those premises, and to look, if possible, beyond them. Yet the critical concern of showing the reflexive consciousness of a text is a necessary premise of deconstructive discourse. It problematizes and suspends the reader's confidence—inspired by the text—that a responsible author is simply narrating a story about a referent. The text of course narrates a story, but it simultaneously reflects its textuality, reads itself as a text among other texts, glances at its compositional conventions, at the protocols, at the constitution of its self-making, at its readers' reading.[46]

In the text I have commented upon there can be no doubts that Sarpedon's glance at the Lycians' appreciation of his *kleos* is almost a glance at the Lycians' reading of the Epic text that is productive of his *kleos*. The *Iliad* gives us empirical evidence—if it were needed—that Sarpedon's *kleos* literally precedes him as a sort of *proklut'epea*.[47] He speaks of himself as if he were borrowing

---

44. It is not necessary today to explain what "writing" means in this context. It has of course little to do with the technique which we call "writing" but with the specific notion that deconstructive criticism has elaborated to speak of the texts. For "writing" names the differential structure of language, the lags and gaps in the process of signification, the unmotivatedness of the sign and its discontinuous signification, the self-referential use of the sign. I refer here essentially to the notions that are illustrated in the writings of Jacques Derrida, and I apologize here for reducing to mere labels such an original and masterful thought.

45. On this "dramatic" oral part that the poem stages and which is as large at least as its descriptive part, see the formal analyses that Carlo Ferdinando Russo has been unraveling in these last fifteen years, in *Belfagor*.

46. Paul De Man has written eloquently on this question (1979).

47. Part of the royal image is conventional and traditional. For instance in Sarpedon's portrait the divine genealogy—he is the son of Zeus—the lion simile, the special epithets are traditional marks of royalty. Together with individual traits and features, the traditional marks compose a royal portrait by which the king is known. When Aeneas answers in *Il.* XX.204ff. to Achilles' mockeries, he says that both of them know each other well through the *proklut'epea*, that is through "the previously heard tales" or "verses" that celebrate them. *Prokluta* is composed by *pro-* and *kluta*, which is connected, through *kluô*, to *kleos*.

some of the traits of his portrait,[48] and finally he accepts it, somehow *a posteriori*, fulfilling an image of himself that, ideally, wants him dead in order to celebrate his posthumous glory. Consequently Sarpedon as a character is a mere function of a structure which precedes him and in which he fulfills the needed role.

Curiously this function does not weaken the representation of his image, but, on the contrary, strengthens it. For the huge superhuman power that his royal portrait outlines lives only as an image. It is as if the real person's immense force of heroic life were drained out and made image. That is why the representation of Sarpedon's power turns out simultaneously to illustrate the power of representation.[49] By this I do not mean that Sarpedon's image is an image: I mean that Sarpedon's portrait represents him already as an image and therefore also already as a text, as other than himself and as dead. For what *kleos* tells of him is what can be said even before and after him. Hector's mother, for instance, will celebrate Hector's death with words similar to those with which Sarpedon celebrates himself borrowing the terms from his portrait.[50] The portrait of the king, therefore, lives only as a dead and deathless image, even while the king is alive. And one portrait resembles the other.

Later in his speech, when Sarpedon simply considers his human destiny rather than his royal image (322–28), he confronts death as any other mortal would. Here the force lies in his capacity to impress on himself the will to confront and somehow master the power of death. Here the text taps a different metaphysical resource, as I have shown, a stronger and more universal one. Yet, by embracing death as he does, he also fulfills the implicit program of his portrait, a program that inscribes his death both in his imperishable glory and in the text of that glory as well.[51]

---

48. Sarpedon picks up the godlike (*antitheon*) feature of this portrait when he says (312) that "all people look at *him* as at a *god.*" This is a rare compliment in Homer. Besides this passage, we have viii.173, for an almost mythical king, and vii.71 for Alcinous! There are several variations on this theme. "To honor as a god": IX.155, 297, 302 (of Achilles); V.78 (Eurypylos); X.33 (Agamemnon); XI.58 (Aeneas); XIII.218 (Thoas); XIV.205 (Castor); XVI.605 (Laogonos); v.36; xix.280; xxiii.339 (Odysseus). "To receive a hero as a god": XVI.434 (Hector); "To be a god among men": *Il.* XIV.258–59 (of Hector, who, a rumor says, boasts of being son of Zeus XIII.54, but the genealogy is denied in X.49–50); "To pray to someone as to a god": XXII.394 etc., Hes. *Theog.* 91.

49. I borrow here the formula which Louis Marin illustrated in his seminar at the Ecole des Hautes Etudes in the spring of 1981 titled the "Portrait of the king." I read there a first version of this chapter.

50. See XXII.433–35.

51. See Loraux 1982, 32: "la mort du guerrier appelle irrésistiblement le chant du poète, la prose de l'orateur, alors il s'avére que *la belle mort est toujours en elle-même déjà un discours.*"

The Structure of Supplementarity

To say that the real person, Sarpedon, is already an image, a text, suspends, within an indecidable logic, the question of his truth. Of course we recall here that *kleos*, the image he fulfills by rushing into the battle, is itself troubled by an unstable meaning. We remain closed within the prison of the text, unable to predicate anything about its referent.

Kleos intimates simultaneously and contradictorily the truthful and imperishable renown (*aphthiton kleos*) and the irresponsible, occasional rumor. As such, *kleos* contains in itself a contradiction in which one term is constitutive of the other while displacing it (supplementing the other), and vice versa. Therefore truth in *kleos* is also constitutive of *kleos* as unverifiable rumor. The oscillating supplementary meaning of *kleos* impinges on the very image the text presents of itself.

Sarpedon's decision to fulfill his *kleos*[52] and to validate it with the evidence of truth, at the price of his life, at once reveals the advantage the text looks after, and intimates the inevitable lack that marks the Iliadic writing. Even if Sarpedon fulfills *a posteriori* his (epic) image, still he becomes the guarantee of its *truth*; by performing the "originary" act that validates his (epic) *kleos*, he demonstrates its truth. Yet, by this same gesture, Sarpedon also shows that epic poetry needs to validate itself as truth.

The supplementary structure of *kleos* does not rest and does not leave any rest to the Iliadic writing. Here we touch the critical move whereby the *Iliad* both intimates its truth and unveils its impossibility to give evidence of truth. For of course Sarpedon's statement merely enlarges his already existing *kleos* which by itself, notwithstanding all its theological underpinning, was already insufficient to prove its own truth. The Lycians suspected it and Sarpedon agrees to add to it the force of truth. But it still remains *kleos*.

The consequences for our interpretation of the *Iliad* resulting from this supplementary force of *kleos* oscillating within the well-built structure of epic self-representation are easy to imagine.

The theological underpinnings, the divine inspiration are as much "evidence" in favor of the truth of *kleos* as Sarpedon's will to fulfill it with his own life. They all hide and expose the supplementarity of *kleos*. But even the psychological characterizations become impenetrable for our analysis. We have already seen how difficult it remains for us to appreciate the way the Lycians read (sarcastically, unreasonably) Sarpedon's *kleos*. Nor is Sarpedon's own appreciation of his *kleos* made evident by his will to validate it. For this does not tell us either how much of his *kleos* he upholds, or what it means for him to validate an image which presents him as a god, as a lion, as a king, while recognizing that only the inevitability of death makes sense of his gesture.

The image of the king could appear to the king himself and/or the *Iliad* to be a noble fabrication—as the king comes to realize his human frailty he would be aware of that fabrication, or, alternatively the text would expose that fabrication

---

52. I pursue here only one of the alternative readings of the passage. The other one, that *kleos* is mere flattery, invalidates already the truth of *kleos*.

without the character's awareness. Or again the portrait of the king could appear to himself and/or to the *Iliad* to be the true image of a superhuman person that only death separates from the gods.

In the former reading the text would exercise a sort of rationalistic criticism; in the latter it would uphold its superhuman heroes with all the theological and rhetorical underpinnings it masters. Both readings are inseparable, and this explains not only why it is possible to speak of the text's awareness of its fiction, but also why the readers are constantly and simultaneously tempted by both views.

The Text's Reading of Itself[53]

We have seen that the Lycians are the first who sometimes admiringly (313) and sometimes suspiciously (318–21) read the portrait of Sarpedon. As readers, they function as mirror figures of us, readers of the *Iliad*. We too, just like the Lycians, are not sure to what extent the *kleos* of the kings is a glorious image the text fully upholds or allows us to feel critical about. We know both that the *kleos* is the main business of the epic song, and that there will be always portraits of kings as long as kings exist. The Lycians of course know also some of the poets who sit at the table of the kings when celebrating their glory.

The text of the *Iliad* with seigneurial assurance and ironic understatement represents the suspicion of those readers of the epic poetry and gives them their due. It has the king recording their relative lack of trust and stating that he must, at the cost of his life, prove the *truth* of that truthful *text*. The Lycians must therefore feel ashamed to be such suspicious readers. And accordingly the text induces us, mimetic figures of the Lycians, to feel like them. We know the success the text has reaped with this strategy.

I have shown that the Lycians' suspicion about Sarpedon's *kleos* arises just because his portrait precedes the king's actions and *bios*. In the eyes of the Lycians, therefore, the precedence of the text with respect to its truth remains unchallenged. First is the word . . .

Yet if Sarpedon (even *a posteriori*) means to validate the implications of his portrait, he is presented by the text as a different reader, an exemplary one, on whom the text has a tremendously edifying effect. Indeed Sarpedon is exemplary of all those noble readers whom the *Iliad* has affected and has persuaded to accept, valiantly, their own death.

The text's awareness of its reflexivity is admirable. It is as though the text knew in advance the possible readings it was offering. On an empirical level it is true that the poets of epic poetry were able to appreciate the reaction of their listeners, immediately, as the reading scene of *Od.* i.325–59 shows.[54] But the

---

53. I follow here some of the critical concerns that Paul De Man has illustrated in his work.

54. Here Penelope intervenes and stops (*apopaue* 340) Phemius's song about "the wretched return of the Achaeans": see my analysis in Pucci 1987, 195ff.

text's rehearsal of its own readings is not an empirical feat: it intimates the sense the text has of itself as a text, of its awareness of itself as fiction.

And yet there is one effect that the text cannot presume and mirror: its unreadability.

At the end of Sarpedon's speech a crossing of possible significations makes uncertain the precise inflection of Sarpedon's thought. I have shown that *eukhos* may designate mere victory or glory (*eukhos* pointing to a *kleos*),[55] and that accordingly an existential and an edifying interpretation of Sarpedon's utterance are possible. For Sarpedon may imply that to die in the battlefield constitutes either one of the countless ways of death that constantly threaten men or a qualitatively different sort of fate. His train of thought from 322 on could follow two different directions. Either he would belittle the importance of *kleos* in the evaluation of the heroic death and would therefore stare at the stern comfort of considering death as that which is proper and close to all men, or he would finally attach heroic death to the exclusive privilege of *kleos* and repeat essentially the train of thought of the first part of his speech. Both inflections are present in the ideological premises of the *Iliad* and, though they are slightly inconsistent, they are oddly readable here in the same words.

Furthermore, even the specific identity of Sarpedon's subjectivity which should be the source of his words and decision is blurred. For the *Iliad* presents Sarpedon as being affected by his own voice which is actually also the voice of the *Iliad*, and, in each oral performance, the voice of its poet. Of course as Sarpedon speaks with the epic poetry's diction and ideas, and he affects himself, his subjectivity emerges as a function of that *autoaffection*. That diction, those ideas, the voice that insistently and solemnly repeats them—and attributes them to a divine source, the Muses—combine in *kleos*, which contradictorily is also what the poets, in their human blindness and ignorance, only hear, a rumor, a voice, which they repeat, insistently and solemnly: "Tell me, now, Muses living in the houses of Olympus—for you are goddesses, you are present and you know (see) everything, but we (poets) hear only *kleos* (rumor) and know nothing—tell me who . . ." (*Il.* II.484–86). The knot of crossing contradictions becomes insoluble: the subjectivity of the hero emerges with the *autoaffection* that is exercised by a discourse/voice which is "other" (*kleos*); glory (*kleos*) is the effect of a repeated voice that insistently declares this effect to be a valuable (divine) voice and a valueless rumor; *eukhos* is either a variant of that same voice, or "victory," which is meaningless since it is a momentary result of the gamble . . . .

The power of the negative that I have liberated with this reading deeply shakes all the articulations that should hold the text tightly together. We are left, to some extent, in a predicament or *aporia* that would seem to force the reader into silence.

---

55. See Griffin's paraphrase of the passage: "If by avoiding death today we could make ourselves immortal, then I should not fight, but we must die some day, so let us go, to win *glory* ourselves or to serve the glory of others" (1980, 73) and his translation: "So let us go either to yield victory to another or to win it ourselves" (92; italics mine).

But this is not the case. The exposure of the power of the negative reveals how the text makes sense, how it holds itself together and how it manages, hides/exposes the negative itself, the difference, the supplementarity, the unreadability. This operation of simultaneous hiding/exposing is the mark of a great text, one that does not offer itself to an easy demystification of its metaphysics, or allow the reader to know exactly where it stands—either on the side of hiding or on the side of exposing.

Furthermore, the deconstructive analysis sharpens our knowledge of the forms (protocols), the power and the effects of all linguistic structures, each staging different strategies and supplementary constructions. The epic language of the *Iliad*, as we have seen, builds its whole immense fabric on the ground of *kleos* and on its several functions and protocols (or "etiquette") as "glory," as "image" of the king, as "repeated voice" (rumor, renown); and therefore it exhibits the "voice" as the main means of its production, and of its effects against death and in taming death.

The *Odyssey*, on the contrary, elaborates its strategies through *mêtis* and polytropy as protocols of a "writing" that seeks to captivate and imprison the most powerful enemy, death, in its own movements and figures.

The power of the negative, of course, also marks the writing that liberates this power in deconstructing other texts. To this extent, the deconstructive discourse cannot assert any truth for itself, but implements a strategy that simultaneously points to truth and suspends it. It gains nevertheless power over the text it deconstructs. The question, then, is whether this strategy is a seductive literary maneuvering or a troubling necessity . . . or both.

CHAPTER 5

Textual Epiphanies in the *Iliad**

In Homeric narrative a god appears to a hero and, by virtue of his presence, determines or intensifies to the highest degree the action that the hero performs. Regardless of whether the god suggests a plan of action (*Iliad* 2.165ff., etc.), prevents the hero from performing a particular act (*Iliad* 1.199ff.) or simply encourages, watches over, and accompanies the hero, his presence—his being there (whether perceived both by hero and reader or only by the latter)—amplifies the action to a heroic scale and places it in an ampler, teleological perspective, directly intensifying its importance, effect, and force.

But this divine presence is characterized by contradictory, ambivalent, and disconcerting elements both from a formal and from a theological point of view. Formally, the appearance of the god is managed through a representation of his physical presence that is always weak and arbitrary. If we compare the epiphanies of Demeter and Aphrodite in the hymns devoted to them with the epiphany of Athena at *Iliad* 1.194ff. (one of the most explicit epiphanies in the poem) we find that the physical presence of Athena is not sketched or represented in any way. She remains a blank figure. In the *Odyssey* the same goddess is described through the rhetorical figure of a simile: "in appearance she was like a woman, beautiful, tall, and skilled at lovely works" [δέμας δ' ἤϊκτο γυναικὶ / καλῇ τε μεγάλῃ τε καὶ ἀγλαὰ ἔργα ἰδυίῃ·] (*Od.* 13.288–89). Odysseus recognizes her, of course. But so arbitrary is the description of this figure that scholars still hunt in vain for an iconographical identification, undissuaded by the disconcerting verdict

* Originally published as "Epifanie testuali nell'*Iliade*," in *Studi italiani di filologia classica*, 3d ser. 3 (1985): 170–83.

of the hero himself—that it is hard to recognize the goddess because she "makes herself like everything" [σὲ γὰρ αὐτὴν παντὶ ἐΐσκεις].

One has to conclude that, although the goddess is indeed present and recognizable, the narrative frames this self-revelation of the divine in an enunciative structure that attests to the arbitrary and surprising nature of her appearance. In general, both in the *Iliad* and in the *Odyssey*, such appearances are marked by rhetorical devices like synecdoche, conspicuous silence ("stone-walling"), and comparison (i.e. metaphor and metonymy). The god, in other words, is not seen in his true form. What goes on is a double or triple process of removal. First of all, the god must divest himself of his invisibility.[1] Then he must reduce the force (luminous or otherwise) of his form—for "the gods are terrible when they appear clearly" [*Iliad* 20.131: χαλεποὶ δὲ θεοὶ φαίνεσθαι ἐναργεῖς]. Finally, the gods in Homeric epiphanies take normal human form and are never portrayed with the enormous, luminous, divinely fragrant figures described in the Homeric hymns (*Hymn to Demeter* 275–80, *Hymn to Aphrodite* 170ff.) and later to be represented in sculpture, but are depicted solely by means of the rhetorical figures described above.

From a formal point of view, it would also be worth examining the different ways in which the Homeric gods enable the heroes to perceive them (sometimes visibly, sometimes only audibly), as well as the specific dramatization of each individual scene. For the presence of the god is as diverse in its significance as the ways in which the self-revelation is performed. If, for example, the god appears first disguised as a human being before suddenly revealing himself for what he is, the epiphany generally signifies an attitude on the god's part that is hostile, critical, or ambiguous. Even where one would least expect it, in the appearance of Athena at *Odyssey* 13.221ff., 288–89, it remains clear that, however benevolent her motives, the goddess of *mêtis* is playing a trick on Odysseus.[2]

Examined from the point of view of content, the self-revelation of the god works on different levels. A god may simply wish to be recognized for what he or she is—as the goddess of *mêtis*, for example. The textual complicities in every epiphany are of the highest importance, and in this case they remind us of the *mêtis* of the Odyssean text itself.

But the difference that we are highlighting between the essence of the gods and the form they take indicates that the text implies a difference between essence and appearance, which—even if not formulated in a theoretical way—paves the way for an important philosophical statement.

---

1. Several scenes will serve to show something of the power that the figures of the gods have when they act without being recognized: the footprint of Poseidon reveals his divine nature (*Il.*13.71–72); Athena descends onto the plain of battle, swift and luminous in the eyes of the two armies as a shooting star (*Iliad* 4.73–83); the presence of Athena in the house of Odysseus reveals itself through a fiery light that pervades the entire room, etc.

2. On this and other epiphanies in the *Odyssey*, see Pucci (1986, 7–28).

Let us begin to disentangle these problems by looking more closely at a particular epiphany, that of Athena in the first book of the *Iliad*.[3] The goddess appears suddenly to Achilles and is immediately defined as "visible to him alone" (οἴῳ φαινομένη, *Il.* 1.198). Such self-revelation of a god in visible form and without any sort of disguise is very rare in the *Iliad*, and with the explicit designation of the verb φαίνεσθαι it is practically unparalleled.[4]

As we know, Athena is sent by Hera to prevent Achilles from killing Agamemnon: the goddess "loved both men in her heart and was concerned for both" (195–96).[5] Athena thus descends and presents herself to the hero as he is engaged in making a decision, a process expressed by the verb μερμερίζειν (1.189ff.) and developed formally in standard ways, as Arend has demonstrated (1975, 106–15). The hero wavers; should he draw his sword, charge forward to disperse the others and kill Agamemnon, or ought he to suppress his anger? As he slowly draws his sword, Athena arrives and without elaborate explanations exhorts him to replace it in its scabbard. The story of the *mênis* has begun.

---

3. By "epiphany" I mean the unexpected self-revelation of a god by means of shapes and signs that are recognizable and identifiable to a human being who is wide awake. I thus exclude dreams, oracles, divine manifestations such as thunder, any divine presence or companionship that is constant or potentially constant (as when Circe becomes the lover of Odysseus), and miraculous or magical visions of gods (like that which Athena makes possible for Diomedes) that are not self-revelations.

4. φαίνεσθαι for the actual appearance of a god is very rare in Homer: *Il.* 1.198; *Od.* 16.159 (with reciprocal allusion between the two texts); *Od.* 24.448 (and cf. *Od.* 19.37–40).

In *Il.* 5.864–67 the verb is used of Ares appearing to Diomedes, but, as mentioned above, this is not an epiphany, properly speaking. The verb is used with *enargês* to speak of epiphanies in *Il.* 20.131; *Od.* 16.161 (these two passages may also be a case of reciprocal allusion); *Od.* 7.201 (cf. 3.218–24 ἀναφανδόν).

Outside Homer, cf. Hesiod fr. 165.5 (Merkelbach-West); Homeric Hymn 7.2; 33.12.

Conversely, even without the verb φαίνεσθαι it is rare for the god to appear in visible form without disguise, e.g., *Il.* 24.169ff. (cf. 223–24) etc.; *Od.* 20.30ff., etc.

In a number of cases it is hard to decide whether the god presents himself visibly or lets himself be recognized solely by his voice: *Il.* 18.165ff.; *Il.* 22.214ff.; 15.243ff., etc.; *Od.* 17.360ff., where Ameis, Hentze, and Cauer believe, without firm evidence, that the goddess is visible to Odysseus; it does appear to be the case that epiphanies by means of voice alone do not appear in the *Odyssey*, whereas they are frequent in the *Iliad*.

Finally, the god may reveal himself visibly or audibly only after divesting himself of a disguise: *Il.* 3.380ff.; *Il.* 22.7–20; 17.333–34, etc.; *Od.* 13.221ff. etc.; *Homeric Hymn* 7.2, *Hymn to Demeter* 275ff., *Hymn to Aphrodite* 81ff. and 170ff.

5. I ought at this point to draw attention to the similarities with the epiphany of Athena, in the second book, to Odysseus (2.165ff.) In this case too it is Hera who sends Athena; the ancient commentators were already dubious about Athena's vicarious role here and about the repetition, cf. von der Mühll 1952, 40.

The difference to which I draw the reader's attention is that at *Il.* 2.165ff. Athena reveals herself to Odysseus and makes herself recognizable to the hero immediately, without any preliminary disguise, but she does so only "by means of her voice" (*Il.* 2.183).

As Mark Edwards has pointed out, the arrival of Athena is as surprising to the reader as the end of line 194, ἦλθε δῷ᾽Αθήνη, unexpectedly replacing the epithet ἀργυρόηλον, which accompanies ξίφος at line-end seven times in the *Iliad* and four in the *Odyssey*. As Edwards notes, "The effect in the audience must have been striking" (1980, 13).

But another surprising detail follows immediately after: Athena arrives and positions herself behind Achilles (1.197 στῆ δῷ ὄπιθεν). This is a unique case; in no other epiphany does a deity materialize behind a hero in quite this way.

What does this unparalleled act imply? Edwards suggests that Athena wishes to attract the hero's attention in a dramatic fashion: "the poet uses a physical action to illustrate powerful emotions" (1980, 14). True enough. But perhaps we can categorize the meaning of the act more precisely.

We observe that Athena places herself behind the hero and from this position pulls him by the hair. In this moment of overpowering astonishment for the hero the goddess is not, as the text erroneously suggests, visible to him alone (οἴῳ φαινομένη, 198), or at least not yet. At this point she remains invisible to the hero. To assure ourselves of this we can appeal not only to common sense, but also to the conventions of the poem itself. When a god is at work behind a hero, he is regularly invisible to that hero. I offer the two most striking examples of this epic convention. In *Il.* 15.694–95 Zeus reinforces Hector as he charges:

τὸν δὲ Ζεὺς ὦσεν ὄπισθε
χειρὶ μάλα μεγάλῃ, ὤτρυνε δὲ λαὸν ἅμ᾽ αὐτῷ.

[Zeus thrust him forward from behind with his enormous hand, and stirred up all his army along with him.]

Naturally Zeus is invisible; some commentators even take the expression as purely metaphorical and assume the god is not in fact present on the battlefield at all.[6]

The most disconcerting example occurs when Apollo places himself behind Patroclus to begin the latter's butchery (*Il.* 16.791):

στῆ δ᾽ ὄπιθεν, πλῆξεν δὲ μετάφρενον εὐρέε τ᾽ ὤμω
χειρὶ καταπρηνεῖ, στρεφεδίνηθεν δέ οἱ ὄσσε.

[He halted behind him and struck him across his back, on his broad shoulders, with the flat of his hand. And Patroclus's eyes whirled.]

This στῆ δ᾽ ὄπιθεν is the same formula we find in the epiphany of Athena: she too touches the hero on the back (at the nape of the neck, to be precise). There is a strange similarity between the two passages, in which one can initially discern no difference of intent. Yet Apollo is a god hostile to Achilles/Patroclus, and thus acts in opposition to him, invisibly, as the text

---

6. Ares at *Il.* 5.595 "comes and goes, now before Hector and now behind him" invisibly.

makes explicit at line 789. Athena, by contrast, is the patron of Achilles; the reader can thus feel sure that despite the disconcerting ambiguity of her action, the goddess's initial intervention will nevertheless resolve itself in favor of the hero. It is perhaps to reassure the audience at once that the text hastens to add "visible to him alone" when the goddess is not, in fact, yet visible to Achilles.

We should recall at this point that epiphanies in which a god manifests himself only after an initial moment of impersonation or disguise all communicate an attitude or intention on the god's part that is at best playful and cautionary, but often critical, hostile, mocking, or even life-threatening.[7]

In our passage Athena is not disguised, but merely invisible. Yet the way in which she becomes visible only after having seized the hero by the hair is nonetheless parallel to the epiphanies in which the god initially appears disguised.

The intention of the text is disconcerting, perhaps even mocking. Athena seizes Achilles by the shoulders from behind, from that anterior space in which the future, for Homeric man, is symbolically situated (*Il.* 12.34, *Od.* 22.55, etc.). Already the future that Achilles does not know and would prevent if he could—the future of the *Iliad*—looms behind him.

While the text asserts that Athena is visible only to Achilles, in reality he cannot yet see her (198): οἴῳ φαινομένη· τῶν δ᾽ ἄλλων οὔ τις ὁρᾶτο. No commentator (so far as I know) has noticed the text's inattention on this point.[8] Ought we to take this inattention on the critics' part as proof of the complicity and blindness that the text knows how to create in its readers, ever eager for reassurances? For the staging of the epiphany is acted for the reader's benefit, while the text is torn between two conflicting goals: on the one hand to tell the reader that Athena has arrived with a disconcerting message for Achilles, and on the other to reassure him that she remains the hero's patron.

---

7. For this reason I divide textual epiphanies into two overarching categories, those in which the god reveals himself from the start as he actually appears or by means of his own voice, and those in which the god reveals himself only after casting aside an initial disguise.

The problematical aspects of this type of epiphany derive from the strategy of the mise-en-scène. The god who presents himself in disguise declares a double proposition, a deception, a piece of cunning. Even in dreams, Artemidorus (*Onirocritus.* 2.40; 4.72) informs us, a god who appears with an erroneous iconography will not tell the truth.

Given the clarity of the Homeric examples (*Il.* 22.7–20; 3.398ff., etc.), there is no need to underline at what critical moments such epiphanies take place, nor to cite still more explicit examples in which the god wishes to be recognized as such, e.g., Dionysus in *Homeric Hymn* 7, Euripides *Bacchae* etc.

8. When I presented an earlier version of this chapter at the Centre de Recherches Comparées sur les Sociétés Anciennes in Paris, Professor H. Wisman informed me that Karl Reinhardt had brought up this problem in an unpublished seminar presentation and argued that φαινομένη must be taken in the broad sense of "perceptible." But this is unsatisfactory; the remainder of the line (τῶν δ᾽ ἄλλων οὔ τις ὁρᾶτο) clearly indicates that φαινομένη must mean "visible."

74 Chapter 5

Returning to the text at 199–200: θάμβησεν δ᾽ Ἀχιλεύς, μετὰ δ᾽ ἐτράπετῷ αὐτίκα δ᾽ ἔγνω / Παλλάδ᾽ Ἀθηναίην· δεινὼ δέ οἱ ὄσσε φάανθεν.
We note θάμβησεν, "he was amazed," which, as noted above, carries a stronger charge than the normal surprise of recognition. Note also μετὰ δ᾽ ἐτράπετο, "he turned": this expression is unique in the Homeric corpus in this sense and certainly the form ἐτράπετο would have been sufficient on its own.[9] I need not stress the possibility that μετατρέπομαι refers to the change or transformation of Achilles himself (Hes. *Erga* 416), as if on seeing the goddess the hero himself alters, or that it indicates Achilles' transfer of his attention to the goddess.[10] We turn instead to the moment at which Achilles sees the goddess or, more accurately, recognizes her. The text describes the blazing eyes of one of the two characters: δεινὼ δέ οἱ ὄσσε φάανθεν. The impossibility of determining whether the οἱ refers to Achilles or Athena is a familiar problem. With this irritating grammatical imprecision, the text solicits our curiosity, tempting critics to decide whom these blazing eyes belong to. It would indeed be worth knowing whether this terrible blaze offers us a reflection of the goddess's splendor. But we cannot know; the ambiguity is irresolvable.[11]

Without the certainty that it is Athena who is described with those terribly flashing eyes, the goddess's presence remains for the reader a blank presence, with no imaginable form. She remains in the sphere of the unexpressed. She is visible, quite literally, only to Achilles. If we could be certain that the eyes described in the text are Athena's, then we would have a description in the form of a synecdoche—a spark at least of the entire luminous form of the goddess.

But the most important point remains this grammatical imprecision, this clumsy negligence on the part of the text. A tiny accident cuts us off from a vision of the divine. The Iliad's enunciation of the epiphany frames it amidst indecision, between silence and synecdoche.

But what is it that Achilles sees? The Athena *promakhos* with spear and Gorgon-emblazoned shield, as she is described at *Il.* 5.733ff.?
The text allows us to imagine so, if we wish, but it seems to me that the "not-said" in our passage signifies precisely that the poets of this text knew no more than they tell us about the form in which Athena appears. It is impossible, in other words, that the reader is here being invited to imagine the figure of the

9. Chantraine (1963, 116) explains the *meta* as "aboutissement de l'action."
10. *Il.* 1.160; *Il.* 12.238; *Il.* 9.630.
11. Most recently Nicole Loraux (1983, 99ff.) has collected the evidence and arguments, among them the recurrent epithets γλαυκῶπις or ὀξυδερκής, to argue that the eyes are Athena's. But however forceful, these arguments cannot explain away *Il.* 19.16–17 where the eyes of Achilles are described as blazing at the sight of arms in terms reminiscent of our passage: ἐν δέ οἱ ὄσσε/ δεινὸν ὑπὸ βλεφάρων ὡς εἰ σέλας ἐξεφάανθεν. One can certainly maintain that these two lines (19.16–17) contain nontraditional elements, such as the expression ὑπὸ βλεφάρων, normally used only with ὕπνος or δάκρυα, and here totally out of context. These lines are perhaps modeled on *Il.* 15.607–8 where Hector's eyes flash ὑπ᾽ ὀφρύσιν rather than under the eyelids, as here. But even if we admit that these elements point to a late date for this passage, it would still be a possible evidence that the expression at *Il.* 1.200 was understood in antiquity as applying to Achilles.

goddess as she is represented, for example, in her role as *promakhos*.[12] To begin with, the epic text allows the reader to know and see more than the characters; in our case, the text tells the reader (1.208–9) what Achilles will learn only later. The text does *not* invite us to imagine that the characters see and know more than we do.

Secondly, there is some evidence that ancient readers found themselves faced with the same kind of perplexity as that outlined above. They must, in other words, have asked themselves what kind of physical presence, what physical actions are implied by a "reticent" epiphany. In Hesiod *Theogony* 22ff. the Muses instruct and inspire Hesiod. The text is perfectly silent as to the nature of their presence; does Hesiod see them or does he only hear their voices? At line 31, however, alternative readings indicate that ancient editors were moved to ask the question:

καί μοι σκῆπτρον ἔδον δάφνης ἐριθηλέος ὄζον

δρέψασαι
        θηητόν·
δρέψασθαι

If we read δρέψασαι, with the papyrus and the *a* family of Mss., the Muses themselves cut and give the laurel branch to the poet, whereas if we read δρέψασθαι, with the remaining Mss., the Muses enable Hesiod himself to cut the laurel branch. Both readings are old,[13] and in my view the reason for their existence is that with δρέψασαι the Muses are conceived of as being physically present, whereas with δρέψασθαι they may be thought of as present only through their voices. In other words, the double reading results from ancient readers' uncertainty about the way in which Hesiod wished to represent the Muses.

The textual crux here is emblematic of an uncertainty rooted in the epic tradition itself and unavoidable once the tradition introduces divine intervention without actually describing its appearance. There are numerous cases in the *Iliad* in which we are unable to be sure whether a god appears in visible form or allows himself to be perceived only through his voice. A case much like that of the Hesiodic Muses is that of Athena at *Il.* 22.214ff.; here the presentation of the scene would favor the idea that the goddess manifests herself to Achilles only audibly, were it not that at 276–77 Athena retrieves the spear vainly thrown by Achilles and brings it back to Achilles without being observed by Hector.[14]

---

12. As described at *Il.* 5.733ff. and *Od.* 22.297.

13. According to the most recent editor of the *Theogony*, West (1966, 165). Though the majority of modern critics and editors read δρέψασθαι, West prefers δρέψασαι, arguing from the rarity of the construction ἔδον...δρέψασθαι.

14. λάθε δ᾽ Ἕκτορα, ποιμένα λαῶν. This would seem to favor the idea that she *is* seen by Achilles. Moreover, the return of the lance would be less fantastic if it remained visible at least to Achilles.

But the visible presence of the goddess here causes difficulties on other grounds: (1) the image of the goddess running shoulder to shoulder with Achilles as she reveals her plan to him (22.215–23) would be ridiculous, and (2) it would be disturbing to

That the text of the *Theogony* reflects uncertainty about our problem even in antiquity ought to give us pause. And although at *Iliad* 1.195ff. the problem we face is not that of Athena's visibility but of the way in which she appears, the uncertainty embedded in the text of Hesiod suggests that on this point too the tradition may know no more than it tells us.

The hypothesis, then, is that the physical figure of Athena appears to Achilles either with eyes flashing terribly (*glaukôpis*), thus implying her divine splendor through synecdoche, or as a figure without a clear iconography, which nonetheless—as also in the first case—acquires attributes and precise powers through her abrupt appearance and tremendous, authoritative gesturality. To this must be added the force and recognizable sound of her divine voice.[15]

What matters, of course, is what the reader sees, since the epiphany does not take place in order to shock Achilles alone, but with him, the reader, who identifies himself with Achilles. Herein lies the importance of the epiphany; it presents not the imaginary and superhuman world of the invisible gods, but the divine as it manifests itself to men. The epiphany carries with it the experience of or desire for the divine which is legitimate or possible for the reader.

The disconcerting textual ambiguity in the description of Athena's self-revelation has a narrative and theological counterpart that has not, so far as I am aware, been discussed. Epic convention in such μερμερίζειν scenes can follow two paths: the dilemma in which the hero finds himself can be resolved either by the character's own decision (in this case the character can even be a god, e.g. *Il.* 2.2ff.) or by the sudden appearance of a god who resolves the hero's doubt. In either case the solution is positive, advantageous, and rational for the character. In the first case, the decision is in fact signaled by phrases like δοάσσατο κέρδιον εἶναι (*Il.* 13.458; 16.652; *Od.* 6.145, etc.), or ἀρίστη φαίνετο βουλή (*Il.* 2.5; 14.161, etc.), or δοκέει δέ μοι εἶναι ἄριστον (*Od.* 5.360) which express the characters' conviction that they are making the most advantageous choice. In the second case, the god who unexpectedly appears to offer a solution to the dilemma is the hero's patron or patroness, and though the god's appearance and advice may sometimes be unexpected, they never threaten the hero. Rather, they work to protect his life, honor, and booty.[16]

In the scene we have been examining (*Il.* 1.188ff.) the epic conventions of μερμερίζειν passages (dilemma, divine intervention and advice) are respected, with a single exception. The goddess intervenes to save Agamemnon at the expense of Achilles' booty, honor, and—ultimately—life. Advice of this kind,

---

have to imagine her visible as Athena at 214ff., and then visible as Deiphobus at 226ff. The best solution is perhaps to imagine that as Deiphobus she is visible only to Hector. She would thus be thought of as visible only in disguise, not in her true form.

15. The voice of the gods has a special quality: Odysseus and Diomedes recognize Athena by ear alone (*Il.* 2.182; 10.512).

16. A typical example is the scene at *Il.* 10.503ff., where Diomedes is torn between continuing his plundering and killing more Thracians. At this point Athena appears and advises him to return, thus ensuring the safety of his booty and life.

in this kind of scene, is unparalleled. How can Athena say that Hera has sent her because she loves both heroes equally? For undeniably she forces Achilles to accept a loss of honor and an offense with no immediate compensation, while when the compensation that she promises is finally offered, intervening events have rendered it worthless to the hero.[17] From an objective standpoint, then, Athena risks appearing to give Achilles fraudulent advice, advice that does not help the hero or salvage his *timê*. Such behavior is exceptional, even aberrant, for a divine patron.

Looking at the matter subjectively, we must ask whether Athena when she appears does no more than suggest the solution that the hero himself would view as advantageous and rational if he were able to resolve his dilemma with his own decision. This is the view taken by critics who, like Snell and Dodds, consider this epiphany to be an external image of Achilles' own decision. Yet in this case too the scene would be an aberration. In cases where a god intervenes to suggest a solution to a hero's dilemma, the suggestion is so obvious, or so appropriate to the situation, that the hero scarcely needs to respond. Here Achilles does respond. But his response by no means assures us that he finds Athena's suggestion rational and advantageous; he says rather that men must obey the gods, and that advantage comes of this obedience (*Il.* 1.218). The advantage thus resides not in the decision proposed by the goddess, but in the power of the goddess who imposes the decision. The goddess and her advice do not represent the hero's mental processes, but the authority of a decision genuinely external to the hero.

If we ask, in fact, who gains from the solution that the goddess offers to Achilles' dilemma, we will have to respond that the gain is the reader's and the reader's only. For from the goddess's solution arises the wrath of Achilles, that is, the poem itself. It is only by condemning Achilles to impotent rage that the *Iliad* fulfills itself as a poem; the poem as immortal monument is founded upon the future death of its hero. In the poem's own terms, Athena forces Achilles to sacrifice his *timê* so that he may later choose *kleos*; in modern terms one would say that the text reveals not the divine but the inscription of the decision Athena makes for Achilles in the metaphysics of its own textuality.

These considerations should help to put in perspective the view of Snell and Dodds that the scene is *exemplary* of the way in which the problem of the Homeric hero's free will is formulated. In fact the scene is clearly aberrant in both form and content. The ironic, mocking appearance of the goddess at Achilles' shoulder and her message (fraudulent on any objective view, a piece of coercion on a subjective one) together form a structure that, as a whole, is ambivalent and ironic.

The scene, then, is scarcely exemplary. Moreover, in order to weigh it as evidence of a world in which the divine and the human combine in heroic decisionmaking, the scene must be compared with all the other μερμερίζειν scenes, as well as the other scenes in which a hero chooses "freely," e.g. the

---

17. As J. Redfield (1975, 103) correctly states: "To attempt a reconciliation is in effect to choose Agamemnon, for a reconciliation would leave the king in place, unpunished for his unfairness to the greatest of the princes."

heroic scenes of *prohairesis* at *Il.* 18.98ff. (Achilles), *Il.* 22.98ff. (Hector), and *Il.* 12.310ff. (Sarpedon).

Achilles does of course resolve to spare Agamemnon following the advice of Athena, and it is clear that this method of making decisions "with the help of" the goddess surely appeared wholly persuasive to the poet and his public. The problem, in other words, revolves around the blindness of the reader before what I have shown to be the aberrant character of the scene. This question can only be answered in the broadest of terms: it is the text and its readers that are the main beneficiaries of Athena's advice. Hence the complicity that ties the reader to the intervention of the goddess. But if we are to respond to recent critics, we must define more precisely what they have to gain from such complicity, and from being less attentive to the discontinuities and ironies of the text.

In Snell's case, the scene responds enticingly to the Hegelian interpretation of the Greek genius that the author offers in his *Discovery of the Mind.* Demonstrating through this scene that Homeric man does not yet consider himself to be the "source [*Urheber*] of his own decisions" (1948, 31), Snell was able to sketch the movement of the Greek mind, beginning with Homer, from a minimal consciousness of subjectivity, thus satisfying not only the Hegelian view of philosophy as a development or as the history of consciousness in the making, but also, perhaps at a deeper level, the Hegelian claim that subjectivity as such was always foreign to the Greeks.[18]

In accord with this Hegelian attitude, Snell's interpretation suggests that there is no real rupture between the goddess's decision and Achilles' acceptance of it, because the goddess's appearance and advice are in a sense the external image of Achilles' own mental processes.[19] This explanation naturally reassures the reader that the relationship between deity and hero is a familiar, rational, and comfortable one, and that the decisions that the hero makes follow naturally from that relationship. The reader's blindness to the disconcerting moments of Athena's appearance and to the aberrant aspects of her advice has the evident advantage of permitting the reader to believe in a comforting and rational Iliadic theology.

That conclusion, of course, is one to which the entire poetics of the *Iliad* does its best to lead us, with notably successful results. The world of the heroes and that of the gods duplicate one another. Naturally they differ in occupying the divergent levels of mortality and immortality, but in other respects they are fully

---

18. On this point cf. Heidegger 1976, 427ff.

19. Or to put it in Snell's terms, all that is said or done by men, even under the impact of divine intervention, is entirely natural and human.

This same thesis is substantially that of Dodds: the epiphany of Athena is the outward and visible representation of an "inward divine monition" which Achilles feels within himself, and to which he attributes his decision—an unexpected decision, certainly, but nonetheless his own.

The claim is still more explicit in the recent work of W. Thomas McCary (1982, 7ff.), who eloquently restates the position of Hegel and Snell. Athena appears as an external image of Achilles' own mental processes. As an *image* she indicates those processes just as the images of dreams do; as a *symbol* of the hero's decision she represents (as Snell also held) the hero's wisdom and rationality.

parallel, without gaps or discontinuities, guaranteeing to one another the sublime virtues of beauty and nobility, attesting to each other's reality (and, I am tempted to add, historicity) and to the wondrous and perfect manner in which both exist and function. Theology, history, and story become a seamless whole.

Yet the observations made here about Homeric epiphanies generally and the analysis of Athena's epiphany at *Il.* 1.188ff. in particular threaten the simplicity of these conclusions. I hasten to add that I am not concerned here with formulating a novel interpretation to replace one so profoundly rooted in the text and developed to such a degree by later critics; my aim is rather to raise questions—questions of a textual, psychological, and theological nature. We will never know what Achilles would have decided if left to his own devices, nor what he would have done or demanded had he chosen to spare Agamemnon. The goddess's intervention obscures forever the decision making process that the text's μερμερίζειν sets in motion. The elements of form and content that appeared to us exceptional and disconcerting conspire to undermine any notion that this scene of decision-making is exemplary or paradigmatic. It goes through protocols that elsewhere signal a reflexive and rational relationship between god and man, and this is why it does not arouse suspicion in the reader.

Yet the epiphany is the condition that gives to the poem the specific plot it has. And this too helps to explain the complicity of the reader with the goddess, who appears essentially to ensure that the story of Achilles' wrath will be told. The text could not show us an Achilles who decides to become the hero of the *Iliad*, for that decision is a textual one, a condition of the composition of the text as such, and is not determined by any rationality or historicity. Hence the necessity for the text to use and simultaneously to subvert the forms and protocols that in general assure a clear and effective representation of an advantageous, rational relationship between a divine patron and a hero. By using such forms, the text attempts to maintain Achilles' decision as a natural consequence of that representation, and correspondingly to conceal the textual character of it. Yet since this is not in fact the case, this representation turns against itself, contradicts itself, subverts itself. For here we are not dealing with a trivial decision, whether to fight or to await another day, but with the wrath of Achilles. He must arrive at the paradox of withdrawing from the battle, losing his *timê*, and emerging vainly, after Patroclus's death, so that he can finally embrace "freely"(!) his own *belle mort*.[20]

On the theological plane one may reasonably ask whether the aspects of divine epiphanies in Homer and specifically of Athena's appearance at *Il.* 1.188ff. pointed out above can be explained only by attributing them to a textual strategy. Certain details in these Iliadic epiphanies, like the reticence with which the deities are represented, might lead one to attribute to Homer a sense of the divine that is far deeper and more profound than the usual claim that the poet

---

20. On the theme of the *belle mort*, cf. J. P. Vernant (1979, 1367–74); "La belle mort et le cadavre outragé," in G. Gnoli and J. P. Vernant, *La mort, les morts dans les sociétés anciennes*, (Cambridge and Paris, 1982), 45–76; N. Loraux, "Mourir devant Troie," in the same collection, 27–43; P. Vidal Naquet, *Préface* to Hélène Monsacré, *Les Larmes d'Achille* (Paris, 1984) 23; Monsacré, *op. cit.*, 51ff.

need not tell us what the gods look like because we already know. Similarly, in the epiphany in question the tremendous surprise of the appearance of Athena, the disconcerting ways in which she makes herself present and perceptible to Achilles, when measured against the canons of other epiphanies, may suggest that the divine has forces in reserve, powers and intentions that escape the control of even the most favored mortal.

This would correspond in turn to the poets' consciousness that their own text creates effects not entirely within their control, and that the Muses, whatever power or function they represent, have a power that surpasses the control of even the most favored θεράπων.

Clearly the solution to these problems, the possibility of breaking through to a level of profundity and complexity at which the theology and its metaphysics are firmly based in the text, is not in sight. The interplay between the deeper and more superficial levels is obvious. What we *can* insist upon is that the text betrays its own textuality—the fact that it is always a text, a fiction, and not a cross-section of truth or reality.

CHAPTER 6

Epiphanic Strategy and Intertextuality*

In the *Iliad* the contact of a human character with the physical presence of the gods is both simple and problematic, edifying and disturbing. A figure of extraordinary power is made visible or audible to a hero. It may bring him a command. It may comfort him. It may deride him and disappear. But always a halo of grandeur, of profundity, of privilege surrounds the character and his action. Yet at the same time, a sense of arbitrariness or insignificance, or an enigmatic message, can accompany these moments of contact. Such reactions strike above all the reader for whom the sudden presence of the god remains theologically difficult, as it never does for the hero, who takes such contact with the divine almost for granted.

The strategy by which the *Iliad* describes the god's physical presence to the reader might almost have been expressly designed to convey the simultaneously simple and problematic nature of the epiphany. We are told that the god moves toward the hero, that he seeks him, finds him, and—suddenly—begins to address him. But we do not learn or see in what form the god appears to the human character. For us the appearance of the god remains a blank.[1] In other cases the text describes for us each stage of the god's approach, repeats the god's message word for word, yet leaves us with the impression that the hero has seen nothing;

---

* Originally published as "Strategia epifanica e intertestualità nel secondo libro dell'*Iliade*," in *Studi italiani di filologia classica,* 3d ser. 6 (1988): 5–24.
    1. Cf. Chapter Five and in general Pfister (1924, col. 282), who draws attention not only to epiphanies that offer little in the way of visible appearance but also those in which a cloud or darkness covers a human character, as at *Il.* 3.380ff.; 5.23ff.; 20.318ff., or the god, as at *Il.* 16.788ff.

he is so familiar with the god that he need only hear his voice to know that the god is at hand and has addressed him.

These epiphanic patterns, which appear only rarely in the *Odyssey*, confine the reader's sensation of the divine presence to a mere voice, with no exterior sign (or almost none) of vitality, producing an abstract presence, a voice which becomes confused with the voice of the narrative and its strategies, and which has no need of a body to animate the poem, a voice at once divine and human which symbolizes the theological-narrative function of the epiphany that is so problematic for the reader.[2]

In the *Odyssey*, by contrast, the sensible presence of the god is realized by means of a divine form visible to the reader as well as the character. But this divine form is absolutely insignificant: Athena appears to Odysseus as a "tall and beautiful woman, skilled at splendid works" (*Od.* 13.289 = 16.157), a formula applied elsewhere even to a poor Phoenician woman. Here we are surely invited to conclude that the goddess of *mêtis* presents herself in an insignificant guise because she possesses a real form that is always different from that which she reveals. This epiphanic strategy corresponds thematically to the poetics of the *Odyssey*, a poetics of disguise and thus of the identity of the hero, continually threatened and reasserted; it has its counterpart at the textual level in the poetics of intertextuality.[3]

It seems worthwhile to try to isolate the protocols and characteristics of these two epiphanic strategies in Homer, both because they play a quite precise textual role in the two poems and because these two distinct approaches continue to be used in archaic texts after Homer: the explicit representation of the god's appearance in the *Hymns* and in comedy, for example, and the "blank" or purely aural epiphany in philosophical poems and, with some frequency, in tragedy.[4]

---

2. On the disconcerting aspects of divinity in the *Iliad*, see Reinhardt 1961, 107ff.

3. On the *mêtis* of Athena, and the capacity for metamorphosis of the gods of *mêtis*, cf. Detienne and Vernant, and Pucci 1987, 105ff. On this epiphanic strategy in the *Odyssey*, see Pucci 1986, 7–28.

4. For the *Hymns*, cf. *Hymn to Demeter* 75ff., *Hymn to Aphrodite* 81ff. and 170ff., where the divine figures appear in all their splendor after a preliminary disguise; for comedy, see for example Aristophanes's *Birds*. The presence of a voice without a description of any physical appearance is evoked by Epimenides (Diels-Kranz 3A I = Diogenes Laertius I.115): "while he was constructing a temple for the nymphs a voice broke from the sky—'Not for the nymphs, but for Zeus!'" Parmenides in his poem evokes the *daimones* as guides (D-K B, 1.3) and the goddess (D-K B, 1.23) as blank figures, quite in the Iliadic tradition though we are dealing not with an epiphany proper but with a young man's visit to the home of the gods. In tragedy the problem is complex and no clear consensus is available. It is highly controversial, for instance, whether Athena in Sophocles' *Ajax* is visible to Odysseus and Ajax; recently Barrett (1964, 396) argues that neither Odysseus nor (presumably) Ajax sees Athena, who is placed above and out of sight of the characters [see now Pucci 1994]. For Aeschylus cf. Taplin (1977, 444ff.) and *passim*, and on the whole question, particularly as it relates to the chorus of the *Clouds*, Lowell Edmunds (1986, 209–230).

So great a sign of divine favor is the epiphany that Athena at *Odyssey* 5.328ff. refrains from appearing to Odysseus lest she undercut the wrath of Poseidon against the hero. She aids him without allowing herself to be recognized by him (*Od.* 7.19ff.; 8.193ff.), but in fact she cooperates with the anger of Poseidon, leaving Odysseus prey to the anxiety her absence provokes.⁵

In Homer the purely aural epiphany is a familiar phenomenon, recognized, for example, by Pfister.⁶ But it is less easy to identify the precise difference of prestige involved (if any) between the full apparition of the god (as of Athena before Achilles at *Il.* 1.188ff., or Iris before the same hero at *Il.* 18.165ff.—in both cases a "blank" apparition as far as the reader is concerned) and his purely audible presence. It would appear that only two (Achilles and Priam) out of all the figures at Troy receive a full divine epiphany, and we can deduce from this that the privilege is reserved for the very greatest hero.⁷

The most elaborate depiction of an aural epiphany, and the one richest in textual suggestions, occurs in the second book of the *Iliad* when Athena approaches Odysseus at a crucial moment. The Achaeans, set in motion by the incautious speech of Agamemnon, are fleeing to the shore to launch their ships and abandon the siege of Troy. Hera sends Athena to restrain the army; Athena descends from Olympus and entrusts the task to Odysseus, using the same words that Hera had addressed to her. The hero obeys and at once goes into action—

---

5. Schwabl (1978, 9–10) rightly notes the cohesion and complicity of the Olympians as against the capricious decisions of minor divinities who, like Circe, aid the hero without worrying about Olympus.

Even antagonistic gods allow themselves to be recognized by the heroes they oppose. Thus Apollo appears to Achilles in order to mock him at *Il.* 22.7ff.

6. Pfister 1924, col. 282: "oder sie werden nur an ihrer Stimme erkannt wie Apollon *Il.* 20.375ff."

7. Priam recognizes only the figure of Iris (*Il.* 24.169ff.; cf. 223). It is hard to say whether the text accords Hector a sighting of divinity; at *Iliad* 15.236ff. he hears Apollo and recognizes that the speaker is a god, but does not know which one. Apollo reveals himself (*ibid.* 254–56) and promises his help, but nothing in the text indicates that the god does more than tell Hector his name. But the question is a vexed one; Ameis and Hentze feel that Hector sees the god in human form, whereas Leaf believes that he sees him in his true form. There are two difficulties. One is the question of how Hector can recognize that a god is speaking but not know which one; this would suggest that the god presents himself in human form but speaks with a divine voice. Secondly, what should we understand by the phrase at 247 ὅς μ' εἴρεαι ἄντην? For some it implies an ellipsis of φανείς (thus "appearing before me"), while for others—for me, for example, and for the author of the *LFGE* article on ἄντην—it corresponds only to an expression of the ἀντίον ηὔδα type. In any case, if by "epiphany" we mean that a mortal recognizes close by him the presence of a god from the latter's appearance or from a divine voice, this is only a partial epiphany; Apollo is recognized as a god, but must still declare his identity.

Ajax at *Iliad* 13.60–72 recognizes the presence of a god—Poseidon appearing in the guise of Calchas—just as the god vanishes, leaving a miraculous footprint in the ground. Similarly Helen has a partial vision of Aphrodite in *Il.* 3. I would not classify as an epiphany proper the isolated (and magical?) case of Diomedes in *Il.* 5 when he obtains from Athena the privilege of recognizing gods (5.127ff.).

action that involves first the kings, then the mass of soldiers and Thersites, and concludes with Odysseus's speech to the army. This is Odysseus's most glorious act in the *Iliad*, and Reinhardt does not hesitate to call it his *aristeia* (1961, 113–14).

But while Odysseus responds with admirable *sang-froid* to the goddess's order, even without seeing her, and thus satisfies without hesitation or surprise both his desire and—all unknowing—the theological-narrative design of the poem, the reader is forced to come to terms with a text that is enormously complex.

To begin with, the reader marvels at the narrator's familiarity with even the smallest details of divine activities. From 151 to 181 all is described from the goddess's perspective as she descends in obedience to Hera's orders, looks for and finds Odysseus, and addresses him. To adapt a famous judgment, we might say not that Homer's heroes are like his gods, but that the text of the *Iliad* itself emanates from a quasi-divine perspective.

Secondly, the repetition of Athena's dispatch by Hera underlines the fact that the text follows the pattern of the epiphany of Athena to Achilles in the first book, thus inviting us to compare the two scenes. In addition, the text is almost certainly aware of the *Odyssey*, so that the two poems here face off against one another, recall one another in subtle counterpoint, make fun of one another. Finally, the choice of Odysseus, a hero hardly suited to the tragic spirit of the *Iliad*, to carry out an action so important to the continued existence of the poem is not a little surprising.

In sum, the epiphany of Athena orchestrates the introductory notes of an *aristeia* that is unique in the *Iliad*, adds to the prestige of a hero who will be *aristos* only in the other poem, the *Odyssey*, and within the score of the *Iliad* sketches unexpected variations upon the epiphanic and heroic themes. Our reading will thus follow a complex textual trail. It will be attentive on the one hand to the aural epiphany (epiphony?) which here recalls strongly and insistently patterns found only in the *Iliad*, while on the other it will follow the intertextual traces, both internal and external, with all their resonances, that mark the text so deeply.

But these traces by no means indicate clear and precise trajectories. To speak of patterns specific to the *Iliad* implies the notion of a fixed Iliadic "code," distinct, for example, from that of the *Odyssey*. This notion is problematic on both an empirical and a theoretical level. What renders the notion of a code particularly fuzzy in our case is the constant linguistic interdependence of the two poems, a dependence that involves not only the two poems but the whole field of epic language. It might be preferable in this connection to speak of a textual "strategy," with all the freedom of movement, the double jumps on a checkerboard, that the notion implies, rather than of a "code."

The paradox of intertextuality or of allusion is inevitable in every text, because intertextual or allusive readings impose a specificity where there are only infinite repetitions and rewritings. But for obvious reasons the paradox is even more unavoidable in the case of epic language. In following the contradictory and paradoxical traces that the scene in *Iliad* 2 leaves us, we will inevitably be venturing onto difficult and rocky ground. But we can only try to respond to the nature of the problems that the text sets us.[8]

The epiphany opens with a hypothetical assessment on the narrator's part: that the Achaeans would have returned home contrary to fate,[9] had not Hera directed Athena to descend onto the field and to halt the flight of the army, using all her persuasive skills: σοῖς ἀγανοῖς ἐπέεσσιν (*Il.* 2.155–65).[10] The reference to these persuasive skills is perhaps an Odyssean touch. We shall defer the analysis of Hera's speech until Athena repeats it to Odysseus; in the meantime we shall consider the similar way in which Athena's epiphanies here and in the first book of the *Iliad* are framed. There too Hera sends Athena (*Il.* 1.195–96) out of concern for Achilles's intentions toward Agamemnon.[11] There too the goddess approaches the hero in a public situation, manifesting herself to him alone. In both cases the goddess's intervention is decisive for the future of the Trojan expedition. These general similarities have the effect of individualizing and privileging these two heroes among all those whose exploits at Troy the poem will shortly describe.

---

8. The concept of intertextuality has received a great deal of theoretical attention since Roland Barthes and then Julia Kristeva, in their different ways, offered a semiotic description of it. In the most radical version, that of Barthes, intertextuality embraces the myriad quotations that constitute the inevitable repetitivity of language. See Culler's analysis (1981, 100ff.). In pursuing intertextuality in this sense one would ultimately have to describe it as a kind of shimmering of infinite reflections and thus rule out the possibility of analysis: cf. Pucci 1984, 283–85. In practice I have made use of O. Ducrot's terminology for the phenomenon of allusion. It seems clear on the one hand that allusion (unlike quotation, for example) does not signal its presence in the text, nor can it be codified via precise diacritical signs; it reveals itself only as an effect of reading. The question how "explicit" and how "implicit" an allusion may be defined is analyzed by O. Ducrot (1980, 1083–1107). Allusive or intertextual repetition is thus a textual effect whose relationship to the other text is made more or less explicit by a series of textual (the rarity or otherwise of the expression) and contextual elements. It is in this sense that I use the terms "intertextuality" and "allusion" here and in my book *Odysseus Polutropos*.

9. ἔνθά κεν Ἀργείοισιν ὑπέρμορα νόστος ἐτύχθη, / εἰ μὴ Ἀθηναίην Ἥρη πρὸς μῦθον ἔειπεν [Then would the Argives have accomplished their return against their fate had not Hera spoken a word to Athena]. On the word ὑπέρμορα, see Leumann (1950, 385), who reconstructs the artificial creation of this word based on a misunderstanding of ὑπὲρ μόρον as the neuter form of an adjective rather than the substantive μόρος, and altered it to an adverbial plural.

In ἐτύχθη the force of τύχη is easily discernible, though the word itself does not occur in Homer: cf. G. Herzog Hauser s.v. "Tyche" (1948, col. 1651).

10. On the interpretation of Athena's mission in ancient and modern scholarship, see Peter von der Mühll 1952, 39–40. Zenodotus wished to make Athena alone responsible for the decision to address Odysseus, and athetized Hera's speech at 155–65. Von der Mühll leans toward the view that this systematization is original to the *Iliad*, and believes that the entire episode belongs to the B stratum of the poem, composed later than the earliest stratum of the *Odyssey*.

11. On Athena's epiphany at *Iliad* 1.188ff., see Aquaro 1984, 143–55.

But these same similarities serve also to highlight differences in detail. Whereas Athena reveals herself to Achilles with a physical gesture and presence, Odysseus senses her only by her voice (*Il.* 2.182): "Ὡς φάθ᾽, ὁ δὲ ξυνέηκε θεᾶς ὄπα φωνησάσης, ("so she spoke and he understood the voice of the goddess speaking to him"). This line, or at least the second half of it, closes three aural epiphanies in the *Iliad*[12] and one in the *Odyssey*.[13] There is nothing numinous, splendid, or surprising in this manifestation of the divine voice;[14] nevertheless, a large proportion of the heroes in the *Iliad* who receive divine advice or a divine message receive it in this way.[15] The *Odyssey*, as I have observed above, keeps this epiphanic mode on the margins of its "code," limiting it to only a few cases,[16] of which the clearest (24.528–35)[17] seems to recall the Iliadic technique intentionally.

At *Il.* 2.166ff. Athena manifests herself to Odysseus by voice alone, in contrast with the scene in the first book and with the epiphanic technique of the

---

12. The same line closes the brief vocal epiphany of Athena to Diomedes at *Il.* 10.512 and the second half of the line closes the epiphany, again a purely aural one, of Apollo to Hector at *Il.* 20.380.

13. The second half of the line closes the appearance of Athena to the two warring Ithacan groups (*Od.* 24.535). The whole passage repeats Iliadic formulas; cf. the commentary of Fernandez-Galiano (1986) and on line 535, Erbse (1972, 228–29).

14. On ὄπα in relation to the gods, cf. Severyn 1966, 38–40, and Clay 1974, 135. For the purely vocal character of the epiphanies closed by these lines, see Ameis and Hentze on *Il.* 2.182: "Danach scheint ihm [sc. Odysseus] die Göttin gar nicht sichtbar erschienen zu sein."

15. Even Diomedes, in *Iliad* 10, receives no special privileges when Athena advises him in a deliberation scene (ὁ μερμήριξε 503ff.) that closes with line 511 = 2.182, though in a previous scene she does send Diomedes a personal sign—a bird. This first scene is characterized by two exceptional elements: first, Athena herself (rather than Zeus) sends the bird, and secondly she sends it without being asked. See Codino *Dolonia* 134–35.

Other examples in the *Iliad* of aural epiphanies are 11.195–209; 15.236ff; 20.375ff., etc. At 22.7–20, Achilles recognizes Apollo, previously disguised as Antenor, as soon as the god declares himself, but we need not suppose a sudden manifestation of the god's form or voice; Achilles is familiar with Apollo's antagonistic stance toward him. At *Il.* 17.333–34 Apollo, here disguised as Periphas (323), appears before Aeneas who nonetheless recognizes him (by his voice? or perhaps by his eyes?).

16. Doubtful cases are *Od.* 17.360ff., where Athena is said to stand close to Odysseus (ἄγχι παρισταμένη) and induce him to beg from the suitors. The use of Odysseus's patronymic at 361 argues for a blank epiphany; the patronymic, insofar as it aggrandizes the character and produces a more elevated tone, suggests an equally elevated move on Athena's part. But nothing rules out the possibility that Odysseus only hears her voice. At *Od.* 18.69–70 the same formula ἄγχι παρισταμένη argues against assuming that Odysseus recognizes the goddess, while at *Od.* 16.455ff. and 24.368ff. Athena intervenes with her staff and must therefore be present and recognizable. Finally, at *Od.* 22.297 Athena holds her aegis aloft from the roof beam, creating panic. Ameis, Hentze, and Cauer ask what shape we should imagine here; if Athena is visible to all, this epiphany would be truly unique, a *coup de théâtre*.

17. See note 13.

Odyssey. Intentional counterpointing here begins to define the goddess's action, characterizing its tones and differences more precisely. The text now describes Athena's route down from Olympus to Odysseus in the Achaean camp (166–72):

"Ὣς ἔφατ', οὐδ' ἀπίθησε θεὰ γλαυκῶπις 'Αθήνη,
βῆ δὲ κατ' Οὐλύμποιο καρήνων ἀΐξασα·
καρπαλίμως δ' ἵκανε θοὰς ἐπὶ νῆας 'Αχαιῶν.
εὗρεν ἔπειτ' 'Οδυσῆα, Διὶ μῆτιν ἀτάλαντον,
ἑσταότ'· οὐδ' ὅ γε νηὸς ἐυσσέλμοιο μελαίνης
ἅπτετῳ, ἐπεί μιν ἄχος κραδίην καὶ θυμὸν ἵκανεν·
ἀγχοῦ δ' ἱσταμένη προσέφη γλαυκῶπις 'Αθήνη·

[So she spoke and bright-eyed Athena did not disobey. She went darting from the peaks of Olympus and quickly came to the speedy ships of the Achaeans. There she found Odysseus standing similar to Zeus in cunning. He had not touched his decked black ship because grief had entered his heart and soul. Bright-eyed Athena stood by him and said:]

The entire passage is constructed on a syntactical and lexical structure that (in the *Iliad*, at least) is built of fixed or formulaic components. This linguistic pattern or "styleme" describes the key stages in the process by which an agent (1) obeys an order (this initial action is optional), (2) seeks the person required, (3) finds him/her (4) in a particular position or attitude, and (5) accosts and addresses him/her. These five stages are represented by the same repeated expressions in the same metrical positions, as in our passage: (1) οὐδ' ἀπίθησε, (2) βῆ δὲ...ἵκανε, (3) εὗρεν, (4) ἑσταότ', (5) ἀγχοῦ δ' ἱσταμένη προσέφη. As the passage shows, the key verbs of the structure tend to appear at the beginning of the line, thus leaving the poet free to vary or add details as the situation requires. The styleme in its full form appears four times, all in the *Iliad*: 2.166ff.; 4.198ff.; 11.195ff.; 15.236ff. (with two minor substitutions). More often we find four or fewer of the five stages: *Iliad* 4.74ff.; 13.458ff. (with a minor substitution); *Odyssey* 5.149ff.; 15.1ff., etc. In complete or fragmentary form the pattern appears twenty times in Homer, leaving aside an exceptional case at *Iliad* 10.507–8. Sometimes it describes the visit of a hero to another hero; more often it refers to the visit of a god to another god or to a mortal, and as such it appears frequently in epiphanies.[18]

There is no doubt that this pattern is the one preferred by the *Iliad*, nor that the fullest examples of it are found in that text. But these two facts are not enough for us to be able to define this pattern as originally Iliadic, nor to

---

18. Of the eleven examples in the *Iliad* in which a god appears to a mortal in stages described in this styleme, only Achilles at 18.165ff. almost certainly sees Iris, since he recognizes and speaks to her. In all the other cases the text either allows one to conclude that the epiphany is an aural one (*Il.* 2.165ff.; 10.507ff.; 15.236ff.) or declares that the god appears in disguise (4.74ff.; 2.790; 3.121ff.; 22.226–27). Doubtful cases are 5.121ff., 11.195ff., and 22.214–15, on which see my comments above, p. 86 n15.

describe it as an element of a code. On the one hand, the various fragmentary forms and synonymic versions obscure the clear boundaries of the basic pattern, so that in at least one case (*Il.* 10.507–8) it is not easy to say whether we are even dealing with an example of the styleme at all.[19] On the other, these variations on the pattern conspire with contextual elements to create an uncontrollable variety of meanings and nuances in each of these passages. By way of example I draw attention to the unique contextuality of our passage, in which the comparison with the epiphany of Athena in the first book is bound to override all the meanings that the styleme in itself has, even assuming that the phrase "in itself" has any sense in terms of real linguistic phenomena. Finally (though the list of difficulties could go on), the contextual aspects also relate to the presence of the pattern in other poems, most importantly for our purposes in the *Odyssey*.

This poem uses the pattern in question on a few occasions, but in two passages uses it in a way which makes it impossible to be sure whether their clumsiness is genuine or hints at parodic intentions.

The first example (*Od.* 5.149ff.) describes four of the prescribed stages by means of which Calypso, after Hermes' visit, brings Odysseus the news that he may return home. By using this styleme for Calypso, instead of Hermes,[20] the *Odyssey* invests Calypso with an ambassadorial function, just as if she were Iris in the *Iliad* or Hermes in the *Odyssey*.[21] But the text's malice—if that is what it is—lies in the fact that Calypso does not relay the message brought by Hermes at all. She is a false messenger, an impostor who distorts the message—hence the unusual use of the pattern here. But in fact such dissimulation is so tightly woven into the thematic and textual web of the *Odyssey* that one is tempted to consider this effect of the repetition as explicit and coherent with the larger meaning of the poem.

The second case (*Od.* 15.1ff.) is even more unusual. Four of the five stages appear as Athena travels to Lacedaemon, where she will advise Telemachus to return to Ithaca.[22] She finds him awake beside the sleeping Pisistratus. The text here seems to make Athena visible to Telemachus, while by attributing the participle εὕδοντ' to Pisistratus (rather than the addressee, Telemachus) it confuses the relationship between visitor and visitee, which the styleme normally makes quite clear.[23]

---

19. Note also that I have described only the general outlines of the pattern, but for an analysis that would evaluate the fixed and recognizable terms of the code one would have to consider the numerous variants of each stage, and especially those of the final one, which appears in at least four variant forms; cf. *Il.* 2.172; 4.92; 13.768; 15.173.

20. The text begins to place Hermes in the formular structure (5.43), but at that point descriptive elements accumulate and the various stages of the styleme are never in fact reached.

21. The *Odyssey* uses Hermes, rather than Iris, as a divine messenger.

22. Note that here too the god's advice concerns a return home. See also a partial use of the pattern in *Od.* 1.102–6 again for Athena.

23. Athena finds Telemachus beside the sleeping Pisistratus (εὕδοντ') and accosts the wakeful Telemachus (Τηλέμαχον δ' οὐχ ὕπνος ἔχε γλυκύς). The participle εὕδοντ'

This analysis has brought us to two important conclusions: (1) Both poems use the pattern by which Athena is described as she descends from Olympus to Odysseus to articulate the themes of the visit or embassy, but this styleme appears more often and in a fuller form in the *Iliad*. Without wishing to speculate as to why the *Odyssey* seems to make an irreverent or awkward gesture, or one of deliberate rupture, one might nevertheless be tempted to say that through this process the *Odyssey* seems to "read" the *Iliad*, to rewrite it and distance itself from it.

(2) Through its prescribed stages the styleme allows the audience to anticipate the outcome of the goddess's visit to Odysseus and ensures that her intervention can be pleasurably savored in its various phases, without the listener being surprised or unpleasantly startled.

Within the formulaic bloc described above, certain details are expressed in lines and formulas marked as Iliadic. Consider line 167: βῆ δὲ κατ' Οὐλύμποιο καρήνων ἀΐξασα·. This physical evocation of Olympus is normal in the *Iliad* and recurs often; we find it at 2.167, 4.74, 7.19, 22.187 referring to Athena, and at 24.121 referring to Thetis. In the *Odyssey*, on the other hand, despite Athena's constant coming and going to and from Olympus, we find it only twice: 1.102 and 24.488.[24]

The Iliadic flavor of the style here becomes more obvious and more significant with the formula Διὶ μῆτιν ἀτάλαντον at line 169: εὗρεν ἔπειτ' Ὀδυσῆα, Διὶ μῆτιν ἀτάλαντον. The formula is applied in the *Iliad* to both Odysseus (2.169; 404; 636; 10.137) and Hector (7.47; 11.200) but never appears in the *Odyssey*, even though the poem's hero is explicitly celebrated as intelligent and *polutropos*. One can only speculate as to why the *Odyssey* ignores this formula. It may be that the *Odyssey* prefers to downplay any potential similarity to Zeus *mêtieta* in favor of the special relationship of *mêtis* between Odysseus and Athena; Odysseus's *mêtis* is not to be shared with other heroes like Hector, but is to be exclusive to him. At the same time, the *mêtis* of Odysseus, which recalls Athena's and vice versa, becomes a salient and personal heroic trait, one that is never developed in the *Iliad*. The predominance of this specular relation of *mêtis* between patroness and hero reduces even the presence of Zeus *metiêta* to three occurrences in the *Odyssey*, as against seventeen in the *Iliad* and five in Hesiod. Here too, then, the process of differentiation between the two poems and the individuation of each develops on the basis of a shared

referring to Pisistratus is aberrant; in all other examples of our pattern the participle refers to the person sought by the visitor, and ought therefore to refer to Telemachus here. Although the text at 7–8 assures us that Telemachus is awake, doubt is still possible. (Or can it be the poet who is nodding?) As to the possibility that Telemachus can see the goddess, we should remember that the scene takes place in the middle of the night (8; 48–50) and that the goddess may, for all practical purposes, be invisible.

24. The *Odyssey* offers weaker and less specific physical descriptions of Olympus in general.

linguistic system. The difference between the two flickers paradoxically in the iridescence of the common epic language.

Understated as the formula is (it is not exclusive, and occupies only part of the line), no reader could fail to notice its importance in this case. It is precisely because Odysseus possesses *mêtis* equal to Zeus's that he remains by the ships without fleeing, and that he alone (or so it seems) remembers Agamemnon's instructions to the *boulê* (2.75). It is precisely because Odysseus is the hero of *mêtis* that Athena selects him and, indeed, substitutes him for herself. For Athena gives Odysseus word for word the same order that Hera had given her to carry out; he is her human substitute and the character who in the *Odyssey* will display the *mêtis* that is proper to her. Even as they exhibit mutual jealousy and suspicion, the texts yet converge in this way. Here the *Iliad* translates into action, and thus confirms, the extraordinary intellectual communion of Athena and Odysseus, highlighted, for example, at *Odyssey* 13.296–99, when Athena recognizes in the hero her own virtues:

ἀλλ᾽ ἄγε, μηκέτι ταῦτα λεγώμεθα, εἰδότες ἄμφω
κέρδε᾽, ἐπεὶ σὺ μέν ἐσσι βροτῶν ὄχ᾽ ἄριστος ἀπάντων
βουλῇ καὶ μύθοισιν, ἐγὼ δ᾽ ἐν πᾶσι θεοῖσι
μήτι τε κλέομαι καὶ κέρδεσιν·

[But why say more? We both know many wiles, for you are far the best of all men in planning and words, and I am renowned among the gods for intelligence and wiles.]

The extraordinary convergence of these two texts might suggest that the *Iliad* is conscious of the *Odyssey*, and of the *mêtis* of Odysseus in that poem; but the hypothesis is not a necessary one, for the word *mêtis* with its connotations and ramifications grows out of elements already present and well-embedded in the epic code. The *mêtis* of Odysseus is compared to that of Zeus in the *Iliad* and to that of Athena in the *Odyssey*. A difference seems to shimmer on the surface of the similarity, but only a complete interpretation of *mêtis* will lend to this difference the force and meaning of a different poem in which indeed the *mêtis* of Odysseus allows him to survive and return home. This moment of contiguity and difference that centers on the word *mêtis* is repeated in the case of many other expressions, as for example in the case of those built on the *tlh$_2$- root and attributed to Odysseus. Such expressions in the *Iliad* can always bear the meaning either of "audacity" or of "endurance," whereas in the *Odyssey* they tend to signify only the latter, with a semantic closure that produces a new text.[25]

When *mêtis* interferes in things, the sense of gravity and urgency is lost, for shrewdness, deception and eloquence can finesse the most difficult situations. Thematically and generically speaking, the incarnations of *mêtis* are comic, communicating the comforting sense that all will work out for the best. But how is it that this pleasurable and reassuring tone crops up here? To begin with, it becomes clear that if Odysseus can handle the situation on his own it cannot

---

25. See Pucci 1987, 44–53.

be all that serious. In fact, the initiative passes from the concerned Hera to Athena, from Athena to Odysseus, and with him branches out to encompass first the *basileis*, then the common soldiers, and finally Thersites. The theme progressively divests itself of nobility, even as the tone is progressively lowered. The action remains Odysseus's *aristeia*, but it is the *aristeia* of an efficient factotum.[26] Consider above all that just as Thersites apes Achilles and Odysseus punishes him with Agamemnon's scepter, their encounter reproduces in a different key the explosion of hostility between Achilles and Agamemnon in the first book of the poem. The entire scene thus alludes to the first book and, as such, it damages somewhat Odysseus's prestige, his heroic splendor. His *mêtis* is here played against the *mênis* of Achilles, the full-blown epiphany of Athena in a deliberation scene (μερμήριξεν) against the aural epiphany here. Two strategies are played off against one another in conformity with or quite beyond authorial control, producing what is in effect a contrast in *ethos* between the two heroes. Remarkably, within the rhetorical strategy of the *Iliad*, Odysseus is already drawn with the shadings and nuances that characterize him in the *Odyssey*—though, to be sure, the tones become more marked and definite in the other poem. Even within the *Iliad*, then, the text intends a contrast between two different sorts of *ethos*, Achilles' and Odysseus's; the text of the *Iliad* has been palimpsested, so to speak, over the *Odyssey*.

A comparison of these two texts dealing with Odysseus's use of *mêtis* suggests potential implications and overtones of all sorts. For example, the *Iliad* may be implying that its own Odysseus, who possesses *mêtis* equal to Zeus's, does not abuse it for selfish, personal gains, as the Odysseus of the *Odyssey* does (we shall look in a moment at the poem's allusion to an Odysseus who tells stories to win himself a cloak), but rather for the good of the community, thus behaving as a heroic king ought.

Let us leave this point for the moment and continue.[27] Odysseus's affliction (ἄχος, 171), inscribed in a snatch of Iliadic phrasing (8.147; 15.208; 16.52; cf.

---

26. It is hard to define exactly the tone produced when the soldiers agree that of all Odysseus's *aristeiai*, his silencing of Thersites is the greatest (2.273–75). Irony? Or the good-natured approval of the soldiers?

27. The nexus εὗρεν/εὗρον ἔπειτ' 'Οδυσῆα...(ἑσταότ') is found outside the styleme described here at *Il.* 11.473 (toward the end of Odysseus's *aristeia*) and at *Od.* 22.401 (repeated at *Od.* 23.45) at the most Iliadic moment of the *Odyssey* when the hero, victorious over the suitors, is celebrated with a heroic lion simile. The simile is Iliadic in style but nonetheless original, as Marzullo 1970, 302, argues: "These passages [sc. 17.176ff. and 22.402ff.] treat the violent and bloody struggle with the suitors in the splendid manner of the *Iliad*, and in the style of that poem." Consider also the extraordinary convergence of the two texts at this nexus. The *Odyssey*, reading the *Iliad*, "finds Odysseus standing" in the two Iliadic passages in which he is at the center of the action, while the *Iliad*, reading the *Odyssey*, finds him doing the same at two Iliadic moments in that poem. Mere coincidence?

Note in addition that this ἑσταότ', "upright, standing" at line 167 is not an otiose descriptive detail, but essential, since in the context of the general flight it marks Odysseus as immobile. A different context can thus reanimate a most stereotyped formula. Even here the textuality does not necessarily imply authorial intention, but

19.307, with an unusual Odyssean example at 18.274), repeats, without formal repetition, that of Achilles at 1.188. Indeed, as Nagy would have it, the ἄχος echoes and confirms etymologically the name of Achilles, and determines his decision to draw his sword from his scabbard; here it keeps Odysseus from laying hands on the ships.

At this point Athena makes herself known to Odysseus and addresses him, following the normal stages of the styleme. The reader here feels none of the violent surprise provoked when, in the first book, she arrives at the end of a verse (ἦλθε δ᾽ Ἀθήνη, *Il.* 1.194), replacing the expected epithet, and places herself at Achilles' shoulder, thus breaking in a dramatic fashion certain "protocols" of the epiphanic code in such deliberation scenes.

The reader is already familiar with the words that Athena passes on to Odysseus; with a few alterations they are the same as those addressed by Hera to Athena herself. But at this point the surprises come thick and fast (*Il.* 2.173–81):

διογενὲς Λαερτιάδη, πολυμήχαν᾽ Ὀδυσσεῦ,
οὕτω δὴ οἶκόνδε φίλην ἐς πατρίδα γαῖαν
φεύξεσθ᾽ ἐν νήεσσι πολυκλήϊσι πεσόντες,
κὰδ δέ κεν εὐχωλὴν Πριάμῳ καὶ Τρωσὶ λίποιτε
Ἀργείην Ἑλένην, ἧς εἵνεκα πολλοὶ Ἀχαιῶν
ἐν Τροίῃ ἀπόλοντο, φίλης ἀπὸ πατρίδος αἴης;
ἀλλ᾽ ἴθι νῦν κατὰ λαὸν Ἀχαιῶν, μηδ᾽ ἔτ᾽ ἐρώει,
σοῖς δ᾽ ἀγανοῖς ἐπέεσσιν ἐρήτυε φῶτα ἕκαστον,
μηδὲ ἔα νῆας ἅλαδ᾽ ἑλκέμεν ἀμφιελίσσας.

This reference to the flight of the Achaeans, when made by Hera to Athena, had a purely constative function. As Reinhardt has observed, it is linked to the theme of the revenge Hera and Athena intend to take on Paris and Aphrodite (1961, 108). But once the phrases are directed to Odysseus, the kind of enunciation involved alters profoundly; the words become a bitter or ironic reproach.[28] Indeed, the opening lines suddenly recall the reproach that at *Odyssey* 5.203–5 Calypso directs to Odysseus when he decides to abandon the goddess to return home:

διογενὲς Λαερτιάδη, πολυμήχαν᾽ Ὀδυσσεῦ,

---

the paradoxical tension between the repetition that is conditioned by language and a contextuality that, by marking language, continually produces difference.

28. There are additional changes in details. The question οὕτω δὴ...φεύξεσθ᾽ is not quite at home here, since Odysseus is *not* fleeing, and knows that this is not Agamemnon's plan. The phrase σοῖς δ᾽ ἀγανοῖς ἐπέεσσιν at 180, according to Kirk, looks forward to the persuasion that Odysseus will use when dealing with the *basileis* (188ff.), but is inexplicable in Hera's mouth since "there is no need for the Goddess to be gentle" (1985, 134). Although there is in fact no reason why Athena too could not have been persuasive and gentle with the *basileis*, Kirk's argument is not valid; words like ἤπιος and ἀγανός are often used to describe the ideal monarch (cf. *Od.* 2.230; 5.8, etc.) and the expression ἀγανοῖς ἐπέεσσιν is thus more appropriate to a king than to a goddess.

οὕτω δὴ οἶκόνδε φίλην ἐς πατρίδα γαῖαν
αὐτίκα νῦν ἐθέλεις ἰέναι;

Text and situation work to confirm the hypothesis that the two passages are in dialogue, as I have argued recently.[29] Once the message has been delivered, Athena departs. The epiphany has ended, and the action is henceforward described from the perspective of her surrogate, Odysseus. All the same, the effect of the epiphany is not exhausted either in terms of the action, or the linguistic traces that it leaves, or even in the play of allusion, which remains in full force. The action unfolds following the goddess's orders, and traces of her appearance remain for example in the reprise of line 164 = 180 at line 189, and in Odysseus's evocation at line 197 of μητίετα Ζεύς (cf. 169). Note finally that Odysseus reins in the flight of the army by repeating for each of the characters to whom he turns the epiphany that Athena has performed with him.[30]

---

29. Pucci 1987. I summarize here the strongest arguments put forward in my book for mutual allusion between the two passages. (1) The repetition is not limited to the formular apostrophe of *Il.* 2.173 = *Od.* 5.203, but extends to the two lines that follow, involving the idea of a sudden and ill-conceived return. (2) The repetition of the initial lines opens the way for repetitions of other types. For example, in both passages the goal of the undertaking is represented by a woman. In the *Iliad* this is Helen, the boast (εὐχωλὴν 2.176) that the Achaeans in departing will leave to Priam, while in the *Odyssey* it is Calypso who boasts (εὔχομαι 5.211) of the immortal endowments that Odysseus will be giving up. I would add here that the phrase εὐχωλὴν Πριάμῳ... Ἀργείην Ἑλένην, which appears twice in the Iliadic scene (2.160–61 and 176–77) reappears at *Il.* 4.173–74 in a speech of Agamemnon's, again in the context of an unhappy and involuntary return. (3) A further repetition links the two passages (*Il.* 1.114–15 and *Od.* 5.211–12). (4) Both passages are crucial to the continued progress of the two poems.

30. Odysseus's speech to the army (*Il.* 2.278ff.) has certain peculiar characteristics, and although absorbed into the atmosphere of the *Iliad* has Odyssean traces, as for example the supporting role played by Athena at lines 279–80 (cf. *Od.* 8.193–94) or Odysseus's exhortation to endure (299: τλῆτε, φίλοι, καὶ μείνατ'), the formulaic expression of which recurs in connection with other heroes, but addressed to themselves and apropos of immediate concerns. Thus, for example, Diomedes undertakes to endure and remain in the front rank and withstand the Trojan assault (*Il.* 11.317: ἐγὼ μενέω καὶ τλήσομαι), and Achilles with the same formula vows to continue his fast (*Il.* 19.308). Here, however, the hero of τλῆναι, of the ταλαπενθής heart (*Od.* 5.222) exhorts his companions and the mass of soldiers to embrace his own virtues. It is this same tenacity and patience that, according to Jacoby (1945, 157–221) the poet of the Eion epigram admires when he praises the Athenian soldiers for their tenacity and patience at the siege of Eion. In particular, Jacoby sees in the epithet ταλακάρδιοι, with which the poet praises the Athenians, a reworking of the expression τλῆτε φίλοι which Odysseus directs to the weary Athenian soldiery at the siege of Troy (*Il.* 2.299). Moreover it should be clear that Odysseus in this role of the general who addresses and exhorts the common soldiers individually and forcefully, brutally punishing one of them, is something unique in the *Iliad*. It is particularly difficult to give a specific social/political definition to this paternalistic depiction of the general Odysseus, who represents the aristocracy confronted with the masses. But

There is thus sufficient evidence to state that after the epiphany of the goddess to Odysseus the text continues with the same amused self-consciousness. And we are thereby justified in fixing our attention on the lines that follow and on their intertextual and allusive play. Having heard the goddess out, the hero moves into action without pausing to respond (*Il.* 2.182–87):[31]

"Ὣς φάθ᾽, ὁ δὲ ξυνέηκε θεᾶς ὄπα φωνησάσης,
βῆ δὲ θέειν, ἀπὸ δὲ χλαῖναν βάλε· τὴν δὲ κόμισσε
κῆρυξ Εὐρυβάτης Ἰθακήσιος, ὅς οἱ ὀπήδει·
αὐτὸς δ᾽ Ἀτρείδεω Ἀγαμέμνονος ἀντίος ἐλθὼν
δέξατό οἱ σκῆπτρον πατρώιον, ἄφθιτον αἰεί·
σὺν τῷ ἔβη κατὰ νῆας Ἀχαιῶν χαλκοχιτώνων

[So she spoke and he understood the voice of the goddess speaking to him and rushed to run and cast off his coat which the herald got, Eurybates of Ithaca, who waited on him. Himself, he went to Agamemnon son of Atreus and received the scepter of his ancestors, imperishable forever, and with it he went toward the ships of the bronze-shirted Achaeans.]

Critics from von der Mühll (who describes the lines as "merkwürdig") to Ramersdorfer have been troubled by the passage for a number of reasons. To begin with, there is no good reason for Odysseus to take off his cape, which symbolizes his royal power. In addition, Eurybates in the *Iliad* is Agamemnon's herald, and only here, with the *hapax* Ἰθακήσιος, does he appear as Odysseus's. And finally, Odysseus uses the ceremonial scepter not, as one might expect, in the *agora*, but to punish the soldiers and Thersites; surely his own scepter would have been more than sufficient?[32] None of these objections can be leveled against *Odyssey* 14.499–501. Here Odysseus in the guise of a beggar tells Eumaeus how he found himself sleeping rough under the walls of Troy while on reconnaissance with Odysseus, and how the latter saved him from the cold by arranging for Thoas to take a message to the camp, leaving his cloak behind:

ὣς ἔφατ᾽, ὦρτο δ᾽ ἔπειτα Θόας, Ἀνδραίμονος υἱός,

---

the fact remains that the masses are here (almost uniquely) represented as active and the generals must treat them with caution (cf. 2.24–25). Might it not have been just this aspect of the scene that prompted the Eion poet to recall this episode? As Jacoby makes clear (1945, 204–5), the epigram, composed c. 475 and inspired by Cimon, falls in a period in which Cimon and his aristocratic circle were being forced to come to terms with the strongly democratic current of Athenian public opinion. On the relationship between this epigram and the *epitaphios logos*, see Loraux 1981, 60-61.

31. The Iliadic hero sometimes gives no response to divine advice, but hastens to follow it: thus *Il.* 11.210 (Hector is silent after the visit of Iris, 22.224ff. Achilles is silent after Athena's message) etc. But sometimes the hero does respond, as happens in the epiphanies at *Il.* 1.188ff.; 18.181ff.; 15.245ff.; 22.14ff.

32. Von der Mühll 1952, 40; Ramersdorfer 1981, 49–51. The problem is not even mentioned in Kirk 1985.

καρπαλίμως, ἀπὸ δὲ χλαῖναν θέτο φοινικόεσσαν,
βῆ δὲ θέειν ἐπὶ νῆας·

[So he spoke and Thoas sprang up, the son of Andraimon, quickly and he cast
off his purple coat and rushed to run to the ships.]

On the basis of close comparison, Ramersdorfer argues for the priority of the
Odyssey passage which then influences *Iliad* 2.183–85. The philological method
requires a conclusion of this type. But the reasons, as we shall see, are somewhat
flimsy. Let us instead admit, for the sake of argument, that the two texts were
composed in reciprocal consciousness of one another. Suppose, then, that the
Iliad at the moment of its composition was familiar with the passage from the
Odyssey. What would be the effect from the reader's point of view? We might
flirt with the idea, for example, that the *Iliad* is playful in showing us how futile
the *mêtis* of Odysseus is when he uses it to tell parables in order to cadge a cloak
from a poor swineherd. To be sure, in this Iliadic episode, Odysseus has to do
with a character of a not dissimilar social caste, Thersites, but at least his goal is
to safeguard an important undertaking. The irony is devastating.

The Iliadic passage is certainly set in a minor key; the attention paid to the
χλαῖνα is rare in the *Iliad* (Ramersdorfer 1981, 50 n. 158) and the presence of a
herald to retrieve it is a realistic detail that would be more at home in the
quotidian atmosphere of the *Odyssey*. But we should not be too hasty. For the
Iliad has also protected its Odysseus from the Odyssean low tone that this
allusion evokes and mocks. In fact a herald, marked by a *hapax*, augments
Odysseus's importance in this scene. Odysseus takes off his cloak in order to run
faster. And the scepter is Agamemnon's because Odysseus acts as his deputy.
Thus the presence of this passage in the *Iliad* causes no incongruity. Yet these
serious motifs *are* in some way curtailed, corrupted by the ironic allusion to the
Odysseus who charms Eumaeus. Paradoxically, to rehabilitate the Odysseus of
the *Odyssey* the text must evoke that other Odysseus all the more strongly.

Now let us read the allusion taking the *Odyssey* as our starting point. The
episode that Odysseus invents to amuse Eumaeus and to obtain a cloak shows
the *Odyssey* poking fun at the epic principle according to which the story
descends to the poet from the Muses and reflects the truth that they have access
to. As in a few other passages, the *Odyssey* here declares ostentatiously that it is
not the Muses but fiction—and all the economic and psychological factors that
condition it—that brings the epic into being. The reader, recognizing here the
reprise of *Il.* 2.182ff., may flirt with the idea that with this reference the text of
the *Odyssey* mischievously casts doubt on the divine truth of the epic stories
about Odysseus, while at the same time it recalls that this Odysseus, the charmer
of swineherds, has also been described as the hero who really did fight at Troy
and really did persuade the fleeing kings to turn back. The allusion links the two
texts in spite of their very different self-conceptions, and it combines the two
characters, even as Odysseus, dressed as a beggar, invents stories about Troy.
When one considers the feverish paranoia which ought to have ensued as the two
texts speak of the same hero in different ways, though with common formulas,
motifs, and traditions, it becomes easy to see that for the *Odyssey*, which

recounts adventures that take place after those of the *Iliad* (at any rate in the fictive chronology of the narrative), to attach itself to the other text, without ever officially acknowledging its relationship,[33] is paradoxically inevitable. On the one hand the Odysseus of the *Odyssey* merges into the Iliadic hero, while on the other he must perpetually distance himself from him. The curious detail of the χλαῖνα at *Il.* 2.183–84 appears delicious and could well have been the determining factor in the link that the *Odyssey* makes between this scene and its own narrative.

Here then is how the reader can construct the effects of reading that derive from allusion. Naturally this hermeneutic does not claim to offer any sort of empirical proof that the two texts developed in full consciousness of each other's existence, and that at the moment of monumental composition they accepted the "readings" that had been and were still being given of themselves and which arranged matter so that one text "wrote" the other. Indeed, although I have offered examples of allusive readings taking both the *Iliad* and the *Odyssey* as alternative points of departure, there is no need to claim priority for one or other of the poems. And what is most important, the allusive or intertextual dependence of the two poems on each other remains indemonstrable. One can do no more than speculate on the relative explicitness of the effect the poems have on one another.

But even if one of two given passages was not composed with an eye on the other, even if the repetition is due to the fortuitous reappearance of epic formulas, it is implicit in such repetition that the two passages have known one another without realizing it, so that the repetition produces an effect that is neither arbitrary nor ungrounded. One text receives it into its context and is affected and marked by it, and the other does the same; the same expression produces different meanings, differences that must be read.[34] We should note that the notion of a purely mechanical operation is excessively empirical and ultimately naive. It misunderstands the fact that the repetitions are in part inevitable given the nature of the poetic language, and that they haunt the compositional memory of the poets; and that by marking both texts, they constitute them with some coherence of meaning.

The text's effects and intentions are there regardless, suspended paradoxically between the inevitable repetition of the poetic language, which tends to annul the autonomy of a text, and the meanings, effects, and shadings that the repetitions give to the text, and that make it *a* text.

---

33. This is the full extent of Munro's law.

34. When Ramersdorfer in the philological tradition speaks of an "Einwirken von j.500 auf B.183" he means that the effect consists entirely in having induced the *Iliad* to repeat the passage in the *Odyssey*, although in the *Odyssey* it seems to be better integrated. While this formulation correctly rules out the assumption of a nonproblematic random repetition, it offers no satisfying explanation of the possible causes of the repetition and of the rationale and end product of the effects of repetition.

CHAPTER 7

Antiphonal Lament Between Achilles and Briseis*

Since at least the work of Dieter Lohmann[1] the lament that Briseis utters over the corpse of Patroclus and the lament that Achilles delivers immediately after (XIX.282–339) have been compared and considered in a sort of parallelism and responsion since both characters develop three very similar themes. Achilles' lamentation by repeating and enlarging the themes used by Briseis produces an intensification of his language, the "amplifizierende Funktion" that Lohmann (1970, 102) attributes to this type of composition.[2] I do not intend to repeat Lohmann's beautiful analysis of the two passages, nor the perceptive insights of de Jong (1987), but to call attention to some unnoticed points of contact and difference that illustrate an unsuspected relationship between the representation of Briseis and that of Achilles. In the same wake I intend to show some aspects of the oral performance.

One question, often ignored by the commentators, concerns the temporal sequence of the two texts. The first text appears to be repeated only when the second text is uttered or read, and this inevitable temporal succession implies a consequence. It doubles the language of the first text and therefore increases the pathos of the second, reducing the first one to a relatively marginal or weaker

---

* "Antiphonal Lament Between Achilles and Briseis" was first published in the *Colby Quarterly* 29 (1993): 253–72.

1. Lohmann 1970.

2. Lohmann (1970) shows the parallelism between the groups of mourners, eight women (245–46) and seven men (310–11), and compares the scene with the facing group in the geometrical amphorae of funeral subject.

posture. It becomes a sort of "second" text though, temporally speaking, it is the first.

My first point concerns the presentation and the framing by the *diêgêsis* of the two lamentations. Briseis utters her lament as she performs the rituals of mourning that comprehend the *kôkuein* and the scratching of her breast, throat, and face. She repeats ritual gestures that have their own ceremonial reason, intensity, and rhythm. She is a slave, and probably this explains the radical expressions of her mourning as disfiguring her body, an action that no free woman performs in the *Iliad.* Free women perform the *kôkuein* but no self-wounding, and they do it in mourning contexts about a dead husband (xxiv.295, iv.259, viii.527) or son (XXII.407–09, 447, XVIII.37, 71), a relative or a dear friend (XIX.284, XXIV.703, xix.541). On only two occasions a woman screams (*kôkuein*) outside a mourning context (XXIV.200, ii.361).[3]

We have to imagine that Briseis's utterance is fully framed within the ceremonial ritual that the poet represents, and accordingly that she is thought of as delivering her words as she tears her face. This is what we imagine as readers. As we know from Plato's third book of the *Republic,* the rhapsodes in the mimetic parts of the poems were imitating the characters' roles through the performance of their voice and movements (*phônêi kai skhêmati*). Now it is impossible for us to reconstruct the actual modes and effects by voice and by movements in the utterance of this speech by Briseis, but certainly it had an effect. Sometimes, when a character repeats an earlier speech or parts of it, it is just their different inscription, i.e., the different mood and ways in which their delivery is couched, that constitutes their unique distinguishing feature.[4]

Achilles, in his turn, ἀδινῶς ἀνενείκατο φώνησέν τε. (XIX.314). We do not know whether to understand ἀνενείκατο as "drew a sigh" or "lifted up his voice" (see Leaf),[5] nor how to translate ἀδινῶς. We know, however, that ἀδινῶς—a

---

3. On *kôkuein,* see Krapp 1964, 38. *Lig(a) kôkuein* is used three times in Homer (XIX.284, iv.259, viii.527), the last ex. of *lig(a)* being connected with *aeidein* (x.254), evidence that the high pitch tone of the voice can be evoked both for mourning and for joyous occasions. We have in XIX.284 the only ritual use of *amussô* "to tear."

4. For instance the repetition of Agamemnon's discourses in II.111–118 = IX.18–25, II.139–41 = IX.26–28 occurs within contextual elements that produce an initial difference Agamemnon's self-confidence, the presence of the scepter and its history in the *diapeira* speech, and the turmoil in Agamemnon's heart in IX.10ff., his tears "like a dark fountain that from a steep cliff pours down its black water." It seems that Agamemnon's stricken heart from which tears and words pour down is like the rock or cliff that emits a fountain of water. One wonders how it is possible that such an elaborated frame and matrix of Agamemnon's words may have effected the performance of the actual words that are in fact the same as those that Agamemnon uttered in a completely different frame of mind. The answer must be that the matrix and frame would become perceptible in the performance of the poet through his body and voice language and still imperceptibly affect us even when we are reading, as they suggest the mood in which Agamemnon pronounced those words.

5. Leaf quotes Herodotus for the former meaning and Ap. Rhod. 3.635 for the latter. The presence of ἀδινῶς might be in favour of the latter interpretation.

hapax in Homer—is usually used, in the adjectival form, for *gooi* initiated by men and women alike,[6] and has therefore no gender characterization as on the contrary Briseis's *kôkuein* has. This distinction goes along with the distinction between the two groups of mourners that Lohmann has underlined (see note 2). Furthermore the expression ἀδινῶς implies a thick, repeated, intense activity, a repeated throbbing. In two instances, XVI.481 and xix.516, it characterizes the "heart" (in both cases the *kêr*).

The *diêgêsis* therefore distinguishes the modes of Briseis's and Achilles' lamentations, offering the occasion for the singer to produce a specific performance for each lamentation and suggesting even to us readers a different rhythm, a different pitch of voice, a different body movement. Now, both Zumthor (1983) and Meschonnic (1982), speaking on the nature of the oral performance, emphasize the rhythms of the voice and of the gesture, the quality of a specific throbbing and beating of the heart. We have here in the *diêgêsis* a pale but sure indication about these oral features.

Having recognized the oral-poetic frame of the two lamentations, let us hear the first one, that of Briseis, beginning with her first theme (287–90):

Πάτροκλέ μοι δειλῇ πλεῖστον κεχαρισμένε θυμῷ
ζωὸν μέν σε ἔλειπον ἐγὼ κλισίηθεν ἰοῦσα,
νῦν δέ σε τεθνηῶτα κιχάνομαι ὄρχαμε λαῶν
ἂψ ἀνιοῦσ'· ὥς μοι δέχεται κακὸν ἐκ κακοῦ αἰεί.

[Patroclus, dearest to my heart, unhappy me, I left you alive
when I moved from this tent, and now, prince of the army,
I come back and I find you dead. Thus evil always follows
evil in my destiny.]

Both Briseis and Achilles begin by evoking Patroclus, who lies dead torn by the wounds before their eyes (283), through a pathetic apostrophe, i.e., through the ritual and rhetorical construct that engages the dead, as it were, in an impossible dialogue with the living person.

The first word in Briseis's apostrophe, Πάτροκλέ has an exceptional prosody because of the short *o* (Chantraine 1958:1.109), and this anomaly might emphasize the strain and the exceptionality of this last address. In the phrase κεχαρισμένε θυμῷ the heart figures as the place where joy was stored and felt, not as Briseis's subjective center of emotions. In Achilles' words, on the contrary, the heart will be the subject and will produce a deeper and more excruciating pathos. The segment κεχαρισμένε θυμῷ is an expression often repeated in the *Iliad* and used among close friends. Achilles uses it once for Patroclus (XI.608): δῖε Μενοιτιάδη τῷ ἐμῷ κεχαρισμένε θυμῷ, with a stronger complimentary and possessive nuance because of the initial compliment and of

---

6. See for instance XVIII.316, XXIII.17 for Achilles' *goos,* and XXII.430 in XXIV.747 for Hecabe's *goos.* In the repeated form *hadina stenakh(izein)* the expression characterizes only males (XXIII.225, XXIV.123, xxiv.317) and only the waves of the sea (vii.274). P. Chantraine derives *hadinos* from *hadên,* implying a noun *hadê.*

the presence of the accentuated possessive adjective with the article—which is unique in this example. Whether we should remember this line of Achilles to Patroclus when we hear Briseis's phrase is open to speculation, but probably we should; we would begin to see the threads of a dialogue that spins beneath the independent laments of the two characters. In Briseis's speech the pleasure Patroclus gave her is exhibited in a powerful contrast to her despondency (μοι δειλῇ, "unhappy me!"), a contrast that uniquely revitalizes the five times repeated expression and its possibly attenuated meaning. With this innuendo, she begins to outline a "private" characterization of Patroclus which will end with her definition of his kindness, *meilikhon aiei* (300), that is a *hapax* for the Iliadic heroes.[7]

Lines 288–89 picture the unique situation of Briseis leaving Achilles' tent at I.345ff. while Patroclus was still alive and returning now (νῦν δέ 289) to find Patroclus dead, but this unique situation finds its peak in the epithetic form ὄρχαμε λαῶν that is generic and used for various heroes (Agamemnon, Menelaus, and Achilles).[8] Its generic quality, however, is revitalized here too by a contrast: Briseis addresses this emphatic and praising title to a dead hero (τεθνηῶτα), and the verbal and conceptual contrast produces a pathetic effect analogous to the one that Briseis reached with her previous line when she opposed her unhappiness to Patroclus, joy of her heart.

This repeated epithet rhymes with the closing two preceding verses that end with a formulaic expression: κεχαρισμένε θυμῷ / κλισίηθεν ἰοῦσα / ὄρχαμε λαῶν producing a text that at the end of each line receives the stress and the relief of a repeated familiar expression:

Πάτροκλέ μοι δειλῇ πλεῖστον **κεχαρισμένε θυμῷ**,
ζωὸν μέν σε ἔλειπον ἐγὼ **κλισίηθεν ἰοῦσα**,
νῦν δέ σε τεθνηῶτα κιχάνομαι **ὄρχαμε λαῶν**,
ἂψ ἀνιοῦσ᾽· ὥς μοι δέχεται κακὸν ἐκ κακοῦ αἰεί.

I imply that the repetition of a familiar expression—here graphically represented by the boldface types—would have the same effect as the repetition of a refrain and accordingly produce an emphasis and a relief at the same time, since the repetition on the one hand increases the forcefulness of the expression and on the other—as the return to the same—produces a sort of pleasure and relaxation.[9]

---

7. This *hapax* underlined with due emphasis in Codino 1965, 154–55.

8. We do not know the sure meaning of this elusive word, but the examples show that it is used with deference in peaceful (XIV.102) as in military encounters (XVII.12, XXI.221).

9. As is clear from these remarks I do not consider the effect of this rhythm as being physical—though it might have also been so at the moment of the performance—but textual and poetic. Any reader knows what sort of reactions the encounter of the formula creates: for instance, meeting the formula *podas ôkus Akhilleus* at the end of the line means to manage and negotiate the iteration in ways that differ from the usual decoding of the other words, for it means either to skip over it, or to feel the puzzlement of the iteration in such different contexts, or to repeat the

Each verse runs to this effect, and only the last line (290) of this first theme in Briseis's lament closes without familiar repetitions if not for the paradigmatic position of some of its words—here graphically represented by the underline. It closes therefore with a linear rhythm missing the layers of familiar echoes but exhibiting their forceful unrecognized meaning.

Such a rhythm emphasizes the unity of each line, and in fact the meaning runs through each with no enjambments, in a relative simplicity of thought and a strong opposition between the various segments: δειλῇ / κεχαρισμένε θυμῷ, ζωὸν μέν σε ἔλειπον ἐγὼ / νῦν δέ σε τεθνηῶτα κιχάνομαι, etc.

In the second part of her lament (290b–294) Briseis narrates her disastrous experience, the death of her first husband and of her three brothers:

ἄνδρα μὲν ᾧ ἔδοσάν με πατὴρ καὶ πότνια μήτηρ,
εἶδον πρὸ πτόλιος δεδαϊγμένον ὀξέϊ χαλκῷ,
τρεῖς τε κασιγνήτους, τούς μοι μία γείνατο μήτηρ,
κηδείους, οἳ πάντες ὀλέθριον ἦμαρ ἐπέσπον.

[The husband to whom my father and my noble mother gave me, I saw him before our city mangled by the sharp spear, and my three brothers, dear ones— my own mother bore them, who all met their day of death.]

A remarkable feature of this passage is the repetition of the phrase δεδαϊγμένον ὀξέϊ χαλκῷ that is used a few lines before in the *diêgêsis* to describe the corpse of Patroclus as it appears to Briseis (283): ὡς ἴδε Πάτροκλον δεδαϊγμένον ὀξέϊ χαλκῷ, a repetition that might suggest that, according to the poet, Briseis receives an analogous experience from the deaths of both her husband and of Patroclus. The adjective κηδείους, postponed with such an emotional effect (Ameis and Hentze), is a rare word in the *Iliad*. The rhythm of the passage is analogous to the first one: each line closes with a formulaic segment, a familiar expression, while the last verse runs on a different movement, unmarked by commonly repeated expressions, as if to suggest a pause. The expression ὀλέθριον ἦμαρ is found only here and in a few lines (409) in Xanthos's speech when he foresees Achilles' own day of death. This unique iteration, therefore, could be called antiphonal to the extent that it responds to Briseis's expression and unites the death of Patroclus, Briseis's husband, and Achilles in one iterated piece of diction.[10]

---

whole formula by heart, without reading it. In all these and other possible reactions a stress, a quickening, and a relaxation ensue.

10. Of course the use of ἦμαρ with a specific epithet is what is most formulaic in epic diction: see αἴσιμον ἦμαρ (XXI.100, XXII.202, etc.), μόρσιμον ἦμαρ (XV.613, etc.). From this point of view our expression ὀλέθριον ἦμαρ is formulaic, but the uniqueness of the epithet in this otherwise repeated expression makes evident the imprecision of this heuristic tool that we call the "formula." Besides, which texts should be included in order to establish the repeated features of the "formula"? The hexametric corpus? Hesiod included? On the retroactivated nature of this critical tool, on its weaknesses and shortcomings, see Pucci 1987, 238–40.

The last part of Briseis's lament is labeled by Lohmann as "unerfüllte Hoffnung" (1970, 103):

οὐδὲ μὲν οὐδέ μ' ἔασκες, ὅτ' ἄνδρ' ἐμὸν ὠκὺς 'Αχιλλεὺς
ἔκτεινεν, πέρσεν δὲ πόλιν θείοιο Μύνητος,
κλαίειν, ἀλλά μ' ἔφασκες 'Αχιλλῆος θείοιο
κουριδίην ἄλοχον θήσειν, ἄξειν τ' ἐνὶ νηυσὶν
ἐς Φθίην, δαίσειν δὲ γάμον μετὰ Μυρμιδόνεσσι.
τώ σ' ἄμοτον κλαίω τεθνηότα μείλιχον αἰεί.

(295–300)

[But you would not let me ever weep, not when swift Achilles slew my husband, not when he plundered the city of godlike Mynes, no, but you kept promising me that you would make of me the legitimate wife of godlike Achilles, that you would lead me back to Phthia on the ships and hold there my marriage ceremony among the Myrmidons. So I weep without rest for your death, you always kind.]

The most remarkable point of this passage lies in the bold gesture whereby Briseis explains to her listeners—among whom is Achilles—her position between Achilles, of whom she is the concubine, and Patroclus, whom Achilles holds as his "most dear *hetairos*." She uses the authority of Patroclus to assert that it was Patroclus's design and will that Achilles should choose Briseis as his legitimate wife. Briseis's gesture is bold and provoking: she continues to outline a private portrait of Patroclus, and she reminisces publicly about the promises that joy-giving Patroclus, the gentle Patroclus, had given her, the (secret?) plans he was elaborating for her happiness. Because of this reminiscing, Briseis crowns her lament with the view of her marriage banquet and festivities among the Myrmidons. Now Patroclus's death has eliminated the supporter of this plan, the escort of the lady to the legitimate bed of Achilles, but the plan could still be enacted, if Achilles were willing. Patroclus's kindness, the mark of his personality, should only continue to speak to his great companion. We will hear later Achilles' answer to this public display of Patroclus's plan to marry Briseis to Achilles.

The familiar expression ὠκὺς 'Αχιλλεὺς—at the end of the line like the many other ones that qualify the subjects: ὄρχαμε λαῶν (289), πατὴρ καὶ πότνια μήτηρ (291), μία γείνατο μήτηρ (293)—emphasizes Achilles' military virtuosity, since ὠκὺς 'Αχιλλεὺς characterizes him as a warrior, for instance in the specific pursuit of Hector at XXII.188, 229, etc. Yet ὠκὺς 'Αχιλλεὺς makes us think also of Achilles as ὠκύμορος (I.417, XVIII.95, 458), and we have only to wait for Achilles' antiphonal lament, when he will evoke his early death in Troy (328–29), to recognize the appropriateness of this allusive epithet.

The epithetic ending 'Αχιλλῆος θείοιο (297), rhyming in chiasmus with θείοιο Μύνητος (297), declares easily its generic force, but since the chiasmus is never gratuitous it is easy to see what parallels and what contrasts these two kings, Mynes and Achilles, in the terrible experience of Briseis.[11] This closing passage is made emotional and emphatic by the chiasmus (295–96: is Mynes the husband of Briseis? 299), the incredible postponement of *klaiein,* the repetition of *tethnêota* (300 and 289), with the concomitant chiastic opposition of the notions dead/alive in 288–89 and 300, where the last word of *meilikhon aiei* gives an immortal continuity to the living kindness of this dead man.[12]

The whole utterance (287–300) opens and closes with the apostrophe to Patroclus, as if he could listen to her: the abysmal pathos of saying to a corpse: "you are dead, you, joy of my heart . . . you forever kind" is too ritual to shock us and at the same time it should shock us. For this fictive interaction and address is made possible by the speaking "I" in the paradoxical posture of rhetorically denying that death while simultaneously decrying it. Furthermore, this fictive address puts emphasis and directness on the speaking "I," who accordingly narrates to the dead "you" her pain, the past griefs his death reminds her of, the hopes his death now frustrates. All this sum of pain assumes the same irreversibility as that decried death has, but at the same time it is couched in a *fictive* address, and almost in an *imaginary* dialogue. These features intimate the paradoxical nature of the utterance of pity and self-pity, the investment of the "I" in the loss of the other, the rhetorical structure that contains and makes possible that investment. The line by line utterance with emphasis/relaxation at one repeated point outlines a specific rhythm, while each segment takes power and meaning in contrast to the other, as we have seen, joy/pain, life/death.

It remains for us to analyze also and simultaneously the attenuation or dissemination of specific meaning that occurs through the folds and the meshes of the formulaic or repeated segments. They of course produce emphasis/relaxation just because they function as refrains, but they refer to and evoke other contexts and texts. In this way they constitute also the source of an attenuation or indeterminacy of meaning. But I will discuss this point with the analysis of Achilles' own utterance.

---

11. The phrase θείοιο occurs 16 times in the *Iliad* and it is distributed to various heroes: Odysseus (four times), Oileus (two times), Achilles (three times: two after *Akhillêos* and once after *Pêlêidao*), etc. It is interesting that the epithet in the nineteenth book is referred to Achilles (279, 297), but never to Odysseus—who is an important character in this book—as if *ubi maior minor cessat.*

12. Some of the iterated expressions contain new features, for instance in line 296: ἔκτεινεν, πέρσεν δὲ πόλιν θείοιο Μύνητος whose formulaic segment is read at XIV.230 but with a different final name, or line 300: τώ σ' ἄμοτον κλαίω τεθνηότα μείλιχον αἰεί, where the first part repeats with a small variation XXIV.773 τώ σε...κλαίω.... Also the last part of the line is a formula only if we accept the Hesiodic phrase (*Theogony* 406) as evidence of formulaic repetition. Besides, there is always the difficulty of fixing the limit of the paradigmatic repetition: if any form of the verb κλαίειν can stand for the infinitive, then here our form occurs in its fixed slot. Because of all these difficulties, my graphic representation of repeated, familiar expressions intends to indicate only the differential process, not the actual condition of each of the expressions.

After Briseis's mourning in tears, the group of women intone their lamentations and Patroclus for each of them is "a pretext" (*prophasin*)[13] to weep about her own misery (301–2). In consonance with Briseis's emphasis on the loss of her husband and then on the gentle Patroclus who was promoting her marriage with Achilles, the miseries (*kêdea*) that the women weep for should be analogous and refer to the death of their men and their consequent fall into servitude. The text suggests the paradoxes we have already felt in the case of Briseis: (1) the women's crying turns into a mourning about themselves as pity turns into self-pity and the other into an alter ego; (2) the living beings mourn about their future death, while the actual dead is rhetorically alive so as to be told about his past death.

Yet with the remark that Patroclus was for each of them a "pretext" about her own misery (*kêdea*), the *Iliad* reaches a sublime vastness and intensity. It seems to suggest that there is a reason for the specificity of the lamentations of the women in the mourning cries, in their gestures of pain and self-destruction. On the one hand their disfiguring gestures mime the death of the person they mourn for, but, on the other, they lament for themselves, i.e., for the specific female condition, as slaves in this case, or dependent upon a male in many others (see, for instance, XXIV.725ff.). Accordingly, as they decry, by miming death, the loss of their man, they might simultaneously intimate that he represents their servitude and their metaphorical death (often marriage is metaphorically described as a form of death for the *parthenos*), a servitude-death that is paradoxically also their freedom and life.[14]

It is instructive to compare the antiphonal comment of the *diêgêsis* after Achilles' lament (338–39). Here the chiefs do not lament for their own misery (*kêdea*), suffering, or death but for "whatever" (*ta*) they have left at home, we assume their possessions, wives, children, and slaves. The comparison is antiphonal and differential: as the women hear Briseis mourning for Patroclus, they weep for their lost men, miming their deaths, themselves images of servitude and death; but the men, after Achilles' mourning, lament for having abandoned their possessions, of which wives and slaves are a part. We have a perfect chiastic structure: males lament for being deprived of those possessions, the females, and these, in turn, lamenting for their males' deaths, in fact lament also for their own deaths inasmuch as they are "possessions" of the males.

After the presentation of the women, the *diêgêsis* begins to prepare the context of Achilles' antiphonal mourning and it describes the care of the Achaean chiefs for the hero (303–7): "The Achaean chiefs clustered around Achilles begging him to eat. But he, weeping, refused: 'I beg you—if any of you my comrades will listen to me—do not press me to satiate my heart with food and drink, since such dreadful pain has reached me . . .'" [μή με πρὶν σίτοιο κελεύετε μηδὲ ποτῆτος ἄσασθαι φίλον ἦτορ, ἐπεί μ' ἄχος αἰνὸν ἱκάνει...]. A different,

---

13. The Greek word *prophasin* can be understood either as "pretext" or "occasion," "reason," and it is not easy to understand how a commentator can eliminate the first of the two senses when here the word could take both.

14. For the relationship between marriage and death for the *parthenos* see Loraux 1985 and Vernant 1990, 197ff.

gruesome sort of nurture satiates his heart, the blood of his enemy, as the *diêgêsis* says immediately after when the chiefs leave Achilles and only a few of the faithful ones try vainly to console him (312–13): οὐδέ τι θυμῷ / τέρπετο, πρὶν πολέμου στόμα δύμεναι αἱματόεντος [but there was no pleasure in his heart, until he should enter the / mouth of bloody war]. In the same vein the text will make clear that Achilles' heart wants "to glut [*asai*] Ares with Hector's blood" (XX.78, XXII.267).[15] This is a gruesome inversion since Achilles' heart refuses to satiate its appetite with food and drink but needs to glut Ares with the blood of the enemy. He longs for a bloody ritual that deeply upsets the normal biological rhythm of life.[16] In Book 22 Achilles will wish that his heart and his *menos* would impel him to eat Hector's body raw (346–47).[17] The odd centrality of the "heart" in all these passages should not pass unnoticed. Both source of anthropophagous appetite for blood and stern rejection of all food in an ascetic communion with death, the heart is the circulating term that receives here a rhythm and a function contradicting those of the normal biological life.

These are the premises of Achilles' lament for Patroclus. The food Patroclus prepared for him leads Achilles to think of the dear friend now that he, miming the asceticism of death, refuses all food (XIX.315–21):

ἦ ῥά νύ μοί ποτε καὶ σὺ δυσάμμορε **φίλταθ' ἑταίρων**
αὐτὸς ἐνὶ κλισίῃ λαρὸν παρὰ δεῖπνον ἔθηκας
αἶψα καὶ ὀτραλέως, ὁπότε σπερχοίατ' Ἀχαιοὶ
Τρωσὶν ἐφ' ἱπποδάμοισι φέρειν πολύδακρυν Ἄρηα.
νῦν δὲ σὺ μὲν κεῖσαι δεδαϊγμένος, αὐτὰρ ἐμὸν κῆρ
ἄκμηνον πόσιος καὶ ἐδητύος, ἔνδον ἐόντων
σῇ ποθῇ·

---

15. The same expression is used by Diomedes in V.288–89; a similar one for the spear XXI.70, 168, etc. The terms *asai, aatos,* etc., produce a series of generic expressions evoking martial hatred, weapons, animism, animals feeding on corpses, etc.

16. The image πολέμου στόμα is repeated in XX.359 as *stoma husminês* by Achilles himself, as he takes over this expression from the *diegesis*. The antiphonal repetitions between *diegesis* and *mimesis* would deserve a long study.

17. Commenting on these passages and on these connections, Nagy (1979, 136) writes: "The elders of the Achaeans are imploring Achilles to eat (XIX.303–4), but he refuses and insists on keeping a fast (XIX.304–8, 319–21); while he is fasting, he actually reminisces about the meals that Patroclos used to serve up to him (XIX.314–18, especially 316). This grim juxtaposition of two images, the bloody jaws of war and the hero who goes without meals while Patroclos lies unavenged, is only part of a ghastly Iliadic theme that finally comes to a head at the moment when a victorious Achilles is standing triumphant over the sprawled figure of a dying Hector and says: 'I wish that somehow my *menos* and my *thumos* impelled me to slice you up and eat your flesh raw, for the things you did' (XXII.346–47)." Nagy, then, analyzes the famous similes in which Achilles is compared to a carnivorous lion whose *thumos* impels him to its *dais* "feast" of sheep, and correctly concludes that "here the *menos* and the *thumos* of Achilles are bringing our hero to the verge of a bestial deed."

[Truly you too, sometimes, my doomed, my dearest friend, would set before us a tasty meal yourself, here in the tent quickly and expertly, while the Achaeans hastened to carry lamentable Ares against the Trojans, breakers of horses. But now you lie mangled and my heart fasts from drink and food, that are inside the house, for desire of you.]

Like Briseis, Achilles begins by addressing Patroclus with a "thou" and an expression about Patroclus's preciousness for himself, "my dearest friend"[18]— compare Briseis's "joy of my heart." Through this pathetic address Achilles remembers him when he was alive and then he states: "But now you lie mangled" in antiphony with Briseis's "and now . . . I come back and I find you dead."

I touch upon these repetitions Lohmann and others have pointed out to frame the general antiphonal correspondence within which I would like to show striking differences and unexpected responsions. First, the insistence on the heart refusing food. While Briseis had spoken of Patroclus as "joy of my heart," Achilles' heart is the source of sterner, irregular distressing desires and impulses. He mentions the regular meals Patroclus prepared in the domesticity of the *klisiê*, only to state after the recognition ("now you lie mangled") that "my heart fasts from drink and food, that are inside the house, for desire of you." The paradoxical nature of the apostrophe to the dead extends to Achilles' statement since the heart, seat of life, ceases to have its normal desires and longs for death, and with this longing prepares the next procession of deaths, imaginary and real, of the father, of the son, and of himself. The heart dictates its needs and imposes them on Achilles: it is a living organ inside Achilles, functioning as a natural force, impelling as an animal instinct. Its will is not negotiable. Achilles makes it clear: "do not keep pressing me that I should satiate my heart with food and drink . . ." (306–7). "My heart fasts from drink and food . . ." (319–20). In a few lines he will say: "My heart was hoping that only I would die . . ." [θυμὸς ἐνὶ στήθεσσιν 328].

This repetition, this insistence, could be judged in different ways. Truly, by being the repeated subject of will and desire, the heart becomes a sort of label for the whole person, a melodramatic substitute for Achilles, and accordingly risks becoming a subject for all seasons, a dead figure of speech. On the other hand, however, the melodrama is serious, emotionally raised to its highest diapason, producing itself with a tremendous directness and unbeatable simplicity. Accordingly, this exhibition of the heart produces a double-bind effect. On the one hand it becomes the figure of speech that allows a simple or naive psychology to operate. One may say that the heart allows Homer to give account of many decisions without troubling to find psychological motivations. As the lion's heart impels him to attack the sheep, so the warrior's heart impels him to fight the enemy. The heart in this interpretation would function mechanically as a symbol for human instinct and dim awareness.

On the other hand, however, this exhibition of the heart can be felt as increasing the depth of pathos and as enhancing the hero's deeply felt awareness

---

18. On this *philia* in the mournings, see Ecker 1990, 118 n. 314.

of his existential destination. For Achilles' heart would be symbolic of his extreme sensitivity, of his readiness to expose and parade his emotional temper and whims, his existential attitudes. Let us notice for a quick contextual comparison that Sappho in her poem *I* (*poikilothron' athanat' Aphrodita*) mentions her heart three times (*thumôs* 4, 18, 27) as the center of her emotional reactions. Especially when his heart impels Achilles to pulsate in accordance with the frightening and ascetic companionship of death, to read in it the hero's existential awareness is stronger than simply recording the mechanical repetition of the heart as a dead or vague figure of speech. But the menace of this dead, vague symbol does not vanish easily from our reading.

The double-bind effect that I am describing for this repetition of the notion of "heart" affects of course all the repetitions of familiar phrases, "formulas," iterated segments, verses, etc., that constitute so largely the epic diction. These iterations, on the one hand, ennoble and aggrandize—as already Milman Parry had pointed out—the pathos or the effect of the diction and define by way of repeated contexts some specific area of meaning or rhetorical emphasis. But, on the other, they connect and evoke too many contexts, and in the act of accommodating themselves to all these contexts they are forced to assume some indeterminacy. Accordingly, the singular signification or emphasis is lost and the repeated phrase sounds attenuated, a vague indicator, a mere ornament. In extreme cases its stressing power is tonal rather than cognitive. Within these double-bind effects, however, the readers are not completely powerless. They may favor what may finally be the stronger way of reading the text, the cognitive aspect of the repetition, its allusive, antiphonal, polemical function, though they remain aware of the metaphysical complicity upon which this choice depends.

Let us begin with an interesting example. After the pathetic address to Patroclus and the linear text of lines 316–17, Achilles utters line 318: Τρωσὶν ἐφ' ἱπποδάμοισι φέρειν πολύδακρυν Ἄρηα.

It is used only one other time in the *Iliad,* by Hector (VIII.516), and in Hector's mouth it is of course correct because the Achaeans bring a war that, as such, is always full of tears, but it is especially so for the Trojans. In that passage (VIII.516) Hector incites the Trojans to make the war full of tears also for the Achaeans, but it remains clear that the war is the source of griefs for the Trojans. It is therefore understandable that Priam may naturally speak of the *polemon poludacrun,* the *lacrimabile bellum* (III.165), and that so does Andromache (XXII.487), and even Iris speaking to Helen (III.132). But why should Achilles care that the war bring tears to the Trojans if it were not for the fact that the war against the Trojans has brought tears also to him? Achilles is the only Achaean in the whole *Iliad* to term the war full of tears. Through Achilles' use of this line we realize that Achilles is the only *aristos* among the Achaeans to suffer a loss comparable to that of the Trojans. By way of sharing the same dictional treasure, Achilles and Hector are shown to share an analogous destiny in the war and Achilles and Priam to enter a spiritual community well before Book XXIV.

This conclusion is strengthened and supported by another remarkable feature, the use of δυσάμμορε in line 315. This word is repeated by Priam to define

Hecabe as the unlucky mother of Hector (22.428) and by Andromache to define herself and Hector together ("I and you *dusammoroi*," 22.485 and 24.727). It is therefore a word used by mourners for themselves and also for the dead. In all Homer nobody else but these characters and Achilles uses this adjective.

These allusions would discriminate Achilles among all the Achaean heroes and label him as the only one who is not ideologically fully determined by the political tenets the poem stages. He is represented as being insensitive to the political allegiance of which Agamemnon or Odysseus are described as champions, and accordingly he is viewed by the poem either as an emotional individualist, even as a possible traitor, or as the hero who more closely symbolizes the *poetic* tenets. In this passage Achilles' negative position toward the common goal of the war is strongly emphasized when he will say (324–25): "I fight against the Trojans in a distant land for the sake of blood-chilling Helen," labeling Helen with a violent *hapax*. We are reminded of Achilles' uncompromising rejection of the war in Book IX.

To some extent Achilles must appear within this spectrum of characterization, from traitor to sublime hero, because of the difficult posture of the epic poet. The poet in fact cannot disentangle the poem from the political implications it has for the kings he is singing for, and accordingly he cannot disavow the political principles of the war. On the other hand, however, he is essentially in complicity with the hero who, by choosing to die, perfectly implements the function of epic poetry, i.e., to grant immortal *kleos*. If his song must be immortal, the death it magnifies must have the same immortal grounds, namely no real, immediate purpose, but the same gratuitousness and necessity as those of the song.[19]

The reader may suspect that I am deriving a lot of heavy implications and consequences from the mere repetition of a verse. But I am purposely activating the effects of the repetition in order to produce a full and meaningful reading of it. Let us see some other examples. We have summarily described the phrase κεχαρισμένε θυμῷ that Briseis addresses to Patroclus. The same phrase is used for Diomedes three times in a whole formulaic line that is successively addressed to him by Sthenelos, Athena, and Agamemnon in the fifth and tenth books; then it is uttered by Achilles in an affectionate address to Patroclus in XI.608; finally we encounter this κεχαρισμένε θυμῷ in Briseis's utterance in her lament. To the extent that Achilles too calls Patroclus "dear to the heart," Briseis's expression has some quotational or antiphonal force. As we have seen, the remaining part of the line: Πάτροκλέ μοι δειλῇ πλεῖστον increases the expressive force by a semantic contrast, while putting all the terms in their fixed paradigmatic slot.

The line that Achilles stitches together by using three separate formulas: ἐμὸν κῆρ, πόσιος καὶ ἐδητύος and ἔνδον ἐόντων is new because these phrases are never used together, and because some of the expressions are loose, I mean unrepeated, as ἄκμηνον (*hapax* in Homer) and σῇ ποθῇ, which never occurs with that rhetorical emphasis. Besides, the expression adheres fully to the sentiment Achilles has already expressed twice.

---

19. On the gratuitousness and necessity of epic poetry as *kleos,* see Chapter Four and Chapter Ten.

The combination of syntagmatic and paradigmatic iterations creates the final *adonius* in line 319 αὐτὰρ ἐμὸν κῆρ that metrically corresponds to the familiar formula αὐτὰρ Ἀχιλλεύς. The identification of Achilles with his heart is metrically suggested.

The position of σῇ ποθῇ at the beginning of the line and with strong enjambment is unique. But the force of the expression lies also in its internal rhyming, σῇ ποθῇ, and in the stop after this rhyming, as the expression closes the sentence. This expression of sorrow and desire for a person is also used, for instance, for Odysseus (XI.471), but it is used in the conditional mode, "if he dies." For Patroclus, on the contrary, it is real (XVII.690). Finally the audience is forced to reach the pathetic conclusion that the desire (*pothê*) Achilles wanted the Achaeans to feel for himself (IX.240) has been transformed into Achilles' desire and sorrow for Patroclus.

These allusive and discriminating repetitions, like all the precedent analogous cases, whatever the intentions of the poet, emerge and take textual force through a combination of contingency and determination, chance and necessity, choice and mechanical routine. I have read them favoring the positive aspects of these features (determination, necessity, choice), aware that this reading is authentically threatened by the contingency, chance, and mechanical routine that combine in the production of these repetitions. This condition increases also the spectrum of the possible significations of these allusive repetitions. But this reading is today necessary, for its metaphysical force has been too often ignored, both by the proponents of Homer's mechanical formulaic diction and by the readers of a Homeric "written" text. In other terms, this way of making sense of the Homeric repetitions has to be proposed and tried in order to assess fully the force and the creativity of this poetic means, though the reader should also be aware of the negative side, along which, of course, the repetition cannot declare and sustain a specific set of intentions.

The next theme in both Briseis's and Achilles' lament is the idea of an evil succeeding an evil (290 and 320), and Achilles' recognition that Patroclus' death is more grievous for him than the death of his father and even of his son is a much more poignant assertion than Briseis's. However, his assertion, by treasuring personal emotional attachments over family connections, remains in the wake of her ideology. It would be impossible to hear a similar statement from an Odysseus, for instance. He develops this idea with great intensity for seven lines (321–27) through inserted details, additions, and crescendos. One has the impression that he simply cannot achieve a sufficiently cumulative effect to express his despair:

οὐ μὲν γάρ τι **κακώτερον ἄλλο** πάθοιμι,
οὐδ᾽ εἴ κεν τοῦ πατρὸς **ἀποφθιμένοιο πυθοίμην**,
ὅς που νῦν Φθίηφι **τέρεν κατὰ δάκρυον** εἴβει
χήτεϊ τοιοῦδ᾽ υἷος· ὃ δ᾽ ἀλλοδαπῷ **ἐνὶ δήμῳ**
εἵνεκα ῥιγεδανῆς Ἑλένης Τρωσὶν πολεμίζω·
ἠὲ τὸν ὃς Σκύρῳ μοι ἔνι τρέφεται **φίλος υἱός**,
εἴ που ἔτι ζώει γε Νεοπτόλεμος θεοειδής.

[There is no more evil blow that I could suffer, not even if I
should learn of my father's death, who now in Phthia pours tender
tears in the absence of such a son of his, myself, I who fight
against the Trojans in a distant land for the sake of blood-chilling Helen; or
the death of my dear son, reared for me in Scyros, if godlike Neoptolemos is
still living.]

Achilles places himself between his father and his son, both of whom he
imagines possibly dead, in order to emphasize the exclusive pain he feels for the
hetairos who lies really dead before him. He tells him and himself that he would
prefer them to be dead rather than him, his comrade. This devaluation of his
family ties before Patroclus seems to feminize Achilles and make of him a
mirror image of Briseis. His pitiful description of Peleus's grief (322ff.) hinges
around the formula of line 323, τέρεν κατὰ δάκρυον εἴβει, which is used
elsewhere for female characters, and here is used for the old Peleus. Achilles had
already used this phrase with an ironic innuendo referring to Patroclus in
XVI.11, when he had compared his comrade in tears to a little girl who runs
weeping to her mother (himself!). In this feminine transfer of his and his
comrade's attitudes, one could read the socially and politically marginal position
of the hero, rejected by and refusing political power; but, with the deepest
implications for Achilles' characterization, we could read in that feminine
transfer the sign of his fully emotional suspension to his unique destiny of
death. This pitiful transfer of feminine tears to the old father Peleus goes along
with Achilles' violent accusation of Helen as "giving the chills," a *hapax*, and
his dismissing the war as a senseless fight for such a creature.

After the father and the son, he extends this funeral parade to himself in the
last part of his lament (328–37):

πρὶν μὲν γάρ μοι **θυμὸς ἐνὶ στήθεσσιν** ἐώλπει
οἶον ἐμὲ φθίσεσθαι ἀπ' Ἄργεος ἱπποβότοιο
αὐτοῦ ἐνὶ Τροίη, σὲ δέ τε Φθίην δὲ <u>νέεσθαι,</u>
ὡς ἄν μοι τὸν παῖδα **θοῆ ἐνὶ νηι μελαίνη**
Σκυρόθεν ἐξαγάγοις καί οἱ δείξειας ἕκαστα
κτῆσιν ἐμὴν δμῶάς τε καὶ ὑψερεφὲς μέγα δῶμα.
ἤδη γὰρ Πηληά γ' ὀίομαι ἢ κατὰ <u>πάμπαν</u>
<u>τεθνάμεν,</u> ἤ που <u>τυτθὸν</u> ἔτι <u>ζώοντ'</u> ἀκάχησθαι
γήραί τε στυγερῷ καὶ <u>ἐμὴν ποτιδέγμενον</u> αἰεὶ
λυγρὴν ἀγγελίην, ὅτ' ἀποφθιμένοιο πύθηται.

[For, before now, my heart in the breast had hoped that I alone would die far
from horse-pasturing Argos, here in Troy, and that you would return to Phthia
and would lead my child home from Scyros, fast in the black ship, and show
him all my possessions, the servants and the large house with its high roof.
For I fear that Peleus is already utterly dead, or perhaps in his last breath of life
suffers for hateful old age, forever waiting the sad news until he learns that I
am dead.]

Achilles answers indirectly to Briseis's intimation that Patroclus had wished that Achilles would marry Briseis in Phthia and was intending to organize this marriage. The answer is the most radical negation a man can give, for it involves Achilles' own death here in Troy: "No," he implies, "it has never been a question for me to think of marrying Briseis in Phthia, since my heart hoped that I alone would die in Troy and that you, Patroclus, would take care of my son in Phthia." Briseis is unmentioned and silently excluded from the expectations and the projects Achilles had formulated about himself. The answer to Briseis's intimation and hope is crude, but not cruder than the assertion Achilles applies to himself as he repeats twice the recognition of his close death. Pathos ensues again from the mention of the *thumos* that hoped for the death of Achilles only. Other heroes of course speak of their hearts conceiving and holding a hope, but the hope is always that of winning glory (XII.407, *diêgêsis*), destroying the enemy (XIII.813, XV.288), and analogous feats, not a hope of one's death.

Achilles recognizes that Patroclus will not lead Neoptolemos to Phthia to show him his father's "possessions, the servants, and the large house with its high roof": line 333 is repeated two times in the *Odyssey* and is *hapax* in the *Iliad*. But it has the resonance of an "internal repetition" in this passage because of Achilles' mention of Patroclus leading Neoptolemos on the black ship to Phthia to show his domestic possessions: θοῇ ἐνὶ νηΐ μελαίνῃ / Σκυρόθεν ἐξαγάγοις καί οἱ δείξειας ἕκαστα / κτῆσιν ἐμὴν δμῶάς τε καὶ ὑψερεφὲς μέγα δῶμα constitutes another indirect answer to Briseis's hope that Patroclus would lead her on the (black) ship to Phthia, as Achilles' legitimate wife: κουριδίην ἄλοχον θήσειν, ἄξειν τ' ἐνὶ νηυσὶν / ἐς Φθίην δαίσειν δὲ γάμον μετὰ Μυρμιδόνεσσι. Since Achilles knew that he would die in Troy, he had planned another trip and a different escort for Patroclus. But Patroclus is dead and he will not be able to escort Neoptolemos either. In this context Achilles' possessions seem abandoned, and at any rate lost for him, and the point contrasts strongly with the nostalgia the Achaean chiefs feel for their possessions as they cry in antiphonal response to Achilles (338–39).

In his closing words Achilles fears for the death of his father: Achilles' last remarks verbally close with a ring compositional repetition, as Nagy notices when he illustrates the meaning and the role of the root *phthi-* (with the play on *Phthia*) in building the basic principle that the hero must die: see τοῦ πατρὸς ἀποφθιμένοιο πυθοίμην 322, ὅτ' ἀποφθιμένοιο πύθηται 337, with the perfect reversal of roles (Nagy 1979, 185 and notes). This ring composition privileges here the internal relation between father and son, and it softens Achilles' previous statement that Patroclus's death is more painful for him than his father's death, but it does not exclude the death of Patroclus over whose corpse this mirrored death is evoked. The phrase with ἀποφθιμένοιο in line 322 and in the closing line 337 is repeated only in these two spots, a sort of "internal quotation" whose force becomes evident only at the end of the passage and remains exclusively active within this passage of Achilles.[20]

---

20. Likewise the formula of line 319 κεῖσαι δεδαϊγμένος partially recalls the more frequently repeated one that has been used by Briseis (283): δεδαϊγμένον ὀξέϊ

The rhythm of Achilles' antiphonal lament has larger waves than Briseis's speech: two or three lines without any strong, repeated, familiar element are followed by one, two, or three lines fully or almost fully formulaic. The motion is slower, more majestic, the breathing more powerful. Let us now read in the rhythm of this passage the several effects that result from it. First, the high pitch zones are those at the end of some themes: see 318, 337, at the development of the theme of fasting (319b, 321a), at the representation of the old Peleus 323–24a, etc. I do not mean that these zones are more powerful and more expressive than the others, but simply that their accent has a different pitch. In fact, as I have shown, very few expressions in this text have the force and the pathos of σῇ ποθῇ (321), which is in no way accented by repetition and metrical fixity. The intensification/relaxation in contrast with the linearity (or lack of familiar echoes) of the unrepeated parts is significant only on a rhythmic register, in terms of more or less chanting, in terms of more or less familiar, pleasurable echoes. If we inscribe these terms in the body language of the poet who "chanted" them, we must imply the tension of his body and soul as he moves through these rhythmic alternations.

Achilles' antiphonal lament leaves no hopes to anybody: the planned marriage to which Briseis makes allusion is denied, the awaiting of Peleus and Neoptolemos for the return of Achilles is frustrated, the normal rhythm of life of the hero himself is threatened, and Zeus must send him some nectar to save him from destitution (341ff.). Though Achilles' mourning lamentation contrasts with some of the themes of Briseis's lament, it harmonizes with it in some specific aspects. Both lamentations move from a posture of marginality, express an intense emotional force, and point to the mourners' own death. This analysis has shown the posture of political and existential suspension from which Achilles speaks and I do not need to enlarge on it. I prefer to comment on the last point. Briseis recalls the real death of her husband and brothers and symbolically mimes her own death by disfiguring and staining with blood her face, neck and breast. Achilles, in an ascetic fasting that mimes death, evokes the imagined death of his father and son and mentions his close real death. He is therefore lamenting from the posture more radically marginal and suspended from all human connections, that of his community with death. The readers are better able to perceive in this extreme posture also the signs that point to Achilles' marginal position in the earlier parts of the poem, his relative detachment from the political allegiance, his commitment to *kleos* rather than *timê*, his unique leaning to private attachments (Patroclus, Phoenix, Briseis), and his display of unchecked emotions. It is then not a mere chance that the greatest hero mourns over his comrade in an antiphonal lament with his slave and concubine.

χαλκῷ, but because of this proximity Achilles' phrase takes on an almost antiphonal force.

CHAPTER 8

The I and the Other in Odysseus's Story of the Cyclopes*

The aim of this study is to examine the figures, themes, and concepts that represent and define the I and the Other in the story Odysseus tells of his encounter with the Cyclops. The ways in which the I (Odysseus, the narrator, and with him the civilized man) and the Other (the Cyclopes, particularly Polyphemus, as well as uncivilized man in general) are represented possess a polarizing power and thus tend to construct two opposed figures. In examining the themes and modes of representation that characterize this dichotomy, we shall find that, despite the clarity and force of the polarization, the representation of the civilized man and the savage is founded upon mutually contradictory rhetorical figures, which end by superimposing themselves on one another and which thus cease to offer precise epistemological definitions at all.

Odysseus finds himself among the Phaeacians as both guest and stranger (in Homeric Greek both connotations are present in the word *xeinos* and are distinguished only by context), and an uncooperative guest at that, one who refuses to give his own name as etiquette requires, yet asks as a suppliant for an escort home, without even communicating where that home might be. But such outstanding hosts are the Phaeacians that they promise him his escort even before learning who their guest is and where they are to take him.

At the close of the second day, Alcinous, the king of the Phaeacians, finally compels Odysseus to reveal his name and homeland, to tell the story of his

* Originally published as "L'io e l'altro nel racconto di Odisseo sui Ciclopi," *Studi italiani di filologia classica*, 3d ser. 11 (1993): 26–45.

travels, and to reveal who among the peoples he has encountered "those who are harsh (*khalepoi*), savage (*agrioi*) and not law-abiding (*ou dikaioi*)/ and those who are hospitable (*philoxenoi*) and god-fearing" (*Od.* 8.575–76). Here we see the anthropological coordinates already set. According to both Alcinous and (as we shall see) Odysseus, the world is divided into two polarized groups, one being that of hospitable and pious men of whom the Phaeacians would be the ideal representatives—as they benefit and admire their guest Odysseus—and the other that of the impious, savage, and inhospitable.

Odysseus offers only one description of this second group: the Cyclopes. To be sure, the other peoples he describes are often judged in relation to their respect for hospitality and for the gods—thus Aeolus is the perfect host, Circe an anti-host—but as gods and magicians they transcend the human scale and represent another level of alterity altogether from that of the savage man. Such an alterity also characterizes the world of the dead. Here man is no longer really human, and the rules of hospitality lose all force.

In the course of his story Odysseus, by matching himself against gods, sorcerers and the kingdom of the dead, defines man and humanity in contrast to the divine and to death; so too when he faces the Cyclops he defines the social and civilized man in contrast to the savage.

His visit to the land of the Cyclopes represents the third stage of Odysseus's voyage home. His companions, normally represented as rash and imprudent, are here uncharacteristically reluctant to disembark. Odysseus chooses a small group of them and addresses them with the same formula already used by Alcinous, claiming that he wishes to see "what sorts of men these are, whether overweening (*hubristai*)"—Alcinous had used *khalepoi*, savage (*agrioi*) and unjust (*ou dikaioi*) or hospitable (*philoxeinoi*) and god-fearing (9.174–175).

The repetition here seems programmatic, rather than purely mechanical. On the one hand anthropological coordinates are introduced (in particular the dichotomy between the civilized man and the savage) in preparation for the specific encounter with the Cyclopes, for which these coordinates thus serve as the interpretative norms. On the other hand, the repetition enables the narrator to demonstrate his solidarity with his audience—Alcinous and his peers. They agree on the definitions of civilization and barbarity, the determining factor being a respect for hospitality of the kind that the audience has itself displayed. This definition is formulated by Odysseus himself before having heard it from Alcinous (see vi.120-21) and after xiii.201-202. One can thus say that Odysseus uses the same coordinates as Alcinous, but, by referring here to Alcinous's position, the guest pays his host a subtle compliment, seducing the storys listener with this *captatio benevolentiae*. Finally, by using Alcinous's own words and setting up the Phaeacians as the model of civilization in opposition to barbarity, Odysseus indirectly inserts the Phaeacians into the story of his return. For us, at least, they begin to play a role in his story comparable, and opposed, to that played by the Cyclopes.

The reluctance of Odysseus's companions to investigate the Cyclops becomes explicit when they observe the immense cave in which he lives. They try to persuade Odysseus to steal the cheeses stored there and beat a hasty retreat, but Odysseus wishes to remain (as he explains) in order to see the Cyclops and to get guest-gifts from him (229). In recounting the episode, Odysseus recognizes that he would have done well to listen to his men, and acknowledges his error.

The desire for knowledge that ennobles Odysseus's imprudence in our eyes is inseparable from a certain greed. It might be worthwhile to digress momentarily here and ask ourselves how the reader reacts when confronted with this avaricious Odysseus. Why does the reader accept Odysseus's imprudence while still retaining the essential image of the hero as circumspect, astute, the man of many devices. There are a number of possible explanations for the respectful reading we give Odysseus;[1] I follow Calames suggestion that without the imprudence and greed for gifts, Odysseus would not have encountered the Cyclops at all, and we, too, would be deprived of a gift: the exciting story we are here enjoying. We find ourselves in much the same position as the Phaeacians who listen, enchanted by Odysseus's spell, unwilling for his stories ever to end. They are quick to offer him additional gifts, and here, too, Odysseus shows himself greedy for such gifts, saying that he would remain on Scheria for an entire year:

> Great Alcinous . . .
> if you invited me to stay here even for a year,
> if you prepared an escort for me and gave me splendid gifts,
> I would be willing . . .
>
> (11.355ff.)

The reader receives a gift from the narrator and hastens to return the favor, which he does by reading in full complicity with the narrator, closing his eyes above all when the defects of the narrator are the very condition of his narration.

But let us return from the I of the reader to the encounter between Odysseus and the Cyclops. The episode has been analyzed as a contrast between two human and social types. Focke for example characterizes it through a series of oppositions: "a contrast between culture and savagery, piety and impiety, law and the absence of law, ingenuity and obtusity."[2]

---

1. Focke (1943, 167) argues that the theft and flight proposed by the comrades would be shameful. Podlecki (1961, 128) defends Odysseus on the grounds that the comrades' suggestion would infringe on the laws of hospitality. But in the face of these apologies, one should not overlook the warning of H. Eisenberger (1973, 135) who rightly notes that the narrator Odysseus regrets his decision to await the Cyclops's return, so that even taking into account line 213 we are bound to see a certain imprudence in that decision. Calame (1976, 316) has an excellent analysis of the situation. On the one hand the companions' proposal would avoid an encounter with the Cyclops and on the narrative level this would have brought the episode to a close and frustrated Odysseus's desire for knowledge. In proposing the raid, the companions wish to steal the products that confer on the Cyclops the status of civilized man, and would find themselves facing only this aspect of the Cyclops, without encountering his savage side. They wish to commit at once a theft that is in fact postponed until the end of the episode, after the encounter with the barbarities of Polyphemus.

2. Focke 1943, 167. Similar contrasts in Burkert 1982, 33: "The final superiority [of Odysseus] displays itself in four 'codes': man with weapon against unarmed savage; the sober against the drunkard; the seeing against the blind; the master of

The asocial and acultural position of the Cyclops has been analyzed in recent years by structuralist critics, for example by G. S. Kirk[3] and by Claude Calame,[4] who demonstrate with considerable subtlety the contradictions that mark him: the contrast between his milk diet and his cannibalism, between his role as shepherd/herdsman and the spontaneous production of the island itself, typical of the golden age.[5]

I would add with Siegfried Besslich that the contrast between Odysseus and the Cyclops is developed by means of the norms of hospitality which Odysseus has experienced among the Phaeacians. We have thus a precise contrast between the Phaeacians and the Cyclops.[6] And ultimately, the example of the unhospitable Cyclops is a warning to the suitors, who have the same ungracious attitude toward guests, beggars, and strangers.

Indeed the episode as a whole appears to confirm such readings, and the few exceptions are easily explicable. By entering Polyphemus's cave, for example, Odysseus walks roughshod over the rules of hospitality, which demand that a stranger wait before a prospective hosts door until he is noticed and invited in. But the cave is open; there are in fact no doors or thresholds to cross. This is a primitive habitation, and Odysseus behaves as if the primitive world in which he finds himself gives him license to break some of the more formal rules.

Odysseus and his companions appropriate Polyphemus's cheeses, make a sacrifice, and wait for the giant. This too is a violation of the rules; it should be the host who offers food to the guest, after which he may inquire as to the strangers name. Whether for this reason or because Odysseus and his companions have already dined, we are less surprised when the Cyclops, as soon as he arrives home and becomes aware of the strangers, asks without any preliminaries who they are and where they come from:

---

language against the stupid." Burkert recognizes that we identify with Odysseus—"though a true structuralist, to be sure, is away above any feeling of excitement." Perhaps Burkert here identifies too much with Odysseus (cf. note 16); as we shall see, Polyphemus is not the fool that this and similar readings suggest, nor is Odysseus uniformly astute and lucid in his actions.

3. Kirk (1970, 164ff.) places the sociological position of Polyphemus within the nature/culture opposition, with Polyphemus representing the troubling ambivalence of both nature and culture (168). For Burkert, on the other hand, certain ambivalences do not spring from the deep structure of the myth, but are the "by-product" of a literary crystallization or elaboration. Thus the ambivalence of the savage depends on this crystallization, which requires the idyllic as a basic contrast to the cannibalism (32–33).

4. Calame 1976, 314 and 325ff. Calame demonstrates clearly how the Cyclops's anthropomorphism (*anêr . . . pelôrios* 187) and his activities as shepherd and dairy-farmer are positive characteristics, while in other respects he is portrayed as savage.

5. Eisenberger (1973) stresses the "golden age" aspects of the Cyclopes' life (on which see also Kirk 1970, 164) and notes that these aspects, placed as they are within a generally negative portrayal, themselves become negative. These beneficiaries of miraculous growth are—like the suitors—ὑπερφίαλοι (*Od.* 9.106).

6. Besslich 1966, 69. Schein (1970, 81–82) also stresses the force of this motif.

O guests, who are you? Where do you come from, sailing over the watery
paths? Do you come for trade, or do you rove at random, like pirates on the
sea, who wander staking their life and bringing evil to strangers? (*Od.* 9.252–
55).

I translate the Cyclops's opening words, "*ô xeinoi*," as "O guests," but the
Greek means also "O strangers." The Cyclops here repeats exactly the words that
the pious Nestor addresses to his unknown visitors (*Od.* 3.71–74). Here, too, the
repetition may be significant; for it has the effect of suggesting that the Cyclops
is perfectly familiar with the rules of polite society. As matters progress,
however, it becomes clear that he honors them only in the breach. The Cyclops
is more ironic and more subtle than his gullibility in the "Nobody" scene might
suggest.

   Put on his guard by the enormous size of the man and by his cavernous
voice, Odysseus declares himself a suppliant before the Cyclops. He beseeches
him to give his guests the gift that is due them, and thus to honor Zeus the
protector of guests.[7] Polyphemus mocks him, calls him a fool and rejects his
supplication. The Cyclopes, he says, pay no heed to Zeus the aegis-bearer or to
the blessed gods, for "we ourselves are much stronger" (273–76).[8]

   After a further brief exchange between Odysseus and the Cyclops, the latter
snatches up and eats two of Odysseus's companions. Once more we see the
normal patterns of hospitality inverted; instead of offering a meal to his guests,
the Cyclops makes the guests themselves the meal. The phrase *epi kheiras ialle*,
"he stretched out his hands for" is used a hundred-odd times in banqueting scenes,
and there is no question but that the text here grimly parodies the standard
gesture of stretching out ones hands for food at a normal sacrifice and banquet.

   By consuming the stranger who supplicates him in the name of Zeus, the
Cyclops not only demonstrates impiety but literally annuls the Other who has
arrived at his abode, swallowing him up, incorporating him into himself, as if
the very notion of the Other as something outside himself did not exist. By
engulfing the Other, the I removes itself from the dichotomy and thus from any
potential definition.

   The grim inversion of the norms of hospitality continues throughout the
following day. When evening comes, as soon as the Cyclops has finished his
dinner of human flesh, Odysseus offers him a potent wine. The Cyclops drinks it
down and at once demands more. He thanks Odysseus, asking his name and
promising him a guest-gift. The etiquette of hospitality is here recalled only to
be absurdly parodied. Odysseus gives his name as "Nobody" and the Cyclops

---

   7. Cf. Besslich's excellent analysis of Odysseus's supplication.
   8. Eisenberger (1973, 132–33) is probably right to suggest that these
expressions of disbelief in the gods are mere bombast. The text assures us at line 106
that the Cyclopes "believe in the immortal gods," and at the end of the episode
Polyphemus invokes his father Poseidon. But the Cyclops's bombast does have a real
goal, insofar as it justifies his rejection of Odysseus's supplication and his
cannibalism. Kirk (1970, 163) notes that "Polyphemus professed no use for the gods,
but there are signs that he and his peers were favored by Zeus," and cf. 167.

then grants him the privilege of being eaten last: "this shall be my guest-gift to you" (9.370).

There is a strong case, then, for reading the entire scene between Odysseus and Polyphemus as an opposition, framed in terms of the ritual of hospitality, between the traits of the civilized and socialized man and those of the barbarous and asocial one. We should note, too, that this dichotomy is expressed as the contrast between an I who is cultured, pious, clever, and in control of the story (the narrating I of Odysseus, in other words), and an Other who is violent, brutal and wholly incapable of telling his side of the story.

This representation of the cultured man and his opposite, the primitive and savage man, seems to us wholly conventional, even at the points at which it descends into caricature and fable—it is, after all, based on a long tradition of fables and stories. But though our own experience of primitive man calls into question its anthropological accuracy, it remains true that this representation has a certain amount of conceptual power within a long tradition.

To the degree that the representation of the savage produces by contrast the representation of the civilized man and the cultured I, the Homeric story might allow us to glimpse the Greeks vision of himself, at least in ideal terms, and might instruct us in the ways in which such a vision and definition of man can be obtained. But the text of the *Odyssey* is not quite as neat in its dichotomies, nor as didactic in its moral and social definitions, as certain of its commentators would claim.

To define man, social and asocial, is an operation of extreme difficulty, in which total precision is impossible. Any definition necessarily implies a certain metaphysics, which is to say the importation of delusory concepts, metaphors, and figures of desire. But I do not wish to embark on a close examination of possible definitions of man in general. My goal is rather to analyze the way that the Homeric representation of the civilized man and the primitive man is constructed and rhetorically composed.

Let me begin by saying that the definition of the savage, the definition that frames the entire representation of him and upon which that representation hinges, is composed of three metonymies. The first is that involving *agrios*, in Greek literally a man "from the countryside" (*agros*) and signifying "savage" only by displacement and figuratively, that is, by metonymy. Similarly the Italian *selvaggio*, French *sauvage*, and English *savage* mean in the first instance "a man from the woods" (Latin *silva*), and only secondarily come to mean "savage."

The second metonymy is that involving *khalepos*, "difficult," and in an extended, figurative sense "harsh" or "cruel."

It is impossible to specify the exact force of *hubristês*, since the etymology of *hubris* remains uncertain. But if the Greeks, as Chantraine suggests, thought of it as related to *hyper*, "above," "beyond," "excessive," this, too, would be, at least from their point of view, a metonymy.

Finally, the word for "just," *dikaios*, does not provide an unambiguous point of departure. If we follow Chantraine, Greek *dikê*, "justice," would be literally "an indication," and "the just" that which follows it.

These metonymies thus describe a man who is unjust, cruel, impious, and savage via conceptual fields that are neither fixed nor unequivocal. For example, as an attentive shepherd (which he undeniably is), the Cyclops could perfectly well be described as *agrios* in the words positive sense—as a simple countryman, rustic and unrefined.[9] To be sure, all these terms taken together comprise a homologous description, intended to show us, in the person of the Cyclops, the opposite of the civilized man. And so they do. But for precisely this reason, these metonymies do not add greatly to our picture of the savage; they describe him only as the opposite of the just, hospitable and pious man, and contribute to our understanding of the savage only if we already know what it means to be civilized.

But at this point we face a more serious question: is the Cyclops a man to begin with?

When we turn to observe the similes that describe the Cyclops, the doubt already implanted in the reader increases. We should be aware that a simile is the foundation of a metaphorical substitution, and thus potentially a metaphor itself. A metaphorical simile describes the Cyclops as a beast, specifically as a lion (9.288ff.):

> . . . rushing he reached out his hands for my companions, seized two of them, and crushed them like puppies on the ground. Their brains splattered on the ground and wetted the earth. He cut them limb from limb and prepared his dinner; he ate like a lion reared on the mountains, and he left nothing, neither the entrails nor the flesh nor the bone-marrow.

The reader no longer knows whether this rhetorical figure an accurate description of the Cyclops or is actually a rhetorical figure. If the text did not strikingly identify this animalistic feeding as "dinner" (*dorpon*), thus giving it a cultural connotation, all the images, like the animalization of the companions into puppies, would conspire to cut the Cyclops off from every human attribute.

We are confronted by a rhetorical contrast; the metonymies tell us that the Cyclops is a man situated between the uncivilized and the savage, the arrogant and the brutal, the unjust and the lawless, while the metaphor tells us that he is not a man, but a ferocious animal, a beast.

Metaphor is a substitution that implies some necessary relationship, whereas metonymy implies only contiguity. To use Paul de Mans example, there is a certain truth in taking Achilles for a lion, but none at all in taking an automobile for Henry Ford.

To return to the images. A simile informs us that the Cyclops "did not resemble a man who eats bread (*andri sitophagôi*) but a wooded crag amid high mountains" (190–92). Here the text explicitly denies that the Cyclops has a

---

9. Calame 1976, 134. Cf. Valgimigli 1964, 64: "This immense giant, glimpsed intermittently in his cave stooping to milk his flocks and to prod the lamb toward its mother . . . is not so different from an ordinary herdsman; he is an oversized Eumaeus, but still a Eumaeus of sorts."

human aspect, and instead assimilates him to a raw feature of the landscape.[10] Yet the text contradicts itself, for elsewhere it explicitly calls Polyphemus a "man" (*anêr*) albeit an immense or monstrous (*pelôrios*, 187) or savage (*agrios*, 494) one. But what then is a man?

Another simile compares the Cyclops to a ship (9.383). At this point Odysseus and his companions are twisting the charred stake in Polyphemus's eye: "Leaning over him I twisted it [*sc.* the stake] like a man boring a ships timber with an auger." The image derives from Odysseus's (civilized) field of reference, for although the Cyclopes have seen ships or at least know what they are, they do not own any and do not know how to build them (9.125ff): "The Cyclopes do not have ships with painted prows, nor are there craftsmen among them to construct well-benched ships . . ." Odysseus's metaphor thus takes us out of the Cyclops's cultural horizon and describes him from the point of view of Odysseus's own skills—the skills by which he blinds Polyphemus.[11] By means of such skills the Cyclops is reduced to an object, a ships timber, something that Odysseus can build or dismantle at will. Let us consider now the force of this image and the action it illustrates from the point of view not of the historical antecedents of the motif[12] but of the narrator, Odysseus, who is

---

10. Kirk 1970, 166: "The striking comparison with the mountain peak . . . is designed to strengthen his association with raw nature."

11. In the view of Eisenberger (1973, 140), this image and the analogous one at lines 391ff. illustrate "on the one hand [Odysseus's] methodical exactitude, steady eye and efficiency, but on the other the terrible cruelty of such an act against another living being." But why show such pity for the cannibalistic Cyclops? Here it is the sailor and craftsman who uses these images, derived from his own arts. But he uses them *in his capacity as narrator*, long after the event—of which he is the sole witness—when at a certain distance he describes and evaluates his act. As narrator he has no desire to pity the Cyclops; he wishes rather to demonstrate his mastery, his power over the brute, the object that he manipulates and dismembers at will.

12. Page (1955, 4) sees in the use of a wooden stake hardened in the fire a variant of the more common myth in which a metal spit is used, and of which lines 391–94 are a trace. The criticism of Seth Schein who, following in the footsteps of Charles Segal (1962, 17–64), argues that the mythical variants are completely integrated into their context and into the poetics of the *Odyssey* is a valuable corrective. Schein points out how problematic the notion of "variants" from an "orthodox" myth can be, and shows that supposedly "deviant" details are in fact insistent themes of the poem.

Burkert (1982, 33–34) sees in the fire-hardened stake a sign of the myth's Neolithic origins. Heubeck cautiously describes the hypothesis as "possible." The difficulty with this mythical search for the origins of the myth lies in taking from the text only what suits one's theory; all else is assumed to be literary elaboration or crystallization. This is circular argument. Thus for Page, for example, the wooden stake is a variant of the basic myth, whereas for Burkert it is the wooden stake that is basic and the metal spit that is the variant: " . . . at the center of the Cyclops tale we find the invention of the first weapon described, along with the use of fire" (34). Burkert's only textual evidence for his thesis is that the wooden stake, in the story, is superfluous. For Odysseus has his sword with which he could blind Polyphemus's eye. The tale therefore postulates the primordial weapon of man. This analysis could be

enchanting his audience with his story of the valiant deed he has accomplished by means of his triumphant shrewdness. Is it going too far to suggest that with this metaphor Odysseus hints that he is constructing and dismantling his Cyclops with his rhetorical tools? That Polyphemus is a delusory composition of heterogeneous human, bestial, ferocious and natural elements, all held together by a particular rhetoric?

To continue. Even as the metonymies describe the Cyclops as a man, aberrant in his habits, but nonetheless a man, the metaphors outflank him and transport him into a quite different representative and conceptual field. To be compared to a mountain peak, or a lion, or a piece of wood being bored—what does this have to do with being a man? We can say, then, that there is a contrast between the metonymic images and the metaphoric ones, and that this contrast deepens the purely delusory aspect of the rhetorical construction that is the Cyclops.

To be sure, Homer uses these rhetorical figures to create a persuasive effect; they contribute significantly to a representation of the savage giant as a disgusting figure. But our inquiry also suggests that the metaphorical figures, by preventing the metonymies from asserting the humanity of the Cyclops, present a serious epistemological challenge to them. The persuasive power of the rhetoric is fractured; rhetoric and persuasion separate and diverge. In other words, to the degree that they convey conceptual representations, the tropes or figures resist serving merely as a means of producing persuasive effects.

As a result, the alterity of the Cyclops as the savage man who does not respect the laws of hospitality is fractured into contradictory and inconsistent facets, which call into question, among other things, his very humanity, or at the least render it a purely heterogeneous and phantasmic composition, devoid of any possible referent.

It would only fracture the phantasmic "identity" of the Cyclops even more if we add that there is, readable between the lines, the project of attributing a sort of martial, heroic quality to the monster. He is defined as a man clothed in great *alkê* (215); he is indirectly compared with Hector (240-42; see XII.445-49 with the consequence of placing the Cyclops in the heroic age). In his boasts of being superior to Zeus, the Cyclops sounds like Agamemnon in the quarrel with

---

supported or suspended by Schein's analysis (75–77) of the function of olive wood in the *Odyssey*, and countered by the observation that it would be a weaker narrative if Odysseus attacked the enormous mountain-peak of a giant with his sword. As it happens, when he considers doing so, he thinks better of an impulse which would have left him prisoner in the cave. The story acquires more marvelous traits and greater suitability through the use of a huge weapon, set in motion by Odysseus and his companions, who like him are prospective victims of the ogre. This weapon is an olive branch, and thus linked to Athena under whose protection Odysseus plans his victory (cf. 317). The weapon unites Odysseus and his companions in a joint undertaking of great daring, so great that the text even refers to divine inspiration (381). Neolithic origin, or an opportune Homeric adaptation and re-elaboration of available folktale material? On Homer's extensive innovation of inherited folktales, see Reece 1993, 127ff. and 139ff.

Achilles; furthermore, he uses *thumos* (278) in a heroic way. Indeed the text insists on heroic diction: κλυτὰ μῆλα "famous flocks" (308); δοίη δὲ μοι εὖχος Ἀθήνη "should Athena grant me glory" (317; cf. xxi.338; xxii.7). Also present are the essential elements of the Iliadic *aristeia* (375-94; cf. Heubeck 1989, 33).

All these heroic features produce a jarring note: should we read them as expressions of a certain pathos for their "displacement" in a world that does not recognize them any longer? or as mock-heroic diction? Either way, the monstrous, cannibalistic figure of the Cyclops emerges even more fractured and inconsistent through this heroic coloring: an unstable, merely linguistic composition, an extravagant foil to Odysseus's heroic, smart, human "self."

The style of this analysis may remind the reader of that conducted by Paul de Man (1979) on Rousseaus representation, in his *Essais sur lorigine des Langues*, of the invention of the word *Homme*, "man." Rousseau imagines that the first man to encounter another man feels at once the others alterity, is frightened, and calls him "giant." After further encounters, the first man discovers that this supposed giant is no stronger or larger than himself, and invents another name, for example "man." From now on he will keep the word "giant" for the false object that impressed and deceived him.

The word "giant" no longer expresses the alterity of the second man, but rather, as a metaphor dictated by fear, the unease that the other provokes. And the word "man" is no less aberrant, since it results simply from the observation that the other is no stronger or larger than oneself. It thus derives from a lack of quantitative difference, as if this quantitative indifference were the distinguishing characteristic of man. Derived in this way, the noun "man" is no less metaphorical. It substitutes for the name of that concrete being over there a name that means "I am a quantitative comparison between him and me."

We have observed how the alterity of the Cyclops as "savage, impious man" fragments into a delusory and heterogeneous composition without any precise referent, a composition in which the attribute "man" is the first to be called into question. Given that this impious savage is the correlative of his binary opposite, the hospitable and pious man, let us turn to this second figure. We shall find him in the person of the Phaeacians, who function as the epitome of the ideal, social man.

Nor are surprises lacking here. To begin with, these superlative hosts are notoriously suspicious and hostile to strangers. This at least is what Athena tells Odysseus when, disguised as a little girl, she directs him to the palace of Alcinous (7.32f.): "They [sc. the Phaeacians] cannot endure strangers, nor do they receive welcomingly those who come from another country." Athena may give this cautionary warning in order to justify to the reader the need to make Odysseus invisible and enable him to appear suddenly, like a god, before the king, queen, and nobles in a hall of the palace. Or perhaps the text underlines the natural suspicion that the Phaeacians feel for strangers in order to exalt the effects that Odysseus's presence produces on them. However that may be, the fact remains that the Phaeacians, those paradigms of the civilized man, the god-fearing and gracious host, are initially described in quite a different manner.[13]

But the most disquieting question here, too, concerns their human status. What manner of men are these Phaeacians? They are described as men whom the gods still visit and associate with, as in the golden age (7.201ff.); they possess ships that think for themselves and sail under the guidance of mens thoughts (8.557ff.); they do not make war, but pass their lives in singing, dancing, and listening to the songs of their poet Demodocus.[14]

So superhuman are the Phaeacians that they mistake Odysseus for a god (*Od.* 7.200ff.). This *qui pro quo* (or change of identity) is disquieting in itself, situated as it is in the context of identifications and definitions of the human beings who come in contact with Odysseus and are defined by that meeting. Most significantly, however, this change of identity, as we shall see from the text, is articulated both through figures of contiguity and through figures of similarity and substitution. Here is how Alcinous, addressing his advisors, questions himself on the nature of Odysseus:

> But if he is an immortal who has descended from the sky, then the gods are up to something new, for the gods always appear to us in their true form (*phainontai enargeis*) when we slaughter glorious hecatombs and feast among us and sit with us ... for we are near to them, like the Cyclopes and the savage (*agria*) tribes of Giants. (*Od.* 7.199–206)

This is a remarkable passage. The relationship between the Phaeacians and the gods is a relationship of proximity and contiguity, specified only by analogy with the relationship that the Cyclopes and the savage tribes of the Giants have with those same gods. Suddenly the humanity and civilized character of the Phaeacians have become problematic. On the one hand, the Phaeacians relationship with the gods, analogous to that enjoyed by the Cyclopes and Giants, necessarily rules out any simple humanity like that of Odysseus. On the other hand, this analogous relationship calls into question the strict distinction between pious and impious, for it seems that the Cyclopes (whose "piety" is familiar to us) and the Giants (explicitly described as savages, *agria*) are equal sharers in this contiguous relationship with the gods.[15]

We turn now to the game of similarities and substitutions that the text initiates. When Alcinous says that if Odysseus were a god he would be manifesting himself differently from the way in which the gods normally present

---

13. The scholia offer a different explanation, assuming a difference between the intolerant commoners (cf. lines 16–17) and the refined aristocracy at the palace. But this explanation only calls attention to the difficulty and has no more authority than others; cf. Stanford's cautious note on 7.33, and that of Ameis and Hentze, arguing that Athena wants to make sure Odysseus will behave carefully and prudently. J. Strauss Clay (1980, 163–64) offers a cautionary note about the opposition scholars draw between the savage Cyclops and the cultivated Phaeacians.

14. On the identification of the Phaeacians with the "ferrymen of Elysium" of Indo-European and Egyptian mythology, see Cook 1992, 239–64.

15. On the various facets of contiguity between the Phaeacians and Cyclopes, see J. Strauss Clay 1980, 163–64.

themselves to the Phaeacians, he suggests indirectly that Odysseus does not have the aspect or appearance of a god. Here, as on other occasions, the text enjoys teasing its readers about the nature of the gods appearance. Odysseus, it seems, does not have the appearance of a god, but something about him is such as potentially to identify him with a god. The text offers us no help in identifying the element that appears potentially divine to Alcinous. From the answer that Odysseus will give, one could speculate that the king of the Phaeacians is astonished at the strangers handsomeness, which in some way reminds him of that of the gods, though the stature and the form of the gods are so immense and luminous that Alcinous, who knows them well, could not actually mistake Odysseus's appearance for theirs.[16] Alternatively (though of course these explanations are not exclusive), Alcinous may be thinking of the miraculous way in which Odysseus made his way into the palace and indeed into their very midst. Odysseus soon relieves Alcinous's perplexity:

> Alcinous, do not trouble yourself on that score,
> for I do not resemble (*eoika*) the gods who possess the vast sky
> in aspect (*demas*) or stature (*phuên*), but [I resemble] mortal men.
>   (*Od.* 7.208–10)

Here again, with this enigmatic declaration, the text seems to be toying with us: how can Odysseus say that he does not resemble the immortals? Does he know what they look like? Why does he not say simply that he *is not* an immortal? The text is committed here to keep its audiences attention on the notion of similarity which dominates all the recognition scenes and which thus inscribes in the text the question of the nature of "being." The "being" of the gods, of a father, of a husband, and so forth is always perceptible only through a totality of similarities, of referential signs, of subjective and objective connotations, and does not present itself as a direct manifestation of being. In the passage above Odysseus denies that he possesses a divine nature ("being"), and does so by defining and articulating relationships of contiguity and contingency (metonymy) and similarity/substitution (metaphor), but refusing to engage in any expression that would indicate his "being."

As is well known, the gods are able to change their "natural" appearance and resemble anything they like (*Od.* 13.313), thus rendering their nature and definition unreadable. Now, inasmuch as they are near to the gods, the Phaeacians are almost gods from the point of view of contiguity, but men from the point of view of appearance. Metonymically, then, these beings are gods, but metaphorically they are not. What are they, literally?

But a man can only be called a god metaphorically, as characters in epic are often complimented on a godlike characteristic or spirit. There is no nearness between men and gods, but the heroic epic, like that of the *Iliad*, praises the beauty or other characteristics of a hero or a woman by assimilating them metaphorically to those of the gods. Here, however, the hero denies that he possesses characteristics assimilable to those of the gods. Neither his appearance or bodily strength (*demas*), nor his stature (*phuê*), he says, are like those of the

---

16. On the natural appearance of the gods, see above 73–75 and 81ff.

gods. He rejects the epic metaphor that describes the superior hero, rejects it with violence, and asserts his mortal nature with a long and exceptional identification of himself with his belly (7.215–21). Here one can see clearly the extraordinary divergence between the Odyssean and the Iliadic hero.

What sort of beings are these Phaeacians? They are described and defined by a game of shifting shapes analogous to the one that describes and defines the identity of the Cyclops. Here, too, metaphor contradicts metonymy. Metonymically speaking—in terms of proximity—the Phaeacians are *almost* gods. But metaphorically—in terms of appearance—they are *like* men. What they *actually are* vanishes in a game of contradictory images. Like the Cyclopes, they become rhetorical, delusory creatures, mere names devoid of any precise reference. In this rhetorical prism, the identity of man, and then of the pious and civilized man (represented in the figures of Alcinous and the Phaeacians) is endlessly refracted.

It might seem that in this shipwreck of identity and definitions the sole survivor is Odysseus, whose I is clearly defined, as we have seen, both in regard to Alcinous's inquiry as to whether he might not be a god, and in relation to the delusory nature of the Cyclopes. In this second case he has the advantage of our complicity as readers. For in reading we conspire with him, our attention directed to his interests and triumph.[17] The text explicitly invites our collaboration by representing a scene of reading in the eleventh book of the *Odyssey*. Right in the middle of his story, Odysseus pauses, and the text describes the fascination felt by the Phaeacians, his first readers (*Od.* 11.353ff.). Such a scene, obviously, creates an effect of psychological mimesis in us as readers.

Odysseus's I appears in relief when contrasted with the apparent obtuseness of the monster. The two high points of the heros cunning and shrewdness are his blinding of the monster with a stake of wood hardened in the fire, and his concealment of his own name and invention of the name "Nobody."

I have already discussed the first trick, and will limit myself here to the second.[18] Polyphemus has tasted with delight the special wine that Odysseus has offered him and he wants more of it.[19] Odysseus is happy to oblige, and says (9.364ff.):

> Cyclops, you ask me my famous name and I will tell you all,
> but be sure you give me my guest-gift, as you promised.
> My name is Nobody (*Outis*). My mother and father

---

17. Valgimigli 1964, 66: "The special tone of the Polyphemus episode is . . . the triumphant, victorious, mocking cheerfulness of Odysseus the narrator. The poet identifies himself with his character, rejoicing in his cunning, preening himself on his victories." Burkert (1982, 33): "The immediate, exciting effect consists, of course, in our imaginary identification with Odysseus."

18. The invention of the name "Nobody" is a unique variant here; in this type of story the hero generally gives his name as "I Myself": cf. Page 1955, 18–19, and Schein 1970, 79ff.

19. On this wine, itself a guest-gift, see Eisenberger 1973, 134.

both call me Nobody and so do my companions.[20]
So I spoke, and he answered with impious heart,
"I shall eat Nobody last, after all your companions,
after all the others; this shall be my guest-gift to you."

The text is studded with felicitous details. Odysseus describes his name, "Nobody," as "famous"—a contradiction all the more ironic given that the Cyclops's name is "Polyphemus."[21] The relationship between guest-gifts and the giving of ones name has already featured in the scenes with the Phaeacians, where Odysseus refuses to give his name for as long as he can. For the hero of masquerades, false names and imposture, to give his name is almost to display himself as the hero of a heroic tradition that has no influence in the *Odyssey*. Here the goal is to hide, to pretend, pose, and dissimulate in order to survive, not to flaunt oneself conspicuously in the front lines to kill or be killed. Hence Odysseus strives to conceal his own name, and critics have on occasion explained this concealment on the grounds that a name carries with it, magically, something of its bearers power, so that one gives it only cautiously and with a good reason. Be that as it may, here, too, Odysseus has played his trump card at the last possible moment.

The well-known scene follows. Odysseus and his companions blind the Cyclops, who cries out and calls the other Cyclopes. They come running and from outside the cave ask whether someone (μή τις) is carrying off his sheep, "Or is someone (μή τις)[22] killing you by guile or force?" (9.405–6). To which Polyphemus naturally responds: "Nobody is killing me by guile, and not by force." The Cyclopes then bid him farewell and go on their way, while Odysseus laughs with joy: "I laughed within myself since my name and my outstanding shrewdness (*mêtis*) had deceived them" (413–14).

The text here makes an untranslatable pun on the *mêtis* ("shrewdness") shown by the hero in calling himself Outis (9.410). Odysseus will recall this trick, his masterpiece as it were, when before the battle with the suitors he reflects disconsolately on the invasion of his house and the treachery of his serving-women (20.18ff.):

> Endure, my heart! You endured far worse than this
> the day when the Cyclops's uncontrollable violence
> ate your strong companions. You endured it
> until your shrewdness [*mêtis*] brought you
> out of the cave when you thought you were going to die.

Nearly all that he has—possessions, kingdom, palace, the loyalty of his countrymen, of his maid-servants and slaves—appears to be lost or denied to him. Only his I is intact, and in this extraordinary scene he duplicates himself,

---

20. Valgimigli 1964, 67: "He tells him smoothly (cf. 366, hiatus and spondee in the third foot, spondee in the fifth): 'I am called Nobody, Nobody is what my father and mother and all my relations call me.' He repeats himself to make sure that the groggy Cyclops will understand and not forget."
21. On the name "Polyphemus," see Burkert 1982, 23 and 153 n. 11.
22. On this double μή τις, see Schein 1970, 79ff.

creating an interior image of himself in which to take comfort and courage. It would be well worth examining this figure of the heart as the double of oneself and analyzing both the connotations and the instability of meaning implicit in it. But this is a task for another occasion.

Clearly, Odysseus here identifies himself with his ingenuity, the spiritual structure of his I that directed and made possible the expedient of the name Nobody. But curiously, although he recognizes himself in his invention, he is absolutely unwilling to accept the name "Nobody" on which he bases his escape. He cannot bear the idea of leaving the Cyclops without first having revealed to him the identity of the man who deceived him. He must re-establish his own identity and cancel the name "Nobody," the name which cancels his own fame, his own self.[23] Thus as he departs from the island he shouts out to the Cyclops, at great risk to himself and his companions: No, it is not Nobody, but Odysseus, son of Laertes, who has blinded you.

The dialogue between Odysseus and Polyphemus that follows would richly repay a detailed analysis. To exemplify, I cite only the passage in which the Cyclops, in response to Odysseus's declaration, describes his own error. To be sure, he had been told that one day Odysseus would come and would blind him

> but I was expecting that a man would come here
> who was immense and handsome, possessing great strength.
> But instead it is a little man, a man of no account, a weakling
> who has blinded me after overpowering me with wine.
>
> (9.513ff.)

Here is our cultivated and civilized man from the Cyclops's point of view: a dwarfish shyster. A true nobody! For this is what Polyphemus means by his *outidanos* ("a man of no account"), a word which conceals *outis* ("nobody") within it. So the Cyclops, too, can play with words and engage in a rhetorical vendetta.

This *bon mot*, which ridicules Odysseus's pseudonym by applying it to him literally, shatters any image we may have had of the Cyclops as an ingenuous, stupid savage. Polyphemus mocks Odysseus in the most Odyssean way. The contiguity between nature and culture here reveals itself on cultures own ground, and disposes of that dichotomy once and for all.[24]

The negative hyperboles that Polyphemus uses produce a portrait that corresponds to the opposite picture of himself and betrays the sentiments that he

---

23. See Horkheimer and Adorno (1972) on Odysseus's constant consolidating his "self" and making it an enlightened master. For Eisenberger (1973, 141) Odysseus's desire to re-establish his name and glory corresponds to the motif of the *eukhos* in the Iliadic hero's *aristeia*.

24. We have already noted other examples of rhetorical cleverness on the Cyclops's part, like his parody of the etiquette of hospitality, or his boasting of his disrespect for the gods (273ff.), intended, probably, to terrify his prisoners. In addition, the quickness with which Polyphemus asks where Odysseus has beached his ship (279–80) shows considerable subtlety. Polyphemus is stupid and intelligent by turns, as the narrative may require. Contrariwise, the shrewd Odysseus fails to realize that by giving his name to Polyphemus he exposes himself to a formal curse.

feels toward the other, the stranger. Here, too, the portrait is formed of appearances that compare and contrast, but indicate nothing other than the Cyclops's desires. Like the cultured and civilized, who describe the savage as the antithesis of themselves, so the savage sees the civilized man as the antithesis of his own characteristics.

The specular image instructs us how each produces his knowledge of the other, but not what the I and the Other are once we discard our own fears and desires.

A nobody! Is this the great hero whose adventures so fascinate and enchant us? A dwarfish shyster, a nobody who saves himself by assuming a name that corresponds to his real stature? Here we measure the potential perilousness of the Cyclops's definition. If we pay no heed, if we remain attached to the enchanting I of Odysseus, it is because we read stubbornly closing our ears to the words of the Cyclops. In so doing we construct the consistency of Odysseus's I and thus prefigure the coherence of our own.

But let us turn to the name of Odysseus.

Odysseus redoubles his verbal attack on the Cyclops and regrets ostentatiously that he did not send him dead down to Hades. But now Polyphemus possesses the heros true name and can thus attach to it a formal curse, invoking his father Poseidon the Earthshaker. This curse will be fulfilled, and Odysseus will arrive home alone, without companions, immersed in troubles.

It is at this point that the name Odysseus acquires the unlucky meaning that the text attributes to it at certain points. Let us examine one such instance. Following the shipwreck that Poseidon has brought upon him, Odysseus is swimming toward the land of the Phaeacians, when he realizes that the coast is rocky, and that he can reach the shore only at the risk of being thrown onto the rocks. He laments to himself and closes his monologue by saying (*Od.* 5.423): "For I know how the famous Earthshaker hates me (*odôdustai*)." The verb *odôdustai* (he hates me), from *odussomai*,[25] plays on the name Odysseus. And it is quite true that Poseidon the Earthshaker, with his wrath against Odysseus, activates the name, makes it significant, as if "Odysseus" meant "he who is hated by Poseidon." Elsewhere the poet explains how Odysseus as an infant received his name. The child has just been born and has not yet been named, when Autolycus, his maternal grandfather, arrives and is naturally consulted. Here is his response: "My son-in-law and my daughter, give him the name I tell

---

25. Ὀδύσ(σ)ασθαι, "hate," "be angry with" derives according to Frisk from a root **od-* found also in the Latin *odium*; see Chantraine *DELG*. But there is no agreement among scholars on the meaning of the word and the force of the word play. Dimock (1963, 58) takes the name to mean "he who causes pain" and is followed by Schein 1970, 82–83; in this case the word would be related to ὀδύνη or ὀδύρομαι. See Russo 1985, 248–49. Whatever the exact sense of Ὀδυσσεύς here, it is worth noting that the meaning is activated not only in the famous episode at *Od.* 19.406ff. but also in this scene where Polyphemus attaches Poseidon's curse to Odysseus's name. See now Peradotto (1990).

you. Since I come here hating (*odussamenos*) many men and women on the fruitful earth, let him be named Odysseus" (19.406ff.).

Odysseus's name is given him in accord with epic convention, which demands that sons take their names from some special quality, contingency, or event in the life of their fathers. On this explanation, then, Odysseus is so called because at the moment of his birth it happens that his grandfather Autolycus hates many men and women, rather than because Odysseus himself is the object of such a hatred.

The curse that the Cyclops attaches to Odysseus's name alters matters. As we have seen, the hero himself makes a pun on his own name and the wrath of Poseidon. His name no longer refers to the hatred that his grandfather nurtured at the moment of Odysseus's birth, but to the hatred that Odysseus has earned from Poseidon for having blinded the latters son Polyphemus.

When we hear Odysseus's name, then, what is it that we think of? Of his grandfather or of the Cyclops? Or of his martial virtues, through which he has ennobled his name in the *Iliad* and created a reputation for himself? To think of Autolycus is to read in Odysseus's name facts that are wholly extraneous to its bearer, and quite alien to his own experience. In what sense is this a "proper name"? How can it be "proper" to Odysseus, when it refers to another?

If we think of the Cyclops, on the other hand, Odysseus's name will recall as well the name "Nobody," the diminutive trickster, and the heros guile. Can we even recognize in this narrative the heroic splendor of the character from the *Iliad*?

Odysseus's name would thus appear to embody diverse narratives which present various facets of the hero—whichever meet the storys needs at a given point. Indeed, when Athena wishes to extort from Zeus a decision favorable to Odysseus, she too plays on the verb *odussomai*, asking reproachfully whether the father of the gods feels odium for Odysseus (*ôdusao*, 1.62).

Since the name Odysseus takes its meaning from the adventure in which the hero finds himself, it functions now as cause, now as effect of his narratives. It is thus not at the root of his adventures, the immutable author of them, but merely reflects them. The name Odysseus becomes part of the story, a narrative element, and like all narrative elements mutable and arbitrary. It replaces a simple pronoun, "I."

We saw above how the concept, the representation of Homeric man, as described in the Cyclops episode and in the atmosphere of the Phaeacians civilized hospitality, is fractured and dispersed into phantasmic representations lacking consistency of reference. But even the "I" of Odysseus, this more personal and intimate representation of Homeric man, and one that we as readers seize upon out of desire and anxiety, mimetically recognizing ourselves in it— even this "I" can be pinned down only as that which at every moment of the narrative says "I."

One could go further along these lines—I have tried to do so in my book *Odysseus Polutropos*—and recall other instances of this fracturing of the "I," of the consciousness and wakefulness of Odysseus. It is enough to recall his sudden lapses into sleep, as when he falls asleep a few miles from Ithaca and his jealous and curious companions open the bag of winds and destroy their chances of returning home; or when on the Phaeacian ship he falls into dreamless slumber and finds himself on an unknown shore which is, in fact, Ithaca. Nor should one overlook his visit to the kingdom of the dead, his exploration of the bottomless secret of the nature of death, and the phrase applied to him by Circe when she calls him "twice-dead." Odysseus seems to live on the borderline of twin existences. On one side he has an alert consciousness of himself and others; on the other he lives within the eclipse of self, a state bordering on sleep, the brother of death (Pucci 1987, 153–54).

It may seem at this point that we have embarked on a fruitless expedition and returned with little or nothing to show for it. But that is far from being the case. This construction and dissolution of the epistemological schema implicit in the story of the Cyclops is not simply an exercise or parlor game, but a necessity. And the necessity is that of respecting the principles that make up great literature. For its task is nothing but to weave and unweave endlessly the significations of our life, the representations of our being. The work of literature is prodigious, setting in motion the most elaborate and sophisticated epistemological and linguistic mechanisms to penetrate the impossible secret of our existence. And this it does over and over.

CHAPTER 9

Odysseus Narrator:
The End of the Heroic Race

The familiarity we feel we have with Odysseus, the knowledge we share of his adventures and so to speak of his mind and habits, depends in some measure on the fact that it is Odysseus himself who narrates and fabricates the Odysseus we think we know. Through four books and through many accounts of himself, later in the poem, Odysseus narrates his own adventures, presents himself as a solid character, and tells us his troubles, anxieties, and hopes. Few characters in ancient literature speak of themselves so openly and clearly, or at such length, as he does.

As he narrates his adventures he opens up a space in the Homeric narrative, and we become his immediate listeners: we learn about him from his voice and words that, as Eumaeus affirms, are like those of a poet.

Let us recall that one of Odysseus's traditional epithets, *poluainos*, characterizes him as a "man with many *ainoi*," that is, as a man able to tell many significant, relevant stories.[1] We find this epithet of Odysseus in XI.430, where Socus so addresses Odysseus: ὦ Ὀδυσεῦ πολύαινε δόλων ἆτ' ἠδὲ πόνοιο

---

1. It is interesting that the epithet *polumuthos* is never applied to Odysseus. This epithet occurs at III.214 to characterize Menelaus, who is not *polumuthos*, and at ii.200 to characterize Telemachus, who in the eyes of Eurymachus is *polumuthos*, that is, "too talkative" or "a big mouth." On the etymological origin of *muthos*, Gregory Nagy accepts the proposal that it derives from the same root as *muô*: "I have my mouth closed," namely from an onomatopoeic *mu*, with the primary meaning of opening and closing the lips (1990, 32). See also Chantraine *DELG*, 728.

[O Odysseus, skillful in many stories, insatiable of tricks and toil]. Here the stories (*ainoi*) that Odysseus can narrate and tricks that Odysseus can use are combined to describe the typical heroic "being" of Odysseus.[2] The epithet *poluainos* occurs in the *Odyssey* only once: in the invitation the Sirens address to Odysseus, in a passage that, as I have shown, mimes Iliadic diction:[3]

δεῦρ' ἄγ' ἰών, πολύαιν' 'Οδυσεῦ, μέγα κῦδος 'Αχαιῶν,
νῆα κατάστησον, ἵνα νωιτέρην ὄπ' ἀκούσῃς.

(xii.184)

[Come here, come, Odysseus, skillful in many stories, great glory of the Achaeans, stop the ship in order that you hear our voice.]

It is relevant that the Sirens call Odysseus *poluainos* in the context of the stories that Odysseus is narrating to the Phaeacians: for Odysseus, the narrator, by telling the Phaeacians that he was so defined by the Sirens—who are Muses of Hades, Muses of death—delivers to his listeners the high appreciation the Sirens have of his skill as a narrator. A subtle doubling of the image looms for an instant through this epithet. Even though they are Iliadic Muses, they have the Odyssean power of charming (*thelgein*). They choose, therefore, the right epithet for Odysseus, who is telling the story of his encounter with them in the house of Alcinous, charming all his listeners and obtaining immense gifts from them.

The implication of *ainos* as a profitable speech becomes emphatically clear during the *homilia* of Eumaeus and Odysseus, when the swineherd praises the *ainos* of Odysseus (xiv.508–9):

ὦ γέρον, αἶνος μέν τοι ἀμύμων, ὃν κατέλεξας,
οὐδέ τί πω παρὰ μοῖραν ἔπος νηκερδὲς ἔειπες·

[Old man, the story you have narrated is perfect: you did not speak an improper (or unprofitable) word.]

In the story that Odysseus tells disguised as an old man, he presents himself as a retainer of Odysseus, a fellow soldier, who, during a cold night under the walls of Troy, badly needed a cloak. He tells how Odysseus, with a clever fiction, obtained the desired cloak for him. Odysseus invents this story presently in order to obtain a cloak from Eumaeus for himself. And, of course, he gets it.

---

2. For *ainos*, see Pucci 1977, 76n3, and Nagy 1990, 31, where he writes: "*Ainos* is authoritative speech: it is an affirmation, a marked speech–act, made by and for a marked social group." *Poluainos* may mean both "famous" and "with many stories"; and for the specific use in this latter sense, implying that Odysseus uses the stories as weapons, see Meuli 1975, 2:742; Heubeck 1983, 323–24; and Pucci 1987, 60.
3. See Chapter One.

Yet to begin a narrative, notwithstanding the desire of the narrator, is not an unproblematic action if the narrator is not invited to speak. Thus, in the passage we are examining, Odysseus begins by asking for a sort of permission to speak and by excusing himself for doing so (xiv.462–67):

κέκλυθι νῦν Εὔμαιε καὶ ἄλλοι πάντες ἑταῖροι,
εὐξάμενός τι ἔπος ἐρέω· οἶνος γὰρ ἀνώγει
ἠλεός, ὅς τ᾽ ἐφέηκε πολύφρονά περ μάλ᾽ ἀεῖσαι
καί θ᾽ ἁπαλὸν γελάσαι, καί τ᾽ ὀρχήσασθαι ἀνῆκε,
καί τι ἔπος προέηκεν ὅ πέρ τ᾽ ἄρρητον ἄμεινον.

[Listen now Eumaeus and all you other companions what tale I will tell, boasting. For silly wine bids me, which drives even the wisest to sing and to laugh idly, and rouses him to dance, and makes him drop a tale which were better untold. But since I raised my voice, I will not hide it.]

Interpreters are puzzled by εὐξάμενος which here could be understood as "wishing," as Stanford suggests: "I have formed a wish and will speak" (1962, 234); or "boasting," as Hoekstra prefers (1989, 226; but see Muellner 1976, 97). The participle most likely refers to the boldness from the wine, which allows the disguised Odysseus to speak and tell a tall tale about himself and Odysseus.

Wine here is personified as foolish and as giving orders: Odysseus therefore speaks boastingly under the order of wine. Surely Odysseus fakes this intoxication, perhaps for the purpose of an authorization, a pretext, a justification to speak, especially about himself. He fakes his intoxication, but the *diêgêsis* makes clear that he speaks in order to test the swineherd and to obtain either his mantle or that of one of the others.

The tale, therefore, is not an innocent or simple affair; it seeks not only to please the audience with a well told and proper story, but also glimpses at gain. The tale is invented, of course, but Odysseus knows that his audience has no way to check its truth. For the audience, then, truth and fiction are indistinguishable. The fictional and "autobiographical" narrative therefore invents its own truth, and its own narrator. And further, this narrative invents its own trusting audience, for instance, the gullible Phaeacians.

It seems therefore that while Odysseus's audience implies that he speaks about a real event (although he is excited by wine), we extratextual readers/ listeners realize that both the narrator and his audience are mere *functions* of the narrative itself. They have reality and place only within the narrative.

As the protocols of the *Odyssey's* poetics underscore the production of pleasure and enchantment through the intelligence and ruse of *mêtis*, Odysseus is here a function of this poetics.

His four books of tales (ix–xii) will see him both as their plot–agent and as their narrator, and yet these tales precede him. Ethnological research has empirically shown (Germain 1954) that most of his tales have deep roots in folklore, so that Odysseus is the plot–agent and narrator of stories that precede him. Nor does he need to have lived through in order to narrate them. But we do not need empirical evidence to realize that Odysseus in these four books assimilates the tales through his persona, becoming, so to speak, the character appropriate to those tales. Homer uses Odysseus as Odysseus uses his own character in his tale to Eumaeus. Again he serves the poetics of the *Odyssey*.

By having him as narrator before a larger audience, the master narrator produces the scene essential in all narrative: an author, master of his narrative, and of his audience.

To think of the scene in this way, as a fiction, does not decrease our pleasure. On the contrary, the mirror effects of this *ainos* are deliciously gripping: Odysseus invents himself as a sympathetic rogue, presenting an iconoclastic portrait of himself that we find not infrequently in his stories[4] and that the swineherd cannot fail to appreciate; he tells a tale about getting a cloak—in order to get a cloak! Our pleasure, as *extratextual* readers, is increased by the double cunning that Odysseus performs, for he dupes Eumaeus and his companions, who consider Odysseus's fiction to be history, while winking at us.

Eventually we recognize an allusion to a passage of the *Iliad* in which Odysseus is performing his best Iliadic *aristeia* (II.182–83). Or is it the reverse and is it the *Iliad* that refers to this passage of the *Odyssey*?[5] Be that as it may, this allusion intimates that part of the meaning of Odysseus's tale lies outside his text and therefore outside his intended effects and purposes. Homer, accordingly, whether he intended it or not, puts in Odysseus's mouth an expression that acquires full meaning through another text, producing effects of reading that Odysseus could not intend. The notion of intertextuality emerges and shatters the image of narrator as full master of his story, fully responsible for its meaning. To the extent that the intertextual significance emerges through a mere repetition of epic diction, whether or not Homer wanted it, this diction becomes the apparent author responsible for this effect of reading we have traced.

This reading scene with its intricate complications provides a paradigm for our analysis of one group of Odysseus's narrations in the *Odyssey*, the *Alkinou apologoi* (Books 9–12), Odysseus's long narrative to the Phaeacians.[6]

---

4. One instance is his recognition scene, xxiv.266–79.

5. For the intertextual relation between the *Iliad* and the *Odyssey* in this story, see Chapter Six.

6. The other collection of stories is generally called "the Ithacan stories," which Odysseus tells, disguised as a beggar and in order to protect that disguise, while learning the situation in his house. The one we have just analyzed is part of this collection. These two groups are different in their function and rhetoric: the Ithacan stories are explicitly false (xiii.254–55; xix.203), whereas the *Alkinou apologoi* are presented as truthful. The Ithacan stories are lying tales with the purpose of hiding Odysseus's identity: they are both perlocutionary and constative speech acts (see Todorov 1977, 59ff.). For an analysis of the Ithacan stories, see Goldhill 1991, 37–47. The two series of speeches have, however, a common quality: they are discourses about the past of the narrator with limited relevance to the immediate actions and deeds of the people concerned.

The concerns that guide this interpretation of some aspects of Odysseus's narration essentially stem from the structure of the "reading scene."[7] Such scenes are dramatizations, within larger narratives, of an event in which one character becomes a narrator and the other(s) becomes listener(s). These roles are textually determined. The narrator is not the generator of his tale, but is inscribed in it; he is a fictional being, referred to as "I," who through that "I" acquires the same solidity that we, the readers, imagine in ourselves.[8]

The Narrator

I am concerned here with describing how Odysseus becomes a narrator, and what sort of narrator he is, since he does not speak as the hero he was but as the wanderer he has become (νόστον ἐμὸν πολυκηδέ' ἐνίσπω, ix.36). What were Homer's purposes (to the extent that they can be determined) in having Odysseus deliver this long narrative; what are Odysseus's own purposes (his *doloi?*) as he takes the floor?

On the last day of Odysseus's stay in Alcinous's palace, Odysseus invites the poet Demodocus to sing about the famous horse which Epeios and Athena built and Odysseus conveyed into the city. During this narration Odysseus cries, and though he tries to hide the tears, Alcinous notices and insistently urges him to reveal his name. At ix.19–20 Odysseus reveals his identity, carefully protected all the previous day: "I am Odysseus, son of Laertes, an object of care for all men because of my wiles, and my glory [*kleos*] reaches heaven."[9]

---

7. I accept the expression Narrator I for Homer and Narrator II and III for each narrator embedded in Narrator I. Accordingly, I call the audience and readers of Homer "narratees," at, what Calame calls, the communication level. However, when no confusion emerges I have preferred to avoid technical terms. Also, instead of "focalization," I have often used the more traditional expression "point of view," following Richardson 1990.

8. For an exemplary analysis of such a type of scene, see De Man 1979: "The necessary presence of a moment of utterance and of the interpretive moment of understanding has nothing to do with the empirical situation naively represented in the scene: the notions of audience and of narrator are only the misleading figuration of a linguistic structure. And just as the indeterminacy of reference generates the illusion of a subject, a narrator, and a reader, it also generates the metaphor of temporality. A narrative endlessly tells the story of its own denominational aberration on various levels of rhetorical complexity."

9. On these two lines, a great deal has been written. See especially Rüter 1969, 254; Pucci 1987, 61–62; Peradotto 1990, 141–42; and Segal 1994, 90–101.

Translated in this way, the text shows by what hyperboles Odysseus depicts his truly universal notoriety: everyone, on earth and in heaven, knows him and his tricks.[10]

The first clause: "I am Odysseus" (*eim' Oduseus*) is formally unique in Homer, and implies that Odysseus thinks that his name is very well known, as the mention of his *kleos* confirms.

His name is significant—the "hated one," as the narrative will later explain—and accordingly the name "Odysseus" in the phrase: "I am Odysseus" is an epithet and a metonymy of "I": "I am the hated one"; "I, the hated one"; "the hated one is a figurative way of saying I".

This implies that the name does not really identify anything and that, in order to know who Odysseus is, one has to know that he is really the very person that the legend about him speaks of. Accordingly Odysseus would be the Odysseus of the legend, but how can he prove that he is that one? Luckily the Phaeacians do not ask and have a poet who sings that *kleos*.

With this heavy emphasis on the tradition in which Odysseus is inscribed, the *Odyssey* perhaps intends to disclaim that he is an historical, real person. Or better said: the *Odyssey* only claims that he exists in the tradition, whatever historicity this tradition may have.

The hyperbole shocks as a proud presentation of himself. Yet it might have also a sort of performative function. I mean that Odysseus's glory reaches heaven because he has pronounced it so, here on this line and now on this occasion. In fact, in the four passages in Homer in which the *kleos* of someone or of something reaches heaven, this someone or something is perfectly unknown.[11] The hyperbole is doubly enhanced by the very anonymity of the person or thing so glorified, but it produces for the first time a fame. It becomes performative. The case of Odysseus's *kleos* is different because he is certainly already well known: his wiles (*doloi*) have also an Iliadic tradition (XI.430), and Demodocus has sung the story of the wooden horse. The adaptation, therefore, of this hyperbole to him is odd: it may suggest an ironic smile inviting the audience to think that Odysseus's fame must be really most powerful and at the same time a pure invention, since it has reached even the fabulous (imaginary) Phaeacians. It is indeed a reason for wonder. The Phaeacians themselves must think so: they certainly never expected a sacred monster like Odysseus to land on their shores.

The question whether the performative force of the statement should imply that Odysseus will gain glory (*kleos*) as a character of the *Odyssey*, through the tricks and ruses he performs in this poem, is difficult to answer. In effect these

---

10. Alternatively: "an object of care for men because of all my wiles." Pazdernick (1995, 348 n.5) notes that the double meaning "demonstrates the hero's trickiness at a verbal level."

11. I borrow this argument from Segal 1983. In *Il.* VIII.191, Nestor's shield, whose *kleos* reaches heaven, "has not been heard before and will not be heard of again" (Kirk 1985, ad loc.); in viii.74 the quarrel between Achilles and Odysseus reaches heaven, but is nowhere else attested in Greek epic (Nagy 1979, 21–25); and finally in xix.108, Odysseus attributes a *kleos* that reaches heaven to his wife Penelope, in an expression obviously hyperbolic and complimentary.

tricks become known and famous especially through the traditions whose monumental poem is the *Odyssey*. Yet it is unclear whether the *Odyssey* ever attributes *kleos* to its hero on account of these fabulous ruses, and in general for the sufferings and struggles of his return (*nostos*).

My feeling is that the *Odyssey* can only bestow an ironic *kleos* on Odysseus for his adventures, since this notion does not play any important role in its poetics, as we will see.

If all these remarks are correct, the audience should be able to perceive the fictional marks of Odysseus's self-presentation, and appreciate the amusing innuendoes that the name and the boasting trigger and that in effect play down the seriousness of the proud statements.

The narrative that follows is attached to Odysseus's name and reputation as a trickster, and flows, so to speak, from the identified *persona* of its author.[12] Whatever the ontological nature of the narrator, we have his name ("I am Odysseus") and his voice. His speaking in the first person creates the necessity of an intersubjective reading, that is, one that puts in contact two subjects, two "I's"—the narrator's and the reader's. This intersubjective relation provides the grounds for us readers to attribute to Odysseus's "I" the same consistency which we attribute to our own. A necessary complicity ensues.

Speaking in the first person, Odysseus distinguishes himself from professional bards, such as Demodocus and Phemius. He is a hero, not a poet, and as a guest of the Phaeacians is asked to tell the story of his return. Polite, he begins his response with praise of the banquet and its festivity (2–11; here, too, wine is not far from his narrative, 9–10); he praises Demodocus's song, which celebrated him as the destroyer of Troy (*ptoliporthos*) in Book 8.

Odysseus also politely praises the poet's voice, with a generic hyperbole,[13] and celebrates the whole festive event as a "beautiful accomplishment" (*telos khariesteron* 5) and as the most beautiful thing (*kalliston* 11) in his mind. By using the expression *telos khariesteron*, he refers to and corrects Alcinous's previous judgment; earlier, when Alcinous realized that Odysseus was weeping at Demodocus's song, he said that Odysseus was not enjoying it (*ou gar kharizomenos* viii.537–39). Odysseus now assures him that the song was beautiful, even if he was weeping. The *kharis* of song is a conventional compliment,[14] but an important one in this connection: it distinguishes Demodocus's

---

12. Goldhill, after having shown the representative force of the name Odysseus, writes: "To say 'I am Odysseus' is not simply self–reference but also self-representation—it begins to tell the story of Odysseus" (1991, 36).

13. θεοῖς ἐναλίγκιος αὐδήν "similar to the gods in his voice." This epithet is generic because it also refers to the voice of the herald (κῆρυξ; see e.g., XIX.250). (A separate question is raised by the fact that Homeric κῆρυξ is cognate with Sanskrit *kârú* "singer," "poet.")

Odysseus therefore uses a formulaic expression that repeats the epithet θεῖος used by Alcinous at viii.539. A slightly inconsistent feature of this formulaic expression is that it assimilates αὐδή, which means "human voice" (see Clay 1974, *Hermes* 102:129–36), to the divine voice. See Ford 1992, 174.

14. *Kharis* conveys the notion of "pleasure, mirth" in conventional descriptions of poetry and its effects. See Nagy 1979, 91; MacLachlan 1993, 105.

song from Odysseus's defining it as beautiful, pretty, while no one will say the same of Odysseus's story. Instead, his story will produce a much more powerful effect: it will enchant and bewitch his audience (xi.333–34). Since this is the effect the *Odyssey* praises in poetry, Odysseus, as narrator, functions as the representative of the *Odyssey*'spoetics.[15]

After his praise of the banquet and the poet, Odysseus lays the ground for his narrative. Alcinous's heart desires to learn Odysseus's lamentable pains, but they are so many that Odysseus does not know where to begin (ix.12ff.):

σοὶ δ᾽ ἐμὰ κήδεα θυμὸς ἐπετράπετο στονόεντα
εἴρεσθ᾽, ὄφρ᾽ ἔτι μᾶλλον ὀδυρόμενος στεναχίζω.
τί πρῶτόν τοι ἔπειτα, τί δ᾽ ὑστάτιον καταλέξω;
κήδε᾽ ἐπεί μοι πολλὰ δόσαν θεοὶ Οὐρανίωνες.
νῦν δ᾽ ὄνομα πρῶτον μυθήσομαι

[Your heart is turned[16] to learn my grievous woes so that I may weep and lament more. What shall I tell you first, then, and what last? For many are the woes the gods of heaven have given me. First I will tell my name . . .]

The question of where to begin the narrative defines Odysseus as a skillful narrator. The *Odyssey* began in just the same way: the poet asked the Muse to begin "from whatever point of that narrative" (τῶν ἁμόθεν γε, i.10).[17] Odysseus, just as the poet of the *Odyssey*, assesses the possibility of beginning the narrative from a certain point, amid so many woes, a point that will not necessarily mirror the real flow of things and events.[18] With the verb καταλέγειν of line 14 (cf. vii.15), Odysseus shows that he can order his woes in a catalogue,

---

15. See Pucci 1987, 191ff. At xvii.518ff., Eumaeus equates Odysseus to a divine poet; here too Odysseus is said to θελγεῖν (enchant) his listener.

16. With the exception of Alcinous in this passage and Helen in iv.260, the subject of the metaphorical use of τρέπω with an activity of the mind is limited to gods, Zeus in particular; see e.g., XVII.546; V.676; iii.147; xix.479.

17. Victoria Pedrick recognizes in the poet's gesture of i.11 a self-confident authority: "Behind the seemingly modest gesture of asking for a starting point, lies a confidence in his own [the poet's] powers: anywhere the Muse decides, the narrator expresses himself ready to begin. So much is evident; but a further self-confidence is at work, since by stipulating the *termini* the narrator is *not* leaving the choice strictly up to the Muse. She is constrained by a plan suggested by the information in the proem: the narrator wants to start after the fall of Troy, but before the slaughter of Helios' cattle" (1992, 49). I surmise the same self-confidence in Odysseus who, however, as Pedrick writes, "makes very different choices from the main narrator in the epic's opening. He begins directly with his name, and the verb he uses— *katalegein*—reflects his intent to proceed straightforwardly in his intent" (60).

18. "À la recherche" of Proust begins with the famous phrase: "Longtemps, je me suis couché de bonne heure." Paul Ricoeur writes: "Ce 'longtemps' suivi par le parfait accompli renvoie à un anterieur quasi immemorial. Il n'empeche que cette phrase est la première du livre et vaut commencement narratif" (1990, 189).

not necessarily following any chronology. Thereby a rhetorical effect emerges, capable of impairing the truth of the narrative.

Odysseus is the narrator not of his *bios*, but of his *nostos* (return); in this he follows, naturally, in the wake of Narrator I and supports the fiction that in the *Odyssey*, Odysseus is only the hero of return (ix.37–38, x.14–15, xi.369).

Having named himself as author and given his return as the theme, Odysseus ponders the effects his narrative will have on him (lines 11–12). He foresees that he "will weep and lament more" [ὄφρ᾽ ἔτι μᾶλλον ὀδυρόμενος στεναχίζω], that is, presumably more than he had during Demodocus's song about the fall of Troy. Then he had cried like a woman taken into slavery, prodded by the soldiers as she sees her husband lying dead on the ground (viii.521–31).

Yet Odysseus does not cry any more. In fact his narrative mesmerizes the Phaeacians. His words, ὄφρ᾽ ἔτι μᾶλλον ὀδυρόμενος στεναχίζω, then function to announce the woeful theme of his narrative to his immediate audience; and to the extratextual readers, it indicates that a new and unexpected Odysseus is taking the floor.

This line occurs also at xi.214 and xvi.195. In the former passage, Odysseus tries three times to embrace the *psukhê* of his mother, but fails each time; embittered, he asks her why she does not stand firm so that he may embrace her. He then asks: "or is it a phantom [*eidôlon*] noble Persephone has sent, so that I may weep and lament more?" [ὄφρ᾽ ἔτι μᾶλλον ὀδυρόμενος στεναχίζω].

Odysseus expects a certain consistency and presence of his mother. When he feels frustrated by its replacement with a shadowy form, he expresses his terrible frustration in a line that promises more tears, but no tears come.

In the second passage, Telemachus, amazed and skeptical about Odysseus's sudden and miraculous change from an old man to a young and vigorous one, shouts (xvi.194–95):

οὐ σύ γ᾽ Ὀδυσσεύς ἐσσι πατὴρ ἐμός, ἀλλά με δαίμων
θέλγει, ὄφρ᾽ ἔτι μᾶλλον ὀδυρόμενος στεναχίζω.

[You are not Odysseus, my father: a daimon charms me so that I may weep and lament more.]

Telemachus cannot believe that this person, who has been mysteriously and suddenly transformed, is not some god or daimon; here, too, the tag line ὄφρ᾽ ἔτι μᾶλλον ὀδυρόμενος στεναχίζω indicates the likelihood of a lament to follow. But none does; on the contrary, after a few words from Odysseus, Telemachus recognizes his father. Both father and son cry only for joy.

It seems therefore that this tag line occurs in contexts of a person's unexpected metamorphosis. In its denotational value, the line promises more tears; but connotationally, it foretells only a change, which, because unexpected, is deeply frustrating and threatens—but does not produce—many tears. When we apply the thematic context evoked by this formula to our passage, we may infer that the idea of a change is not far away from Odysseus's mind. He was the subject of Demodocus's song as the heroic destroyer of Troy (*ptoliporthos*); now he must speak of himself as a castaway. The line therefore conveys his frustration about this change, about the near-unrecognizability of his being. He refers as well to the new role he assumes as he is beginning to narrate his griefs, a role that transforms him from doer into raconteur.

The meaning of this transformation is clearer when it is read in the context of the scenes over which Odysseus weeps. The famous simile that compares Odysseus's weeping at the end of Demodocus's song (viii.521ff.) with that of the wife of a fallen Trojan (of an Andromache, according to Nagy) has been interpreted in many slightly different ways (see Nagy 1979, Pucci 1987). In my view the simile intimates the death of Odysseus as a doer, and his emergence as a "reader" (Pucci 1987, 221–23). Now the pitiful reader of his heroic deeds becomes the reader/narrator of his long series of losses and gains. His narration, with the demise of the old tradition about the heroic race, opens up a new fascinating and pleasurable poetry.

Odysseus's I-Narrative and Odyssean Poetics

When we inquire why Homer wanted Odysseus to tell his own story, we find some critical response. It has been suggested, for example, that by narrating this story and thus re-living his experience, Odysseus restores himself to himself after the long period of self-oblivion on the island of Calypso.[19]

Though this view has an outstanding pedigree and powerful advocates, I prefer to read Odysseus's story of his return as the unveiling of an identity impossible to grasp. Though the *Odyssey* tempts us to read it as a Bildungsroman, or a novel of the self, explicitly superimposed on that narrative of return is the story of an obsessive repetition of figures of difference. For the return is neither a return to the same nor a journey to discover an identity, but rather a voyage in which the recuperation of the self is constantly promised and compromised. The

---

19. Charles Segal, for instance, puts this quite eloquently: "The very act of recounting his adventures is a mark of Odysseus's readiness to return. He has lived through a full complement of experiences, carrying him from the heroic to the fantastic, from the intelligible to the nonhuman, from war to inaction, from his position as a leader of men, surrounded by his companions, to total isolation in the seas off Thrinacia and Scheria. Now, no longer immediately involved, he has reached a point of integration for reentrance into his humanity. In his tale to the Phaeacians, he is making the synthesis final and strong, fixing the past in readiness for the future" (1994, 19).

phases of the repeated themes are diverse in measure, intensity, and relative results, but the variations do not upset the basic coherence of the motif. As some of these essays make clear, the humanity of Odysseus is not easy to define. In the *Odyssey*, the notion of his humanity rotates around his determination to return home, as a mortal, as the husband of Penelope. He is presented as a lost image of his heroic past, a castaway who is the last returning hero of the heroic age ("Now all the heroes, as many as escaped sheer destruction, were at home . . . but Odysseus alone was longing for his return and his wife" i.11–12). He is shown as the sole survivor in a culture that no longer shares, unless in the narrative, the frame of mind of the old heroic times.[20]

Even in his home, only Penelope belongs spiritually to his heroic age. And, rightly so, she shall be granted *kleos*.

What humanity, then, which self, is Odysseus recovering during his narrative? How to describe them, unless through the many lapses, temptations, and obscurations that make them tentative and fragile? Let us recall the Odysseus who rushes to snatch two companions from lotus-induced forgetfulness, and then remains one year with Circe, and seven with Calypso! The return then is the story of alluring temptations to forget, and of forgetfulness. The poetry of this return celebrates the power of enchanting, of luring and bewitching: Odysseus himself is the master of enchantment, and is tempted by the enticing song of the Sirens. But even so, he nevertheless resists and returns. Yet a song that constantly prizes its power of enchantment, and that successfully enchants us even by keeping death away from Odysseus, depicts a specific humanity: not so much the self-awareness of mortality which defines our humanity, but rather the wishful escape from it, the pleasurable traps in which to ensnare death, the tricks for survival. By enchanting us in this way, Odyssean poetry indulges in our fear of death, and, like the song of the Sirens, lulls our awareness of being toward death.[21]

The goal of escaping the jaws of death induces Odysseus into a zigzagging movement that always removes him from any stable form of himself. The many recognition scenes, in which Odysseus's disguises and concealments are dramatized and exposed, produce only new differences that mark him and suspend his self-identity. And difference only triggers new scenes of recognition in an ever baffling recuperation of Odysseus's self. The hero and the reader get pleasure from each adventure (loss of the self, disguise and recognition), and this succession of the analogous episodes could continue forever (Pucci 1987).[22] In

---

20. Of the surviving heroes—Nestor, Menelaus, Diomedes, and Idomeneus—the *Odyssey* shows the first two. The melancholy of the encounter with Menelaus reveals that the heroic past is only an obsessive memory of pain, while for Nestor it remains a narration to edify the young Telemachus and Pisistratus.

21. The sameness of effects that the *Odyssey* and the song of the Sirens produce should logically require that either we readers stop reading the *Odyssey*, or that we be allowed to hear the Sirens' song.

22. Also see Detienne and Pucci 1988; and Pedrick 1994. I insist on this endless process: even in Book 24, after his successful fight against the suitors and reunion

this endless pursuit of an impossible identity for its hero, the text discloses its own anxiety about its own identity and difference in relation to the heroic epic, for instance to the *Iliad*.

Odysseus himself spins the humiliating and exhilarating narrative of his losses.[23] However, Odysseus's most important possession, his life, is never lost. Thus the I-narrative and its discourse of *mêtis* bring into light the very success of his survival, the modes of his being for survival, his mistrust, his isolation, his specific tone of resignation and endurance. Only the voice of the I could manifest so directly the continuity and the very presence of the self. Only the voice of the I could express so freely the pleasure of narrating the triumph of intelligence over the dark power of death, as for instance Odysseus does, with exhilaration, after having tricked the Cyclops (ix, 413–14). It is the discourse of Odysseus's being as care for survival that the *Odyssey* ceaselessly likes to repeat in total syntony with his audience that would never want to stop listening to him.

Odysseus survives in the world of fairy tales, of long sailings, and of civic strife. Homer has chosen that the I-narrative should describe the world of the fairy tales, the world of total otherness, to depict which the heroic traditional language would have been more betrayed. For Odysseus is not represented in relation with his peers, in dialogue with the other kings, and in military fights, but in situations in which he must invent his own language, with bold adaptations from the traditional one.

Furthermore the I-narrative bestows the narration of fabulous encounters with the sense of a lived experience. As Reinhardt 1948, 68 writes: "The I-narrative is the form through which the old fabulous lore becomes new in so far as it becomes rapture and at the same time life-experience; it acquires the remoteness of the fairy tales and simultaneously the closeness of the self."

The newness of the new world, spiritually removed from the heroic age, is represented by the old world of fairy tales, as though the complete oblivion of that glorious epoch were leaving room for the monstrosity of what is totally unexpected.

---

with his wife, Odysseus again plays the perverse comedy of disguising himself before his old father. He presents a roguish impersonation of himself, as a sort of ladies' man, a successful guest; he declares that Odysseus is dead, and provokes his father to such a point that the poor old man swoons. To anyone who dismisses this final act in Odysseus's perverse comedy as a late addition, I say that this new poet—if indeed he was a new one—understood Odysseus perfectly well. Already Aristotle (*Poetics* 1459b, 15) saw that the *Odyssey* has a complex plot as "it has recognitions throughout."

23. According to Stewart, Odysseus's "misfortune at the beginning of his adventures with the Cyclops, began a process that actually amounts to the destruction of Odysseus the epic hero" (1976, 34). According to Most (1989), the Ithacan stories "are uniformly tales of misfortune."

Between fairy tales and true experience

Homer lets his character have the floor and frees the Muses of any responsibility for Odysseus's story. The Muses of course tell Homer exactly what Odysseus recited on that precise occasion (I analyze the textual strategy in accordance with Calame's 1986 elaboration), but whether those words are true is up to Odysseus. The Muses vouch for the words, not for what they relate. If Homer had presented Odysseus's adventures in the third person—that is, if he had declaimed that "Odysseus found a cave, wherein a monster slept," and so on—it would have meant that the Muses had seen Odysseus finding a cave with a monster sleeping in it. But Homer grants the floor to Odysseus and limits the Muses' responsibility to repeating Odysseus's words. Thus Odysseus is guarantor for what he narrates, and his story becomes a purely "literary" narrative. (Reucher 1989, 25.)

This does not mean that Narrator I (Homer) denies the truth of Odysseus's story, for, in fact, he sustains it in the following places: in the proem, outside therefore the Muses' inspiration (i.6–9); in Zeus's reference to Polyphemus (i.68–69); in the *diêgêsis* of ii.19–20; in Odysseus's reference to the Cyclops (xx.19–21); in conversation between Odysseus and Penelope (xxiii.248–84); and in Odysseus's summary of his adventures to Penelope (xxiii.306–41).

Homer sustains Odysseus's role also by recalling oracles about him: Polyphemus and Circe have been foretold of Odysseus's arrival and success, and Alcinous's father knows in advance the danger that ensues from the Phaeacian habit of escorting foreigners.

In ix.507ff., the Cyclops remembers that Telemos Eurymides had prophesied that one day a certain Odysseus would arrive and blind him. Naturally the Cyclops was expecting a big man, beautiful and strong, not the sort of dwarf he sees Odysseus to be. The smallness of Odysseus only adds insult to his defeat (see Chapter Eight).

In x.325ff., Circe confesses that Hermes had told her that Odysseus Polutropos would arrive, coming back from Troy. She does not need to tell Odysseus that Hermes had foretold her defeat, since she confesses the prophecy after his victory over her magic. Finally in Hades, Teiresias's prophecy awaits Odysseus.

These prophecies constitute a sort of retroactive recognition of Odysseus's identity. They produce several effects.

First, they seem to confirm the truth of Odysseus's narratives. I say "they seem" because in principle Odysseus could have invented these prophecies to reinforce the credibility of his narrative.

The question of for whom Odysseus's stories are true is a complex one. The Phaeacians believe him. They are completely bewitched by his words (xi.333–34) and shower him with gifts. However, the words that Homer—for at this point Narrator I has the floor—puts in the mouth of Alcinous in praise of Odysseus's stories (xi.363–69) should sound ironic to the extratextual audience. Alcinous emphatically declares: "as we watch you, we judge you to be no cheat, no liar, such as many are that the dark earth breeds and scatters far and wide, who fashion false stories out of what no man can see." We, who know Odysseus well, know that he could be just one of those men.[24]

For the actual audience of the poem, the truth of Odysseus's stories depends on their faith in the Muses, for only the Muses may know what Zeus said in council about Odysseus blinding Polyphemus. And though, of course, the text professes to be inspired by the Muses (i.1ff.), there are conspicuous signs that the poet of the *Odyssey* uses them as a literary contrivance. The presence of Muses in the poem is faint; they are often forgotten before the beginning of a song; and they are sometimes taken as fictionalized objects.[25] Accordingly, the actual audience of the *Odyssey* would find in Zeus's mention of the Cyclops little real evidence to support the truth of Odysseus's stories.

For us, the extratextual narratees, the whole scene—narrator, narrative, and narratee—is a masterful fiction. Fiction, however, does not mean absence of truths. What is most difficult to ascertain even in a self-declared fictional narrative is that it expands and elaborates notions and categories such as "subject," "self," "man," and "society" that have referential determinacy in real life. In the present case, the cognitive reference is to the notion of the narrator itself, as that person who speaks, knows what he is saying, and is fully master of his story.[26]

In order to show that in our text the *notion* itself of narrator—and not simply the narrator Odysseus—is fictional, we have to indicate how the text empties the solidity of its function. Thus, for instance, when Odysseus tells Eumaeus the story of the cloak, that story is enhanced by reference to an external text that the narrator does not control. We will see analogous effects in the *Alkinou apologoi*. The disjunctions between Odysseus as narrator and as character, the intertextual effects that the narrator cannot master, and the phantasmic coherence of his "I" put into question the mastery of the narrator over his story.[27]

Second, since these prophecies reveal that Odysseus's narratives were already written in the folds of the oracular utterances and cosmic order, he discovers—and we discover with him—that he is simply repeating a story already "written."

---

24. Nitzsch 1840 (III.262) remarks that while Alcinous's statement absolves Odysseus from the suspicion of lying, it induces Homer's listeners who know Odysseus to consider the plausibility of his narrative. The poet seems to have intended this effect.

25. See Pucci 1987, 215–16. Pedrick (1992), after analyzing the interaction between the poet and the Muses in i.1–21, writes: "He [the poet] is aware all along of the real nature of his project and the approach he should use; the exchange between himself and the Muse is an artful, staged enactment of the process of inspiration, and his willingness to participate as the lesser voice is testimony to his confidence that, although he is corrected, he suffers no less glory, since the help is divine." See also Crotty 1994, 128–29.

26. Though the context is fictional, these notions appeal to us as not being fictional, since they have extratextual epistemological reference. For examples of this cognitive reference to notions such as "man," "primitive man," "civilized man," and so on, see Chapter Eight.

27. On the instability and fragmentation of the "self" of Odysseus, see Chapter Eight.

Thus he both acts and reads his own adventures. After blinding Polyphemus, he learns that Telemos Eurymides had already told this story; and after he has escaped Circe's nasty magic, he learns that Hermes has already told that story. Thus the stories he tells the Phaeacians have already been told many times. The identity of writer and reader is confirmed at the level of Narrator II's experience.

To my knowledge, the critics have not seen the effect of these embedded voices of prophecy. Heubeck (1983) writes concerning ix.507–21 that "the Poet loves such inventions that have no link with the tradition." On the Circe episode (see x.330–31), the same critic opines that the use of the prophecy motif brings the fable—that knows no such features—closer to the epic. Stewart, not mentioned by the commentators of the recent English Commentary, more astutely implies that Circe reveals to herself, through the prophecy, the name of Odysseus (1976, 34).

These prophetic voices turn Odysseus's adventures into scenes of recognition. The cultural and human background changes, but Homer remains obsessively concerned with disguising and *un*disguising Odysseus. Hidden, unrecognizable, unexpected, Odysseus must be disguised and revealed again and again, in a sort of continuous aberration of his identity.

The aberration in the plot parallels the aberration in the writing. The poem intimates, in this obsession with the identity of its character, its own obsession with its own epic identity, its endless rewriting of the epic poems in a mode that forever alienates it from the *Iliad* and makes it a half-and-half epic poem, a perverse epic poem, a bastard epic poem . . .

Practical Functions of Odysseus's Narrative

Critics have rightly shown that Odysseus's stories have other goals besides amusing the audience.

Glenn Most (1989) maintains that these stories "are aiming at the securing of practical ends" and describes these practical ends as defining the precise measure of hospitality civilized people should grant. Odysseus tells the Phaeacians, through his narratives, how he expects them to behave. Most proposes that the Cyclopes and the Sirens function as examples of destructive, negated hospitality, whereas Circe and Calypso function as examples of protracted hospitality, one that refuses leave to the guest. The hosts should behave neither as the Cyclopes nor as Circe. Most writes: "Just as the Phaeacians surely do not want to be like the Cyclopes (6.2–8) and have no intention of eating him, so too Nausicaa should not be like Circe and Calypso, and her parents should let him go home when he wants to" (1989, 29).

Most is certainly correct that this was one of Odysseus's concerns. Besides, his analysis is a healthy antidote to the suggestions by other critics that Phaeacian society represented the highest degree of civilization. Most describes the desire that Nausicaa and Alcinous seem to share, that Odysseus remain in

Phaeacia, a desire that Odysseus could find threatening. He does not refer to another passage that would give his argument even more power. Odysseus meets Nausicaa on his way to the banquet at which he will tell his stories. It is to be his last encounter with her and her last word to him. She greets him as follows (viii.461–62):

χαῖρε, ξεῖν', ἵνα καί ποτ' ἐὼν ἐν πατρίδι γαίη
μνήσῃ ἐμεῖ', ὅτι μοι πρώτῃ ζωάγρι' ὀφέλλεις.

[Farewell, stranger/guest, so that even living in your fatherland you may remember me, since you owe your rescue to me first of all.]

The primitive meaning of ζωάγρια must have been the ransom that the prisoner, captured alive, pays for his rescue, and the verb ζωγρέω in fact means to capture alive (Luppino 1971, 73ff.). Thus Nausicaa lets Odysseus understand that he has been her prey.

The practical purposes of Odysseus's narratives, however, are not limited to this definition of hospitality and to this warning to his hosts. William F. Wyatt suggests that Odysseus had an eye on the gifts from the beginning of his storytelling (1989, 240). Wyatt vigorously underlines Narrator I's concern to present Odysseus in Hades facing his old comrades:

> Are we seriously to believe that Odysseus (or Homer) had intended not to tell the fate of the heroes of the Trojan War in the underworld? . . . Surely not. Homer had intended all along to tell us these things, and he had planned the interlude at least in part as a prelude to the climactic and very gripping scenes, with the Achaean dead in Hades. Those scenes are, in fact, the real reasons for Odysseus's journey, for they are the scenes in which the average Greek audience would have been most interested.

Wyatt also insists that after Odysseus replaces Homer as bard, we, not the Phaeacians, or perhaps we *and* the Phaeacians are the audience:

> When the hero replaces the singer, the audience replaces the fictional audience. We have up till now—quite consciously—been listening to Homer tell us the story of Odysseus. In book nine however, and thereafter, we are listening to the hero tell his adventures to us. We, not the Phaeacians—or rather we as well as the Phaeacians—are listening to Odysseus, it is we who are spellbound by his tale . . . The interlude has the added function, therefore, of reminding us, the audience, that it is not really Odysseus who sits before us bewitching us with his tales, but the poet Homer. (256–47)

What Wyatt describes here, without defining it, is a "reading scene" with the mimetic effect that such scenes inevitably produce on the extratextual readers.

Wyatt sees Homer's purpose in interrupting his story as the same as that of Odysseus's, to get gifts and money from his actual audience: there is sufficient anthropological literature to support this point of view.

A reading scene performed by a *poluainos* narrator cannot fail to have this sort of purpose. Odysseus says that if he were asked to remain even a year at Alcinous's palace and would receive splendid gifts, he would happily comply. His desire to hurry home becomes less intense when he espies the prospect of gifts. Indeed, the prospect of gifts certainly stimulates his desire to create among his listeners amazement and enchantment.

Discontinuity Between Narrator and Character (Plot-Agent)

As Odysseus the adventurer becomes Odysseus the raconteur (Narrator II), we note two kinds of split between the narrator and the doer.

First, as his own narrator, it seems unlikely that Odysseus should know more about his story than as plot-agent; but Homer grants him this magisterial position—the position which is Homer's own and that of the Muses, and which defines a narrator.

Ann Bergren (1983) and others have described the proleptic and analectic knowledge that Odysseus the narrator has about his past experience as plot-agent. It has been noticed by many how the narrator criticizes himself (see ix.228) for having disregarded the advice of his companions.

Second, the narrator is not always able to explain himself as a character (plot-agent) that either loses control of the action or has become different from the one he has been in his heroic past. I will analyze later some cases, but I present now a pair of examples

I find it particularly disquieting that Odysseus cannot always explain why the plot-agent acts as he acts. He falls asleep when the ship is a few hundred yards from his homeland, abandoning the control of it to his companions. How is it possible? Is not the excitement of the desired return keeping him awake for a few more minutes?

Thus, he abandons the control of the ship to his companions who come home after so many years of war and piracy empty-handed. Is that true? Odysseus earlier assured us that the booty was divided amongst him and his men (ix.41–42), and now he does not care to straighten out the matter.

His companions, observing the bag of winds and believing that it contains gifts Odysseus received from Aeolus, are envious (x.40–42):

πολλὰ μὲν ἐκ Τροίης ἄγεται κειμήλια καλὰ
ληΐδος· ἡμεῖς δ᾽ αὖτε ὁμὴν ὁδὸν ἐκτελέσαντες

οἴκαδε νισόμεθα κενεὰς σὺν χεῖρας ἔχοντες.[28]

[So many treasures and booty he carries for himself from Troy: but we who have accomplished the same expedition come back home with empty hands.]

However, as a narrator, he is unable either to contest this disparity between his fortune and his companions' poverty, or to think of a way to punish their miserable envy. The man who stopped the stampede of the whole army in the second book of the *Iliad* now sits resigned to his men's foolishness. He even derives a sort of grandeur from this resignation by repeating some of the high-minded phrases that the *Iliad* and Narrator I of the *Odyssey* have occasionally attributed to him. Describing himself as divided between killing himself and enduring in silence, he chooses the latter alternative (x.53–54):

ἀλλ᾽ ἔτλην καὶ ἔμεινα, καλυψάμενος δ᾽ ἐνὶ νηὶ
κείμην.[29]

[But I endured, and I remained, and covering myself I laid down in the ship.]

Yet what in the *Iliad* was a heroic attitude of firmness is here rather a pathetic surrender.

On another occasion he falls asleep when the companions are impiously slaughtering the cattle of the Sun: it is the will of the gods, he surmises as narrator—after the fact. But when he describes the development of the action, we readers sense some reticence and odd silences. He tells us that he came back to the beach where his companions were feasting and remained for six days watching them as they ate (ἑξῆμαρ μὲν ἔπειτα ἐμοὶ ἐρίηρες ἑταῖροι / δαίνυντ᾽ Ἡελίοιο βοῶν ἐλόωντες ἀρίστας: xii.397–98).

What did he do? What did he say in these six days? How did he resist the torture of hunger that had driven his companions to sacrilege? He gives us no details. He tells us nothing about what must have been at best a terrible silence, or at worst a most disgraceful dispute between him and his men. The ubiquitous narrator disappears while the plot-agent suffers the torments of hunger and the mockery of his impious companions.[30]

---

28. Though the position of χεῖρας is almost regular in this position of the line, the epithet κενεὰς is unique in Homer.

29. For a comparison with similar expressions in the *Iliad* and *Odyssey*, see Pucci 1987, 46–53.

30. It is during these six terrible days that the narrator might have meditated on the combination of fate and human error that ruins his companions. With this meditation, he would be able to produce for us that "tale of grief" which Crotty (1994), in his otherwise sensitive and provoking book, considers to be the experience the *Odyssey* delivers to its readers. But Odysseus tells nothing of these gruesome six days. Probably the reason is that the destruction of the companions and the suitors, for all its grief, is a foil to Odysseus's own survival through his *mētis*,

This silence certainly breaks the pattern that Auerbach (1957) describes for the Homeric narrative. Unlike the elliptical narrative of the Bible, exemplified by the long silence in the story of Isaac's sacrifice, Homer, Auerbach argues, fills his narrative with foregrounding details, leaving no void at all. Clearly that is not the case on the island of the Sun.

The Stories

An analysis of the content of the tales within the perspective of the "reading scene" would be too long an undertaking. Still, a few remarks on some aspects of Odysseus's tales may be useful to my discussion of the subjects covered in this book.

First of all, Narrator I gives clear signs that his Narrator II (Odysseus) narrates events that the Muses have not witnessed or in any case have not repeated to him. Deprived of their vision, Odysseus does not know what the gods plan for him. He introduces a scene in Olympus (374–90), but immediately adds that he heard it from Calypso. Ove Jörgensen (1904) has studied theological expressions in Odysseus's speeches of books 9–12. He shows that with the exception of Hermes in book 10 and of Helios in book 12, Odysseus does not mention any specific god as being the agent of an event. Instead, when he attributes an event to some theological power, he mentions θεός, δαίμων, θεοί, or Ζεύς. These, in conventional language, are four names for the same thing.[31]

The comparison between Narrator I and Narrator II shows how much less the latter knows. Yet there is a specific realm in which perhaps Odysseus's ignorance about theological interventions and responsibility might be an asset for Homer. When he describes the magical and perverse places where hostile divinities and monstrous beings threaten his life and that of his companions, the distance of the Olympian gods is welcome. These places and beings are

---

his disguises, and his painful self-control. These are the experiences the *Odyssey* cares about and embroiders endlessly.

31. For instance when the bowstring of Teukros breaks, the cause of this accident is a daimon for Teukros, a god for Ajax, and Zeus for Hector (XV.468, 473, 489). Homer as Narrator I makes much of the difference between his own theological knowledge and the limited one of his characters. For instance Homer says, οὖρον ἵει ἑκάεργος Ἀπόλλων, (I.479) [Apollo, the far-darter, sends them a favorable wind], but Nestor says, οὐδέ ποτ' ἔσβη οὖρος, ἐπεὶ δὴ πρῶτα θεὸς προέηκεν ἀῆναι, (iii.182) [Nor did the favorable wind once come, after the god first sent it to blow], and so on. Homer knows that Athena has sent sleep to Odysseus (v.491), but Odysseus himself says that a god has done it (vii.286); the poet knows that Athena is harassing the suitors (xviii.346), but Telemachus speaks of a *theos* (xviii.407); the poet narrates that Athena comes personally to help Odysseus (xxii.205ff.), but when later Amphimedon relates the event he speaks of a god who came to Odysseus's help (xxiv.182), and so on. See Jörgensen 1904, 364–66.

surrounded by an uncanny and sinister atmosphere that seems to be alien to the Olympians.

The stages of Odysseus's travels are twelve, a number of structural importance in Homer, and in the *Odyssey* in particular. They design a certain rhythm, with their turnings toward west and toward east, in almost alternate movements. Recently Chiarini 1991, 90ff. has assimilated this rhythm to the turns and shifts of a labyrinth. The geographical places these travels reach and describe have been often scrutinized by critics to ferret out the possibility of an historical reconstruction, but the success of this scholarly enterprise remains uncertain.

The Cicones

The story of Odysseus's return is placed by Odysseus himself under the agency of Zeus (ix.37–38); but along the way, as we have already remarked, the responsibility for the wandering and the losses is ascribed to various other agents: in particular to Poseidon, but also to the *atasthaliai* of the companions, to the will of some anonymous *theos*, or sometimes even to the wind itself.

It is the wind that takes Odysseus with all his fleet to the Cicones (ix.39–61). This episode is the first of Odysseus's narrative, and the last to describe a known geography and an historical, real—within the fiction—people.[32] After this episode, through the line: ἔνθεν δὲ προτέρω πλέομεν ἀκαχήμενοι ἦτορ (62), which is a line used especially in books 9–12,[33] we enter the fabulous places of the journey with their fabulous characters.

This episode is paradigmatic: it shows the plurality of agencies, the oscillating point of view, and the problematic relationship of the *Odyssey* and the *Iliad*.

Odysseus knows only that the wind drives him to the Cicones, but he attributes the losses he and his companions suffer both to his companions' foolishness (44) and to Zeus's evil decree of fate (53–54).[34] A sort of oscillation

---

32. The Ciconians are mentioned as allies of the Trojans (II.846–47); Apollo disguises himself as one of their chieftains to incite Hector (XVII.73).

33. This is not the place to record the special expressions that are typical of the four books in which Odysseus is narrator (ix–xii). Let it suffice to note that some epithets of address are found only here, as for instance φαίδιμ' Ὀδυσσεῦ: x.251; xi.100, 202, 488; xii.82; this epithet is essentially devoted to Achilles in the *Iliad*. As Odysseus narrates, he appropriates the heroic epithet for himself. Some phrases are used in the *Odyssey* only, or mainly, in these books: καμάτῳ τε καὶ ἄλγεσι θυμὸν ἔδοντες ix.75; x.143, 379 (cf. VI.202; XXIV.129); ἄσμενοι ἐκ θανάτοιο ix.63, 565; x.133 (cf. XX.350), etc. A large number of *hapax legomena* can be found here: σιτοφάγος ix.191; φύσις x.303; etc.

34. Lesky's theory of double motivation perhaps may be applied here: the companions' foolishness detains them on the Cicones' land longer than was prudent;

bctween Odysseus and his companions, as subjects of the actions and as points of view, traverses the episode:

39–40	I destroyed the city and killed the inhabitants.
41–42	We took the spouses and riches and shared the booty.
43–44	I gave the good advice, but they did not obey.
45–46	They drank a lot of wine; they slew many sheep and oxen.
47–55	The Cicones received help and attacked the Achaeans.
53–54	The evil doom of Zeus stood by us, ill–fated men.
56–57	We resisted their assault.
58–59	The Cicones overcame the Achaeans.
60–61	Six companions perished from each ship; the remnant of us escaped death and destiny.[35]

This distribution of the actions according to different subjects and objects shows that Odysseus ascribes first to himself the heroic actions (39–40) and wise behavior (43–44); to "us" the capturing of booty and the losing fight against the Cicones; and finally to *them* the kind of orgy the companions enjoy (45–46) and the final loss (60–61).

This distribution is sufficient to show how Odysseus glorifies himself in his account[36] and how, from the very onset of his narrative, characterizes his companions as foolish and prone to orgies. This beginning already prefigures the companions' six days of debauchery at the end of the journey with the cattle of Helios.

Odysseus's point of view could not be more explicitly revealed. Whether the disaster was caused by Zeus or by the foolishness of the companions, he at any rate is without fault and guilt.[37]

Notwithstanding the heroic role that Homer carves for Odysseus's ego, it is clear that Odysseus, the narrator, cannot explain what is happening and why. He speaks of his companions as "they," without being able either to feel community with them, or to exercise the commander's control over them. The

---

Zeus's evil fate occurs as a large contingent of hostile Cicones engages Odysseus and his men in battle, and defeats them.

35. Notice the composition of the narrative mainly by snippets of doublets, as though each doublet were the summary of more extensively described actions.

36. Pazdernick (1995, 350) underscores that Odysseus's description of his assault is "stately and direct, the aorists conveying a marked finality and an epigrammatic force: 'there I sacked the city and destroyed them.'"

37. Pazdernick (1995, 350) notices how "Odysseus turns a defeat into a parable of character that shares clear affinities with the manner in which his entire saga is presented in the prologue of the work." See Nagler 1990, 335–36; on νήπιοι, see Edmunds 1990, 60–97.

king who punished Thersites and won favor with the whole army in doing so, now accepts that his men do not "obey me" (ix.43). What a shame!

We are reminded of Nestor's description of his raid in XI.670ff. How clearly and significantly the differences stand out! Nestor names the heroes he slew (672f.); he lists precisely the number of horses, sheep, and swine he captured. His tone is confident, and the goddess Athena is present and helpful. Finally, the "I" and "we" narratives combine in triumphant unison. There is no separation between Nestor and his companions. While the raid must be a traditional epic theme, making it vain for us to look for a model, Nestor's example allows us to measure the difference of tone.

Odysseus's raid is not only defeated, but also to some extent inconsequential: we never hear, for instance, of women that were captured at Ismarus. This Iliadic feature of the heroic raid remains here inconsequential for the later narrative. The heroic age is over: concubines are a thing of the past; faithful wives are the new order.[40]

The Iliadic resonances function further in another way. Lines ix.45–46 describe the eating and drinking of the companions:

ἔνθα δὲ πολλὸν μὲν μέθυ πίνετο πολλὰ δὲ μῆλα
ἔσφαζον παρὰ θῖνα καὶ εἰλίποδας ἕλικας βοῦς.

[There a lot of wine was drunk and they slew on the shore many sheep and oxen with trailing feet and shambling gait.]

This sounds in part like IX.466ff.:

πολλὰ δὲ ἴφια μῆλα καὶ εἰλίποδας ἕλικας βοῦς
ἔσφαζον .../ .../
πολλὸν δ' ἐκ κεράμων μέθυ πίνετο τοῖο γέροντος.

The word μέθυ "wine" is basically Odyssean.[41] It occurs in Phoenix's somber description of the feast at his father's house, before his exile. Scholars disagree on which passage is the model of the other.[42] What I find curious is that the remake—if it should be one—allows Odysseus to introduce the third person plural "they" for his companions. Notice that when Odysseus speaks of himself in the first person he may use a language less marked by previous diction (see

---

40. M. Steinrück, forthcoming in "La pierre et la graisse," develops some of these themes with original insights. The only part of the booty we hear about later is the Ismarian wine (ix.195ff.).

41. It occurs twice in the *Iliad* (VIII.471 and IX.469) and fifteen times in the *Odyssey*. Nine of these fifteen occurrences appear in the journey books (ix–xii). On the word, corresponding to Sanskrit *mádhu* and its poetic use, see *DELG*.

42. Heubeck, without hesitation, states that the model is IX.466–69. Ramersdorfer (1981, 245ff.) is more cautious; his arguments make improbable the assumption that *Iliad* IX directly refers to the *Odyssey*.

ὤλεσα δ᾽ αὐτούς, which is without precedent). But when he describes their *common* activity he has at hand more conventional diction. Thus for instance the scene of the battle "is described in the language of the *Iliad*" (Heubeck 1989, II.15).

This feature occurs also in lines 54–55, where the repetition of XVIII.533–34 breaks the narrative "we" of 53, 57, and 61.[43] When the text appropriates fixed phrases from the tradition, the adaptation of the personal pronouns may become infelicitous.

By this phenomenon, the persona of Odysseus's "I" emerges stylistically enhanced. But the representation of the companions, especially when the expressions attributed to them refer to drinking and eating, portrays them as more common and trite.

Because of this tremendous bias in favor of the narrator, we are attached to that "narrating I," who makes us see him in a privileged light, different from the others, suffering because of the others. It may not be ethical how this effect is reached, but it is totally pleasing. It flatters what we take to be the consistency and the desired invulnerability of our "I's."

Yet this enhancement of the speaking I does not gloss over the pervasive feeling of frustration at defeat and for loss. The initial energy of the narrative—"I sacked the city and I destroyed them"—promising the reenactment of a heroic deed, melancholically peters out in the witless drinking and eating of the companions. The mention of food and drink, conjuring up the analogous tale of Phoenix's companions, highlights the inability of the Achaeans (59: how sad and nostalgic a name at this point!) to resist the Cicones, the ancient allies of the Trojans. To think that the Achaeans with their leader, the destroyer of Troy, are now routed by Trojan allies!

Later, in book ten, when the whole fleet enters the harbor of the Laestrygonians, Odysseus's failure as a commander comes under sharp light. No god and no foolishness of the companions account for their ruin. They confidently enter the hollow harbor, but Odysseus alone moors his ship outside it. Why he does so, the "omniscient" narrator does not tell us; why, if he had some premonition or suspicion, he did not speak to his companions, the narrator does not tell us either. And yet Odysseus's unique strategy saves his ship while all the others are lost (x.87–132).[44]

The leader has completely failed in his duty, but the narrator does not say a word about it. Hesiod here would perhaps comment that the *laoi* pay with their

---

43. See Usener 1990, 122ff. This phenomenon occurs other times in other episodes: see e.g. IX.86; X.57 where the formula changes the subject of the narration.

When Odysseus is reunited with his companions, the "we" may have the tonality of the *Odyssey*'s suffering (52–53 with the Odyssean ἄλγεσι πολλὰ πάθοιμεν, on which see Mawet 1979, 179).

44. A parallel situation occurs at x.257 when Eurylochus says that the companions entered Circe's house because of their inexperience or ignorance (ἀϊδρείῃσιν); this moralizing comment however is deserved also by Odysseus when Hermes mocks him for his inexperience (x.281–82).

lives for the foolishness of their kings; this comment would form a better corrective than the one that praises Odysseus's consciousness and responsibility.

In this case the narrator does not invoke either a theological principle or a psychological one. Eleven ships are destroyed, and, though we expect, relying on the coherence of the narrative, that the same principles of causation intervene, this is not the case. If the theological principle lacks coherence and continuity, then it is unaccountable, and depends on the narrative agenda or on the narrator's whim to mention it.

As concerns the companions' foolishness and wickedness (*atasthaliai*), we find them sometimes to behave in a wiser and more responsible way than Odysseus (e.g., ix.224–30, where the narrator recognizes their wisdom; x.198ff.). If therefore their foolishness and their wisdom is again inconsistent, but sometimes the one and sometimes the other, or even if no psychological ground prevails in accordance with a certain narrative agenda, we cannot trust the moralizing of Odysseus, since it lacks coherence and responsibility.

So Zeus, Poseidon, and the companions' foolishness (*atasthaliai*) comprise the theological and psychological "grounds," or simply the "dummy pretexts," for a ruin necessitated or favored by the narrative.[45] Odysseus, and with him Narrator I, use those grounds or those pretexts, or do not use them at all, as though the narrative had *at any rate* to go on with the demise of the companions.

The Goats' Island

The description of the Goats' Island (ix.116–65), lying off the coast of the land of the Cyclopes, has troubled interpreters. Rhetorically it has been defined as a "descriptive pause";[46] but it is too long should it serve, as Reece correctly writes, "to facilitate the adaptation of the folktale to the theme of the seafaring wanderer,

---

45. Odysseus, in accordance with the Cyclops's prayer to Poseidon, is destined to arrive home alone, having lost all his companions and in a foreign ship (ix.534–35). Accordingly, the accidents of narrative that explain the loss of the companions simply fulfill that prediction. For ultimately it was the plot-agent's taunting of Polyphemus that revealed his name and made it possible for the blinded Cyclops to curse him.

The theological causation seems either overdetermined, since the narrative provides sufficient explanation, or underdetermined, since it is insufficient or contradictory to the plot. See Chapter Ten.

46. Richardson 1990, 53; 217–18. We visualize what the visitor sees and what passes through his mind: accordingly the action never really comes to an absolute standstill during this descriptive pause. This is true even in our passage, though by a sort of *hysteron proteron* the island is described (116–41) before Odysseus reaches it (141ff.). The narrator precedes the plot-agent as if he wanted to show that he knows more and better than the visitor.

whose fleet must somehow be preserved for later adventures."[47] The island has also a curious particularity in that it is inhabited only by wild goats. No explanation is given.

Critics often explain the long and enthusiastic description of the island—of its fertile ground, well watered meadows, harbor, and so on—as the appreciative glance of a prospective settler.[48] They therefore see a relationship between this passage and the age of colonization.

A sort of epistemological necessity determines that the description of what is completely new and unexplored can only be expressed with a reference to what is known and familiar. Hence this description shifts between what the visitor's eye finds missing among things that are familiar (119–24; 125–29) and what the same eye imagines possible to create or build in these given conditions (130–41). The odd presence of the wild goats [ἐν δ' αἶγες ἀπειρέσιαι γεγάασιν/ ἄγριαι ("there are countless wild goats" 118–19)], with the insistent repetition of the α(ι)γ– sound and the ironic use of ἀπειρέσιαι, from phrases like ἐν δ' ἄνθρωποι / πολλοί, ἀπειρέσιοι xix.174–75), is preposterously balanced by the absence of men,[49] specifically hunters, shepherds, and farmers. Only goats and more goats.

The eye of the *homo faber* realizes that the absence of people relates to the absence of ships: the Cyclops have no "red-cheeked ships" nor do carpenters "who might build decked ships, which would perform all tasks, voyaging to the towns of men, as often men cross the sea on ships to visit one another" (ix.126–29).

When Odysseus considers the absence of this locomotive tool, it is the *homo faber* who speaks, the builder of rafts, who, possessing that tool, is now visiting places others never could. The auto-reference is direct, since the νέες μιλτοπάρηοι "red-cheeked ships" (125) are his own.[50]

Now the same *homo faber*, conscious of his power and creativity, imagines what this land could produce (131ff.):

> It is in no way a sorry land, but would bear all things in their season; for there are soft, well watered meadows by the shores of the gray salt sea; there the

---

47. Reece 1993, 127. See already Reinhardt 1960, 63ff. Race 1993 has shown that Odysseus's descriptive technique does not diverge deeply from Homer's. He correctly sees anticipation, repetition, and silencing of details to create surprise as specific features of Odysseus's descriptive pauses.

48. Heubeck 1989, 22.

49. The absence of man is evoked by the lack of any πάτος ἀνθρώπων, path (or ways) of men (119); to describe man by his steps, his walking on the ground, evokes his earthly destination, his marking the ground by all his activities. In Homer (V.442) and Hesiod (*Th.* 272) men are *khamai erkhomenoi* "walking on the ground," in contrast with the immortal gods. See also *Hymn to Hestia* 1–2.

50. See II.636–37, where again Odysseus's twelve ships are described with this epithet μιλτοπάρηοι, a *hapax legomenon*. See Usener 1990, 40–41. Odysseus as Narrator II cannot find a different epithet for his ships: a series of authors precede him.

vine would be perennial; the land is level for plowing and people would reap a deep crop in due season, because there is richness beneath the soil.[51]

This reads as a positive description; before it was purely negative (122–23):

It is possessed neither by flocks nor by plowed lands, but the soil is unsown (ἄσπαρτος) and untilled (ἀνήροτος) all the time . . .

To describe the "new," Odysseus adds an alpha privative to what is familiar to him. In this way the new looks also old, to the extent that it appears as the unfamiliarly familiar. If this island had attributes and potentialities other than those inscribed in Odysseus's polarized spectrum of absent features and prospective opportunities, neither he nor we would ever know.

But what other attributes and potentialities? The text suggestively describes Odysseus's arrival to the island and his next day's hunting: the *homo faber* appears completely overcome and abused by an aspect of the island which could only be called its uncanniness and magic.

Let us begin with Odysseus's arrival (142ff.):

There we sailed and some god guided us[52] through the dark night, without appearing so as to be seen.[53] For a deep mist was lying around the ships, nor did the moon show her light from heaven but was covered with clouds. No one, then, perceived that island with his eyes, nor did any one of us see the long waves rolling to the beach, until our well-decked ships landed.[54]

The day after, Odysseus and his men hunt: "the Nymphs, daughters of aegis-bearing Zeus, roused the mountain goats . . . And a god soon gave us goats in plenty" (154ff.).

We realize two important points. First, the island offers more wondrous aspects than the positive/negative list of features reported by Odysseus. And second, the master carpenter, the proud sailor who extols the possession of ships, is no master at all. He reaches the island without guiding the ships, since they run by themselves. An old image, from the *Rig-Veda* to Pindar, assimilates

---

51. Wine and bread are the two main products Odysseus thinks of in agreement with a fundamental choice that remains rooted in Greek culture; see Euripides *Bacchae* 274–75 with Dodds's commentary. We wonder here at Odysseus's agricultural concerns and skills: are the heroic princes, who were accustomed to produce richness through booty and raids, becoming farmers?

52. A similarly guiding god is mentioned when Odysseus reaches Aiaia, Circe's island (x.135ff.); calm and *galênê* occur in xii.169 when approaching the Sirens' island.

53. The god, *theos*, is the subject for some scholars; see Heubeck 1989. But the verb is impersonal for other interpreters; see AHC.

54. As AHC note, the ships are considered to be animated; they run into the shore, here at 148 and in the next line, 149.

carpentry to the construction of a poem. The *Odyssey* uses it (xiv.131–32) for "forging a tale."[55] If now the control of the master carpenter over his ships parallels his control over his narrative, we understand why he can hardly give an account of how the ships reached the land, who drove them, and so on. It seems that just as some external, uncontrollable force drives the ship, so some other narrative, an unknown one, lies behind Odysseus's. As an effect of this switch, the *homo faber*'s bold utterances about what this island lacked and could produce are humbled by a power no technology can cope with and no *logos* can account for.

The sailing is so automatic that Odysseus must assume the help of a god. But he does not really know nor is he able to say whether it is a benign or a malevolent god: nor can we.[56] Perhaps the intervention of the Nymphs and again of an anonymous god the day after, during the hunt, may suggest a benign presence of the gods. But the animation of the ships is more than what the Homeric gods usually do. And we may suspect that this divine help during the hunt, which gives Odysseus confidence about the place, makes him well disposed in favor of the next, disastrous visit to the Cyclops.[57] Is this help then a snare?

To leave Odysseus overwhelmed by the uncanniness of the island may be however a rhetorical trick; whether benign or malevolent the effect of the unaccountable (magic?) power enhances the charm of the narrative. This sailor and *tektôn*, who becomes the narrator and describes such an enchanted place, must have been in contact with forces that are superior to all *tekhnai* (arts) and accountability. He has known the touch of magic, the premonition of sinister forces, the trap/help of the undecidable, and has survived it. He, too, must be powerful. The image of an Odysseus both in contact with magic and in control of the *tekhnai* is adventurous and appealing. Readers will encounter it again and again. Yet they may ask themselves whether this magic island with its ensconced powers could really be cultivated as the *homo faber* has assumed. A possible contradiction or unsuitability between the two orders looms disquietingly.

The function that we are attributing to the descriptive pause of the Goats' Island can be ascribed to several other descriptions of magic places. The islands of the Laestrygonians, the Cyclopes, Circe, and the Sirens have certain features in common: magic presence, suspicious stillness, and uncanny beauty hang over them like a numinous atmosphere. Again a god leads Odysseus and his ship toward the island and its harbor (e.g., x.141; cf. xii.169); on other occasions a god helps Odysseus to hunt (beside ix.154–55, 158 see x.155–57). The woods and forests in some of these islands constitute a peaceful and sacred element

---

55. Rousseau 1995a, 16ff. See also in Chapter Eight how Odysseus's metaphor of ship construction as he blinds the Cyclops relates to his rhetorical composition of the Cyclops's figure.

56. Heubeck 1989 assumes that it is benevolent.

57. To assume that the Nymphs roused the goats so as to have an abundant hunt may correspond to a pious reflex of Odysseus, who would justify in this way the brutal intervention of man in the idyllic and uncanny island.

mingled with uncanny ambivalence (ix.118, x.99, x.149–50). The stillness of the sea (γαλήνη) in x.94 is not less treacherous than the stillness which descends upon the sea and puts all the natural elements in a deathlike sleep close to the Sirens' island (xii.168ff.). Odysseus describes this stillness in the Laestrygonian harbor:

οὐ μὲν γάρ ποτ᾽ ἀέξετο κῦμά γ᾽ ἐν αὐτῷ,
οὔτε μέγ᾽ οὔτ᾽ ὀλίγον, λευκὴ δ᾽ ἦν ἀμφὶ γαλήνη[58]

[for no wave swelled in it, large or small, but a clear calm was all around.]

The stillness of this clear sea has the immobility of a Socratic concept, but implies also an unpredictability, like the calm that precedes the storm. Instead of surmising, with Stanford and Heubeck, that Odysseus describes here a fjord,[59] we realize that the features of these islands are the same and point to their magical, sinister—and at the same time generous—nature: they have good natural harbors; there is a γαλήνη when our sailors approach them (or an alluring singing voice in the case of a garden); no work is done in these settings, though occasionally smoke is visible—a welcome sign of domesticity for the mariners; divine intervention occurs at several moments to bring the sailors into the harbor, or to grant them a prodigious hunt, and so on; and there is a fountain for water. Our sailors are also thoroughly lost, having no idea, for instance, where is east and where west.

These uncanny and ambivalent features become evident as soon as we compare the description of these magical islands with that of another island, Pharos, where Menelaus encounters Proteus. Though that island, too, is the setting of a divine encounter, no "descriptive pause" elicits ambivalent and uncanny features. The geography, name, and position of the island are known and real; Menelaus knows immediately why he is detained (he did not sacrifice a perfect hecatomb for the gods iv.352); and he is never at a loss about where he is. The island is inhabited (358–59) and the harbor is not natural; these elements of culture constitute some familiarity even in the midst of the most fabulous encounter. Finally, the only reference to mortal danger is uttered in a contrary-to-fact conditional sentence that already contains its own resolution (iv.363): "Now had the food been fully consumed and my men's courage, had not some goddess pitied and preserved me."

---

58. The word γαλήνη occurs exclusively in the *Odyssey*, where it is found five times: in some of these cases this stillness serves as a narrative springboard for something unpredictable though in itself alluring and salvific (v.391, x.94, xii.168). It denotes a fully positive calm in v.452 and vii.319.

59. "The description of the harbor in 87ff. is dimly suggestive of a Scandinavian fjord with its high encircling cliffs, narrow entrance 'white calm' (94, a memory of frozen seas?), and possibly yodeling ἠπύει, 83" (Stanford 1959, 368). Also see Heubeck 1983, 226.

In contrast, Odysseus's descriptive pauses are the springboards of the subsequent narrative: they prepare the readers for a magic presence or for a monstrous potentiality of nature; an uncanny mingling of excessive reassurance and terrifying aggression, they function like the traps and the baits of a mysterious *mêtis*. They then become foils for Odysseus's encounter with magic: readers and listeners are induced to expect that Odysseus is no longer in control, and that his *mêtis* is overwhelmed by the uncanny one of the place and of its gods.

But the foil simply increases the reader's emotion and pleasure when Odysseus masters the monsters and the magicians. The contest, of course, is rigged: pure wine (still the wine!) overcomes the feeble mind of the Cyclops, Hermes' *molu* defeats Circe's potions, and Circe's trick masters the Sirens' seduction.

Though the contest is rigged, the outcome is however felicitous and pleasurable. For the unexpected help does not diminish Odysseus's performance nor does the recognition that since time immemorial he had to come and to succeed in mastering the magic. He enters that world and dispels its powers like a master magician.[60] But notice that the recognition occurs after he has mastered the Cyclops and Circe: the recognition is the result of his performance of *mêtis*.

The magic which Odysseus overcomes is not lost; it is simply transferred to the narrative. The enchanted place (*topos*) becomes therefore the foil, the *figure* (*topos*) of magic that the narrative both exposes and controls through its rhetorical *tekhnê*, the *tekhnê* of fairy tales.

Circe

The wild animals, lions and wolves, which fawn like dogs around the visitors, embody the power and effect of Circe's magic *pharmaka* (x.210ff.). She tames wild and savage nature. However, she changes Odysseus's human companions into pigs, whom she feeds with acorns and mast and the fruit of the cornel tree (241–43); and she tries to change Odysseus, too, into a pig (318–20). It is an odd politics: in the conventional folktale, the witch first has intercourse with the hero and then changes him into an animal.[61] Hermes intimates that she will follow that expected strategy when she realizes that her magical potions have no effect on Odysseus; but this strategy could well be simply what Hermes suspects, and not what she might really do.

At first and literally, it seems therefore that she tames the wild animals in order to have them around as inverted pets, as magical embodiments of her power. It seems furthermore that she transforms men into pigs in order to avoid

---

60. Odysseus leaves the enchanted places he approached by magic power in full control of the situation.

61. Germain 1954, 272.

sexual intercourse with them! It is only when her magic fails that she consents to have sex with the invulnerable hero and to become a benevolent lover.[62]

Let us read the scene at the precise point at which Circe fails to transform Odysseus into a pig and Odysseus rushes upon her (318–25):

> And now, when she gave it [the drug] and I drank it off and I was not bewitched, she hit me with her wand, spoke to me, and addressed me: "Go now to the sty and lie there with the other companions." So she spoke and I drew my sharp sword[63] from along my thigh and I rushed upon Circe[64] as though[65] I were furiously eager to kill her. Then she, with a great cry fell down and clasped my knees and weeping spoke to me winged words: "Who are you of men and from where . . ."

Circe then wonders how Odysseus could have been insensitive to her drugs (*pharmaka* 326) and surmises that he is Odysseus, as Hermes had prophesied; and then she continues (333–35):

> "Come on, put your sword into the sheath and let us go up to my bed, so that meeting in sex[66] and love we may trust each other."

That Odysseus's sword is a symbol for his male sexuality seems evident to many critics;[67] what is disputable is the meaning of this symbolism.

Many interpretations have been given of this encounter,[68] and my favored one is that "it is played out on the level of an archetypal conflict between sexes. The

---

62. The situation is deeply ironic: Hermes, the *polutropos* god, has forewarned Circe that Odysseus will come and master her magic; of course, by arming Odysseus with counter-magic power, he manages that the *polutropos* Odysseus may realize that prophecy and defeat her. She is therefore twice the victim of *polutropia*. For *polutropia* is a kind of magic and counter-magic.

Was Hermes spending all his time (αἰεί) mocking Circe with his prophecy without enjoying the favors of the Nymph?

63. Hermes had used the word ξίφος for sword (294); now Odysseus uses the word *aor*, and the wording is Iliadic (XXI.173, said of Achilles drawing the sword). Is it malicious to remark that ἄορ, etymologically connected with ἀείρω and signifying "a suspended object" may facilitate the sexual metaphor that seems inevitable at this point?

64. The proper name Circe occurs here, as if the personal relationship would begin just with this pretended assault. The recognition precedes the love scene; cf. Papadopoulou-Belmehdi 1994, 181 n.41.

65. Notice ὥς τε, while in the *Iliad* the hero is simply μενεαίνων. In the *Odyssey* the heroics is make-believe.

66. μιγέντε is dual, and a *hapax* in Homer; it underscores the dual participation in love, as in III.441: εὐνηθέντε.

67 See Segal 1968, 425–26 with bibliography.

68. See Germain 1954, 249–74; Crane 1988, 31–85; Heubeck 1989, 50–52. The whole episode is structured on the general lines of Priam's visit to Achilles in *Iliad*

companions who do not go as far [as Odysseus] succumb to a lower appetite (see x.234–35, 237); they meet gentler charms, but are made brutes."[69] In this and analogous interpretations, Odysseus would confront Circe's seduction with a stronger power, through a heroic attitude. His brandished sword would represent his heroic self embodied also in his physical male power.

There is no doubt that this gesture is ingrained in that sort of mock-heroic, or paraheroic diction and action that enhances Odysseus's "I," especially in his own narrative—for example when he thinks of attacking the Cyclops with his sword, or stands up on his ship provoking Polyphemus after having blinded him, or stands tied to the mast listening to the Sirens' song. In all these cases, Odysseus stands erect and defiant, an image of his swollen ego.

However I wish to add a detail that produces a less anthropocentric reading and one more consistent both with the literal text and with the oath Odysseus requests. Circe's initial transformation of Odysseus's companions implies her seduction and scorn for human lovers, for the goddess who tames wild animals into pets has a sexual power well beyond human capacities. She begins to seduce/scorn Odysseus in the same way, but she fails. Odysseus raises the sword as a sign of his heroic and male power. He can, supposedly, kill her or become her lover. The sword, however, is also symbolic of castration. This symbolic meaning, together with the oath he requires from her, signal to her that the sexual relationship he imposes on her should be inscribed into the economy of castration, that is, into one of controlled, marital sex, which is socially accepted and erotically domesticated. She must tame her divine sexuality, allow him to lead the sexual game as he can, and ultimately accept his mortality.

The scene suggests both her fear before the sword and her acquiescence to Odysseus's request. On 323–24 she falls at his knees as a suppliant, in a posture more dramatic and powerless than what Hermes ὑποδείσασα "fearing" (296) let us suppose. She is genuinely distressed by the θαῦμα "marvel" of her failure (326).

We do not need to recall that Odysseus boasted that Circe "was desiring to make [him] her husband" (ix.32) in order to realize how quickly she decides to accept his conditions, to give up her ruses and schemes, and free his companions so that he might be ἤπιος "gentle" with her (337).[70] When Odysseus requests an analogous oath from Calypso, the goddess smiles and gently mocks him and then utters the oath (v.180ff.); but here Circe is not shown to reflect or comment. She simply does it (345–46).

XXIV (see Beck 1965); this consistent echoing has encouraged critics to interpret Circe as a sort of "queen of the dead."

69. Segal 1968, 425–26. On the nature of the Odyssean nymphs, see Papadopoulou-Belmehdi 1994, 23: "female figures using enchantment and ruse in order that men may forget and be absorbed into the feminine world, focused on weaving."

70. ἤπιος describes family relationships, just as those of a father toward his children (e.g., VIII.40 = XXII.184; XXIV.770; etc.); or of a husband toward his wife (e.g., xi.441; etc.)

The text is maliciously astute: ostensibly it extols and magnifies Odysseus's male power of seduction, while discreetly suggesting that his threat and his sexual compromise are more persuasive than his sexual power. For it is legitimate to surmise that Hermes' suggestion (301) that the goddess could make him *kakon kai anênora* (dastardly and unmanly 341), which Odysseus repeats, might refer to Odysseus's inability to confront the full sexual power of the goddess.

Through the oath, therefore, Circe agrees to love Odysseus as a mortal, as a sort of husband, a domestic pet.

Circe's reception and love for Odysseus, and his companions, builds up a subtle suggestion that her house constitutes his return home. The text provides clear signals toward this suggestion. Let us begin with the most explicit passage (x.410–17) which describes the joy with which Odysseus's companions see him alive:

> And as when calves of the homestead gather around the cows of the herd that have returned to the stables when they have their fill of pasture, and all together jump before the cows and the fences do not detain them, but with a ceaseless bellowing skip around their mothers, so they [my companions] as soon as they saw me with their eyes poured tears about me. Yes, to their mind it was as though[71] they had reached their homeland and their city of Ithaca where they were born and reared.[72]

Was it indeed worth all the trouble Odysseus took to transform his companions from pigs into men, if in this simile he makes them calves? Surely we may smile. The extraordinary point is that he feels that they see him as the king of Ithaca and behave as if they had returned home. No wonder they remain for an entire year.

The companions that had been metamorphosed into pigs recover their human shape, and become bigger and more handsome (395ff.), a transformation that intimates a special encounter, or a favorable, privileged situation. Like a return.

As concerns Odysseus himself, the bathing scene suggests an atmosphere of domesticity, repose, and homecoming with powerful emotional echoes (x.360ff.). A maid, or possibly Circe herself,[73] bathes him. The bath quenches and wipes away the "heart- or life-consuming weariness from my limbs" (ὄφρα μοι ἐκ κάματον θυμόφθορον εἵλετο γυίων 363). This heart-breaking or life-consuming weariness is that of the return journey; in iv.716 it is Penelope's grief.

---

71. "Their minds were in the same state, they felt as if they had arrived home," Heubeck 1989, 66.

72. The emotions the companions feel of being back at home is conveyed even more clearly, immediately after, in direct speech (419–20): "we were made as happy at your return as if we had arrived back to Ithaca, our homeland."

73. In iii.464 Nestor's own daughter helps bathe Telemachus. So Stephanie West uses the bathing scene of Book 3 to confirm Circe's own action here in this book; her view seems plausible. But for Heubeck (1989, 63) the bathing in Book 10 is done by a maid.

Finally the dinner, whose preparation begins at 370 and is delayed by the return of the companions, takes place at 456ff., with the encouraging words of Circe: "eat and drink, she says, so that you recover the courage (*thumos*) you had when first you left the homeland of Ithaca." She implicitly intimates that they will recover the *animus* of their youth, and she completes the circle of their journey:

> So she spoke and our noble hearts were persuaded. Here we sat all days to complete one year, feasting on abundant meat and sweet wine. (466–68)

If to be transformed into pigs symbolized being reduced to brutes, the Circean "paradise" reduces Odysseus and his men to grazing animals without any drug or touch of the magic wand. It is of course a false and only momentary homecoming: Odysseus must return to his wife Penelope, a real wife, who saves him from the destructive relationship of the nymphs. For the nymphs not only threaten the heroes as Circe does, but by making their lovers immortal, they shut them within the heroic age and its closing time.

The innuendoes and suggestions that Circe's house functions as the place of homecoming sound ironic and pathetic. It is but a moment of rest after the terrible losses of the previous encounters. Yet Odysseus's self-exposure, with that heroic, mock-heroic sword, sign of a great power and simultaneously of a terrible weakness, which leads him to tame a queen of ferocious animals and to forget himself, fractures the image of Odysseus's self into kaleidoscopic fragments.

Circe recognizes him as *polutropos*, just as the Cyclops recognized him from his being "Nobody." He arrives always unrecognizable even if announced many times. The *polutropos* man moves around, has many ways, is polymorphous and undetainable: he cannot be identical to himself unless it is in his disguising and in his *polutropia*.

Agamemnon and Achilles

Many excellent analyses exist on the characters—Teiresias, his mother Anticlea, his old comrades in arms Agamemnon, Achilles, and Ajax—whom Odysseus meets in Hades,[74] but a specific interpretation of Odysseus's reaction to these encounters, deserves renewed attention, particularly in view of my focus on Odysseus as narrator.

---

74. Reinhardt 1960, 126–31; Rüter 1969; Marzullo 1970; A. Edwards 1985; Crane 1988; Peradotto 1990. See also Steinrück 1994, 83ff. for an insightful paper on the rhythmic interaction among the characters Odysseus meets.

Odysseus's reaction to Teiresias's long prophecy, which theologically
explains Odysseus's disasters and tells him of his death,[75] is extremely cool:
"Teiresias, all these things the gods themselves have somehow spun"[76] (139).
Not a word more. The tone is one of resignation (ἄρ που "somehow") or of
condescension ("certainly"), but not of sadness, for he is alive among the dead.
And furthermore the prophecy, notwithstanding its many hypothetical clauses
that threaten dangerous narrative turns, assures him that he will survive his
return and that his death is far away.

Alive amid the shadows of the dead, Odysseus will meet the men of his age,
the dead heroes of his generation whom he is surviving.

The first soul he meets is the chief of the Achaean army, the ἄναξ ἀνδρῶν,
Agamemnon.[77] He is not alone, but is accompanied by the souls of those who
died with him in Aegisthus's house. As soon as Agamemnon recognizes
Odysseus, he breaks into tears, and weeping loudly, stretches his arms to
embrace Odysseus, in a display of deep, uncontrollable emotion (xi.390ff.).[78] At
this violent explosion of affection, Odysseus, also in tears, is taken by pity[79] and
questions Agamemnon on the cause of his death.

Odysseus can only imagine and mention ways of death conceivable in the
heroic life: death caused by shipwreck or by wounds during some heroic raids; he
cannot bring himself to think of illness, accident, or murder by one's kin.[80]

---

75. As Reinhardt (1960) has noticed, only Teiresias prophesies Odysseus's death.
This, of course, is an important epic theme. The prophecy unravels through a sort of
ring composition, within which Odysseus's fate begins under the negative sign of
Poseidon, passes through Helios, and returns to Poseidon and the final reconciliation
with that god. It is however odd that Odysseus will placate Poseidon and his cosmic
order (= the sea) in a distant country to which he will arrive walking and where the sea
is not known. Of course Poseidon controls other cosmic realms: he is the earth
shaker, for instance, but Odysseus has related to him as the god of the sea.

76. ἐπικλώθω "to spin," "to assign by spinning" is basically an Odyssean verb
(7x Odyssey; only once in the Iliad at XXIV.525). It is used often in a sententia, to
indicate the will of the gods, without any particular emotion, toward men in general:
xx.196; vii.579; or toward one's personal lot: iii.208; xi.139.

77. Already in the presentation of the souls that gather around Odysseus (xi.38–
41) the emphasis is on the heroes. Two lines are devoted to gender and age classes:
women, young men, old people, delicate young women, and two lines to warriors:
"many torn by the bronze weapons, men slaughtered in battle, carrying their weapons
splattered with blood" (40–41).

78. Notice the repetition of the action of weeping in chiastic position on 391,
and the repetition of the idea of stretching the arms in 392 with the unique phrasing
πιτνὰς ἐς ἐμὲ χεῖρας which is explained by the more conventional ὀρέξασθαι (I.351;
XXII.37; XXIV.783).

79. Burkert (1955, 139) suggests that Odysseus's pity for his dead companions
corresponds to the pity the companions feel in the Iliad when one of their friends is
killed.

80. Illness is almost never mentioned in the Iliad. There is of course the "plague"
sent by Apollo (I.10) and then the strange destiny of a certain Euchenor who had to
die either of a sore disease at home or go to Troy and be killed there by the Trojans
(XIII.667–70). In the Odyssey, on the contrary, disease is recognized. Even the

Agamemnon, in response, repeats all the heroic ways of death Odysseus has suggested and then adds the unexpected one: death caused by the wife and her lover.

Agamemnon narrates his death, with his concubine, Cassandra, at the hands of Aegisthus and Clytemnestra.[81] He contrasts heroic battle with the murder that killed him, a murder accomplished amid festive tables laden with food. He curses women.

Odysseus's answer exemplifies Agamemnon's point but frames it into a larger and theological plan (436–39):

> Alas! Verily loud-voicing Zeus has terribly hated[82] the seed of Atreus through the females' plans.[83] For Helen's sake so many of us vanished[84] and now Clytemnestra has ambushed you while you were far off.

The violent hatred of Zeus (ἐκπαγλῶς ἤχθηρε 437) will again be evoked by Odysseus, with the same phrasing, when he attributes the ruin of Ajax also to Zeus (xi.558–60):

> No one else was responsible but Zeus: terribly he hated the army of the spearholding Danaans and imposed on you this fate.

Together the two texts manifest Odysseus's awareness that Zeus caused the destruction of the heroic race of the Danaans. The women's plans, just like Ajax's defeat and suicide, are only instruments of Zeus's will to destroy the whole Achaean army of which Odysseus himself had been a champion. Also in the *Iliad* he is aware of this final doom of the heroes when he answers Agamemnon (XIV.85–87):

> Would that you were . . . not the leader among us to whom Zeus has given it, from youth to old age, to weave grievous wars until each of us perishes.

Cyclops is told by his neighbors that he cannot avoid illness (ix.411); see also v.395ff., xi.200; xv.408; etc.

81. Only on this occasion does Clytemnestra receive the epithet *dolomêtis* (422), which is exclusive to Aegisthus: i.300; iii.198, 250, 308; iv.525. But in at least one of these passages Clytemnestra is not far away: in iii.250 (τίνα μήσατ᾽ ὄλεθρον Αἴγισθος δολόμητις), the verb (μήσατο) recalls Clytemnestra by etymology; just as in ix.429, the same verb evokes Clytemnestra. The verb μήδομαι is most often used to designate a cruel, violent deed (ἔργον). On Agamemnon's *nostos*, see Katz 1994, 52f.

82. This formula occurs again at xi.560.

83. γυναικείας διὰ βουλὰς "through females' plans" is a *hapax*, the adjective γυναικεῖος occurring only here in Homer.

84. Notice how Odysseus speaks as if he were sharing the fate of the dead heroes.

Odysseus's awareness of the destructive will of Zeus coincides with the plan of Zeus, of which we read in *Cypria* (fr. 1 Allen). According to this plan, Zeus decided upon the destruction of the heroes in the Trojan War.[85]

This plan may be alluded to in *Iliad* I.5 ("and so the plan of Zeus was accomplished"), though its sure and immediate reference is to Zeus's will to help Hector and the Trojans until the Achaeans give Achilles his due honor (τιμή).[86]

As Odysseus perceives the death of Agamemnon, besides that of the heroes he already knows, he interprets Clytemnestra's will, like Helen's will, as Zeus's instruments of terrible hatred against the Achaean heroes.

Odysseus himself could still be a victim of Zeus through Penelope or through a shipwreck, for example. Agamemnon reassures him that Penelope is a good wife, but Odysseus seems hardly to listen and dismisses him rather abruptly (462–64). This abruptness raises questions. Is he confident in Teiresias's prophecy? Or is he distressed by the violence of Zeus's hatred? Perhaps the latter is the more compelling if we can derive full force from the closing lines (465–66): "Thus we stood, exchanging painful discourses, sorrowful, and pouring copious tears." This last phrase (ἐπέεσσιν ἀμεβομένω στυγεροῖσιν) is used only at the end of the sad encounter with Elpenor,[87] and line 466 is found in x.570; xi.5; xii.12, on occasions of deep distress.

Agamemnon produces an atmosphere of doom through his distrust of the wife, upon which Odysseus meditates as he refers to Zeus's terrible hatred. But he will be given the chance to correct this distrust and utter a full praise of Penelope in xxiv.191ff., in the second *Nekuia*:

> Blessed son of Laertes, resourceful Odysseus, you certainly got a wife with great virtue. How noble was the mind of blameless Penelope, daughter of Icarius. For she kept a good memory of Odysseus, her legitimate husband. Therefore her fame (*kleos*) will never die, the fame of her virtue (ἧς ἀρετῆς) and the immortal gods will produce a most beautiful song in honor of wise Penelope for mortal men . . .[88]

---

85. Zeus took pity on Earth weighed down by countless tribes of mortals, and "devised a plan to lighten the burden caused by mankind from the face of all-nourishing earth, by fanning into flame the great strife that was the Trojan War..." (tr. Davies, 1989).

86. The connection between I.5 And Zeus's plan in the *Cypria* was suggested by ancient critics, according to scholia A and D. See Davies 1989: the phrase 'and the will of Zeus was accomplished' occurs both in *Cypria* fr.1 and I.5, "where it seems calculated to convey a rather complex effect, impressive but rather mysterious, potentially reassuring but also potentially disturbing."

87. The epithet στυγεροῖσιν "hateful" attached to ἐπέεσσιν is particularly strong and exclusively used in xi.81 and 465. Line 466 is one of those phrases repeated only in books ix–xii.

88. This is an extremely sophisticated passage, deliberately suggesting the sharing of the virtue between Penelope and Odysseus: *hoi kleos ou pot'oleitai* could be referred to Penelope or Odysseus, and *hês aretês* could again mean her or his virtue (see for instance II.292: *hês alokhoio*, "his wife"). Many scholars discuss this passage: Foley 1978, Nagy 1979, Segal 1983, A. Edwards 1985, Papadopoulou-

Here the *Odyssey*, through the voice of Agamemnon, recognizes that Odysseus, the survivor of the heroic age, was blessed by having such a wife as Penelope. The comparison that Agamemnon draws between Penelope's virtue and Clytemnestra's murderous mind (199ff.) should not encourage us to restrict the significance of this passage to the praise a man betrayed by his wife utters for the good wife of a friend.

Rather, the passage should be read in connection with the previous praise of Achilles (xxiv.93ff.), where the conventional Iliadic *kleos* is attributed to him (κλέος ἔσσεται ἐσθλόν xxiv.94). In this parallelism, Penelope's *kleos* assumes a distinctive meaning, but one which continues an epic significance. Furthermore by presenting Penelope's virtue as her firm memory of Odysseus, and her epic renown (*kleos*) as attached to it, the text suggests that this μνήμη saved him.

Penelope saved Odysseus by refusing to marry a suitor. She constituted the safe harbor of his return and represented the only ground on which he could remain hero-king, rejecting the role of demigod that was part of the enticement of the nymphs.

That Penelope should obtain the fame of the Iliadic demigods is not the last irony. The text (just as in ix.20) creates further irony by extolling or promising fame and glory (*kleos*), and thus becoming performative as it actualizes that *kleos*. It becomes the vehicle that recycles *kleos*. This is an Iliadic gesture.

The complex field of ironies that frames this passage should be clear at this point of our reading of the oblique shades and innuendoes which the *Odyssey*'s relationship to the *Iliad* produces.

The insertion of Penelope within the tenets that control the *kleos* of the Iliadic demigods is only formal. In fact, after the mention of Achilles's *kleos* (xxix.93ff.), we expect Penelope's *kleos* to be grounded on the same values and austere principles. As we know from Nagy (1979), Iliadic *kleos* arises from excellence in the performance of *klea andrôn* (the deeds of men). A special shield (VIII.191) and an exceptional wall (VII.451ff.) may win *kleos*, and Helen, daughter of Zeus, together with Paris may become matter for songs in the future. These are the few exceptions. Iliadic poetry, defining itself through the semantic

---

Belmehdi 1994. This last scholar develops the point that "Penelope est la contrepartie féminine d'Ulysse dans le domaine du *kleos*" in so far as she embodies, just like Odysseus, anti–Iliadic values. She represents not only the *nostos*, but also the refusal of the war. Accordingly Penelope is the ideal character to symbolize a new kind of *kleos*, a new song (199).

Notice the ambivalence of construction in line 193, whereby the "great virtue" could be also the "means" through which Odysseus got his wife; it is also possible that in line 196 we read: "therefore his *kleos* will never die, his *kleos*, due to her virtue." In this case his *kleos* would refer to the *kleos* "renown" acquired through his return; but then *kleos* would be even more ironically used in a stronger non-Iliadic fashion; while the opposition which follows between this *kleos* and the στυγερὴ ἀοιδή for Clytemnestra confirms, as Segal has well seen, that this *kleos* belongs to Penelope.

and thematic connection of *klea andrôn* and *kleos*, presents itself as a song that repeats and expands the glory for accomplished heroic deeds. Penelope, on the contrary, gains *kleos* through the excellence (*aretê*) of her memory and loyalty to Odysseus: no famous deeds are hers. Besides, the *Odyssey* systematically discounts the *klea* of men. While Penelope asks to hear the "deeds of men and gods which the poet makes famous" (ἔργ' ἀνδρῶν τε θεῶν τε τά τε κλείουσιν ἀοιδοί i.337–38), Phemius, on the contrary, sings the sad return (νόστον λυγρόν) of the Achaeans (i.326–27). Demodocus, who sings the *klea andrôn*, is replaced by Odysseus and his enchanting narrative. The *Odyssey*, therefore, would not define itself as a song that produces *kleos*, but rather as one that produces enchantment (*thelxis*), or a song-tale (*muthologeuein* xii.450, 453). These indeed would be the terms that bring to full light the most genuine features of Odyssean poetry.

If then both in ix.20 and in xxiv.196–97 the *Odyssey* mimes an Iliadic gesture, we must realize, here again, that the *Odyssey* unfolds its text, so to speak, on the back of the *Iliad*; this "symbiosis" entails also a polemic against the *Iliad* and an attempt to preempt it. In this paradoxical relationship which the *Odyssey* entertains with the *Iliad*, the insertion of Penelope into the demigods' type of glory constitutes both a recognition of the other epic and also a strong distancing of the *Odyssey* from the *Iliad*. Penelope is granted heroic value by Agamemnon, but the reader knows the difference between the protocols of the Iliadic and the Odyssean *kleos*, between the centrality of the *kleos* in the *Iliad* and the *ironic, marginal* function of *kleos* in the *Odyssey*.

This marginal ironic value of Iliadic *kleos* appears in all its sadness in the narrative Odysseus offers of his encounter with Agamemnon. As he interprets the death of his old companion, he realizes that Zeus's hatred and ruinous plan are much stronger than any imperishable song of glory. He had attributed the greatest *kleos* to Agamemnon when speaking to the Cyclops in ix.264, and now he sees that this fame and renown of the conqueror of Troy did not save him from the most miserable, unglorious death, as Agamemnon himself laments (θάνον οἰκτίστῳ θανάτῳ xi.42).

The brooding Agamemnon and Odysseus are interrupted by the soul of Achilles, who comes surrounded by those of Patroclus, Antilochus, and Ajax— the very best. On the character of Achilles in this scene, much has been written, both on its content and on its difficult tone. For here, more than ever, the pathos the text exuded in Achilles's words is tinged with some tartness and some polemical intent. To measure the precise combination of these notes seems impossible, and their jarring vibrations cannot be checked or silenced.

I will again focus on Odysseus's reaction and especially on the first part of Odysseus's and Achilles' conversation.

Achilles speaks lamenting (472) and questions how Odysseus could dare to come to Hades.[89] Odysseus explains that he came for the sake of Teiresias, and then unexpectedly utters an extravagant praise of Achilles (481–87):

> But for you, Achilles, none other was ever more blessed[90] in the past and in the future. For before, when you were living, we Achaeans honored you as a god and now you have a great power here among the dead.[91] Therefore do not grieve for your death, Achilles.

Achilles' reply is well known (484ff.):

> Do not comfort me about death, splendid Odysseus.[92] I would prefer, as a hireling, to serve another man, a landless man who has no great livelihood,[93] rather than be the lord among the departed dead.

Achilles' somber view of his death and his confession that he would prefer to be alive as a working man rather than enjoy honors in Hades has led readers to feel that he is explicitly rejecting the heroic life and the *kleos* that accompanies it. But this conclusion is oddly paralleled by the pride Achilles later manifests for the heroic behavior of his son, Neoptolemos (538–40).[94]

Perhaps we will find a richer signification in Achilles' words if we start from Odysseus's extravagant praise. Extravagant, because there is no indication that

---

89. πῶς ἔτλης: the verb echoes with the typical epithets of Odysseus, πολύτλας, τλήμων; see Pucci 1987, 44ff., and it wavers between the meanings: "to dare" and "to withstand" and "to suffer."
The land of the dead is described by Achilles in the most pathetic way: "where dwell the senseless dead, the phantoms of mortals outworn." Odysseus appears to be an audacious survivor among his old companions, phantoms of the doomed race.

90. Manuscripts and editors waver between μακάρτατος and μακάρτερος. This attribute is difficult to explain here as it is ascribed to the dead Achilles. See Heubeck 1989.

91. A strong chiastic position emphasizes the opposition between life and death (484–86a):
πρὶν μὲν γὰρ σε ζωὸν
           ἐτίομεν
                    ἶσα θεοῖσιν
                    μέγα
           κρατεῖς
ἐνθάδ᾽ ἐών

92. In φαίδιμ᾽ Ὀδυσσεῦ, notice the epithet φαίδιμ(ε), which in the *Iliad* is never attributed to Odysseus, but only to Achilles (IX.434; XXI.160, 583; XXII.216).The *Odyssey* forces Achilles to pay to Odysseus a compliment that the *Iliad* always refuses to grant.

93. Perhaps here Achilles ironically alludes to Odysseus's own capability of assuming all sorts of low and undignified roles.

94. Schmiel 1987.

Achilles enjoys a special *kratos* in Hades. In fact, the succession of souls presenting themselves to Odysseus intimates that Agamemnon is still the supreme leader.

Furthermore, Achilles has not condemned his own death: he is lamenting (472), but so are also other souls (391ff.); and his description of Hades (475–76), dark and ominous as it is, does not contain any personal note.

Finally, from the point of view of the *Iliad*, Odysseus's assertion that the Achaeans "honored" (ἐτίομεν) Achilles like a god is only partially correct. During the quarrel and the *mênis*, Achilles's *timê* (honor and privileges) were brutally offended by Agamemnon and very feebly defended by the other Achaean leaders.[95]

The extravagant aspect of Odysseus's praise sounds more surprising if we compare it with Agamemnon's praise of Achilles' death in xxiv.36ff. Agamemnon values the traditional markers of heroic death: the great heroic battle of "the best of the Achaeans" around Achilles's body, the extraordinary funeral rites with Thetis and the Muses singing the *thrênos*, the funeral games with marvelous prizes, the building of a great tomb high on a jutting headland over the wide Hellespont "that it might be seen from the sea by the men who are now and those who will be in the future" (83–84). And Agamemnon concludes: "Therefore not even dead have you lost your name, but forever your noble fame (*kleos*) will be among all men, Achilles" (93–94).

This is the correct epic consolation and praise for heroic death; in exchange for his life, the hero gets a renown that will never be extinguished in the world among all living men and gods. Odysseus, on the contrary, tries to praise Achilles as though some heroic distinction were marking the death itself of the hero, the status of his death in the underworld. This attempt sounds as an improper way of placing in Hades some sort of heroicization of Achilles that, according to Proclus's account of the *Aethiopis*, occurred in the Island of Leuke.

Is Odysseus then simply unskillful in this desperate attempt of imagining or suggesting a special *kratos* in the death itself of the hero? Or is Narrator I using Odysseus in order to level an ironic and crude reflection at the small value of worldly fame if some sort of status is not assured the hero in his death? It seems that the latter better explains Achilles' response. For the hero seems ironically to suggest that even if there were some sort of recognition among the dead, this would not compensate the loss of life. It would be better to be alive even as a hireling, rather than to reign among the dead. In other words, the privileged status a hero may enjoy among the dead would not make his death worthy.

Of course, in the parallel between the hireling and the king of the dead, the contrast between life and death is implicit and cannot be erased. It seems as though the ironic meaning has been crossed by the bitterer one and the two significations hang somehow together in Achilles' answer.

---

95. Also in xxiv.24ff, in the second *Nekuia*, the theme of the quarrel and the *mênis* seem forgotten; Achilles speaks to Agamemnon only with lavish compliments, and Agamemnon returns them. The reconciliation between the two heroes is already evident in the *Iliad*; still, at XXIII.890–94, some readers find that irony is leveled at Agamemnon by Achilles. See Postlethwaite 1995, 95ff.

Whether or not Achilles asserts the idea that the real compensation for heroic death is provided by the epic *kleos,* spreading among all men and gods, remains undecidable.

Surely Achilles's desire to return as a hero to defend his father, and his pride in Neoptolemos's heroism suggest that for him there is no other life than the heroic one. But Odysseus's odd praise resonates with upsetting questions: has the epic *kleos* any sense for the dead hero? Has the epic *kleos* any sense *at all?* The *Odyssey*'s answer, to say the least, is oblique, or, presumably, negative.

The End of the Heroic Race and Tradition

Though in the previous pages I have underlined the motifs that present Odysseus as a survivor of his generation and as a sort of link between two ages, a stronger emphasis has certainly fallen on the narrative's rhetoric, fictional structure, pleasurable and edifying purposes. I wish now to collect some of the passages that more explicitly illustrate the *Odyssey*'s awareness that, with Odysseus's *nostos,* the heroic age is over and that its poetic tradition is finished.

The *Odyssey* insistently aligns Achaeans and Trojans in the same doom and destruction. Time and again the poets and the characters of the poem comment on this common destruction as though the Achaean triumph over Troy had created no difference, no distinction between the fate of the two peoples.[96]

In the first book, after Phemius has sung about "the sad return of the Achaeans," as it was ordered by Athena (326–27), Telemachus paraphrases this theme by calling it "the harsh fate of the Danaans" (*Danaôn kakon oiton,* i.350). This phrasing needs commentary.

---

96. In the few Iliadic passages that explicitly refer to the end of the war (II.36ff.; VIII.431ff.; XV.59ff.) we hear, from the divine perspective, no sure plan of the final demise of the heroic race. In II.38–40 and VIII.431 the destiny of the Achaeans and the Trojans is conjoined through the phrasing *Trôsi te hai Danaoisi*—which we will find also once in the *Odyssey* viii.8. But the reference is to their labors and sufferings.

Cypria fr. 1 makes explicit mention of Zeus's plan (*boulê*) to destroy the race of the heroes (*hêrôes*) in order to lighten the earth of the excessive human burden. Whether *Iliad* I.5 refers to this *boulê* is mooted since Antiquity (see n. 86). Hesiod, fr. 204, 96ff. (MW) unequivocally states Zeus's plan and will to destroy the demigods (*hêmitheoi*) in order to prevent the children of the gods from mating with the wretched mortals. In short, Zeus enacts a neat separation between the human and divine races by eliminating the race of the demigods.

The idea that the *Odyssey* signals the end of the heroic tradition is familiar. I select two of the recent authors who have underlined this point, Reucher 1989 and Martin 1993. See particularly Martin's statement on p. 240: "...the poem itself speaks of the end of a tradition." My analysis unravels some of the ways in which this end is represented.

First, Telemachus does not limit this harsh fate of the Danaans to the troubles of their return. Their ruin is general. In fact the expression *Danaôn kakon oiton aeidein* (i.350) echoes the one Odysseus will later use on viii.489: *Akhaiôn oiton aeideis* to speak of the Achaean fate in Troy, and the one Alcinous will employ on viii.578: *Argeiôn Danaôn êd' Iliou oiton akouôn* ("listening to the fate of the Argive Danaans and of Ilios") to refer to the common doom of the two peoples.

Moreover Telemachus replaces the word *Akhaiôn* (i.326) with the word *Danaôn* (i.350): the substitution is significant, since *Danaoi* in the *Odyssey* refers only to the Achaeans as characters of the Trojan war and never as characters acting in the *Odyssey*. *Danaoi*, therefore, is for the *Odyssey* the name of a past people, no longer surviving as such in the fictional time of the poem. In i.350; viii.82, 578, xi.559, this name occurs in the context of their destruction.

Finally Telemachus attributes this harsh fate inflicted on the Danaans to Zeus (i.348–49) and not to Athena, as Phemius had sung (i.326–27). It is difficult to assess correctly this different attribution. Whether Telemachus implies that Athena is simply enacting the plan of Zeus, and whether this plan is the one that envisages the destruction of the Danaans, is impossible to decide, but it is plausible. If all this is correct or plausible, Telemachus would interpret "the sad return of the Achaeans" as a chapter of the general theme of "the destruction of the Achaeans" thanks to the will of Zeus.

This theme is picked up by Demodocus in the Phaeacians' palace, when he sings of the first episode, the quarrel between Achilles and Odysseus, that had to be the sign of the beginning of the great disaster (viii.81–82):

Then the beginning of the ruin (*pêma*) rolled over[97]
Trojans and Danaans alike,[98] thanks to the plans of great Zeus.

We notice here the use of the word *Danaoi*, as a name of the past, and the mention of Zeus's plans. Whether Demodocus intends to refer to the Cyprian or Hesiodic theme or to allude to a version of his own, remains undecidable.

Line 82 stitches together two formulaic expressions, the second of which *Dios megalou dia boulas* is built on the metrical pattern: u — uu —uu — — in the final part of the verse. This pattern occurs four times in Homer (XV.71;

---

97. The image of a "calamity that rolls over (*kulindei)*" is also Iliadic: XI.347; XVII.29, 99, 688. The word *pêma* implies suffering and calamity, often in defeat. It refers sometimes to the calamity produced by the death of a great hero, as in XVII.688 where Menelaus says that "the gods roll a great *pêma* [the death of Patroclus] over the Achaeans..." In *Odyssey* xi.535, *pêma* indicates the calamity that the gods inflicted to the Argives through the death of Patroclus.
98. The phrase *Trôsi te hai Danaoisi* occurs in *Iliad* II.40 and VIII.431, in the context of the same theme.

viii.82; ix.276, 437) and designs a filigree of allusions in contexts of the same theme.[99]

While Demodocus sings this lay on the origin of the great ruin for Trojans and Danaans, Odysseus begins to cry. When later the hero praises the poet for this song and truthful recounting, he rephrases the theme of Demodocus' lay, saying (489–90): *Akhaiôn oiton aeideis* ("you sing the fate of the Achaeans"). Odysseus disregards the common destiny of Trojans and Achaeans, and focuses, with this formulaic phrase, on the ruin of the Achaeans. The Trojans are absent from this passage and also from Odysseus's encounters in Hades.

But Alcinous, in reverse, when referring to the third song of Demodocus, the one on the destruction of Troy by the Achaeans and on the deeds of Menelaus and Odysseus, enlarges the horizon of the song, as he asks Odysseus (viii.577–80):

> Tell me why you weep and lament in your heart
> when you listen to the ruin of the Argive Danaans and Ilios.
> The gods produced it, they spun threads of death
> for mortals, in order to have matter for song also for those who shall come.

The word *Danaoi* indicates again the Achaeans of the past; the notion of *kleos* ("glory") is absent and in its place we read the word *aoidê* ("song"), though of course this *aoidê* is thought as a song spreading in the future and therefore functioning like *kleos*.

It is suggested by the *kai* ("also") of line 580 that Alcinous and all those who are listening to Demodocus's song are contemporaries with the events the poet has narrated. In fact Alcinous assumes that Odysseus is weeping because he lost a close relative in that war (581ff.).

The distance that separates the experiences and the poetics of the *Iliad* (and of the other poems on the war) from those of the *Odyssey* is therefore presented by the *Odyssey* not in chronological, but in spiritual terms. Alcinous does not comment on the quality and nature of this song; he simply terms it a song also for future generations, implying Iliadic poetics; but this restraint must be contrasted with the lavish praise he gives of Odysseus's own narrative (xi.366–68).[100]

Alcinous attributes the destruction of the whole generation of warriors to the gods.[101] He presents his own version of the reason why the gods wish this ruin. In comparison with the grounds presented by Odysseus when he speaks of Zeus's

---

99. Line 82, therefore, by its two formulaic segments, could refer to the Iliadic passages with the analogous theme (II.38–40; VIII.43l; XV.71) and puts together the theme of Troy's destruction (XV.71) and the theme of Zeus's will concerning the suffering of Trojans and Achaeans alike.

100. I am reminded of Telemachus's praise of the new song that men applaud more (*epikleiousi*, i.351), when he rebukes his mother who wanted to listen to the deeds of heroes and gods (*erg'andrôn te theôn te*, i.338).

101. See Nagy 1979, 101 and 113 who argues that *Iliad* I.5 is treated as a foil by this passage (viii.577–80).

hatred, Alcinous's explanation is idyllic, if not frivolous.[102] It is in tune with the Phaeacians' appreciation of Demodocus's poetry that simply amuses them. They have to hear the sacred monster Odysseus and fall bewitched by the fascinating power of the new poetic voice.

It is in his dialogue with Agamemnon that Odysseus gives this harsh explanation for the ruin of the Achaeans (xi.435–39):

> Alas! Verily loud-voicing Zeus has terribly hated the seed of Atreus through the females' plans. For Helen's sake so many of us vanished and now Clytemnestra has ambushed you while you were far off.

The hapax *gunaikeias dia boulas* ("females' plans") deserves some attention. First, it is inscribed in a fixed pattern that occurs three other times in this specific theme. In particular the phrase recalls a line, *Iliad* XV.71, at the end of a passage where Zeus declares his intent to pursue his plan until the destruction of Troy:

> "I will cause a new pursuit from the ships
> that will endure continuously until the Achaeans
> will take steep Ilios, thanks to the plans of Athena (*Athênaiês dia boulas*)."

What are these plans or decisions of Athena? Presumably Athena's help in the construction of the Trojan Horse (viii.193). It remains enigmatic why Zeus wants to mention the complicity of Athena: perhaps to win the favor of Hera to whom he is speaking?

In the Odyssean passage, Zeus's hatred comes to fulfillment thanks to the active decision and will of Helen and Clytemnestra. Though Helen is indeed Zeus's daughter and therefore in some way analogous to Athena in the Iliadic passage, nevertheless the coupling of Helen and Clytemnestra with the epithet *gunaikeias* suggests that Odysseus is thinking of mortal females. The adaptation, if this is an adaptation, is therefore subtle and felicitous.

The new role that the *Odyssey* attributes to women is here clearly exemplified. In comparison with the Iliadic Helen, who is mostly represented as a passive element in the play of male intrigues, here Helen acquires the same active determination as Clytemnestra. The misogynistic streak of the *Odyssey*, however, emerges here too, since this active participation of the two women in the destruction of the heroes functions as a pretext and a foil for Agamemnon's advice against trusting women.

In the encounter with Ajax, Odysseus indicts Zeus's hatred as responsible for Ajax's death (xi.558–60):

---

102. Marg, 1971, 20 f. notes the importance of the final clause (580: "in order that..."): it implies the purposeful transformation of pain into song. For Marg, Alcinous and the Phaeacians enjoy poetry as "poesie pure."

> No one else was responsible but Zeus: terribly he hated the army of the
> spear-holding Danaans and imposed on you this fate.

With the appearance of the name of the past people, the Danaans, Odysseus
evokes indirectly the ruin of the whole army.

Ajax does not answer, because he still feels enmity toward Odysseus (562),
but had he wanted to answer, what could he have said after such a statement by
Odysseus? That his fame was still alive? Not even Achilles can say so. And had
Odysseus wanted to flatter the two heroes, could he have sincerely assured them
that their name and reputation were spreading in the world?

Hardly so, in accordance with the *Odyssey*. The only place where Achilles'
glory is extolled is, again, Hades (xxiv.93–94). Otherwise, only the Phaeacians
feel the pleasure of listening to those glorious deeds, but the Phaeacians are a
fabulous people outside history. In another fabulous setting, among the
Cyclopes, Odysseus boasts of having been a man of Agamemnon, whose "glory
is the greatest under the sky" (ix.264). In the real world, however, Agamemnon,
the victorious leader of the Achaeans, returns home and is slaughtered at a festive
occasion like a bull. His great *kleos* does not give him any privileges, nor even
respect.

And what about the remembrance of the glorious past in the houses of the old
heroes? In Ithaca, in the house of the *ptoliporthos*, Phemius does not sing the
κλέα ἀνδρῶν (the glorious deeds of the heroes), but their sad return and death
(i.325–59). This is what the young men like to listen to. And Telemachus, too,
likes it (i.351–52). Is this the spreading of the praise poetry and *kleos* to *all*
men? In Menelaus's house, the recalling of the past is insufferable for the new
generation (iv.190ff.). The heroic past can finally be told by Menelaus and Helen
only because Helen drugs the listeners and speakers and makes them immune to
a suffering that otherwise would be unbearable (iv.219ff.). Even Athena must
recognize that no one of the peoples Odysseus ruled still remembers him (v.11).

There are no privileges in heroic death. The doom that weighs upon the
whole heroic generation remains without any consoling remedy. Only life, any
sort of life, counts.

The Sirens

In Chapter One, I have shown the Iliadic texture of the passage in which the
Sirens urge Odysseus to stop his ship and listen to their song (xii.184–91). I
deduced that they invite him specifically as a hero whose *kleos* is the Iliadic
kleos. In that brief analysis, uncovering the use of vocabulary from the *Iliad* was
my major object, so I did not consider the whole context of the episode. I
returned to it in my *Odysseus Polutropos*. Here I have seen that the promise of
the Sirens' sublime and seducing song is embedded in the *Odyssey* in such a way
that this poem appropriates it for itself: "No text can incorporate the titillating

promise of a song as sublime as the Sirens' without implying that this same sublimity resides in the incorporating text itself" (212). To dramatize the promise of such a song is to become the text of that song.[103]

These Iliadic Muses thus urge the Iliadic Odysseus to stop and to enjoy the recounting of his *kleos;* but because he has become the Odyssean Odysseus, he refuses, though powerfully tempted by the power of recollection and the excitement of that story. Like the Muses and the bards of the *Odyssey*, the Sirens are represented as able to seduce and charm (*thelgein*), even when they sing Iliadic themes.[104] Thus the Sirens have affinities with those magic and erotic enticements which Odysseus encounters on his long, difficult journey home.[105] As Odysseus succeeds in mastering Circe, only with the help of a magic potion, and in escaping the Lotus-eaters, only by binding his companions, so he is equally powerless before the enchantment of poetry. He wants to listen, but he knows that it will master him. No poet has ever portrayed poetry as corrupting and dangerous in more powerful terms than Narrator I does here through the voice of his embedded narrator, Odysseus.

The corrupting and dangerous moment lies in the Sirens' promise: for the symbolic meaning that takes shape around their unrealized promise produces the expectation of an impossible song and the utopia of a unique song. As Blanchot writes, they lead Odysseus toward the space

> where singing would really begin ... The enchantment, through an enigmatic promise, was inducing men to become unfaithful to themselves, to their human song and even to the essence of the song, as it was rousing in them the hope and the desire of a marvelous beyondness. This beyondness was nothing other than a desert as though the motherland of music would have been the only place deprived of music ... (10–11)

Odysseus would indeed betray himself if he were stopping at the Sirens' island, where he would meet the vastness of an eternal song of glory (*kleos*) and simultaneously its desert. He would remain under the seduction of the nymphs, and encircled by their modes of being that shut the mortals within the heroic age and its closing time.

Odysseus, with his experience and his knowledge of the world, meets the Sirens with their promise of a song that possesses knowledge of the world and

---

103. See Blanchot 1959, 12ff.: the Sirens induced him to undertake the successful unsuccessful journey which is that of the narration i.e., the song which is no longer sung, but told ... "ode that has become episode."

104. It is odd that the *Odyssey* attributes the power of charming (*thelgein*) to the heroic (Iliadic?) song (see *thelkteria* i.337). The *Iliad* never attributes that power to song, only to sexual attraction and magic. The Sirens' power to enchant (*thelgein*) Odysseus produces, of course, a mimetic effect and charms Odysseus's listeners, the Phaeacians, and us. See Goldhill 1993, 147–50.

105. Segal elaborates this point: "In this temptation of 'forgetting the return' the Sirens' magical spell has affinities not only with Circe, but also with the Lotus-eaters. There too a man forgets his return ... The victims of the Lotus, like Odysseus in book 12, have to be bound forcibly in the ship" (1994, 102).

bewitches with pleasure and enchantment. Both he and the Sirens cannot coexist, and one must disappear. The Sirens disappear in the *Odyssey*, and yet their promise haunts Odysseus, and Homer, and enlarges his text beyond Odysseus's world and knowledge, into a tension toward an unfathomable wondrousness.

The long reading scene Homer stages in his poem between Odysseus (Narrator II) and the Phaeacians, his readers, could not end with a more appropriate caution against or a more fitting praise of the power of poetry. With the representation of the Sirens' encounter with Odysseus, the text embeds a new reading scene in Odysseus's narrative. Odysseus tells us that he listened to a promise told by the Sirens (Narrator III). With an extraordinary economy the text consolidates all the terms of the reading scenes: the integrity, the knowledge, the seductive power of a narrator, the titillating promise of a vast, sublime story to be told, and the unavoidable enchantment of the eager reader.

All our careful inquiries suspecting the integrity and solidity of these terms would seem to be swept away by this grand gesture. There is such a master storyteller, there is such a sublime story, and there are such readers, who cannot withstand the magic of the poetic voice. Accordingly there is such a song that produces heroic fame, a song that never dies and keeps the memory of the hero alive forever.

However the song of the Sirens remains a promise. The singers never deliver that unfathomable poem of delight and knowledge and the listener is only bewitched by his desire for such a song. In fact, Odysseus had already decided that he would not listen to it.

All the terms in question—author, song, and narrative—would acquire fullness only in the perspective of that unsung song. But Odysseus never stops in the region where that song would be possible, where the song of the fallen heroes would result in their immortal life. That region would be a place of death and life, where endless repetition of the whole of things would be equivalent to their silence, and vision would be parallel to blindness.

That is why Odysseus must escape that Master and that scene of reading. Outside that fatal condition, the scene of reading stages the narrator, the story, and the reader in the fragmented, recycled, and suspended figures that we have shown through our careful inquires.

CHAPTER 10

Honor and Glory in the *Iliad*

The origin of the opposites, *good* and *bad,* is to be found in the pathos of nobility and distance, representing the dominant temper of a higher ruling class in relation to a lower, dependent one. (The lordly right of bestowing names is such that one would almost be justified in seeing the origin of language itself as an expression of the rulers' power. They say, 'This *is* that or that'; they seal off each thing and action with a sound and thereby take symbolic possession of it.)

—Nietzsche, *The Genealogy of Morals*

When Achilles complains that in Agamemnon's camp there is the one and the same lot for the man who stays back and for the man who rushes to battle, and the same honor (*timê*) for the coward and for the brave—ἴση μοῖρα μένοντι καὶ εἰ μάλα τις πολεμίζοι· / ἐν δὲ ἰῇ τιμῇ ἠμὲν κακὸς ἠδὲ καὶ ἐσθλός (IX.318–19)—he expresses his resentment that a greater *timê* (honor and privileges of status) does not await the man who accomplishes glorious, warriorlike deeds.[1] As Hainsworth puts it: "For Akhilleus there is an equation between *kleos, kudos,* and *timê.* In the real world that equation is a pretense because distinctions in rank are not established by the achievement of fame, and the possession of status *ipso facto* confers *kudos,* cf. I.279" (1993, 104).

---

1. The privileges of status are both material goods and symbolic signs of deference. They map a large series of services, gifts, and gestures of respect and admiration that the man with *timê* receives: see van Wees 1992, 69ff. In the case of Achilles' present statement, he resents that the apportionment of booty—with the symbolic signs of respect and recognition that are attached to it—is not allotted in accordance to the measure of each fighter's military prowess.

A stronger reading of the passage (IX.315ff.), however, would infer that a *timê* that is the appanage both of the brave and of the coward is not, in any case, a worthy *timê* for one like Achilles, who consecrates himself to an early death. Death, he continues, catches both the coward and the brave (320). Most likely[2] he means that before the undiscriminating arrival of death, there should be something exciting and powerful that justifies the choice of the brave. He may have in mind something akin to *kharis* (316), which should be understood not merely as "a thanks for fighting," but "a gracing reason," "a delightful reason" for fighting.[3] To be sure, Achilles asking for an equation of *kleos* and *timê* advances an impossible request. But for him, this request means also the social recognition of his absolute uniqueness, of his privileged (IX.323ff.) and cursed (IX.410ff.) personal situation.[4] Yet Agamemnon and the Danaans have not listened to his request (IX.315-16).

It is problematic for us that someone destined to die young and acquire immortal glory should care so much about status and its prerogatives. It seems that the lesson the text has Achilles learn—that Agamemnon is the more powerful—is a bitter one and that the learning of it forces him to discover disconcerting truths, such as the questionable value of *timê*.

The grounds for Agamemnon's exclusive claim to supreme power are not fully clear to modern scholars.[5] To this extent, Achilles' reasons for his frustration cannot be correctly assessed. Yet, as we will see, his word does not command the same authority as Agamemnon's; it does not have the same institutional recognition. Therefore, Achilles' disobedience, however nastily or imprudently provoked, is a breach of authority and threatens to unsettle the whole hierarchy of the Achaean army. Indeed, as the proem tells us (I.1–5), it will cause countless Achaean deaths.

If we consider the prerogatives of *timê* and *kleos* as two parallel but distinct systems of power, we realize first of all their contiguity, osmosis, and

---

2. Line 320, however, has often been bracketed because of its recent Attic grammar and its supposed "weakness." See Leaf's commentary.

3. On this *kharis* see MacLachlan 1993, 13ff.

4. Zanker 1994, 81: "the incommensurability of effort and reward is dispiriting enough, but in his choice of the word *moira* "portion" Achilles is thinking to death . . ." Zanker's attempt at finding in Achilles' text traces of his singular condition seems to me justified, though his reading of ambivalent meanings in *moira* and other words leaves me skeptical.

5. Hainsworth comments on IX.160, with Agamemnon's declaration that he is "more kingly" (*basileuteros*) than Achilles, that: "it would be natural to take *basileuteros* to mean that Agamemnon in some way outranked Akhilleus (as is generally implied), not merely that he could mobilize more ships and men. However this aspect of the politics of the Heroic Age was unknown to the poet or at least not clarified by him. There was no reason why he should define it, for if he did the rights and wrongs of Akhilleus' dispute with Agamemnon would be defined also, and instead of a quarrel, there would have been a rebellion. In that case Agamemnon would have had, what he evidently lacks, sanctions. Instead we have an insoluble moral issue, the relative respect-worthiness of social eminence and martial excellence" (1993, 104).

parallelism.[6] But soon we discover that each system has its own vocabulary and protocols. In the assembly, the *commanding* word belongs only to Agamemnon as *anax andrôn*, and, there, his *kudos*, too, is unique. In the field, he is responsible for the expedition: if it succeeds, the *kudos* "glory" will be his (IV.415); but if it fails, his will be the scorn (II.285) or dishonor (IX.22=II.115). He urges on the whole Achaean army (V.529; XI.153-54; although Nestor does also at VI.67-71). The marshaling (*epipôlêsis*) of all the troops[7] and the distribution of food and wine to the other *basileis* is his prerogative and duty. As the senior and as the leader of a larger contingent, Agamemnon's status is higher than that of Achilles. Seniority is important: Nestor owes his authority to his long experience, and even Zeus is superior to Poseidon because he is older (*Iliad* XV.165–66). On the other hand Agamemnon has no military *kudos* and no *kleos*,[8] while the brave warrior has both. The brave man acquires this reputation by constantly risking his life, as Achilles says of himself. Therefore, while relatively marginal to the power structure, the courageous warrior is uniquely close to the awareness of his personal destiny.

This situation implies an unsettled tension between the protocols of the two systems of power, an imbalance crucially important in the *Iliad* because the poem bestows—and knows that it is the bestower—of glory (*kleos*), as Nagy 1979 has shown. While it can only nod at and occasionally extol the *timê* of the kings and assent to their commanding word and privileges, this dispenser of

6. Martin (1989, 97) illustrates exactly the terms of this interrelation: "The problem of the *Iliad* appears to be rooted in the clash of two systems: status-based *timê* and performance-based judgments, the latter an almost economically pragmatic 'market-value.' But in a different view, this is really just one system, in which status must always be recreated anew by performance, while it is concurrently threatened by the performance of other heroes. (Thus in Agamemnon's view, Achilles' offense is to wish 'to speak as an equal' and 'be likened openly' to the king I.186–87). The two systems overlap in that all brave fighters are simultaneously kings or princes (*basileis*) with their own scepters and prerogatives, and that the supreme commander is himself at times a good fighter. Zanker (1994, 11ff.) strongly underlines the fluid interrelation between the two systems.

7. See, for example, IV.231ff., XI.264, and XI.540. Odysseus, another "political" leader, is described in this function in III.196. Achilles marshals only his own troops, the Myrmidons, once (XVI.166ff.), and then only to send Patroclus to the battlefield. He remains behind waiting for the results. On Agamemnon's precise authority, see Sale 1994, 21ff.

8. Critics often take Agamemnon's *kudos* (I.278–79) as a manifestation of generic glory, but I believe that it is a *kudos* that is attached only to his commanding word. There are a few instances in the *Iliad*, in which a king is said to possess a certain *kleos*, but in these cases *kleos* means perhaps a glorious image rather than specifically military glory. At any rate, as we shall see, Agamemnon is never granted any *kleos* in the *Iliad*. The privileges of *timê* derive from status and not from military prowess. See Collins (1988, 89): "Nestor's reference to a distinctly royal *timê* and *kudos* (I.278–79) reminds Achilles that a king's status is not a mere reflection of his achievements." Also see van Wees (1992, 353n55): "It must be stressed that they do not acquire these privileges [of *timê*] by fighting bravely: they receive these privileges by virtue of their status as princes."

kleos needs characters that embody and recycle its voice of *kleos*, that is, the voice that gives reputation and glorious fame.

Two Voices: The Commanding Word and the Pathetic Autopsy

Critics generally agree with Nestor that an important reason, perhaps the most important reason, that Agamemnon is more powerful than Achilles is that Agamemnon commands a larger number of men (I.281). This is certainly the case, and it is a reason that Achilles must consider. But despite its *realpolitisch* weight, this cannot be the real source of Agamemnon's supremacy, for he shows no fear of any possible coalition against him. During the quarrel in the first book, he addresses the assembled "lords and captains of the Argives," threatening to take Odysseus's captive girl, or Ajax's, or Achilles', adding that he will enrage the man he will so deprive. In one breath, he insults three kings whose combined military strength might seriously upset his numerical superiority. But he fears no such coalition of forces.

Furthermore, he asserts that taking another's prize is his right.[9] And as he speaks he obviously fears neither rebellion nor personal assault (Achilles was tempted to kill him). And he is sure, when Achilles does rebel, that the other leaders (*basileis*) will remain on his side and will "honor me, and especially wise Zeus (will honor me)" [πάρ' ἔμοιγε καὶ ἄλλοι / οἵ κέ με τιμήσουσι, μάλιστα δὲ μητίετα Ζεύς (I.174–75)]. It is clear that his power lies in the honor that all the other Achaeans render him, without contesting his invocation of privilege, without protesting his apparent insolence. His commanding word persuades them. The honor he receives from Zeus is the religious counterpart to the human deference he expects from the Achaean chiefs.

It is this power of Agamemnon's commanding word that Achilles puts into question when he protests Agamemnon's plan to seize his prize, exclaiming (I.149–151):

ὤ μοι ἀναιδείην ἐπιειμένε κερδαλεόφρον[10]

---

9. Later, Agamemnon is reproached for his high-handedness toward Achilles by Nestor (XI.111), by the Greeks at large (XIII.108–14), and by Thersites (II.240). And finally, of course, even he himself regrets his folly (XIX.88–89), but these later and not disinterested judgments—the absence of Achilles creates havoc among the Achaeans—only enhance the uncontested authority that Agamemnon possesses in the assembly, when he speaks and says that it is not proper that he alone remain without a gift.

10. Notice the scream ὤ μοι of indignation and anger. In this first book, this utterance will be used again, as an expression of grief, only by Thetis at 414.

In the *Iliad* the warriors wear bronze armor and (metaphorically) *alkê* (XX.381, etc.). On this line, see Lowenstam (1981, 10ff.), who analyzes the conjunction "of honorific and pejorative terms" and the mingling of a traditional fixed segment with an ad hoc expression.

πῶς τίς τοι πρόφρων ἔπεσιν πείθηται¹¹ Ἀχαιῶν
ἢ ὁδὸν ἐλθέμεναι ἢ ἀνδράσιν ἶφι μάχεσθαι;

[You, armored in shamelessness, greedy mind, how can any Achaean warrior
be gladly persuaded by your words to begin an expedition or to go to fight full
force?]

Achilles' question is a bombshell. He wonders how any warrior, any other
basileus, can be persuaded by this man when so few of them have a reason for
hostility against the Trojans, and besides, when he shares so little of the treasure
that his fighting peers produce for him. How is it possible? How can Achilles
obey him?

The silence of the other *basileis*, equally threatened by Agamemnon, is his
answer. To quote Michael Naas (1995, 38):

> The commander is not honored and obeyed because he is a commander; he is a
> commander because he is honored and obeyed. Command is not, then, some
> mysterious or unactualized power that resides in a present or would-be king; it
> is the sum of the relations of obedience which already exist, and is thus
> inseparable from the obedience it elicits. Command is based not in the poten-
> tial to gain obedience, but in the relations of obedience themselves. Hence to
> declare oneself commander or King is not merely to give an external sign of a
> state already realized, but is in large part to realize that declaration.

It is sufficient for Agamemnon to say, "I am the stronger," and it is so,
because this commanding word both embodies and gathers the deference and the
acquiescence of the others. Being and word coalesce, and the identity between the
authority of the king and that of the community is guaranteed. That is why he is
anax andrôn.

Let us now take a closer view of the passage (I.149–51).

The obedience, the acquiescence of the kings is described by Achilles as being
"freely," "gladly" given (*prophrôn*, I.150): "How can any Achaean warrior be
gladly persuaded [*prophrôn . . . peithêtai*] by your words?"

The adjective *prophrôn* most often qualifies the king (I.77; XXIII.647; ii.30 =
v.8),¹² the person in power who receives a needy person or a guest (IX.480, and
other times, in the *Odyssey* for the amiable host), or the god who listens to

---

Only Agamemnon and Odysseus (IV.339, where *kerdaleophrôn* must mean
"scheming") merit this epithet in the *Iliad*. These two political chiefs have the same
virtues.

11. Notice the emphasis on "be persuaded *by your words*" (ἔπεσιν falls between
two caesuras): Agamemnon has no other means to gain obedience but his words. A
strong alliteration of 'p' unites the larger part of the line.

12. In these passages the adjective qualifies the protective, kindly attitude of the
ideal scepter-holding king: an ideal portrait that is proper to the *Odyssey*, where he is
prophrôn, aganos, and *êpios*.

prayers (VIII.175, XIV.71, 357; XXII.303, XXIV.140),[13] and often, in the
Odyssey, those who obey gladly and willingly. This means that Achilles
deviates from the normal *Iliadic* use of the adjective and grants to the obedient
warrior that graciousness which the *Iliad* normally attributes to those in
command. By doing so, he subtly underlines the absurdity of such a willing, free
obedience to a man like Agamemnon and tries to provoke the other *basileis*.
Simultaneously, the text hints to the reader about the oddity and newness of the
question that Achilles raises. This is his explosive discovery.

   After this unheard-of question, "How can any Achaean gladly obey
Agamemnon?" Achilles enumerates all the arguments that should provide this
question with the answer that no Achaean should, for no Achaean has any
personal reason to be here. Notice how, with *ou gar* (152), he drives home the
point that the Trojans were never guilty of anything toward him, and how
emphatically he describes the remoteness of Phthia from all Trojan activity (154,
with a new *ou gar* on line 157). But then, why did he obey Agamemnon freely?
He answers this question with an insult and implies that he speaks for all the
other Achaeans (158–60): "But it is you, great shameless one, whom we all
followed, in order to please you [*ophra su khairêis*], to win honor from the
Trojans for you and Menelaus, you dog-face! You think nothing, you care
nothing about all this."[14]

   So, this is why all the Achaeans are expected to obey him gladly: they
followed (*hespometha*) Agamemnon, wanting to give him pleasure and favor
(*kharis*) and wishing to obtain honor for him and Menelaus, that is,
compensation for and effacement of the received insult. By describing the alliance
and the help of the Achaeans as *kharis*, Achilles also suggests that the
relationship between the commanders of the Achaean contingent and their
supreme commander has been one based on friendship (Latacz 1966, 91).[15] Such
a basis explains why Agamemnon's word carries so much authority.

   Achilles, who has committed himself in this war more than anyone else,
denounces that behavior in a pathetic tone, while the other Achaeans keep silent.
Already his statement that the Trojans have never offended him, and that Phthia
lies far away from Troy, underscores the discovery of his marginality, and even
separateness, from the whole business of this war.[16] But, as he goes on, he
accentuates his solitude and marginality and emphasizes his suffering:

---

   13. It is curious that this adjective takes on the specific shade of "in full
earnestness" essentially when, as in XXIV.140 and elsewhere, it is an epithet of
thumôi.
   14. Naas (1995) underlines the importance of this care, *ou ti metatrepêi oud'
alegizeis*; the expression implies a turning toward the other, a flexibility that, by
quarreling, Achilles, too, is eliminating.
   15. The point is made also by Odysseus in the *Odyssey* v.306–7.
   16. Griffin aptly comments on the last line of that description (I.156-57):
"because there lies between us large space of shadowy mountains and resounding sea."
Griffin says that "the rhythm of the ... line οὔρεά τε σκιόεντα θάλασσά τε ἠχήεσσα
suddenly opens a wide and inhuman vista, a world of empty space far from the quarrels
at Troy" (1980, 75). The theme of the distance of Troy from Achilles' concern returns
in IX.337ff. in a more intense and polemical tone. Notice that Sarpedon too has no

And now you yourself threaten to strip me of my prize, for which I toiled so much [ᾧ ἔπι πολλὰ μόγησα] and the sons of the Achaeans gave it to me! Never is my prize equal to yours [οὐ μὲν σοί ποτε ἶσον ἔχω γέρας], when we sack some populous Trojan stronghold: my arms accomplish the greatest part of the fierce fight, but when it comes to dividing up the plunder, your prize is always larger, and I go back to my ships with a little and dear share [ἐγὼ δ᾽ ὀλίγον τε φίλον τε] after I have fought to exhaustion. Now I will go back to Phthia, for it is better to go home on the curved ships, nor do I deem it proper to remain here, deprived of honor [ἐνθάδ᾽ ἄτιμος ἐὼν], and draw riches and wealth for you. (I.161–68)[17]

The tone, content, and conclusions of this passage are surprising and unexpected. The tone is almost Odyssean in its awareness of suffering and its precise expression of that suffering: πολλὰ μόγησα.[18] In the *Iliad* this verb is very rare, and, in *mimesis* (in dialogue) it is used only by friends in a warm exchange (IX.492 and XXIII.607); whereas in the *Odyssey* it often describes (with *paskhô, epathon,* and so on) Odysseus's sufferings and toil.[19] Also the expression *oligon te philon te* has an Odyssean ring: it is found there twice in contexts of giving and helping a poor man (vi.208 and xiv.58), where the phrase fits much better than this one occurrence in the *Iliad*.[20] Here, accordingly, it depicts an unexpected Achilles, one who withdraws silently from the assembly, like a subdued retainer, happy with the little he gets.[21] The pathos is sustained by Achilles' claim that by his own hands (*kheires emai,* in enjambment) he accomplished the largest part of the fierce fighting—belittling therefore the efforts of all his peers—with the rare, alliterating *poluaikos polemoio* (only twice in the *Iliad*); the emotional tone is powerfully sealed by the awareness of his exertion in constant fighting. He is already the *oizuros peri pantôn* (I.417),

---

private reasons to fight in Troy, and yet he justifies his staking his life on heroic grounds (see Chapter Four).

17. Some of his phrases return in the great expression of pathos and deception that he utters in the ninth book: see I.162 and IX.492; the alliteration is strong at lines 165 (πλεῖον πολυάϊκος πολέμοιο) and 167 (ἐγὼ δ᾽ ὀλίγον τε φίλον τε). The metaphor of "drawing water" (*aphussein* 171) reminds us that slave women drew water for their owners.

18. Cf. *Odyssey* v.223 and viii.155; also see Ramersdorfer 1981, 198.

19. Note that one of the few other occurrences of the expression in the *Iliad* is also *polla mogêsa,* a reference to Achilles. See II.690.

20. See Ramersdorfer 1981, 142–43, who finds the expression utterly unfitting to its context in the *Iliad*. On Achilles' special language, similes, unique words and expressions, short and staccato speech, and so on, see Griffin 1980, 75; Schein 1980, 129, and 1984, 108; and Martin 1989, 146ff.

21. Redfield (1994, 13) finds that the phrase *oligon te philon te* is hardly fair considering the value and the high epic reputation of Chryseis and Briseis. The fact is correct, and it underlines Achilles' hyperbolic rhetoric as he seems to discover and condemn Agamemnon's outrageous behavior only now, for the first time. Only now does he wonder: "Why have we all obeyed him?"

"the most lamentable and lamenting" hero of all, as his mother will define him with a unique epithet (Pucci 1987, 57–58).[22]

The tone, in short, suggests that Agamemnon's decision has made Achilles suddenly and acutely aware of the suffering the war has cost him, the violence of this treatment, and the marginality of his position. It strikes a strong personal accent, almost a private note, as if suddenly he had freed himself from all "entangling alliances" with Agamemnon and his peers. He glances at himself in relation to the work of war and decides to cease from it. This is the first step toward the later realization that the business of war is a dismaying waste of energies and human affections. In other texts and times, we would speak of the first step of a conversion.

How should we read this conversion, this emotional outburst and self-exile from the common goal? It has been customary in modern times to interpret Achilles' lucid awareness of his suffering and his disgrace as the first step toward a negative assessment of the business of war, its vanity and absurdity. This critical line has recovered, from under the violence of Achilles' reaction, a strong streak of human concerns, and has presented a humanistic portrait of the hero.

But, on the other hand, Achilles discovers how absurd it is for him to place his frail mortality at the service of a common business that does not sufficiently aggrandize his image of himself. The uniqueness of his mortal destiny, the absolute singularity of his birth, and the magnitude of his deeds should be compensated for by some *kharis*, some unanimous recognition. His expectation is great, and his frustration at the upsetting of his *timê* is enormous. As he reflects on his own efforts and toils for the war, he reaches a sort of self-reflection that gives pathos to his voice; this same self-awareness and pathos mirror his difference from the others and deepen his isolation from them.

Through this violent dispute between Achilles and Agamemnon, the assembly has become the space that both gathers and creates their voices. I mean that it is in this space that something like the "subjectivity" of the characters comes to light and becomes visible. For it is from the interferences which this space gathers that the "subjectivity" emerges.

Agamemnon's subjective voice is composed and molded by the voices of the men who would eventually offer him a compensation (135–136) and who meanwhile do not contest the legitimacy of his decision to take the prize of one of the kings. By their silence, the men produce Agamemnon's authority and somehow they say with him that it is not proper that the supreme leader sits in his tent and remains without his precious prize (134ff.) Let us notice that only after Achilles swears to abandon the war (234–44) does Nestor rise to speak. Meanwhile Agamemnon has ordered that Chryseis be sent back to her father, and this concession, of course, must please the assembly.

Agamemnon's subjective voice is therefore his and not his: it comes from him as the echo of his men's acceptance and acquiescence. As we will discover later, this voice, by retroactivation, will appear to be also dictated by *atê*

---

22. Notice that this epithet constitutes a new link between Achilles and Odysseus in the *Odyssey*.

(blindness and ruin). Agamemnon's subjectivity emerges in this space of many interferences of otherness.

Achilles' subjective voice appears, at first, to interpret the assembly's feelings (150ff.), but little by little it turns toward his frustrations, and becomes the pathetic response to the army's acquiescence to Agamemnon. At this point, Achilles' voice sounds even as the voice of another poem. For indeed, as he fathoms the idea of going back home, he is in tune with a poem of return (*nostos*), with the nostalgia of peace in the far-removed territory of his fatherland. This attuning is impossible for Achilles, for his poem, and yet it is from this that Achilles' subjective voice acquires its unexpected singularity and novelty—what we call his self-consciousness.[23] In harmony with this voice and consciousness, Achilles will produce strong statements against the war (I.352ff.; IX.307ff.), and he will in fact cease being a character of the *Iliad* (with the exception of book nine) until book eighteen.

The split that this other-voice, that of a *nostos,* produces in him is so radical that it cannot in any way negotiate with the voice that is proper to the *Iliad* itself. Accordingly his consciousness remains decentered and disjointed. Thus, for instance, if his feeling that he has lost honor leads him to abandon the war, he should feel a simultaneous loss of glory (*kleos*); however, if he wins honor, he should see in his mind's eye the loss of his life. His goals and his feelings cannot be reconciled.

The Word That Gathers Acquiescence

In this section I will present the specific features of the two voices, those of Agamemnon and of Achilles; then I will examine first the protocols of Agamemnon's voice and then those of Achilles.

Agamemnon's irritation with Achilles is different at different times, variously ironic,[24] dismissive, and finally fearful. After attributing Achilles' prowess to his mother,[25] Agamemnon insists that he is superior in power, and that Briseis shall be his: "So that you learn well how much greater I am than you [ὅσσον

---

23. This is one of the main points of Whitman's interpretation of this scene (1958, 193): "The whole quarrel with Agamemnon was merely . . . the impetus which drove Achilles from the simple assumptions of the other princely heroes into a path where heroism means the search for the dignity and the meaning of the self."

24. See Leaf (1960) on line 173, where Agamemnon urges Achilles to "run away by all means." Of course, only cowards and slaves run away. The power of this φεῦγε μάλ', "run away," becomes obvious when one compares IX.42–43, where Diomedes answers Agamemnon's plan to leave the war and repeats I.173–74, but uses ἔρχεο, "go," instead of φεῦγε μάλ'. Notice in both cases the use of the present tense. Agamemnon agrees with Achilles that he does not care about him and repeats the same word used by Achilles (180).

25. For Segal, Agamemnon's attribution of Achilles' courage to his divine mother is meant scornfully, since it "suggests that Achilles' *karteria* is an accidental rather than an essential attribute of his character" (1970, 98). But Nestor repeats the comment (I.280) without any desire to insult Achilles.

φέρτερός εἰμι σέθεν], and that another man may shrink from speaking equal to me [ἶσον ἐμοὶ φάσθαι] and from likening himself to me openly [καὶ ὁμοιωθήμεναι ἄντην]" (I.185–87).

The important word here is *phasthai* (speaking), if we are correct in translating it in this way. Commentators are divided: some follow the scholiast, who interprets this expression as a breach of the *isêgoria* in the assemblies,[26] whereas others interpret it to mean "to deem himself equal to me."[27] The scholiast who refers to IX.33, where Diomedes asserts the right of free speech, supports the first interpretation. Besides, Homer often uses *phasthai* with *epos*, to indicate the "speaking" in the assembly. Especially telling is IX.100, where Nestor advises Agamemnon how to behave in the assembly at a crucial moment:

τώ σε χρὴ πέρι μὲν φάσθαι ἔπος ἠδ᾽ ἐπακοῦσαι,
κρηῆναι δὲ καὶ ἄλλῳ

[Therefore you must speak your word more than we, and listen to, and enact the word also of another person . . .]

In I.187 instead of *epos* we have *ison*, adverbially "to speak equal to me" (cf. XV.50 ἶσον ἐμοὶ φρονέουσα at the beginning of the line, just as in I.187 ἶσον ἐμοὶ φάσθαι).[28]

If, on the contrary, we follow the second translation, we have a repetition of the same notion: "to deem oneself equal to me and to liken oneself to me," which, though not impossible, is much less interesting speech.

As in I.187, in IX.100 Agamemnon's speech is defined as something more than that of the others, *peri*: perhaps more powerful than the speaking of the other *basileis*. For Achilles, then, it is impossible to speak with the same weight and power as Agamemnon, for only Agamemnon's "speaking" gathers the others' deference (*timân*), and therefore, *ipso facto*, commands.[29]

---

26. Leaf 1900–1902; Kirk 1985; Martin 1989, 97; Taplin 1992, 65.
27. Ameis and Hentze, Janko 1992 on XV.167: "His heart does not shrink from deeming him equal to me whom others dread." The context in XV.167 is slightly different: there is no assembly, no ὁμοιωθήμεναι ἄντην, though there is the scholiast's same paraphrase of φάσθαι as ἰσηγορεῖν. Reinhardt (1961, 285) translates "sich mir gleich zu nennen" where "sich . . . nennen" means "to name himself."
28. Compare Themis' description of Zeus's power in XV.106–8:
ὁ δ᾽ ἀφήμενος οὐκ ἀλεγίζει
οὐδ᾽ ὅθεται· φησὶν γὰρ ἐν ἀθανάτοισι θεοῖσι
κάρτεΐ τε σθένεΐ τε διακριδὸν εἶναι ἄριστος
[And he, sitting apart, does not care and does not have a qualm for us, for he declares that among the deathless gods he is distinctively the best in strength and power.]
Let us observe how here too Zeus's act of saying "I am the best" makes him so in the eyes of Themis and the other gods. Of course the translation "For he deems himself to be the best" is also possible, but I think it is weak, since it presents an opinion rather than a statement.
29. There is no need to emphasize that *phêmi* in Homer usually implies a strong declaration, often with an accent of menace, and that even in its weakest sense it means "to assert." Examples of *phêmi* in threats are II.248, V.652, XI.443, and

According to this interpretation, therefore, the expression ἶσον ἐμοὶ φάσθαι does not refer to the *themis* of *isêgoria* (IX.33), as the scholiast implies: Agamemnon does not deny Achilles the right to speak; he denies him the same weight, the same commanding power, the same authority of speech that he enjoys.

The interpretations that imply "deeming" rather than the speech act, "I say," lack two important associations. They miss not only the specific force of asserting as an act of power, but also, metatextually, the force of the speech act in general, since the oral performance of the poem certainly identifies itself with the represented acts of speaking and saying. One can only imagine the inflection and innuendo the bards gave these verbs of saying when actually reciting these passages before an audience.

The point is clear: in stating that he is greater than Achilles, Agamemnon does not give himself any special title,[30] nor does he mention any material force on which he relies. He simply states a fact before an audience that already consents.[31]

The same expression, ἶσον ἐμοὶ φάσθαι, in XV.167, seals Zeus's assertion of his own superiority over Poseidon.[32] It is significant that Homer decides to

---

XXI.316. For this verb, see Benveniste (1969, 2:135). In Agamemnon's speech (I.183–87) Agamemnon uses three enunciating verbs: "I do not pray you" (173–74), "I do not care" (180), "I will threaten you" (181). By beginning with an imperative (φεῦγε) and ending with a lesson (so that you may learn, 185), Agamemnon demonstrates the conscious authority of his speech acts and the structure of a commander's φάσθαι.

30. He uses the word *pherteros*, as Nestor will use later at 281, and as Zeus will use for himself at XV.165.

31. This does not mean that the audience likes what Agamemnon says: in I.23ff., after the priest Chryses has spoken to the Achaean assembly, all the Achaeans agree to respect the priest and to accept the ransom for his daughter, except Agamemnon, who alone rejects the proposal and who brutally sends the priest away. Not one Achaean protests; not one Achaean thinks that he has strong enough reasons, claims, or power to question Agamemnon's decision.

32. Zeus sends Poseidon a message through Iris (XV.158–67), ordering him to cease from war and battle. Let him obey,

ὡἐπεί ἑο φημὶ βίῃ πολὺ φέρτερος εἶναι
καὶ γενεῇ πρότερος· τοῦ δ' οὐκ ὄθεται φίλον ἦτορ
ἶσον ἐμοὶ φάσθαι, τόν τε στυγέουσι καὶ ἄλλοι.
[. . . since I declare that I am much stronger in force than he, and older in age. But his heart does not worry to speak equal to me, before whom the other gods shudder with fear.]

". . . The verbal parallels between XV.165–67 and I.186f. are no accident," Janko writes (1992, *ad loc*). Still, there are differences between Zeus and Agamemnon. Zeus can afford to tolerate his rival because he knows that in the end Poseidon will yield. Zeus reminds Poseidon of the formidable fear the other gods feel before him. Agamemnon cannot afford to tolerate Achilles because his word, and only his word, *is* his power.

bring together Zeus and Agamemnon.[33] Initially, at least, this correspondence enhances Agamemnon's prestige in the view of the readers. And this is not the only protocol that compares Agamemnon's superiority over his fellows with Zeus's superiority over his own peers.

Agamemnon's superiority is confirmed by the fact that everyone "shrinks from speaking equal to him," except Achilles, who will be defeated. In fact, in the face of Agamemnon's declaration, Achilles has only one recourse, namely to kill Agamemnon. And probably he would have, had Athena not stopped him (I.188–222).

And yet the superiority of Agamemnon's word has an internal weakness: it does not command because it is powerful; it is powerful because it gathers the sum of the relations of friendships and deference. Accordingly, *any* word that could satisfy this condition could be equal to his and could command. If Achilles' word could contain the deference of his peers, Agamemnon would no longer have power. This process had already begun. It is *Achilles* who gathered the assembly (54) and permitted Calchas to indict Agamemnon's mistreatment of Chryses as the cause of the plague.[34] But, as the quarrel explodes, the others stick to their deference to Agamemnon and obey his word. Achilles has no chance to persuade them.[35] Indeed, for better or worse, it is Agamemnon's word that realizes the common purpose and will of the Achaeans.[36]

---

33. There are at least three verbal parallels: neither Zeus nor Agamemnon cares about his antagonist (I.180–81 = XV.106–7); each claims to be more powerful (*pherteros*) than his antagonist (I.186 and XV.165); and both refer to their rivals' ἴσον ἐμοὶ φάσθαι (I.187a = XV.167a). Furthermore, both Zeus and Agamemnon are addressed as *kudiste*, "most glorious."

34. Achilles has been inspired by Hera. He already knows that Apollo has caused the plague (64) and that the protection Calchas requests is against Agamemnon (90–91).

35. Agamemnon characterizes Achilles' ambition and competition as follows: "But this man wants to be superior to all the others, wants to rule all and to be the lord of all, and to signal orders to all (*sêmainein*): which I think nobody will acquiesce to (*peisesthai*). If the gods, who exist forever, made him a spearman, is this a reason that his insults should run forward for him to be told?" (I.287–91). This is Aristarchus's understanding of line 291, and see Kirk 1985, *ad loc.*

Schmitt 1990, 184 recognizes that Agamemnon is specifically outraged by what he takes to be Achilles' desire to be superior.

Agamemnon knows that all his peers will not acquiesce (*peithesthai*) to Achilles' ambition—to be the lord of everybody, to *sêmainein* "to signal words, orders." *Sêmainein* and *sêmantôr* qualify Agamemnon's command over the Achaeans in XIV.85 and identify him again with Zeus who is *sêmantôr* in Hesiod's *Aspis* 56 and frag. 52.

Collins has collected the important documentation about *sêmainein* in relation to power and has correctly suggested "an identification of kingship with what are verbal functions" (1989, 90–91).

36. When Odysseus intervenes to stop the stampede of the army, he formulates the will of the Achaean army in a famous passage (II.203–6): "We are not all masters, we Achaeans, here, and multiplicity of rulers is not a good thing. Let there be one ruler, one king only, to whom the son of crooked-minded Cronus gave the scepter and the

When Agamemnon, in book 2, explains the encouraging dream from Zeus and proposes the most incredible plan, Nestor intervenes and comments: "If any one else of the Achaeans should tell us this dream, we would assert that it is a lie [ψεῦδός κεν φαῖμεν], and turn away from it. But now the man who saw it has every claim to be the best of the Achaeans [ὃς μέγ' ἄριστος 'Αχαιῶν εὔχεται εἶναι]. Come on! See if we can arm the sons of the Achaeans" (II.80–83). If the phrase with *eukhetai* were in direct discourse and in the first person it would say something like *phêmi gar einai aristos Akhaiôn.* That sort of dream in all other circumstances would be considered a lie: it has the unmistakable quality of a lie, but since it is uttered by Agamemnon who is the best of the Achaeans, it cannot be a lie. The king's word may be irresponsible or groundless, but this does not matter, for it must be true and it must be carried out.[37]

The irresponsibility and amorphousness of the king's word parallel therefore its commanding power. Moreover, no matter how false, weak, and hysterical, no matter how copiously watered by tears of impotence, it is the word that represents the will of the whole army and, to the extent that it reflects the continuity of the Iliadic action, the word that secures the continuity of the narrative.

One could object to this neat equation between word and power by citing instances when Agamemnon is disobeyed. This happens, of course, and the case of Achilles is only one example; yet, in all other cases, no rebellion ensues. As we shall see, the insignia of power, namely, the scepter and the *kudos* from Zeus, may help him; and when disagreement does occur, it is generally not in the assembly. Agamemnon is contradicted not when uttering a declaration of power, but only when giving advice or asking for help.[38] I leave aside the episode in the ninth book (9ff.), in which Agamemnon weeps (13–16);[39] instead I turn to a few lines in book 14.

Agamemnon, meeting a few of his most faithful peers, Nestor, Odysseus, and Diomedes, like him wounded in battle, proposes to launch the ships into the sea, in view of a possible withdrawal (XIV.65–81). This is his usual theme in moments of distress (II.110ff.; IX.17ff.): now the situation is worse, for it is not simply a question of renouncing the capture of Troy, but of saving the army

---

customs so that he may counsel his people." One function of the *Diapeira* is to show that the silent agreement of the army with their leader, Agamemnon, during the quarrel, turns out to be an explicit and solid accord.

37. Thalmann (1988, 7ff.) has shown the tissue of lies on which this passage depends: Zeus's promise of victory is a lie; Agamemnon recites it believing it to be true, but tests the troops by presenting the Achaeans' defeat, which is the true intent of Zeus's lie (with the caveat, however, that if the stampede of the army had been successful, Zeus's whole plan would have been baffled).

38. The case of flyting is different, in which it is part of the ritual that the provocation be answered with the same degree of insolence.

39. The text is not clear on whether Agamemnon's display of despondency occurs in the general assembly (*agorê*), or in the council of the elders (*boulê*). Leaf (1900–1902) on IX.17 and Janko (1992, 157) favor the council; Hainsworth (1993) on IX.9–78 and IX.17, the general assembly.

from total destruction. His advice is given to fewer people than ever. He introduces the proposal: "Come on, as I am saying, let us all obey [*peithômetha pantes*]" (74). One might think that such a proposal should command obedience. But things are never simple in Homer: expressions derive their meaning from a complex and refined code. In fact this very line, repeated eight times in the *Iliad* (and twice in the *Odyssey*), is used only for offering proposals, never for making commands. It is used by Agamemnon, Diomedes, Poseidon, and Thoas; retainers use it to advise their chief commanders, as Diomedes advises Agamemnon (IX.704) and Polydamas advises Hector (XII.75). The verb *peithômetha* in the first person plural, which includes the speaker in the act of obeying what he proposes and in the jussive subjunctive, invites agreement to a proposal rather than obedience to an order. In short, it does not assert "I am the commander and you honor and obey me."[40]

Odysseus sharply disagrees with Agamemnon's proposal to launch the ships and withdraw (XIV.83–102), but how he disagrees makes clear the power of Agamemnon's word of command:

Atreides, what word has escaped from the barrier of the teeth! Curse you! Would that you were giving orders [σημαίνειν] to an army of cowards [ἀεικελίου στρατοῦ ἄλλου],[41] instead of ruling us [ἄμμιν ἀνασσέμεν] to whom Zeus has granted to carry out terrible wars [τολυπεύειν ἀργαλέους πολέμους] from youth to old age until every one of us perishes! So eager are you to leave the wide-avenued city of Troy, for which we are suffering [ὀϊζύομεν] many evils? Be silent, lest one of the Achaeans hear this word [σίγα, μή τίς τ' ἄλλος Ἀχαιῶν τοῦτον ἀκούσῃ μῦθον], which no man would allow at all to pass

---

40. Agamemnon utters this line three times and is obeyed only once (II.139, in the *agorê*). The other two occurrences (IX.26 and XIV.74) are exceptions to the norm that, after this invitation to agree on a course of action, agreement follows.

41. Odysseus is made to speak in full accordance with his specific diction, as we know it from the *Odyssey*. *Aeikelios*, "unseeming, unworthy," occurs twelve times in the *Odyssey* (four times uttered by Odysseus), whereas it is *hapax* here in the *Iliad*. Also the expression *polemon tolupeuein* seems Odyssean (four times), whereas here it is hapax (but see XXIV.7). Also *argaleos*, as epithet of *polemous*, is *hapax* in the *Iliad*. The first part of line 90, *Siga mê tis allos*, repeats xix.486, where Odysseus orders Euryclea to be silent about the scar she has discovered. Most remarkable, the use of *stoma*, "mouth," with reference to voice and language (91), occurs only in II.489 (the poet's invocation to the Muses) and in II.250 (Odysseus's scolding of Thersites). These two occurrences and our example in line 91 constitute the only three examples where *stoma* has reference to voice and language, out of twenty examples in the *Iliad*. See Chapter One. *Ozuô* (89) represents a lamenting that describes Aphrodite in love (III.408), while it is twice used in the *Odyssey* for Odysseus's suffering and grieving during the war: iv.152 = xxiii.307. These examples should be sufficient to convince us that here the *Iliad* has the Odysseus of the *Odyssey* in mind. Perhaps the *Iliad* here telescopes the end of the war, of which Odysseus is the craftsman, as *ptoliporthos*; as such, Odysseus is correctly represented as giving the advice to remain and fight. There is also in Odysseus's words (85–87) the forecasting of the demise of the heroic race fighting at Troy. The irony is that Odysseus will be the survivor. See Chapter Nine.

through his mouth [διὰ στόμα πάμπαν ἄγοιτο], a man who knew in his mind how to say the right things, who is a sceptered king and whom so many people obey [πειθοίατο], as many as are ruled [ἀνάσσεις] by you among the Argives![42]

The passage confirms that Agamemnon's word of command can compel obedience by itself. Again *sêmainein* and *anassein* are used as synonyms; his word is called *muthos*,[43] and Odysseus asserts that Agamemnon, knowing the power of his word, should not let it pass through his mouth.[44] The fact that Agamemnon rules so many men is not the source of his power, but simply a condition that grants to the unconditional power of his word greater consequences.

With this illuminating example we realize both the power and the weakness of Agamemnon's commanding word: even when it is heedlessly blurted out, it compels obedience. It is therefore a dangerous and powerful engine driving the Achaean expedition. As a consequence it is this same dangerous and powerful engine that also drives a certain skeleton of the Iliadic narrative (*muthêsasthai* II.488). Its amorphousness, that is, its unpredictability, constitutes certain features of the narrative of the *Iliad*. I am referring to the passages in which Agamemnon's decisions, uncertainties, and doubts loosely structure the narrative and complicate the direction of its plot.

---

42. There is a potential optative in the first relative clause, ἄγοιτο (Chantraine 1963, 96) and an optative with a conditional sense in the next one, ἐπίσταιτο (248): "a man who knew in his mind" = "if he knew in his mind." Martin (1989, 121) praises the fluidity of Odysseus's tone.

43. On *muthos* as "authoritative speech," see Martin 1989, 59ff., and 66.

44. Notice, with Janko, the beautiful correspondence between the formulaic "what word has escaped from the barrier of the teeth!" (83) and the metaphor "let pass through the mouth" (91). Those words really escaped from Agamemnon's mouth. But this is not all. Here for the second time in the *Iliad,* Odysseus accuses Agamemnon of speaking without first thinking. Agamemnon had already "taken back his words" [πάλιν δ᾽ ὅ γε λάζετο μῦθον] in IV.357 after having uttered vain accusations against Odysseus. Notice the extraordinary pertinence of the formulaic expressions. For in both passages Odysseus opens with the line: "Atreides, what word has escaped from the barrier of the teeth!" [Ἀτρεΐδη ποῖόν σε ἔπος φύγεν ἕρκος ὀδόντων, IV.350 = XIV.83]. This tag line, implying reproach, is frequent in the *Odyssey,* where it is uttered by Zeus, Athena, Euryclea, and Antinous (but *not* by Odysseus), while in the *Iliad* it occurs twice, in the two passages we are comparing, and Odysseus utters it each time. This tag line therefore is used in the *Iliad* only when Odysseus is showing that Agamemnon's word did indeed escape too quickly and heedlessly from the barrier of his teeth! And finally, to complete the picture of this pertinent play of references, the *Odyssey* alludes to line IV.357 and, of course, to its theme (see Chapter Four and Pucci 1987, 103–4).

The Marginalization of Achilles

We return to the first book, when (186f.) Agamemnon has spoken almost as Zeus and declared his disgust for someone like Achilles who has tried to speak as his equal.

Then Achilles ponders whether or not to kill Agamemnon: he is slowly drawing his sword, when Athena appears and stops him. He obeys her command to limit his rage to insults (I.188–222).

From our viewpoint this scene is central to Homer's representation of Achilles. In it Achilles is singled out as one of the very few heroes to whom the gods make themselves fully manifest—again in powerful contrast with Agamemnon. This special intimacy between Achilles and the divine is underlined elsewhere by his mother Thetis and their mirror-like relationship. Likewise, the epithet "godlike" refers to Achilles most frequently, raising him above all the others.

Achilles' edifying proximity with the divine makes the shortness of his life seem even more bitter and arbitrary and produces a pathetic paradox.[45]

The splendor of this intimacy should not blind the eyes of the readers and prevent them from recognizing that something unique and utterly exceptional occurs in this scene, as though the poetic voice absolutely needed to legitimize, against the complicitous silence of the whole assembly, Achilles' moral claim. In fact this scene has the quality of other scenes, in which a digression or a reflection—as Slatkin 1991, 110 defines them—takes place, and the line of the main action is momentarily suspended or deviated.

I will shortly analyze here two other scenes of these kind, in order to show some characteristics of this type of divine intervention. I intend to prove that in these scenes the god's decision responds to narrative concerns or reflections, leaves little room for mortal options, and exposes the poetic voice's need rather than account for the human character's reflections. By a drastic shortcut, the text with its divine device allows itself rapid and circumstantial digressions, often of tremendous power and effect.

In III.129ff. Iris comes to Helen and advises her to go up to the wall to watch the duel between Paris and Menelaus. Through this divine device Helen is brought in contact with the leaders of the Trojans, and she is inspired with nostalgia for her earlier husband. The text reflects on various aspects of Helen's presence in Troy: for instance, by having Priam defending Helen, the text preempts what will later be Herodotus's argument against Helen's presence in Troy, that is, that some Trojan leaders would have certainly returned Helen to the Achaeans before the destruction of the city.

In XV.59ff., Zeus, after having been seduced by Hera and lost control of events, awakens and gains again the upper hand in the direction of the affairs and of the narrative.

---

45. See Slatkin's valuable remark: "the exacting mortal aspect [of Achilles] . . . exerts its leveling effect on the immortal affiliations and expectations of the hero." 1991, 49.

In Athena's epiphany to Achilles (I.194ff.), the poetic voice needs to explain why Achilles would not have killed Agamemnon and would have accepted humiliation and a dishonorable marginalization.

In all three scenes the divine intervention occurs in surprising, unaccounted ways; it is known only by one character besides the god (and by the audience/readers) and is marked by some aberrations. In III.129ff., for instance, Iris secretly visits Helen, without having been sent by anybody, and in an unprecedented way takes the responsibility of inspiring Helen with nostalgia for Menelaus.[46] In XV.59ff. Zeus gives to Hera an account of events until the capture of Troy, running the risk of killing the curiosity of the audience and committing some odd mistakes in foreseeing the future.[47] In I.194ff. the formal oddities of Athena's appearance are many, as I have observed in Chapter Six,[48] and the aberrations in content are no less singular. Athena's intervention is biased in favor of political power: she unfairly forces Achilles to accept his defeat, his loss of honor, in view of a later compensation that will have no value for him.[49]

I want to add here a few considerations on the word *hubris,* which occurs during the dialogue between Achilles and Athena (203, 214). This word, which is found only here in the *Iliad* and a few other times in its correlated verbal forms, proves unmistakably that Athena's intervention and message communicates a private and legal character to Agamemnon's political aggression before the assembly. For the noun and the verb characterize always a personal insult, and the creation of an unsettled relation between parties in which one party becomes "creditor" and the other "debtor," with legal rather than political implications.[50] Accordingly, by this repeated definition of Agamemnon's *hubris,*

---

46. These aberrations have been noted. Certainly Aphrodite did not command Iris to produce in Helen this "sweet desire for her former husband, her city, and her parents," nor did Zeus, who has promised Thetis to give victory to the Trojans. It is evident, as George Kennedy writes, that "Iris is the agent of the poet" (1986, 7; see also Mark Edwards 1987, 192). Also clear are the advantages the text derives from this heavy manipulation. First, as I have suggested, Helen is represented under the protection of Priam. Furthermore she can be shown in an edifying resistance against an immoral Aphrodite, becoming, in short, an Iliadic heroine. But this inspiration by Iris is costly: it adds a pathetic flavor to her visitation, and confuses Helen's genealogy, for, suddenly, when "the daughter of Zeus" feels nostalgia for her parents (*tokêôn* 140), she acquires human parents! Zeus is certainly not waiting for her in Sparta.

47. See Janko 1992.

48. To my analysis of Athena's gesture to grab Achilles' hair while standing behind him, Acquaro (1984) adds that this gesture is proper to rape.

49. She offers Achilles the same sort of compensation (I.213: "splendid gifts will lie before you three times over") that Achilles had offered to Agamemnon (I.127ff.: "we will compensate you three and four times over"), a compensation that Agamemnon had refused, and one that Achilles too will refuse in the ninth book and will not care about when, in the nineteenth, it is offered to him.

50. On IX.368, Achilles, speaking to the ambassadors, describes the insult of Agamemnon by the verb *ephubrizein* ("the prize that he himself gave to me, he snatched away from me, with insolence (*ephubrizôn*), the mighty son of Atreus,

the text opens in the parenthesis of Athena's exclusive appearance a second private parenthesis, within which Agamemnon's gesture of authority and disregard of Achilles' role and status assume the quality of a private offense. This offense opens up a credit for Achilles and the possibility of a legal, moral solution, as Athena suggests.

Achilles will not be able to accept Athena's solution, to attack Agamemnon only with words, though he promises that he will, and this point already shows that Athena's decision and command do not correspond to Achilles' feelings and determination. Had Achilles behaved in accordance with the compensating plan of Athena, he would have accepted the gifts that are offered to him in book 9; he might even have refrained from a whole-scale desertion from the war. The only certain success of Athena's bid consists, therefore, in sparing Agamemnon's life and in gaining time; and this is essential for the plot of the poem. In fact, if Athena knows, when she comes to Achilles, that the only effect of her intervention will be to spare the life of Agamemnon, clearly she must think that Achilles would otherwise slay Agamemnon. Accordingly she is literally right when she says: "I come to check your fury" (207).

Because of the goddess's intervention, we will never know what are the real feelings of the hero. In this case, even more than in the other two examples of digression and reflection that I have briefly evoked, the divine takes over the responsibility of deciding and leaves to the audience and the readers the task of inventing some plausible human reasons that could be aligned to the divine one.[51] Of course it is not difficult to find many: it is possible that Achilles' character is such that he would never have killed Agamemnon; but the question

---

Agamemnon." The verb underscores the privacy of the dealing Achilles evokes, while most often he and others emphasize the fact that the prize was a present of the entire army (I.162, 276, 299, 392), as also Taplin 1992, 63–66 has emphasized. In Nestor's narrative (XI.695) the verb describes a situation that opens a debt (see *khreios* 698) for which finally the citizens obtain repayment, or compensation. In XIII.633, Menelaus terms the Trojans *hubristai* ("insolent"), and the personal, sexual, insult he refers to is explicit to everyone (623 "all the shame you heaped on me," Fagles translates).

51. Schmitt 1990, 76ff. analyzes with care and abundance of examples the scholarly views: as a whole, the strong humanistic inclination that guides the Homeric interpretations from remote times encourages the sensibility of the critics to find out, for Achilles, good and persuasive reasons, in order to be able to pronounce the perfect alignment of the hero and the goddess. Hegel wrote an epigrammatic assertion of this alignment in *Vorlesungen über die Philosophie der Religion* II Theorie-Werkausgabe 17, 127: "Pallas, who checks the outbreak of Achilles' rage, is his own levelheadedness." This statement is exemplary of many others that follow: Schmitt shows how the modern interpretation finds a parallelism between Achilles" autonomous psychic development and Athena's decision. He analyzes the positions of Snell and Lesky, who, despite their differences, join in the general tendency. He himself proposes that Athena's intervention occurs just in the instance in which, as Achilles moves from rage to execution, measures the consequences of his action, and suddenly searches for a way out, Athena provides it. Schmitt's analyses are subtle and psychologically complex, often plausible, but their plausibility does not prove their correctness.

remains why Homer did not express this point. Achilles, compelled by a terrible sorrow, will decide to rush to his death without any divine interference, and so also will Hector after a long introspective speech to himself. Many other emotional decisions occur in the *Iliad*, motivated and accounted by the hero's words.

Besides, the theory of the alignment between man and goddess disregards the specific protocols of this epiphany, the violence of Athena's grabbing from the back Achilles' hair, her becoming visible to us before him, her irony, her too simple order, his too simple obedience, and the infelicitous sort of compensation she promises.

In my view, therefore, it cannot be stated that Athena represents the divine counterpart of Achilles' own decision, as Lesky, Schmitt, and Dodds, though in importantly different shades, suggest. Nor does she simply decide for Achilles, as Snell intimates, since Achilles' acquiescence and agreement must mean something. Rather, she represents the violent intrusion of textual concerns. In short, she represents the theological support of a narrative decision, as does Iris in the third book (see note 46). By so intruding, the narrator renders Achilles' "actual" decision forever suspended and unaccounted for, but he saves Agamemnon and puts in motion the moral legitimacy of Achilles' rage. This legitimation is not a simple affair in view of the complicitous silence of the whole army sustaining Agamemnon's right, and, as we will see, forces the narrator to various manipulations. The first one is this epiphany.

By the violent gesture of Athena who grabs Achilles by his hair, he is drastically turned toward the divine and removed from the alliance and equality with his peers.[52] He ceases being an active character of the *Iliad*—though he acts through the effects of his absence—until the moment in which he will gaze into his death, his failure, and glance askance at his glory.

Two other consequences are implicit in the interpretation I have presented.

(1) In these scenes of digression or reflection, the divine intervention serves the plot rather than the psychology of the characters, or if it serves also the psychology of the characters as when Iris and Aphrodite manipulate Helen's feelings, its effects remain circumscribed, produce a limited scene, but do not tamper with the general economy of the poem.

In the case of Athena's intervention, as we will immediately see, her order and advice are superseded by Achilles' decision to involve Zeus in his rage. This new development raises the question how Hera's and Athena's decision and advice integrate with Zeus's long term plan.[53] The problem is complex: on the one hand, by saving Agamemnon's life and therefore also the Achaean expedition against Troy, Athena, intentionally or not, saves Zeus's plan to lighten the

---

52. On a different interpretative key, but with a similarly negative assessment of Athena's role, see Naas 1995, 81: "By turning toward the gods, the gods turn toward Achilles, automatically, bringing with their gaze the spotlight of glory and the blinding Augenblick of death. Just after this scene Achilles will separate himself from the community to pray to his mother for a vengeance that will open up the space of narrative."

53. See Chapter Nine.

burden on the earth through the bloody war of Troy (*Cypria* fr.1). On the other hand, however, she presents herself and Hera as φιλέουσά τε κηδομένη τε (loving and caring) toward both Agamemnon and Achilles. How could they declare such love and care if they were complicitous with Zeus's plan that aims for the destruction of the whole race of heroes? Of course we know that Hera is ready to let her beloved cities be destroyed in order to have Troy captured and ruined. One can easily see the complexity of this question.[54]

(2) If we consider this kind of divine intervention as the theological support of narrative decisions, digressions, plot's needs, and so on, we face the manipulative strategy of the text. The god does not function as the aggrandizer of a human decision, fury, military prowess, and so on, but as a narrative device, a sort of narratological contrivance to legitimize a textual point. This occurs even at the price of silencing or suspending the usual accountability of the character's decisions and moves. This would eventually explain why there are so many aberrant features or novelties in these interventions: Iris deciding by her own whim to call Helen and inspire in her nostalgia for her past, Athena producing a solution to be immediately superseded, Zeus's foreseeing and dictating an incorrect course of the events. Is the text calling attention to its innovative, reflective, or digressive point?[55] Or does it run into trouble when it adapts traditional motifs to new situations?

This contriving and aberrant use of the theological scene implies also a certain abuse of theology itself. As we have seen, Athena's and Hera's love for Achilles is asserted but not proved. Accordingly this deployment of the theological motif has the effect of showing the relative callousness of the text in using the theological scene. One can advance the assumption that in these scenes, the poet, more than ever, could become aware of his own manipulation. Though the question whether he did or did not remains unanswerable, my feeling is that he did.[56] The *Iliad* signals its fictionality.

---

54. It is not my purpose here to pursue the analysis of Athena's and Hera's behavior in relation to Zeus's limited and the larger plan. While the two goddesses are violently opposed to Zeus's agreement with Thetis, they seem unaware, for a time, of the other plan of the father of the gods.

The thesis that the *Iliad* unravels as a theodicy orchestrated by the larger *boulê* of Zeus, and that instead of being a mere *Achilleis* the poem telescopes the whole war of Troy and the demise of the heroic race—therefore correctly called an *Iliad*—has been brilliantly elaborated by Philippe Rousseau 1995. The implications of this thesis for the relationship of the two goddesses with Achilles are not dealt with in this work.

55. However, the fact that an epiphany interrupts a scene of introspection (a *mermêrizein* scene), is traditional; see V.668ff., X.503ff., etc.

56. An episode of the *Odyssey* perfectly illustrates that the poet is aware of the use of divine intervention as a contrivance to sustain a fictional story. In xiv.470ff. the disguised Odysseus narrates a fictitious event and shows how he invented the appearance of a divine dream (*theios . . . oneiros*) in order to send away one of his men. (495ff.)

Furthermore, the cases in which the poet could choose a divine or a human motivation are many. In the first book of the *Iliad* we are told that Calchas led the Achaean ships to Troy through his divination (*mantosunê* 71-2), while the poet

At the end of Athena's intervention, the audience realizes that the kiss of the gods is a kiss of death. But in this case, as I have tried to show, the kiss of the gods is really the kiss of the poet. The text itself traps and shapes Achilles' hard destiny and prepares his funeral monument through its theological masonry and carpentry.[57]

Existential Rhetoric

> In Kant, all that remains of the subject is the "I" as an empty form (a pure grammatical necessity, said Kant, a grammaticalexigency, Nietzsche would say) that accompanies my representations . . .
> —P. Lacou-Labarthe and J. L. Nancy, *The Literary Absolute*

The quarrel between Achilles and Agamemnon acquires vast proportions and deadly quality when Achilles meets his mother and requests that she persuade Zeus to give victory to the Trojans. Some consequences ensue:

(1) Athena's early command and solution are overruled by Achilles' one-sided decision: he wants to humiliate Agamemnon with blood and defeat, not by merely abusive words.[58]

(2) Thetis must display a tremendous power of persuasion in order to convince Zeus: whether the story of her help to Zeus (I.396–405) was traditional or composed for this occasion (see Kirk) does not change its exceptionality. Hera rages and Zeus's long-term plan runs into some trouble. What Achilles asks for goes against the grain of the events, the plan of the gods.

I wish to analyze three moments of the interview between Achilles and his mother Thetis in order to show how the text produces the conviction that Achilles should be honored by Zeus with the defeat of his own companions. These three moments are

(1) Achilles' weeping on the beach of the sea
(2) Achilles' invocation to his mother and his summary of the events
(3) Thetis's words.

---

knows very well that Odysseus can sail by the help of the stars. Clearly the poet wanted to aggrandize the feat of his aristocratic warriors and eventually to suggest that with the help of Apollo the sailing would be certainly surer and quicker. The Achaeans however would have reached Troy, as the poet knows well, also without that help. Finally, in many other cases, the presentation of events and stories is made without any support of the Muses: Helen pictures the Trojan war in a large web and Odysseus tells his owns travels without any divine inspiration.

57. For these images of Iliadic writing, see Svenbro 1976, 193–212, and Ford 1992, 35.

58. I disagree with Schmitt's interpretation that Achilles' refusal to fight and his request from Zeus translate Athena's advice to abuse Agamemnon with words (1990, 78).

(1) Achilles chooses a solitary place on the beach of the gray sea, gazes at the "boundless ocean" while crying and appealing to his mother (348–51). Though the setting repeats the one in which Chryses retires to pray to Apollo (I.34–5), and other analogous settings in the *Odyssey*, here we have two particularly emotional features, Achilles' gaze into the boundless sea and his weeping.

Truly, the epithet for the sea on line 350 presents a variant in our textual tradition: the manuscripts read *oinopa* ("wine-colored") and only Aristarchus reads *apeirona* ("boundless"). Almost all the recent editors, however, prefer Aristarchus' reading even if in the *Iliad* it is the unique example of such an epithet for the sea. It occurs in *Odyssey* iv.510; it is an epithet of the Hellespont in *Iliad* XXIV.545, but this is not strong internal evidence. The reason for this preference lies of course in our modern sensitivity, which appreciates that nature be described here in a sort of spiritual consonance with the boundless grief of Achilles.[59]

These two variants propose an exemplary case of the process through which the text produces its own reading of the sublime in relation to Achilles. On the one hand, the presence of Aristarchus' variant ("boundless ocean") proves that the rhetorical presentation of Achilles creates the need for reading a specific spiritual dimension in the sympathetic nature toward which Achilles reverses his limitless grief, his sense of terrible isolation. Whether the "boundless ocean" is the truthful reading or a variant does not change my point, for, even as the right reading, it is in the *Iliad* a unique epithet for the sea. If this is the truthful Iliadic reading—I mean, if it is the reading of the monumental composition at its emergence—the process has begun with it, as a singular process of producing a sublime immensurability for Achilles' passion. If the reading is spurious—I mean, if it derives from the later scriptural tradition—it is clear that this process was already implicit in the text, and the variant has simply made manifest what was latently there.

On the other hand, this gaze of the grieving hero upon the boundless surface of the ocean characterizes perfectly the type of emotional rhetoric that represents the existential mode of the hero. His mother is going to surface from this ocean and is coming to listen to him: nature is animated and spiritualized by her being a goddess of the sea. Accordingly, Achilles' integration into the spiritual mode of the boundless ocean, seat of his mother goddess, monumentalizes so to speak his solitude and grief. The specific claims and reason for his mood are left undetermined, his specific voice is momentarily silent, but the boundlessness of his pain is made visible and perceivable. The voice of the poet takes over that of the hero and speaks in his place.

Homer represents Achilles also crying and crying copiously, as he begs his mother (357 and 362), and while he gives her an account of the events (364). The protocols of male weeping in the *Iliad* imply that weeping is a "language"—to use Hélène Monsacré's definition[60]—of unrestrained grief. It bursts out with the violence of a snow storm from the heart of the subject (X.9–10):

---

59. See, for instance, the sensitive pages of Lesky 1947, 187f.
60. Monsacré 1984, 167ff.

Even so thick and fast in his chest groaned Agamemnon, from the very depth
of his heart, and his *phrenes* shook within him.

Male crying bursts out when the subject is in small, almost private, enclaves,
specifically among friends, and is provoked sometimes by indignation, but most
often by grief, for the death or the wound of a friend, for a ruinous defeat.[61]
While the expression used for Achilles on line 357—*dakrua kheôn*—is
frequent (e.g. IX.14; XVI.3, etc.), the phrase that indicates his groaning while
narrating the events (364 *tên de baru stenakhôn prosephê,* "deeply groaning
Achilles told her") is rarer and more specific. Of the seven occurrences in the
Iliad (it never appears in the *Odyssey*), four times it is used for Achilles
(I.364=XVIII.78, 323, XX.60), once for Patroclus (XVI.20) and twice for
Agamemnon (IV.153 and IX.16).[62]
In appealing to his mother and in recounting the events, Achilles cries for the
grief of his lost honor (*timê*), the only compensation he has for the shortness of
his life. The loss of his honor acquires an ontological quality and deserves the
sharpest manifestation, the violent outburst from the heart that is proper at a
funeral.
(2) It is just for this loss that Achilles weeps as he calls his mother (352–
56):

Mother, since you have borne me to have a short life,
the Olympian should at least have granted me honor (*timê*),
Zeus, who thunders up on high. But now he honors me not at all.
For Atreus' son, wide ruling Agamemnon,
dishonors me. He seized and holds my prize, he deprived me of it himself.

The striking accusation Achilles levels at Zeus is that the god has failed and
betrayed Achilles. He seems to believe that Agamemnon was literally correct
when he had boasted that his own men and Zeus would continue to honor him
even if Achilles should desert (173–75). Achilles now evokes these two complicitous beings, the king of men and the king of gods, responsible for disgracing
him, and qualifies them with their long epithets, as if to underline their
(misused) power.
Achilles gives a theological cause for Agamemnon's behavior and in effect he
seals this theological view by defining Agamemnon's insolence as *atê* (412

---

61. Monsacré 1984, 137ff. shows that sometimes the hero cries out of rage, as
Diomedes in XXIII.385, or for the defeat of the friendly camp, XIV.320 etc., or because of a wound that forces the hero to withdraw from the battle. Achilles, however,
occupies a unique position, as Monsacré notices (140), in using this unrestrained language of grief: "Books XVIII and XX are in large part devoted to the narrative of his
weeping, as though Patroclus's death opened a blank in the development of the
fights."
62. This line prefigures Achilles' weeping for Patroclus's death (XVIII.78, 323;
XXIII.60), and it picks up the force of a tag-line to characterize Achilles' experience
of *akhos* (grief) in the *Iliad*. Yet this line is read also for the cryings of Agamemnon:
an odd, but not meaningless coupling.

"blindness, ruin"). Agamemnon later—and the *diêgêsis* too—will appropriate this definition to justify his attitude and will attribute this *atê* to Zeus (II.111, etc.). Achilles seems to interpret literally the saying that the power of kings comes from Zeus, and he draws the necessary consequences that this belief entails.

All these features conspire to show two points. On the one hand, Achilles must assume that the power of Agamemnon could not have been what it has been against him without the acquiescence of his men, and without the theological props that sustain that acquiescence. On the other hand, this responsibility of Zeus allows the poet to present as a legitimate claim that Achilles should ask Zeus to become directly involved and concerned with the restitution of Achilles' honor. For Zeus literally committed a breach of duty (see *ophellen* 353) in disgracing Achilles through Agamemnon.

But was Zeus really responsible? It does not seem so,[63] and this indictment appears to be a rhetorical manipulation by the text either in order to show the immensity of Achilles' wounded pride or to persuade the audience of the legitimacy of Achilles' request.

Once this question is posed, it becomes correct also to suspect that the odd selection of the events he relates to his mother (365392) is dictated by a certain tendentiousness and manipulation. To begin with, he is silent about Athena's intervention. This allows him to remain silent also about his wish to kill Agamemnon and about the solution of the quarrel presented by the goddess, with which he had promised to comply. He withholds his oath to abandon the war and the silence of the whole assembly, implicitly supporting Agamemnon; in a word, he narrates only the episodes that shape him as a zealous defender of the Achaeans' safety.

Again the poet has Achilles speaking in view of the extratextual audience, for it is this audience—rather than Thetis as De Jong writes[64]—that must retrieve this edifying image of Achilles, and combine this image of Achilles with the one that now feels victimized by Zeus and Agamemnon. The audience must agree that Heaven has the duty to resolve the question of his honor.

We, the audience, of course, agree, blind to the tendentiousness and the manipulations we are uncovering, since the despair that drives Achilles to his mother and the sympathy with which nature and gods respond to him silence all our temptations of criticism; and since the boundlessness of his grief, as he realizes the futility of his honor as a counterbalance of his short life, opens an immeasurable ontological abyss, before which the readers cannot quibble over the sense of his words, cannot assess the meaning of his silences.

Who would dare to say that Achilles is manipulative? And yet the text is so for him: it deprives him of arguments, of simple reasons, puts him in contact

---

63. Nobody except Achilles fathoms this indictment, and he himself does not pick it up again. On Zeus's responsibility for Achilles' short life, as presented by Pindar in *Isthmian* 8, but of which the *Iliad* says nothing, see below.

64. De Jong 1985, 5–22. Thetis knows exactly how the events have occurred, and her persuasion at any rate functions also as the mirror of our persuasion.

with the divine, enlarges his pain to his consciousness of death, and sinks in it every one of his words.

(3) The last passage in Achilles' encounter with his mother I wish to comment upon is the couple of lines Thetis utters as she comes to him (363–364):

> My child, why do you cry? What grief has reached you in your heart? (*se phrenas hiketo penthos*)
> Tell me, do not hide it in your mind (*noôi*) so that we both may know it.

We are so accustomed to read in Homer that feelings and ideas come to the heart, that people speak to their hearts or receive injunctions, hopes, and so on from their hearts, that we do not comment often on the extraordinary power of this image. Yet we should.

Through this image, epic poetry has invented a place, a seat to which feelings arrive inside us, hit us, grieve us, or move us to do things. Though Homer uses various words (*thumos, kradiê, phrenes, êtôr,* etc.) to indicate, without substantial difference, what we translate by "heart," this seat inside us becomes something that we would call self-consciousness or our will, our mind, or our "being" when we see it as a sort of alter-ego. But while our notion of self-consciousness is an image that thinks (*cogito ergo sum*), is aware of its individuality and unity, has, in one word, a cognitive power over the self and the world, the Homeric heart has especially a voice and listens to a voice. Thus in this passage Thetis asks Achilles: "What grief has reached your heart?" and then she adds: "tell me." Achilles obeys, and what follows is the voice of Achilles' grieved heart that recounts the events. For he speaks while weeping (364).

Sorrow reaches the heart just as a voice reaches the ears (XI.466), as *kleos* reaches heaven (XIV.60).[65] The materiality of both images (the *phrenes* which as we know are shaken by crying, and the traveling of the sorrow) increases their effect on the readers, since they are uncertain whether to activate the metaphorical value of at least one of the two images or to take them in their forceful literality.

It is difficult to believe that Achilles' recounting has any other purpose than the discharge of his emotions into his mother's bosom. Yet it expresses more than the simple voice of his troubled heart. For the great master, Homer, does not only know the gestures of motherly care: he recognizes also the need of a fresh rephrasing of the events producing an edifying image of Achilles to persuade his more skeptical audience.

---

65. The phrase *se phrenas hiketo penthos* is rare: it occurs only in XVIII.73, 88, (and see XVIII.64); it is again a tag-phrase for Achilles' sorrow; and it contrasts with the sort of phrases we hear from Nestor: *ô popoi, ê mega penthos Akhaida gaian hikanei* ("alas, a great sorrow reaches the Achaean land") in I.254; VII.124 or analogous usages as in XVI.548, XXIV.708 etc.

Illustriousness of *Kudos*

We return to the scene of the quarrel, though in fact we have never abandoned it. It is not a mere accident that Nestor stands up to speak just after Achilles, who has, with the dramatic gesture of throwing the scepter to the ground, sworn vengeance and broken all relations with his peers.[66] The clever old adviser takes his time to get to the point[67] and finally urges both of them to give in (274–84). As he turns to Achilles he says (277–81):

μήτε σὺ Πηλείδη ἔθελ᾽ ἐριζέμεναι βασιλῆϊ
ἀντιβίην, ἐπεὶ οὔ ποθ᾽ ὁμοίης ἔμμορε τιμῆς
σκηπτοῦχος βασιλεύς, ᾧ τε Ζεὺς κῦδος ἔδωκεν.[68]

---

66. On this scene, and whether the scepter of the first book (233ff.) and the second (II.100ff.) are the same, see Gernet 1968, 241n13. On the two scenes, Easterling 1989, 103ff. clarifies many issues. For Lynn-George the transformation of the branch into a stripped scepter, studded with nails, becomes a sign "of what ends and endures"—and, with the promise and the hurling, "the epic is projected in the future, the indeterminate certainty of 'some day,' a possibility within the epic common to death and oath, language and loss, desire and compensation alike" (1988, 49). Achilles' gesture of dashing the scepter to the ground implies for Easterling (1989, 113ff.) that "the sense of an orderly transmission is being shattered, and *themis* is being contravened." In the light of the distance that Achilles sets up between himself and his peers, his gesture seals his denial of Agamemnon's *kudos*, luster, scepter, order, and word, and, accordingly, it points to his own marginalization from the community. Like the staff alive and blooming in the mountains that dies in the process of becoming a powerful symbol of divine continuity, so Achilles, the son of a goddess, has abandoned Phthia where he grew "as a plant in a fruitful field" (XVIII.56) and will die in Troy in order to become the icon of immortal glory. I do not underline this parallelism only at the literal level of the story, but also at the level of the murderous effects of the poetic craft. For all crafts, artistic or poetic, when they create a symbolic object or a literary character, drain whatever life the referent—the implied "original"—has, and transform it into immutable, immortal forms, objects, and icons. See Austin 1994, 28.

67. Of course, he takes all this time also because Homer must introduce him to his audience, characterize his way of speaking, his relation to memory, as Martin has shown, and his sweet, honey-like talk. What could be read as an ironic hyperbolic presentation could simply be the effect of an unavoidable textual convention.

68. The word σκηπτοῦχος is a generic attribute of βασιλεύς and does not add any technical or legal definition. But Odysseus in XIV.93 refers to Agamemnon simply by σκηπτοῦχος. In the singular it is rare: I.279; XIV.93; ii.231 = v.9. On the various scepterholding functions we find in Homer, see Kirk 1985 on II.109. Nagy sees the function of the scepter in "solemn verbal interchange" and connects it with the function of Hermes "as the god of interchange, verbal or otherwise" (1974, 242). Zanker 1994, 58n8 assumes that Nestor, by mentioning Agamemnon's superior *timê*, "may be tacitly criticizing the king because in Homeric thinking the Zeus-given *timê* of the king imposes on him the obligation to wield the scepter and pronounce *themistes* . . . and that the man with the highest *timê* should exercise the greatest moral and legal force and also act appropriately."

εἰ δὲ σὺ καρτερός ἐσσι θεὰ δέ σε γείνατο μήτηρ,
ἀλλ᾽ ὅ γε φέρτερός ἐστιν ἐπεὶ πλεόνεσσιν ἀνάσσει.

[Nor you, Pelides, try to quarrel with the king, opposing force to force: for the scepter-bearing king to whom Zeus has given glory is not apportioned equal honor. If you are mightier, a mother goddess bore you, but he is stronger because he rules more men.]

In the first three lines, Nestor assesses the symbolic power of authority and in the last two, the material force of both contenders. He implies Agamemnon's superior force, but the way in which he phrases the comparison is such that Agamemnon's rule over more men than Achilles is matched by Achilles' greater individual might: thus neither seems to have a real physical advantage.[69] But the symbolic power, the impalpable tokens of superiority that *kudos* and *timê* from Zeus provide for a man, privilege Agamemnon over Achilles. We find here the ideological ground that allows Achilles later, as we have seen, to reproach Zeus for having disregarded Achilles' honor.

It is now clear what these impalpable tokens correspond to. *Kudos*, the scepter, and *timê* (in its symbolic function) are the metaphysical distinctions through which the *basileis*—whether they know it or not—objectify and symbolically represent their own deference and obedience to Agamemnon. It is not always the case that men are conscious of the connection that exists between their practices and the metaphysical legitimation they attribute to them. And this may be the case with Agamemnon and his peers. But certainly they do know that through these marks of distinction they magnify that commanding word which they hate to dismiss or disobey.[70]

This cooperation between the king's powerful word and *kudos* granted by Zeus presents the normal divine and human counterparts. But such a collaboration, produced by the imaginary cultural tenets of the characters, is fraught with gaps, inconsistencies, and disjunctions.

Ruijgh 1971, 260–61 interprets the *te* of the relative as a "permanent fact" and the aorist ἔδωκεν as a sign of an "earlier fact": the king possesses this *kudos* since Zeus has given him the glory of royalty in the day of his event.

69. It is not sure whether Nestor's "more men" refers to Agamemnon's rule over the whole army of the Achaeans or to the larger contingent of men and ships with which he came to Troy. In the former case Nestor would imply that, just as he is speaking, he is under the rule of Agamemnon and that he speaks with the consideration of his obedience in mind. But probably Nestor implies only Agamemnon's own greater contingent of men and ships, for this is emphasized elsewhere. See, for example, II.576ff.

70. A longer analysis would be necessary to establish how each *basileus* is aware that the same metaphysical prerogatives function in their favor with regard to their subjects, and to question the nature of this belief. Its necessity and usefulness are evident: the divine honor of the king allows the *basileis* to disagree with him occasionally without denying his superior authority.

Kudos has been understood by Steinkopf as belonging to the realm of seeing and shining, Benveniste defines it as the "luster of glory,"[71] and Redfield 1975, 33 summarizes and illustrates this meaning as follows: *kudos* "is a kind of luster or mana which belongs to the successful . . . a kind of star quality or charisma, an enlargement of the persona."

The luminosity of *kudos* is often visible to and accounted for by humans who recognize that a hero has the favor of a god. Yet this luster is not permanent, and it dies with the person to whom it was awarded (XXII.432–36). In the battlefield *kudos* shines for the moment of victory upon the successful person, while in the assembly it lasts only to the extent that it is attached to *timê* and to the scepter.

However, *kudos* is not always a sign of divine favor. Sometimes an enemy, by being defeated, grants *kudos* to the winner. In these latter cases there is still glory, but no divine visible source.[72] Analogously, when *kudos* is obtained (*aresthai*) through victory, it is merely a synonym for victory, not an ostensible sign of divine favor.[73]

What is more important for our inquiry is that *kudos* falls in very different ways upon Agamemnon's and Achilles' heads. To begin with Agamemnon, the mention of his *kudos* in I.279, outside the context of the battlefield, as a general mark of luster and glory in the assembly, is almost unique. The only other analogous example, that is, coupled with the *timê* of the kings and commanders, occurs in XVII.248ff., where Menelaus urges his peers to fight on behalf of Patroclus's body and begins his address as follows: "O friends, commanders and

---

71. Steinkopf 1937, 24; Benveniste 1969, II.57ff. goes on to term it "force rayonnante" or "talisman de suprématie" (60). He shows that *kudos* often implies a divine sign of favor that is visible and appreciated by the winner and also by others: see VIII.140, 175f., etc. Whereas Chantraine records this meaning, R. Führer in *LFGE* ignores it. An excellent formal analysis of *kudos* in Homer is found in Steinkopf 1937, 23ff.: from the start, Steinkopf shows the formal parallelism between *kudos* and *timê:* "The word *kudos* occurs sixty-nine times in the *Iliad* and nine in the *Odyssey*, and it even resembles *timê* formally; it is frequently coordinated with other nouns (*timê, aglaiê, kosmos, kharis, biê, menos, nikê*), and it is accompanied by the same verbs (*eggualizein, didonai, opêdein, tithenai*) or similar verbs (*orexai, proienai, kataneuein, hepesthai, protiaptein*) as *timê*." Though the etymology of *kudos* does not point with certainty to the notion of shining and splendor, the conceptual connections this word invites (with *aglaiê, aglaizô*) seem to confirm it: see xv.78 and X.307, 331. Compare, however, Hoekstra's commentary on xv.78. Furthermore, Steinkopf calls attention to the form *kudioôn*, which defines Agamemnon in the luster of his arms (II.579) or a vigorous, exulting horse (VI.509 = XV.266).

72. See, for examples, XV.664, XX.27, and so on. Benveniste calls this use of *kudos* "a figure of style" (63).

73. Benveniste calls it "une acception nouvelle," and he notices that it is often presented as a future or possible accomplishment (63). According to my analysis, it is true that *kudos*, in any form and meaning, tends to be elusive, and not simply because it is easily lost, as Agamemnon complains in VIII.236–37, but because of the frequency with which it is prayed for (VII.205, XI.78–79, XVI.240–41, and so on) or hoped for (XVII.287), or the object of a contrary to fact condition (III.373, XVIII.166, and so on), or the object of a statement of simple possibility (V.33, 225, 260, IX.303, and so on).

councilors of the Argives ['Αργείων ἡγήτορες ἠδὲ μέδοντες], who by the Atreidai, Agamemnon and Menelaus, drink wine at common expense and who, each of you, utter commands [σημαίνουσι] to your soldiers: from Zeus honor and glory accompany you [ἐκ δὲ Διὸς τιμὴ καὶ κῦδος ὀπηδεῖ].[74]

In this passage each commander possesses *timê* and *kudos* as the conventional appanage of the *basileis*, without any consideration of the intrinsic value of each *basileus*.[75] Notice the verb *opêdei*, "accompanies," which implies that *kudos* follows a person and that it is only there where that person is. On the contrary, *kleos* moves away from the person toward the world (Steinkopf 1937, 25). Menelaus mentions the banquets—where the *basileis* boast of their bravery—and the privileges of the kings, as Sarpedon does in XII.310ff., to remind them of what they are expected to accomplish on the battlefield.[76] Menelaus not only speaks exactly—though without indignation—as his brother does in his flyting (IV.341ff.), but he combines his name and that of his brother as a pair of leaders to whom the other commanders and councilors come for the banquets (*daites*): he points therefore to his role as Agamemnon's colleague in the supreme command of the Trojan expedition.[77]

This "political" sort of *kudos* which shines on Agamemnon[78] is connected to other honorific attributes that insist on the same divine favor. For instance, in a few lines the assembly is defined as *kudianeirê*, "giving *kudos* to men" (I.490). Here Achilles is described as consuming his heart since he does not frequent the "*kudos*-giving assembly." This is the only example in the *Iliad*—in the *Odyssey* the word does not appear—in which this epithet qualifies *agorê* instead of its common noun *makhê*, "battle." This unique expression sounds bitter in this passage, for of course it reminds us that it is not to Achilles, but to Agamemnon, that Zeus has given *kudos* in the assembly.

---

74. The "commanders and councilors of the Argives" are the same as the *gerontes* or "elders" (Finsler 1906, 410). The word σημαίνειν, "to utter, to signal orders," again identifies command with its enunciation, that is, with the word that while signaling an order, establishes also the authority for giving that order. As each basileus is a *sêmantôr* (signaling orders, commander) for his warriors (*laoi*), so, as we have seen, Agamemnon is a *sêmantôr* for his peers, just as Zeus is for his.

75. Steinkopf 1937, 23 emphasizes the juxtaposition of *kudos* and *timê* that together point to the two essential aspects of Homeric royal life. *Kleos* and *timê*, on the contrary, are never coordinated, and correctly so, since they evoke values that are not coincidental in their essence.

76. For the representation of this protocol see Thalmann 1988, 5–6 and Chapter Four.

77. On this collegiality of power between Agamemnon and Menelaus, see Rousseau 1992.

78. This *kudos* could perhaps be the living expression of the frozen epithetic address, *mega kudos Akhaiôn*, which in all of Homer is addressed only to Nestor and Odysseus.

The allusions to Agamemnon's *kudos* are also carried out by the superlative *kudiste*, "most glorious," which is used by Achilles for Agamemnon (I.122), and which is an epithet of address Agamemnon shares only with Zeus.[79]

Monumental Glory (*Kleos*)

> The best [*hoi aristoi*] choose, instead of all else, one thing: everlasting glory [*kleos*] in place of mortal things. The majority, on the contrary, graze like cattle.
>
> —Heraclitus

Though Agamemnon is not a coward, and though he fights well in his own *aristeia*, the gods bestow on him no visible luster (*kudos*), and the poet gives him no epic renown and glory (*kleos*) in the battlefield.[80] This absolute lack of ·luster and renown as a warrior puts him in sharp contrast with Achilles, who is initially deprived of *timê* by Agamemnon, but has greater luster and an immortal glory in reserve. To make the distinction sharper, Agamemnon is granted only a conditional *kudos*, if, as Diomedes says, the Achaeans will destroy the Trojans and capture the city (IV.414–15);[81] on another occasion he is made to see and denounce how Zeus withdraws *kudos* from the fighting Argives (VIII.237–38). This notion that Agamemnon would gain *kleos* only if he conquers Troy is also implicit in the passages in which he recognizes that return to Argos with the loss of many men and without the conquest would be dishonorable (*dusklea*), as he says at IX.22 = II.115.

Achilles, on the contrary, desires to obtain *kudos* (XX.502, XXI.543), reproaches Apollo for snatching the *kudos* of victory away from him (XXII.118 and cf. XXI.596), and prevents the Achaeans from shooting arrows or casting spears at Hector during the last duel, in order to assure the *kudos* for himself. Finally Athena, appearing to him alone, tells him that she expects "to carry off a great *kudos* for the Achaeans, to the ships, as I and you slaughter Hector" (XXII.217). Since Athena sees herself as Achilles' comrade in the killing of Hector, we may assume that Achilles will gain *kudos* together *with* Athena, and not *from* her. This use of *kudos* is deviant, for it refers to the object itself of the victory, in this case the weapons of the slain Hector and his corpse.[82]

---

79. The marks of honor that are shared by the king and Zeus are collected by Collins 1988, 73f.

80. On Agamemnon's claim of being "the best of the Achaeans," see Nagy 1979, 26ff. Postlethwaite 1995, 98–99 takes a skeptical view of Agamemnon's military virtue.

81. Also Menelaus would gain immortal glory (*kleos*) in VII.91 if he were fighting against Hector and conquering him. But this hypothetical boasting placed in his mouth by Homer is of course mere fancy. Menelaus will not be allowed to fight against Hector, for he would be destroyed by him.

82. The dative *Akhaiois* implies that the *kudos*, the glory attached to the victory over Hector, will be "for the Achaeans," "in their eyes," as in IX.303. Notice with Benveniste (1969, 63–65) that here the obtaining of *kudos*, as often, is contingent upon a future or conditional situation.

After the killing of Hector, Achilles announces (XXII.393–94): "We have won a great *kudos*. We have slain divine Hector, the man the Trojans glorified in their city like a god." Though these words echo Athena's previous statement, the meaning of *kudos* has changed. His plural no longer includes only himself and the goddess, but all Achaeans. These two lines could be the lines of the song the Achaeans will intone, celebrating the defeat of their most dangerous adversary.[83] It is in fact exceptional that the expression: "to obtain *kudos*" is in the past tense, as it is here, but in a song the past achievement of the act would be explainable (Benveniste 1969, 65). For the glory of *kudos* lasts only for the moment of victory, and disappears outside the splendid instant of accomplishment (XXII.432ff.).

An interesting feature is that Achilles does not obtain *kudos* from the gods. Thus, the best of the Achaeans does not receive the grace of this visible sign of divine support.[84] Though he is helped in an extravagant way by Athena, who, as we have seen, wants to collect *kudos* with him, Achilles' peers cannot see her. As on other occasions, the divine intervenes into Achilles' life parenthetically, in a narrative that remains known only to the audience and readers of the poem. We confront again the disturbing complicity between divine power and textual strategy that suspends narrative accountability for Achilles. This suspension is probably intended to show how the divine plan takes over and inscribes Achilles' destiny into its unaccountable design; but it intimates also the critical assumption that the theological is inscribed in the textual rather than the reverse. The presence of the divine enhances the stature of Achilles in the eyes of the readers who alone know about this privileged presence. The text takes seriously Achilles' marginality among his peers and Achilles' uniqueness as a mortal. It celebrates his deeds in a sort of exclusive complicity with the divine and with the audience and the readers.

Though his peers are not aware of it, divine help is present for Achilles, and he does desire glory. Modern authors tend to think that after Patroclus's death and his decision to embrace his own impending death, Achilles cares little about

---

83. See Steinkopf 1937, 28 note 95, who quotes Eustathius. Modern scholars uphold this view.

84. The only partial exception to this norm, with its curious deviation from the regular pattern, confirms my point. In XXIV.110–11, Zeus promises Thetis to attach *kudos* to Achilles (*kudos Akhillêi protiaptô*). But the luster that Zeus intends here to bestow on Achilles will depend on his willing restitution of Hector's corpse. This will be his glory (Ameis and Hentze 1884, ad loc.). If this were the meaning, the text would illustrate the exemplary force of this civilized gesture as the source of glory for Achilles. But others critics prefer a more concrete source for this *kudos*. Steinkopf (1937, 29), noticing that it is not ethical behavior that gains glory for Homeric heroes, thinks that both the gifts from Priam, pleasing Achilles' heart (XXIV.119), and the will of the god enter more in the picture. Richardson (1993, 288) speculates that *kudos* must refer at least primarily to the honor that Achilles will receive from Priam's ransom. Steinkopf shows the unique occurrence of the verb *protiaptô* with *kudos*, a connection attested by Pindar *N*. 8.37, Sophocles *El*. 356. At any rate this *kudos* would be neither a victory in battle nor a preeminence in the assembly, but a humane gesture with a glance at obeying the god and obtaining gifts.

honor, prizes, or glory.[85] Though this point is correct concerning honor (*timê*) and prizes, it is not correct concerning the specific glory of victory (*kudos*). On the one hand he is upset with Apollo when that god deprives him of *kudos* by snatching Antenor from his assault (XXII.18); and on the other hand, he moves toward winning noble *kleos* in XVIII.123–25.

Achilles, in fact, is to earn undying glory (*athanaton kleos*). In this he is unique and exceptional. He thus contrasts with the political leaders, Menelaus, Odysseus, Nestor,[86] and Agamemnon in particular to whom the *Iliad* attributes no *kleos* at all. This lack is shocking, since *kleos* is the real *epic* glory, that is, the glory the *Iliad* can produce, wants to sing about, and recycles (i.e. produces through the narrative of deeds) for some of its "heroic" characters: Achilles, Hector, and Diomedes.[87]

To begin with, *kleos* is not visible but audible. It is "what is heard" and is repeated that becomes "reputation" or "glory." It does not remain attached to the person like a halo, but moves around as words do. Thus whenever the word *kleos* is uttered by a bard, his singing of it transmits and recycles the power of this word to be heard, to be heard often, forever, throughout distant lands, and up to heaven. For *kleos* is such (Steinkopf 1937, 4ff.) that it is always specified and labeled: men hear something that spreads around, in the city (*ana astu*, XVI.461), toward Cyprus (*Kupronde*, XI.21), becomes large (*mega*), and spreads to all the army (V.1–3), to all Greece, and even among all men (X.213).

---

85. To illustrate how Achilles expresses his disillusionment with his social world by misusing the language he disposes, Adam Parry gives, among others, this example: "He says that he has won a great victory by slaying Hector, when we know that he is really fighting to avenge his comrade and that he sees no value in the glory that society can confer" (1956, 6–7). In XVIII.79–90, Achilles rejects the pleasure of being honored by Zeus, now that his friend has been killed, and he "will never again, in the *Iliad*, go out to fight for glory, though he is happy enough to bask in it at the moment of victory, 22.393–94" (Hainsworth 1993, 103).

86. Only Nestor's shield obtains the grace of being granted *kleos* (VIII.92). Another object, a tomb (*sêma*), could ensure immortal *kleos* for Hector (VII.91). It is the tomb of the man Hector hopes to kill. See Nagy 1990b, 202–222. As Steinkopf (1937, 14) writes, the tomb preserves *kleos* both in its concrete objectivity and as the thing talked about. In VII.451, the *kleos* of the divine wall is threatened by the coming into being of a greater wall: only the destruction of this competitor will ensure the continuity of the *kleos* of the divine wall.

87. There is of course no equivalence between what we call a "hero" and what archaic Greek calls a *hêrôs* (for which, see Nagy 1979, 114–15, and West 1978, 370–73), and no equivalence either with the image of the great warriors of epic, the *aristoi*. Agamemnon is certainly an *aristos*, but he would hardly be a "hero" for us. Yet an approximation between the two notions could occur when an *aristos* is represented as seeking *kleos* at the risk of his life, or obtaining *kleos* by divine help, as in the cases of Achilles, Diomedes (V.1–3), Hector (XXII.304), Patroclus (XXIII.280), and Sarpedon (XII.318). There are only very few others, Pandaros, for instance, to whom *kleos* is granted (V.172), for whom, however, the attribution of our notion "hero" might not apply. In the *Odyssey*, *kleos* becomes devalued: everybody, from Alcinous to Orestes to Penelope, has *kleos*.

In *kleos*, the glorious survival of the hero after his death and the unending fame of the poem lead to only one conclusion: the poet's fame and the hero's glory are inextricably grafted together.[88] For death is the terrible adversary against which the poem concentrates its imagination and its energy, the enemy that it wants to conquer (or outrun!). Such a superb artifact, this sophisticated product of generations of "virtuosi," depends for its survival on the frail breath of the poets (see II.489–90). This complicity between the poem's survival and the survival of the hero's name is one of the most exciting poetic conundrums, one of the greatest of human inventions, and one of its pitfalls.

The survival of *kleos* in the *Iliad* depends also on the magnitude of the object to which it is attached and on the absence of rivals. The wall that Poseidon and Apollo built around Troy has a great reputation (*kleos*). Yet something threatens the immortality of this wall, as Poseidon says in VII.451ff., when he sees the new wall built by the Achaeans:

The fame (*kleos*) of this [Achaean wall] will spread as far as dawn!
Men will forget the wall that I and Apollo
built with much labor for the hero Laomedon.

But Zeus comforts Poseidon (458ff.):

Truly your fame will spread as far as dawn!
Come on, when the long-haired Achaeans shall leave . . .
then tear down the wall and sweep it all into the sea.

Kleos spreads and lasts only on the condition that it is produced by an unbeatable object that fears no competition: artists and poets therefore must be aware of this cruel rule and raise their monuments always higher, the deeds of their heroes always more exceptional and singular, the poem more monumental. And even so, fashion may change: the newest song and the newest hero may dethrone the old ones, as Telemachus implies in *Odyssey* i.351–52. The competition among poets is ferocious, as Hesiod states in *Erga* 25–6.

Most often the object that conserves and produces *kleos* is a tomb (*sêma*, "monument" and "sign"), before which men may raise their voice and remember the deed of the buried hero (xxiv.80ff.) or the deed of the champion who slew the buried man (VII.87ff.). In these two passages the poem itself becomes exemplary of the way this voice of remembrance arises at the sight of the monument. This memory is in this way twice monumentalized, first by the tomb and furthermore by the voice we hear in the poem.

What deed, what extraordinary action, what singular hero to sing? Would he be the one whose tomb shall not be surpassed by a more visible tomb, whose poem shall not be put into obscurity by a more monumental poem? Should he be a hero of whom the poem sings the glorious deeds or the glorious death, or both?

88. "We may have lost countless other epic compositions, but the *Iliad* has survived and endured. The confidence of the *Iliad* in its eternal survival is the confidence of the master singer" (Nagy 1979, 29).

Hector receives glory for his victories and for his death (XXII.304–5). On a few occasions the *Iliad* grants *kleos* to living heroes as their accompanying reputation (as part of their image). On other rare occasions, the *Iliad* grants *kleos* to heroes for specific deeds. Such is the case of Diomedes in V.1–3: "Now Pallas Athena gave to the son of Tydeus, Diomedes, fury and courage so that he might become conspicuous [*ekdêlos*] among all the Argives and win noble glory [*kleos esthlon*].

The deeds which Diomedes accomplishes in the fight against the gods are extravagant and marvelous and become, so to speak, part of his *kleos*, his glorious portrait. It would be possible to speculate on the particular nature of this *kleos* that seems almost a synonym of *kudos*: for in fact it is bound to visibility (*ekdêlos*)[89] among all the Achaeans, it is granted by a divinity and is attached to a specific series of deeds. These features confirm the absolute uniqueness of Diomedes' performance and the glory (reputation) attached to it.

But of course Diomedes is not the immense hero of the *Iliad*. Its hero is one with a more pathetic and tragic experience: his gripping enigma is why, among all the heroes who earn *kleos* in the *Iliad*, he should be the only one who knows that he *must* die if he wants *kleos*. Why could he not, like Diomedes, get *kleos* and imagine that he could go back home? It is this chance that the *Iliad* refuses to Achilles. Let us analyze the famous passage in the ninth book (410–16):

> For my goddess mother, silver-footed Thetis, tells me that two fates are bringing me to the issue of death. If I remain here and fight besieging the city of the Trojans, my return home perishes [ὤλετο μέν μοι νόστος], but my glory shall never fail [ἀτὰρ κλέος ἄφθιτον ἔσται]; but if I go home to my dear native land, my noble glory perishes [ὤλετό μοι κλέος ἐσθλόν], and a long life shall be for me, and the issue of death shall not get me soon [οὐδέ κέ μ᾽ ὦκα...κιχείη].[90]

All the time Achilles remained in Troy up until now, he must have accepted the dire condition his mother prophesies, and he must have resolved that immortal glory was worth his early death. He had to adjust his existential experience to that uncompromising ideal, quintessence of the Iliadic poetics.

---

89. This word is *hapax* in Homer, and *dêlos, deelos* occur only in two other passages (X.466 and xx.33). In the next lines (V.4ff.) Athena kindles flames from Diomedes' helmet and shield: this light translates Diomedes' luster and reputation into material terms.

90. Line 413, ὤλετο μέν μοι νόστος, ἀτὰρ κλέος ἄφθιτον ἔσται, is held together by a powerful chiasmus that puts the conceptually opposed terms *kleos* and *nostos* in a contiguity full of tension; the beginning of line 413 is repeated with the opposite notion in line 415. Notice the contrast between *ôleto* and *aphthiton* that increases the value of *kleos* in relation to *nostos*. The contrast is emphasized by the particle *atar*; in the corresponding line 415 the contrasting particle *de* is much weaker. The syntax of the conditional clauses is that of the more vivid future: the aorist *ôleto* in the protasis refers to the already settled decision of the fate, or to the perspective of the speaker who puts himself at the future point of his long life. In line 416 the optative occurs, *kikheiê*, reducing the certainty. This line was athetized by Aristarchus as being pleonastic.

But the quarrel with Agamemnon produces in Achilles a profound conversion: he rejects now that terrible alternative and envisages his return home. Such a switch is deep and leaves profound traces even when he will later accept his early death in order to avenge Patroclus. Even at that moment he will not glance at his "immortal glory" as the main motivator for his sacrifice.

The text of Thetis's prophecy with its balanced and opposed clauses, locking up his fate into a terrible either/or, sounds like a splendid and inflexible ideal, a sort of epitaph that Achilles painfully recites at the moment in which he writes it off.

His fate is unique in the *Iliad*. Occasionally great heroes sense that death is not far away from them, or that their destiny is to fight until their death (Hector in VI.447ff., Odysseus in XIV.82-87, etc.) but only Achilles is portrayed as facing either a short life or an inglorious return, and as finally identifying himself with his death. Again and again he is portrayed with a painful, we would say tragic, vision of himself.[91]

It is intriguing that in a poem in which each small change of a character's mood, even his minimal decisions, are often supported and justified by a theological intervention, no theological sign occurs to explain the grounds of Achilles' unique destiny. A sort of enigmatic, funereal silence surrounds this curse of his. While Zeus enters into all sorts of intrigues and quenches others, he has nothing to do with Achilles' destiny in the *Iliad*.[92]

One might assume that his destiny depends on his immortal mother: Achilles' early death would be a sort of sinister counter-effect of a birth which should have been immortal.[93] Such an assumption is certainly supported by the mirroring relationship which the text portrays between Achilles and Thetis. But in this case again no divine will is implicit, only a structural parallelism. No, in

---

91. Even in XVII.404–411, as he anxiously awaits Patroclus's return without knowing that he is already dead, we are told that Achilles knew from Thetis that it was not Zeus's will that he and Patroclus should sack Troy together. Achilles thought that he would die before the sack of the city, not Patroclus, of course. In other passages he asserts that his fate consists of a short life (I.352, 416, *etc.*).

92. Zeus, however, is the plotter of Thetis's marriage with a mortal (XVIII.84ff.). Slatkin 1991, 71–77 refers to Pindar's *Isthmian* 8, where Themis invites Zeus and Poseidon to stop their erotic pursuit of Thetis and declares that Thetis, married to a mortal, will see her son dead in war (29–38). In Aeschylus's *Prometheus Bound*, Gaia, identified with Themis, holds the secret of Zeus's future overthrow if he marries Thetis. Slatkin (77) is cautiously favorable to connecting Pindar's treatment to "mythology present in the *Iliad* in some form and recoverable from it–even if deeply embedded and only allusively evident to us." On page 101, she writes: "The price of Zeus's hegemony is Achilles' death." This is epigrammatically said. However, the *Iliad* wants its hero to be conscious of his alternatives, and at the same time wants him to choose his heroic destination, and to choose with a precise human *prohairesis* in a great act of self-dedication to death. For this reason the text does not mention any divine will for or parallel to his decision, neither in XVIII.84ff. nor in 429–37 of the same book, where there is mention of the gods' or Zeus's ordering Thetis to marry a mortal.

93. I read this assumption in Rousseau 1995, 576.

Thetis's words, he should have chosen *kleos* or *nostos*, without any divine injunction or prerecorded word.

The contrast with Odysseus is sharp: the Odyssean hero, by identifying himself with his tricks, disguises, and *ainoi* becomes ungraspable for death. By baffling his human essence he drifts constantly also from himself (Pucci 1987, 150–54). In this process, by constantly losing himself, he survives and defeats death. That is why the poem enchants its readers in the double sense of the verb *thelgein*, to charm and to paralyze the mind.

In view of this poetics, the *Odyssey*, contravening the protocols of the *Iliad*, grants Odysseus both *nostos* and *kleos* (i.344 = iv.726 = 816, v.311, ix.20, and so on; see Nagy 1977, 35–36). The *Odyssey* diverges from protocols of the *Iliad* also in the cases of Agamemnon and Nestor and grants them *kleos*. Speaking to the Cyclops, Odysseus identifies himself as a man of Agamemnon, "whose *kleos* is now the widest under heaven" (ix.264). Of course, Agamemnon is the conqueror of Troy, and Odysseus grants to the commander that *kleos* which Diomedes had conditionally promised him (IV.414–15). On the other hand, Nestor, seeing the miracle of Athena's disappearance, prays that the goddess may give *kleos* to himself, his children, and his wife (iii.380–81).[94]

The Urging of the Heart: Heroic Death

> I am fully convinced that we are at the end of a subjectivity understood as a self-presence which supports presentations and brings them back as one's own—this subjectivity being, precisely, unpresentable.
>
> Jean Luc Nancy in *Beyond Representations* 1996

When Achilles fully reemerges as a character of the *Iliad*, in book XVIII, he does so only to face his death. Speaking to his mother, he voices his heroic choice (*prohairesis*), by listening to the bidding of his heart (XVIII.90ff.):

> . . . since the heart (*thumos*) urges me
> not to live, nor to be among men unless first Hector,
> hit by my spear, loses his life (*thumon*) . . .

The voice that spreads *kleos* to the light of dawn and to Heaven, the glorious rumor that never ends, starts from a voice that resounds inside the chest of the hero and tells him that he must risk his life in order to avenge Patroclus.

Many questions arise at this point in relation to this text: what sort of agent is this heart that produces such orders? In what way does it command? Does it constitute an image to indicate the autonomous decision of a unified self? Does it gaze at the splendor of the immortal *kleos* when it urges Achilles to die rather than to leave Patroclus unavenged? I will unravel these questions and I will

94. See Pucci 1987, 216–19, and here Chapter Nine. For different views, see Nagy 1979; Edwards 1985; and Goldhill 1991, 96ff. On the Odyssean *kleos*, I rather agree with Segal 1994, 85–109 and Papadopoulou-Belmehdi 1994, 200–203 on Penelope's *kleos*. The survey of *kleos* in this chapter is restricted to the occurrences of the word in the *Iliad*.

maintain that the "heart" is here the metaphorical expression of Achilles' passion, and that this "heart" speaks what we would call the language of passion, will, consciousness.[95] We will find that this heart does not point to any unified idea of self, while the voice does. Finally Achilles makes his heroic *prohairesis* while glancing only askance at his *kleos*, and at any rate the glory he will envisage has a different psychological quality than the immortal *kleos* of Book Nine.

The heroic inner voice resounds also in Hector's heart. It comes from the heart of a brave man (*esthlos*), just as the *kleos* won will be brave and noble (*esthlon*), as he says to his wife in VI.441ff.:

> ... but I feel profound
> shame facing the Trojans and the Trojan women, trailing their long robes,
> if, like a coward, I shrink from the battle,
> and the heart urges me not do so,[96] since I have learned to be brave (*esthlos*)
> always and to fight in the front ranks of the Trojans
> winning my father's great glory (*kleos*) and my own.

In these words we find a cluster of images that combine the urging of the heart (*thumos*), the brave (*esthlos*) hero, and the winning of glory (*kleos*), whose most common epithet is just *esthlos*. Like the voice of the Socratic *daimonion*, this voice of the heart detains Hector and Achilles from doing something shameful or wrong, as shrinking from the battle or continuing to live without first avenging Patroclus's death. We have seen Athena appearing suddenly and violently to detain Achilles from slaying Agamemnon, and now we hear the heart itself of the hero taking the same power of deterrence: this heart is not a god coming from outside, with an ironic voice, but the inside itself of Achilles.

The source of the decision is inside the hero, but the nondetermination or the overdetermination of the heart's urging remain problematic: certainly Hector will tell Andromache that he has learnt to be brave, and Achilles will aver that he

---

95. I take *thumos* with a figural, metaphorical sense for "passion," "will," and the verb *anôge* ("urges," "impels") with either a metonymical force, the internal pressure standing for an "order," or more plausibly with a metaphorical meaning, the internal impulsion being similar to the complex of inner voice, imagining, and thinking that constitute the psychic process or "language." A slight justification in favor of the latter interpretation could be the use of the verb *anôge* with the negative as in *ou phêmi*. Pelliccia 1995, 45ff. has presented some arguments to caution the reader against this metaphorical use of *speech*. His view that "the organs come close to speaking ... but they never actually do" (62) is correct, but it seems to me natural that it is so, for, as we are going to see in the Achilles scene, as soon as the internal voice is made argumentative it must become the voice of the speaking I.

The inner, psychic language is evoked also in other images, for instance in the formular expression *kata phrena kai kata thumon* (e.g., IV.163; VI.447; xv.211. etc.), which constitutes a notorious conundrum for the interpreters and translators: *in mente et in animo* (Latin translation), "im Verstand und im Herzen" (Ameis-Hentze-Cauer), "in heart and soul" (Leaf, translation), "nella mente e nell'animo" (Privitera), "in my heart and soul" (Fagles), etc.

96. The urging of the heart not to do something, in the expression *oude me thumos anôge(n),* is found only in these two quoted passages, in Hector's utterance VI.444, and in Achilles' XVIII.90.

cannot live without first killing Hector, but why and how are questions that are not even allowed to emerge before the stern command of the heart.

In this specific sense the heart is the general powerhouse of the hero's own decisions, the fountainhead of his heroic determination.[97] Different semantic shades among the terms that we translate by "heart" (*thumos, kradiê, phrenes, êtôr*, etc.) are perceivable especially when they are in the nominative case, but, as a whole, modern scholars tend to take them to be almost interchangeable.[98]

This plurality of terms increases, of course, the overdetermination and indetermination of these agents and fragments, at least terminologically, the unity of the self. In Achilles' speech that we are commenting (XVIII.90–92):

> . . . since the heart (*thumos*) urges me
> not to live, nor to be among men unless first Hector,
> hit by my spear, loses his life (*thumon*) . . .

the speaking I refers to the urging agent inside himself, the *thumos*, as to a sort of alter ego, so that the moral injunction seems somehow separable from the speaking I.[99] In this supreme moment of self-commitment the text shows us a plural self, an emotional agent driving the speaking I.

---

97. Often a god inspires the hero with fury and courage so that he may win *kleos esthlon* as in V.1–3. Other times the inspiring voice is that of comrades in arms: Sarpedon rushes into the battle in order to have his Lycians say of him: "They are not without glory, our kings (*ouk aklees*) . . . but they have a brave might (*is esthlê*), since they fight in the front ranks of the Lycians" (XII.319-21). Notice here too the connection between the hero's brave (*esthlê*) might and his *kleos*. The Lycians' voice becomes the voice that urges Sarpedon: it is in fact, as I argue in Chapter Four, the voice of the epic protocols which Sarpedon makes his own, and in which he is inscribed as a character. My interpretation in Chapter Four and here differs from Vernant's 1980 and Wofford's 1992, because for me even in the Sarpedon passage *kleos* and *timê* are not parallel terms of the heroic ideology, as Vernant and Wofford take them to be. These terms are even there opposed or incongruent. We all agree, on the other hand, that there is tension between the ideal of *kleos* and existential concerns, and Wofford expresses it powerfully: ". . . the consolation provided by the promise of *kleos* is at best inadequate, at worst fraudulent" 1992, 46.

98. Jahn 1987, Schmitt 1990, Pelliccia 1995. To exemplify one of these shades, I quote Schmitt 1990, 174ff., who argues that *noos* in Homer constitutes man's clear insight that can however be disturbed, misfocussed, and limited by passions expressed by *thumos, kradiê* etc. It is what founds the unity of the self in Homer (224). *Thumos* inasmuch as it designates thinking stands at the service of attaining a specific desire, or of warding off a specific grief.

99. In Achilles' movement of introspection, when he ponders whether to slay Agamemnon or to calm himself down (I.189ff.), the *diêgêsis* describes a series of emotional seats and states. First Achilles' "*êtôr* in his hairy chest" ponders whether to draw the sword or "to restrain the *thumos* (*erêtuseie . . . thumon*), (his fury)," and "while he was revolving these things in his *phren* and his *thumos*, he was drawing the sword . . ." Whether we have to take the two terms "in his *phren* and his *thumos*" as referring respectively to the calming urge and to the raging impulse or as sort of hendiadys indicating the spiritual place of the decision ("in his heart and soul"), is

Yet the voice that refers to the *thumos* and its stern order agrees with the *thumos*; in fact when the speaking I unravels the reasons why he should die immediately if this is the condition for avenging Patroclus, he finds only arguments to corroborate the urging of the heart. As a consequence, the voice seems to be the unifying principle of the self, while there is a terminological excess or a psychological overdetermination.

The terminological overdetermination risks creating a conceptual conundrum. The term for the driving agent, *thumos*, is here (92) also the term for Hector's life, and this repetition of the same term (*thumos*) with two different meanings is unsettling. Should we interpret this disturbing repetition, this split-meaning, as the casual result of the contiguity of two formulaic expressions? It is certainly legitimate to do so. Yet we should be aware that this repetition produces also the pathetic oxymoron of Iliadic poetics: Achilles' life/heart/breath (*thumos*) urges his own death in view of depriving Hector of his life/heart/breath (*thumos*). A sort of vicious circle ensues, whereby one dies in order to have the other dead, and by doing so both win glory. The *thumos* beats the tocsin of death.

To represent the impulses that drive Achilles to sacrifice himself through the radical ontological terms of life and death is certainly a reduction to a shocking generality, but it produces a tremendous impact since it asserts and contrasts the essential existential principles. Yet the presence and unity of Achilles' "self" through this powerful and essential term are not achieved to the extent that *thumos* evokes too many meanings, heart, passion, fury—and here plays on two significantly different meanings. In the first instance Achilles' *thumos* has a voice; in the second it represents simply the physical life of Hector.[100]

This analysis aims at describing the psychological agents and props that the text arrays in this momentous decision by Achilles; in the next pages I inquire to what extent we can connect his decision to a fundamental motivation, desire of glory, or grief for his failures. My purpose is always the same as from the start of this chapter, the assessment of the specific voice of Achilles and its relation with the poetic voice.

The speaking I of Achilles is weeping. Just as in the first encounter with his mother, Achilles again groans deeply when he tells her of his decision to avenge Patroclus and to accept his own death (XVIII.70, 78ff.). We recall that crying emerges from the bottom of the heart, shaking the *phrenes* of the weeper. A new

---

difficult to say. Yet the formulaic nature of the expression favors the latter interpretation.

100. I am not trying to resolve the long-discussed question whether Homer has the terms to represent a "self" in its unity, a question raised by Snell and still debated by many scholars. I am simply probing the Homeric language in this important scene of decision. It would be futile for me to try to summarize even the general terms of the debate. I will only say that the whole question should be reopened on the ground of current awareness that the terms our culture uses for representing the self, the person, are metaphysical, and that, to put it bluntly with A. Oksenberg Rorty: "There is not such a thing as the concept of a person" 1990, 21. This awareness should bring us to consider Homer's failure to represent the self, if indeed there is such a failure, from a different problematic than the Hegelian one that inspired the work of Snell.

intervention of the heart is here indirectly implied. Then he was weeping for the loss of his *timê*, now for the loss of his friend and the uselessness of his heroic life.

When Hector, speaking to his wife, foresees his death and his future *kleos* emblematized in his wife, he does not weep. He leaves his wife crying, and by her crying she prefigures her becoming the *sêma* ([living] sign and monument) of his *kleos* (see VI.405–59).

In the scene of Achilles' heroic *prohairesis*, Thetis too weeps as she performs over Achilles the funeral gesture of taking the head of the dead person (70–72): Achilles' death is imminent and certain, as her gesture implies. Thetis' crying is defined as *kôkusasa* which indicates the screaming of the mourning ritual.

It is in this funeral frame that Achilles speaks of his heart urging him not to live, and Thetis confirms this destiny by announcing to him that his short life will end immediately after Hector's death [αὐτίκα γάρ τοι ἔπειτα μεθ' Ἕκτορα πότμος ἑτοῖμος, XVIII.93]. Achilles' I answers with that "Let me die at once" [αὐτίκα τεθναίην, XVIII.98] which Socrates recalls in his *Apology*. Now the shortness of his life (XVIII.88–91, 115–16) is no longer some vague projection but close and poignantly real, present (ἑτοῖμος). So Lynn-George (1988, 169–70) writes: "The intensity of the wish would abolish the intervals of time's sequence—even the short succession which will culminate in Achilles' own swift and early death after Hector—in a death which would be present instantly."[101]

Through an emotional speech (98-126), Achilles' I unravels a series of motivations that must have determined the imperious injunction of his heart: shame and grief for his failure to save Patroclus, bitterness and grief for the futility of his heroic life succeeding in nothing, neither in achieving *timê* nor in saving the friend,[102] the urge to take revenge upon Hector, shame for the foolishness of the quarrel with Agamemnon, and finally desire for glory. The overdetermination that the word "heart" implies is mirrored by this overdetermination of themes. Let us comment on some of them.

He sacrifices himself for Patroclus, whom he failed to protect (XVIII.79–82, 91–93, 98–106), and with whom he identifies himself (ἴσον ἐμῇ κεφαλῇ

---

101. On this awareness of an imminent death we may compare the reflections of the Prince in Dostoevsky's *Idiot*: "Yet the chief and the worst pain is perhaps not inflicted by wounds, but by your certain knowledge that in an hour, in ten minutes, in half a minute, now, this moment your soul will fly out of our body, and that you will be a human being no longer, and that that's certain—the main thing is that it is *certain*" [original italics].

102. It is difficult to define exactly the nature of Achilles' feelings: grief, resentment, shame, guilt mingle in decrying his failures and his having been the cause of the death of many of his peers (101ff.). Note that self-scorching and grandiose phrase: "I am sitting by the ships, a vain burden of earth" (104); observe also that ambiguous verb in *ton apôlesa* (82), meaning "I lost him" and "I caused his death." The latter is more plausible in translation, but the ambivalence remains unerasable. See Pazdernick 1995, 363f.

XVIII.82). Through such an identification, Patroclus's death is contiguous to his own death.[103] He curses the discord and the wrath that produced the quarrel with Agamemnon and says (112–13): "Let the past be past, though I am still anguished, beating down by force my fury (*thumos*)." The polysemic value of *thumos* occurs again. It refers to another impulsion and passion of the hero, his not totally extinguished wrath against Agamemnon. A stronger *thumos* now dominates Achilles' "self" or voice and drives him to live no more if he does not kill Hector.

Just as the word "heart" implies the absolute notion of life and a rush of rage, so also Achilles' motivations straddle a sense of bitterness and guilt (as in cursing the dispute with Agamemnon) and a self-consecration to death that will drive him to a sort of sublime asceticism. In this last frame of mind, he compares himself with Heracles and quietly embraces his destiny.[104]

At the end of his speech, Achilles contemplates also his glory (XVIII.120–25):

> Thus I too [as Heracles], if the same fate is prepared for me, I will lie when I die. But now[105] let me win noble glory [νῦν δὲ κλέος ἐσθλὸν ἀροίμην] and induce some of the Trojans and their Dardanian women to wipe away the tears with both hands from their soft cheeks, to cry aloud, and to recognize that I have been long absent from the battle.

As Renehan (1987, 112) notices, Achilles sees his glory not in nobly dying but in slaying a host of enemies. *Kleos*, as we have seen, can go to the victorious hero, as Achilles sees himself now, or to the dying hero who has always been glorious and conquering in combat. Hector, for instance, in XXII.304–5, when he faces his death, evokes his *kleos* as compensation.

The *kleos* that Achilles conjures up at this moment not only does not refer to the *aphthiton kleos* ("immortal glory," IX.413) he is destined to reap with his death, but it is characterized by several disturbing features. For, stated as it is stated, this pursuit of glory (1) implies the creation of a *kleos* also for Hector, (2) exhibits an expression of self-pity, and (3) sounds cruel and perverse.

---

103. Another image represents him as already the prey of death. In XVIII.202ff. Achilles makes himself manifest to the Trojans without any weapons; Athena surrounds his shoulders with an aegis and his head with a crown of golden clouds "and kindles from it a blazing flame." In the simile that follows, this flame is compared to a city almost conquered: the immediate reference is Troy, but it is also and simultaneously Achilles himself who will die forthwith, immediately after Hector and before the fall of Troy.

104. I have illustrated some aspects of Achilles' mourning asceticism in Pucci 1987, 170ff., and in Chapter Seven. See now also Blössner 1991, 28ff. On the sublime in Achilles' figure, see Turolla 1949, 67–68, and Ford 1992.

105. On this "but now" Nagy (1979, 102) comments: "After the death of Patroclus, the Achilles figure uses the expression *nun de* 'but now' no fewer than fifteen times in our *Iliad*. With his *akhos/penthos* over Patroclus, Achilles enters the realm of *kleos*."

(1) By identifying his *kleos* with the crying of the Trojan mothers and wives, whose men Achilles shall kill, he unwittingly evokes the funeral ceremonies for the fallen men, during which mothers and wives in their lamentations (*gooi*) and poets in their *thrênoi* were singing the praise of the dead. Part of Hector's *kleos* will be embodied in the *thrênos* that the poets will sing in his honor during the funeral rituals (XXIV.720ff.), just as the Muses' *thrênos* will initiate Achilles' own *kleos* (xxiv.60ff.).[106]

The paradox in this correlation is that Achilles' *kleos* causes *thrênoi* among the Trojans which shall grant Hector greater *kleos*. This correlation of epic song and *thrênoi* uncovers the textual investment in a narrative that produces them through internecine stories.

This is another formulation of the vicious circle we have seen in connection with Achilles' heart: Achilles' *thumos* (heart/life) urges his death in order to slay Hector's *thumos* (heart/life). The sublime heroic deed and song are grounded in an oxymoronic economy of loss. This loss is preordained, as a structural game, by a chain of relays. This economy of loss moreover fails to differentiate the values and the heroes: the *kleos* of Hector being produced by that of Achilles will forever survive. Which *kleos* shall be greater in the eyes of future audiences will not be absolutely sure.

(2) Achilles transfers his own grief (*akhos/penthos*) for the death of Patroclus into the grief of the Trojan women, who like him will suffer for the death of one of their dearest. In a word he is killing Hector in order to have Andromache and Hecabe crying just as he cries for Patroclus. His pursuit of glory, being so formulated, implies that he creates for himself the condition to pity the women and the family of Hector, since they will suffer his same sorrow. In a paradoxical way this means that he will be able to understand and pity Priam when the old man will come to him. The vicious circle affects also the register of pity.

This sharing of suffering with the Trojan women feminizes him. This representation of Achilles in feminized figures occurs on other occasions. For instance, in IX.323 Achilles likens himself to a mother bird feeding her young, in XVI.7–10 he compares Patroclus to a silly girl and himself to the protective mother whom the girl grabs by the skirt, in supplication; and in general his relation toward Patroclus tends to be expressed by parental metaphors (XVIII.318, XXIII.222—as a father). As Janko observes: Achilles "is usually cast in the protective parental role, Patroclus in that of the protected party. It is all the more ominous when Patroclus is sent out to protect the Greeks" (1992, 316).

---

106. The *thrênos* in fact has two simultaneous aspects: it constitutes the reverse image of the *kleos* reserved for the conquering hero. As such it produces a *penthos* and a *pêma* (grief) for the family and the friends of the fallen hero. On the other hand, however, the poetic song of *thrênos* initiates the song of *kleos* for the hero fallen in the pursuit of *kleos*, and irradiates his name and deeds. See how Hector's heroic deeds are emphasized in Andromache's and others' *gooi* (XXIV.725ff.). At the end of the ritual honors and *thrênoi* for Achilles, his name and his *kleos* are explicitly said to be immortal (xxiv.93–94); cf. G. Nagy 1979, 170–72.

Achilles' relationship to Patroclus is a private and emotional one and accordingly is marked by uninhibited expressions of familiarity and passionate affection. We find here the same features of Achilles' pathos already examined as one of his characteristics. It is just in this moment of familiarity, of uninhibited intimacy of language between Achilles and Patroclus (XVI.7ff.), that Achilles let himself be persuaded to send Patroclus to lighten the Trojan pressure on the Achaeans.[107] As it has often been suggested, Patroclus, initiated by Nestor (XI.762ff.), provides Achilles with the only link of compassion for his Achaean peers and a concern for the survival of the fleet. It is worthy of meditation that such a link is realized through a feeling of motherly pity (XVI.5),[108] defensive irony, and babyish imagining, as though only private, emotional, and joking language could eventually affect the uncompromising and sublime image he has of himself.[109]

Even in this troubling expression (XVIII.120–25) in which he identifies his *kleos* with the pain and laments of Trojan mothers and wives, Achilles focuses on the domestic and private consequences of his heroic action. He does not think of the fall of Troy as a result of his killing of Hector; he hardly envisions the respite his victory will afford to his battered peers. Again he imagines his heroic glory in its extension into domestic and emotional realms, as a private affair between himself and the poor mothers and wives of the Trojan fighters.

(3) For the great hero to contemplate his glory (*kleos*) not in the body of his fallen adversary but in the anguished mothers and wives wiping their tears means a pitiful identification with them and a perverse reward. He wants them to be tortured by the same grief as his own, as though this common pain could be compensation or even glory!

Given all these shades, the vision of glory does not seem the attraction at which Achilles gazes in his *prohairesis*. It sounds rather as a desperate, vain compensation.

Yet, the oxymoronic, self-centered, perverse features of Achilles' pursuit of *kleos* in this passage sustain the tremendous force and pathos with which the text asserts Achilles' acceptance of death. The reader is blinded by the violence of

---

107. For the explanation that the feminine simile covers a traditional feminine role in the persuasion of the hero, see Kakrides 1949 and Nagler 1974, 135.

108. Notice how line XVI.5, τὸν δὲ ἰδὼν ᾤκτιρε ποδάρκης δῖος Ἀχιλλεύς, picks up line XI.599, τὸν δὲ ἰδὼν ἐνόησε ποδάρκης δῖος Ἀχιλλεύς, when Achilles had seen Nestor and Machaon and had sent Patroclus to inquire, happy that the Achaeans were so pressed by toils and defeat. But now (XVI.5) he sees Patroclus weeping and feels pity for him. Martin 1989, 62: "In the poet's image system, the [weeping] performance of Patroclus ... resembles that of the *Iliad*'s weakest rhetorician, Agamemnon, the only other speaker who resorts to such an act (16.3–4 = 9.14–15)." Burkert (1955, 94) correctly shows that Achilles does not feel pity for the ruin of the Achaeans, but for the tears of the friend, and he argues that by the following tone of irony Achilles defends himself from that pity.

109. Pity in the *Iliad* confuses the mind of the pitier. Notice in the passage XVI.7ff. how Achilles describes the ruin of the Achaeans as being caused by their *huperbasia*, forgetting, as Reinhardt (1961, 27) notices, the collaboration of Zeus.

that "May I immediately die," by the ascetic companionship with death which his rush to it implies, and by the pathetic assertion that there will be no return.

Here again, as in the scene of the first book, Achilles' voice conjuring up his death, which now is imminent, sinks into this ontological abyss all the contingent aspects of his words. The scene of the mourning mother for her still living son, of a dying son manifesting his pursuit of glory to his mourning mother, ensconces and hides in its folds all the features that in fact, once they are uncovered, should destabilize its tremendous compactness. In this hiding lies its immense force.

We have underlined these features, the oxymoronic economy of loss, the superfetation of meanings in the images of the deciding self, the fragmentation of its motivations and their overdetermination, the accretion of upsetting shades in the image of *kleos*. As a consequence we cannot say with any certainty whether sorrow for Patroclus, or desire for glory, or ambition for status, or shame and guilt feelings, or all of them drive him to embrace his death. We can only say that what drives him to death is the death of Patroclus. As Nagy (1979, 102) says epigrammatically, "The key to the *kleos* of Achilles' epic is the *akhos/penthos* over Patroclus." What I have added to this definition is an analysis of how this grief (*akhos/penthos*) lodges in the large and polysemic container of the *thumos*. This image would seem to provide conceptual unity both to the notion of the self, to its autonomy, and to the elaborate motivations it contains, but our analysis has shown just the contrary for all these points. This voice of the heart is programmed, so to speak, to fit a prerecorded internecine structure whereby life/heart accepts death in order to kill life/heart, and whereby the song of *kleos* produces a song of mourning that produces a song of *kleos*.

We here have to recognize a subtle distinction, of paramount importance, between Achilles' subjective motivations and the poet's own goal and *pragma*. For the Iliadic song ideally presents itself as the continuity of his poetic voice and Achilles' decision to conquer *kleos*. The song seems only to come after, as a retroactivation of Achilles' exercising his heroic choice.

In fact, as we have surmised all along, it is possibly Achilles' heroic decision that comes after and retroactivates, fleshes out the poetic principles of the Iliadic song. And yet at this point the text is somehow overpowered by the deconstructive threads that disassemble its metaphysics. It is not the uncompromising sublime *kleos* of IX.410ff. that Achilles glances at as the motivation of his early death, but it is the voice of *thumos* that leads him with its abysmally complex urgings.

This being the basic structure that superintends Achilles' voice in his speech of *prohairesis*, it is inevitable that readers and critics are unable to fix the exact motivations and their precise weight in his decision. A mesmerizing overdetermination and simplification are responsible if, beginning from antiquity, Achilles' death is attributed to his desire for glory, as well as to his loyalty to Patroclus. For instance, to restrict our glance to only a few Platonic dialogues, in the *Symposium*, Phaedrus praises Achilles as a darling (*erômenon*) who chose to die for Patroclus: "Having learned from his mother that he would die as soon as he killed Hector . . . he dared to bring help to his lover Patroclus, and avenged him" (179D–E). It is curious that in this erotic version Achilles' motivation for dying is probably closer to *Iliad* XVIII.98ff. than Diotima's version when she says: "Do you suppose that Alcestis would have died for Admetus and Achilles would have died after Patroclus . . . if they had not expected to win 'an immortal memory for their valor' [*athanaton mnêmên aretês peri*] which we now keep? Of course not . . . They are in love with what is immortal" (208D). Here Diotima connects Achilles' decision to avenge Patroclus to his desire for immortal glory. In the *Apology* Plato has an almost similar version: Achilles "disregarded the danger of death in comparison to enduring any shame" [*aiskhron*, or disgrace] which he would have incurred had he not avenged his comrade (*Apology* 28C). Again Achilles' reputation seems to be the engine driving his decision to die.

The fact that the interpretation of Achilles as *erômenos,* as the darling of Patroclus, may come closer to our passage's motivations, brings to light also the indetermination in which the text leaves the nature of the relationship between the two men. The nature of their affection remains suspended and the tremendous power of their *philia* becomes more evident from Achilles' decision to die for Patroclus than from anything else in the poem.

The difference among these versions is not simply the result of the adaptations of Achilles' example into specific arguments, though it is also this, but the consequence of an overdetermined text whose pathos often complements and covers the arguments.

The splendor of Achilles' glory lasting centuries after the song that sang it— "an immortal memory for their valor [*athanaton mnêmên aretês peri*] which we now keep"—has not always invited the readers to question the nature of this *kleos.* Some modern authors who have done it deny absolutely that Achilles dies for any concern of glory, and underscore, especially in connection with the last book, Achilles' awareness that war is a tremendous waste.[110] Other critics assert Achilles' desire for *kleos* in his decision, for in fact he searches for glory (XVIII.123–25), and he knows that *kleos* is at any rate attached to his fate of dying young (IX.410ff.).[111]

My analysis has also questioned the nature of this glory in Achilles' momentous decision and found that it has perplexing features, its strongest one being that it functions as a perverse engine to produce more songs of glory, more pitiful tears over these songs. Accordingly the *Iliad* might be conscious of

---

110. See note 85. Also for Di Benedetto (1994, 306), glory no longer has sense for Achilles in the last part of the poem.

111. Goldhill (1991) states: "*Kleos* is that for which the heroes of the *Iliad* and the *Odyssey* fight" (70); and: "Achilles willingly proceeds to a certain early death for a surety of immortal *kleos*" (80). The overdetermination of which I have spoken also leads some scholars into making ambivalent statements. See, for instance, Griffin 1980, 96: "Achilles chose a heroic fate, short life and endless fame," but Griffin 1980, 100: "[Achilles] does not return to fight for gifts . . . nor does he really regain his belief in heroism. Sitting with Priam, in the last book, he still sees the war in an unheroic light."

this perverse and ferocious production. The pity the poem arouses for the frailty of human life and despairing absurdity of violence and death seems to confirm it.

The search for the hero's autonomous motivations, when a goddess imposes her will and when the heart gives its orders, can only lead the readers to identify these motivations with the scriptural desires of the poetic voice. The poetic voice obsessively desires to become the immortal *sêma* (sign and monument) of the heart (and of the gods) whose voice evokes pitiful laments over splendid deaths.

Kleos and the Poetry of the *Iliad*

If a God had not rolled and turned what is on the earth beneath it, we would have remained invisible and we would have not be celebrated, giving themes to the poetry of future men.

Hecabe in Euripides' *Trojan Women.*

In Chapters Three and Four I initiated an analysis of a certain frailty of *kleos* and its metaphysical underpinnings. My argument, in the wake of Nagy, developed from the famous invocation to the Muses (II.484ff.).

Ἔσπετε νῦν μοι Μοῦσαι Ὀλύμπια δώματ' ἔχουσαι·
ὑμεῖς γὰρ θεαί ἐστε πάρεστέ τε ἴστέ τε πάντα,
ἡμεῖς δὲ κλέος οἶον ἀκούομεν οὐδέ τι ἴδμεν·
οἵ τινες ἡγεμόνες Δαναῶν καὶ κοίρανοι ἦσαν·
πληθὺν δ' οὐκ ἂν ἐγὼ μυθήσομαι οὐδ' ὀνομήνω...

[Tell me now, you Muses who have your home in Olympus—for you are goddesses and you are there, and you know all things, but we [poets] hear only a rumor and know nothing—who were the chiefs and the lords of the Danaans. But I shall not recount and mention the multitude.]

What is this *kleos* that the poets hear? Either it is the rumor that the poets listen to from the Muses, namely the song itself that the poets will repeat (Nagy 1979, 16, 271), or a mere human rumor (from hearsay, or from tradition) that can be equated with the poet's ignorance.[112] The text therefore may leave unclear whether *kleos* is a manifestation of the Muses' presence and knowledge or of the poets' ignorance.

Both interpretations could be supported by some precise indicators, leaving us with an undecidable meaning: *kleos* in the sense of mere rumor and therefore indicating the poet's ignorance is simultaneously the truthful story of the Muses. One meaning constantly displaces the other.

Of course, the text of the invocation should imply that the poets repeat the whole message of the Muses, not the hearsay (*kleos*) of their ignorance. Accordingly, the deeds and the glory of the heroes are enshrined in a truthful

---

112. Kirk 1985, 167: "Men can only repeat hearsay."

voice. Yet even within the truthful voice of the Muses, the word and the notion of *kleos,* once it has been identified with the poets' ignorance, cannot fail to reverberate with this ambivalent association. This irreducible textual connotation surfaces through the theological assurance.

Besides, the Muses, and some divine interventions, have appeared in my analysis as means or contrivances that the narrative needs and manipulates *ad libitum.* While this does not necessarily imply religious skepticism on the part of the poets, it certainly means a thorough integration of epic gods within the epic poetic matter. When we compare the representation of the divine in didactic poetry, for instance in Hesiod, we realize that notwithstanding the same basic poetic and religious conceptions as in Homer, Hesiod emphasizes the untrustworthy nature of the gods, the unpredictability of their will ("if they want" [*Theog.* 28, *Erga* 268] is the pathetic leitmotif of Hesiod's reference to the divine), their doubleness (a good and a bad Eris), the impossibility for humans to know Zeus's ideas and plans. In Homer, on the contrary, we hear the voice of Zeus, his will, his plans, even his inner psychic thinking and torments. Yet the Muses are the same reporters in both cases. It cannot therefore escape us, that the specific nature of the divine in Homer is inscribed within a specific poetic tradition and serves the needs of a precise narrative and poetic voice. Of course the narrative is about the race of the heroes and is produced for an aristocratic society, but this and all that this implies simply fleshes out the principle that the gods are what they are in Homer because the narrative voice, the fiction, needs them to be so.

In the analysis of this last chapter we have better seen how the poetic voice integrates and inscribes in its folds the voice of the heroes dying in a brave way and winning a brave glory (*esthlon kleos*). Because of this inscription of the heart's heroic voice within the modes of the poetic voice we have retrieved some features that assimilate them.

First of all, the voice of the poet also starts from the heart (II.489–90):

Not even if I had ten tongues and ten mouths
and a tireless voice and the heart (*êtôr*) of bronze inside me . . .

sings the poet, as he contemplates his physical limitations. The poet of the *Odyssey* knows also that the heart (*thumos*) or mind (*noos*) of the poet is where the song emerges i.346–49[113] and viii.43–44:

To him [Demodocus] the god gave excellent song
to give pleasure in whatever way his heart (*thumos*) incites [him] to sing.

Hesiod knows that the song of the poet reaches the anguished heart of the audience (*Theog.* 98–102):

For though a man has grief in his recently troubled heart (*thumôi*),
and he is dried up in his anguished heart (*kradiên*], when a singer,
servant of the Muses, sings about the glorious deeds (*kleia*) of men of old

---

113. See Pucci 1987, 201ff.

and about the blessed gods who inhabit Olympus,
at once he forgets his grave thoughts and he does not remember
his griefs at all . . .

Hesiod employs two of the epic words that indicate the "heart" in order to
specify where, in what seat, men suffer and accordingly will be consoled by the
power of the poetic song.[114] From the heart of the poet to the heart of the
listeners, through the mediation of the (Musean) word, there is a link, and a
magic effect is produced.

The glorious deeds (*kleia*) are the deeds that rumor/reputation/glory (*kleos*)
celebrates through the epic poem, as Nagy has pointed out many times.

In my new analysis I have accentuated the frailty and the disquieting nature of
kleos and therefore of the Iliadic song that enshrines it in its own words. This
deconstructive reading does not eliminate anything of the poem's greatness; it
only shows the metaphysical and ideological grounds on which the song is
composed, and reveals the scriptural tenets of this glorious artifact.[115]

I leave aside the fear, the anxiety the poets show about the competition that
could silence the greatest monument or poem. I recall only the edifying example
of Thamyris (II.595ff.), who lost his craft since he defied the Muses, as a
possible figure of a treacherous competitor. The *Odyssey*, on the other hand,

---

114. See Pucci 1977, 18ff. for the consoling power of this poetry.

115. I regularly use the metaphors "scriptural, to inscribe, inscription" in order to
emphasize the compositional features of the poems, the poets' reliance on
elaborations and schemes that allow intertextual effects, etc. Since Derrida, the
metaphor and the notion of "writing" have become popular to imply all the elements
of "textuality." See Pucci 1987, 26–29. The reader should not miss the *programmatic,
polemical* intent (*ibid.*, 27) with which these metaphors from the realm of writing are
used in this book. They mainly oppose the metaphysical thrust that in many
aesthetic readings of the Epic enhances the fullness of the voice, its immediacy, its
presence *etc.* They also reject the idea of a text mechanically produced and processed
by the grammar of the formulae.

As concerns the empirical, historical question how the Homeric poems in the
monumental form we possess were composed by oral singers, we cannot provide sure
answers. Of course in the eighth and seventh centuries, during which the monumental
composition of our poems might have taken place, writing became more and more
present and effective in the life of the Greek cities and in the houses of the nobles. It
is impossible to believe that poets who experienced around themselves the growth of
writing and who probably composed or saw others composing epic lines for
inscriptions on statuary and on other objects, did not pay attention to that
phenomenon. They ostensibly refused to show their utilization of writing, and yet it
is difficult to assess whether and how much they might have learned from it, for
instance, in the organization of the episodes, in the calculated use of repetition even
at great distances, and so on. F. Bader 1989, 17 argues that writing was for the poets a
secret and initiatory practice from which they learned. On the other hand, it is
possible that poets could not find any benefit in the techniques of writing for their
oral compositions and performances. See G. Nagy 1996.

testifies in no uncertain way that competition and new fashion could try to remove a poem like the *Iliad* from its domineering position and success.[116]

The more pertinent features, however, that destabilize the full glory of the epic song are centered upon the questions of the heroic decision and of the nature of *kleos*.

As for the first point, we have seen that even under the guise of Achilles' autonomous *prohairesis*, a certain mechanical and preprogrammed structure functions and determines Achilles' decision. The hero must simply say that his heart commands him to die, and the audience does not need any more words: the reasons for this choice follow without involving that work of introspection that the characters undertake for much easier choices, or without those arguments that even Sarpedon or Odysseus display to their friends or to themselves. For, of course, Achilles does not need to think about it: he arrives at book XVIII preprogrammed to die young and to win immortal glory; he has been burdened by a constant pathetic awareness of his early death; he has been removed from most human contacts, deprived of his insignia of *timê*; he has been turned toward the gods and toward that part of him that is closer to them. It is in this precise frame of mind and being that he faces his own death, prescribed as soon as he slays Hector.[117]

No wonder then that the usual terms Homer employs for expressing heroic decision are here, more than ever, exposing their overdetermination (pre-programmed working) and simplification, their formidable power and their insufficiency. On the side of the insufficiency, we have seen the split of the self, the fragmentation of the arguments, the fact that this famous immortal glory is not even obliquely mentioned. The grief for Patroclus's death dominates his heart. On the side of the formidable power, we list the reduction of the whole issue to a choice between life and death, a death already lamented and here prefigured but not yet occurring. For this is the greatness of Homer: he knows that the power of representation lies in the representation of how death is foreseen, how it is faced, how it is fore-experienced. "May I die immediately" is the voice of this prefiguration, of the courage to face it in its immediacy.

It is this voice that is the avatar of Achilles' "self," the sound that emerges from the heart with groans, shaking the human being and defining his "person."

The voice, in accordance with the analysis made by J. Derrida,[118] is felt, in western metaphysics, as emerging from inside the heart, as a pure signified, namely as pure emotion, concepts, meaning, etc., as though it had no material

---

116. The almost absolute absence of Iliadic episodes in the *Odyssey* (Munro's law) testifies to this paranoiac competition among the texts.

117. The fact that the Muses have nothing to say on the reasons why Achilles should be a victim of early death, why he should constantly be conscious of it and suffer for it, intimates that, while this abysmal condition is true, it is nevertheless without any theological grounds. Accordingly, the hero's most singular feature, with his concomitant overflowing passions and pursuits, is inscribed in the narration that the tradition (the *kleos* of the poets) wove and elaborated. This tradition was unable or did not care to justify the "heroic" condition with any theological argument.

118. Derrida, 1972.

support of sound, of articulate chain, with its gaps and lags, in a word, as though it had no signifier.

The text of the *Iliad* in the scenes of Achilles' crying seems to want to produce just that metaphysical effect of a pure voice and emotion bursting at the edge of man's vision of his own death, echoing an heroic self in its full auto-manifestation and presence. We may imagine that the voice of the performer would have increased this powerful effect.

But our analysis has shown that the signifier weighs heavily on the signified: the disturbing repetition of the word *thumos* at XVIII.90–92 may be the clearest example of the way in which language creates tensions, split significations, and accordingly, in this case, confuses the voice of the heart with that of a physical organ or of life. The oxymoron this confusion creates may still be significant for the Iliadic poetics, but it cannot erase the literal split-signification and accordingly the blurring of this voice of the self.

On Achilles' choice of *kleos,* we have seen that he regards only obliquely the glory of his fighting, and that the nature of this *kleos* presents disquieting features. For *kleos* is not only the ignorant rumor that the poets would listen to, were the Muses not inspiring them, *kleos* is also a rumor/song that, as any rumor, creates more rumor, enlarges news, reputations, and fares on its own repetition. Therefore a chain of relays determines the spreading of *kleos*: Achilles glances at his glory as he slays Hector and gives reason for crying and lamenting to his women, and these funeral cries will enhance Hector's glory. There is never an end to this rumor/song and no real discrimination between the heroes, notwithstanding the incredible singularity of Achilles.

Perhaps what is considered by many critics to be a certain typicality or standard characterization of the Iliadic heroes[119] depends on this nature of Iliadic poetics as voice of *kleos* that essentially reduplicates the same or analogous deeds and reputations, producing them by a chain of relays that maintain necessarily the same registers and therefore the same motifs and themes.

Because of this undifferentiated nature of the heroic deed, the compensatory value of *kleos* vanishes completely: by his glorious deed Achilles, who hates Hector to the point of perverse aberration, will hear the praise of Hector, the song expanding and honoring him forever! The enemies gratify each other by killing each other!

On another level, however, this absence of differentiation between enemies constitutes a trait of Homer's great wisdom, for it focuses on the heroic brotherhood of the enemies. Yet at the point in which Achilles decides to win *kleos*, the recalling of this indifferentiation would be psychologically inconsistent.

This final *kleos* Achilles is glancing at is neither the *aphthiton kleos* he asserts in book 9 as the compensation for his death nor the *kleos* which Sarpedon, for instance, evokes as the result of triumphing over the enemy. In his heroic *prohairesis* Achilles longs for a *kleos* that has destructive, perverse, and paradoxical traits.

---

119. See, for instance, Codino 1965.

We may remember that Sarpedon finds a sort of paradoxical source of consolation in the awareness that death is constantly present in its innumerable ways. He finds consolation in a defiant attitude, in a sort of battle stance against the arbitrariness and anonymity of death and envisions the power of a choice, the splendor (*kudos* XII.325) of glory in battle, and hears in his own utterance the cry of triumph (*eukhos* XII.328) he might hurl against his enemy. Though these consoling elements form a paradoxical conceptual frame, since they also parallel the chance of a death without any distinction, the positive significance of *kleos* nevertheless comes to light.

But the *kleos* which Achilles contemplates as he decides to pursue Hector and therefore to embrace his own death, has none of this positive significance. It spells tears and grief for the sake of compensating another destruction and another grief. It spells out Achilles' own self-pity. For by equating his glory with the tears and the laments of the Trojan women, he indirectly equates "glory" with his own "tears and laments" for Patroclus. To be sure the text shows us the "brotherhood" of victims in this extraordinary expression, but at the same time it has Achilles perversely indulging in the image of mothers' and wives' despair. The splendor of "glory" is quenched in that perverse pleasure and that problematic consolation.

With these points we touch upon the destabilization of the underpinnings that sustain the poetics of *kleos* in the *Iliad*. *Kleos*, with its poetic connotations, straddles a contradictory structure of both positive terms (compensation, immortality and truth) and negative ones (mere repetition, with its passivity and valuelessness, frailty of the human being, voice, purposes, and mere rumor). It functions as the "supplement" of Iliadic poetics. Whenever *kleos* appears, one set of terms displaces the other and vice versa.

The questioning of this poetics in the direction of destabilizing some of its principles and grounds already begins with the *Odyssey*. If our analyses have been correct, the poetics of the *Odyssey,* by privileging *mêtis* aimed at survival, and enchantment and pleasure, discards the importance of a song that enhances glory (*kleos*) if this glory, by coinciding with death, ultimately becomes an insufferable funeral song.

Like a model of the human existential condition, Achilles experiences the frailty and the anxiety of being, keeps alive in his heart the expectation of his death, and accepts it with a violent assertion. His brooding, his tears, his pathos are the expression of the unhappiness of this condition. In the trace of Aristotle we may add that his consecration to death telescopes not only the innumerable other deaths of heroes, but essentially the whole Trojan War with the fall of the city.

This is the sublime, vast and absolute conception that makes Achilles' heroic stature, his heroic decision, however grounded, so alluring and irresistible. A magnificent pathos makes us blind to the perversity, destructiveness and unaccountability of Achilles' *kleos*, and lets us fall accomplice to its tremendous and splendid brutality. For its metaphysics is grounded in fierce and dire corollaries and protocols.

If we discount the series of negative or disquieting elements we have uncovered in this metaphysics, that is, in the nature of *kleos*, and if we, accordingly, forget that heroic decisions are made by simplifications and cutting off alternatives, we realize why the text has been taken, in its long history in the West, to answer conundrums of life and death. It specifically proposes that what is proper to man is his awareness of mortality and that to live with this awareness is man's authentic or heroic stance; it intimates that no conscious part of a person survives and that though the business of life is ungrounded, one should follow precise protocols: to privilege one's individual—even idiosyncratic—choices, to accept a short life and to burn it in a noble deed, and therefore to ensure that one's individual reputation survives after death. These protocols have shaped that formidable ideological engine whose success we all know.

Through Homer's interpretative machine, the West, in a formative period of its history, incorporated this formidable fictional engine. All other alternative or contemporaneous interpretations of life and death, such as hedonism (foregrounded in the *Odyssey*), survivalism, mysticism, and so on, are rejected in this unfathomably severe system of protocols for the conduct of one's life.

And indeed, Achilles' fame has survived, and it has become his truth. But is it truly glory? Or is it just a stern lesson of severe fathers? A lure and a bait of tremendous fascination? A perverse justification of relays of violence or the consoling song winning over the anonymity and arbitrariness of death? A shrewd rhetoric of asocial self-enhancement or the magnifying of a man through the divine song?

By inventing the gods to serve as its narrators, this marvelous story denies textuality and conceals its authors, their compositional work, and the difference between narrative and event. Even the formulaic style can be justified by the need to ensure perfect immutability of expression. There is only one right way to say a thing, and that way is right once and forever.

Yet someone composed this monumental word, this vision of the Muses. It carries differences, changes, contrivances, it exposes the protocols it needs to assert, and exposes and ensconces its frailties and its predicaments. On each occasion of its performance, a human author is behind it, effacing himself before the divine voice he himself creates, attending to the narrative with sublime modesty and enormous virtuosity.

Reference List

Acquaro, Giovanna. 1984. "Alle soglie dell'*Iliade*: Quel fascino accecante." *SIFC*, 3d. ser., 2.143–55.

Ameis, Karl F., and C. Hentze. 1884. *Homers Ilias für den Schulgebrauch erklärt*. Leipzig: B. G. Teubner. [=AH]

Ameis Karl, F., Carl Hentze, and Paul Cauer. 1920. *Homers "Odyssee."* Dreizehnte Auflage bearbeitet von Paul Cauer. Leipzig und Berlin: Teubner. [=AHC]

Arend, Walter. 1975. *Die typischen Szenen bei Homer*. 2d ed. Berlin: Weidmann.

Ariès, Philippe. 1977. *L'homme devant la mort*. Paris: Éditions de Seuil.

———. 1985. *Images of Man and Death*. Cambridge: Harvard University Press.

Aristides. 1964. Ed. W. Dindorf. Darmstadt: Georg Olm.

Auerbach, Erich. 1957. *Mimesis: The Representation of Reality in Western Literaure*. Trans. Willard Trask. Garden City, NY: Doubleday.

Austin, Norman. 1972. "Name Magic in the *Odyssey*." *California Studies in Classical Antiquity* 5.1–19.

———. 1990. *Meaning and Being in Myth*. University Park: Pennsylvania State University Press.

———. 1994. *Helen of Troy and Her Shameless Phantom*. Ithaca: Cornell University Press.

Bader, F. 1989. *La langue des dieux ou l'herméneutique des poètes indo-européens*. Pisa: Giardini Editori.

Barmeyer, Eike. 1968. *Die Musen: Ein Beitrag zur Inspirationstheorie*. Munich: Fink.

Barrett, W. S. 1964. *Euripides Hippolytos*. Oxford: Clarendon Press.

Beck, Götz. 1965. "Beobachtungen zur Kirke-Episode in der *Odyssee*." *Philologus* 109.1–29.

Behr, C. A. 1973. *Aristides.* Loeb Classical Library.

Bekker, I. 1863. "Über den Anfang der *Odyssee.*" In *Homerische Blätter.* Bonn.

Benveniste, Emile. 1969. *Le vocabulaire des Institutions Indo-Européennes.* Paris: Les Éditions de Minuit.

Bergren, Ann. 1983. "Odyssean Temporality: Many re(turns)." In Rubino and Shelmerdine.

Besslich, S. 1966. *Schweigen-Verschweigen Übergehen.* Heidelberg: C. Winter.

Blanchot, M. 1959. "Le rencontre de l'imaginaire." In *Le Livre à venir.* Paris: Gallimard.

Blössner, Norbert. 1991. *Die Singuläre Iterata der "Ilias."* Stuttgart: Teubner.

Brandestein, W. 1961. *Kratylos* 6.167–70.

Burkert, Walter. 1955. "Zum Altgriechischen Mitleidsbegriff." Ph.D. diss., Erlangen.

———. 1982. *Structure and History in Greek Mythology.* Berkeley and Los Angeles: University of California Press.

Calame, Claude. 1976. "Mythe grec et structures narratives: Le mythe des Cyclopes dans l'*Odysée.*" *Ziva Antika* 26.316.

———. 1986. *Le recit en Grèce ancienne.* Paris: Méridiens/Klincksieck.

Canfora, Luciano. 1972. *Totalità e selezione nella storiografia classica.* Bari: Laterza.

Carlier, P. 1984. *La royauté en Grèce avant Alexandre.* Strasbourg: AECR.

Chantraine, Pierre. 1958. *La grammaire Homerique.* Vol. 1. Paris: Klincksieck.

———. 1963. *La grammaire Homerique.* Vol. 2, *Syntaxe.* Paris: Klincksieck.

———. 1968–80. *Dictionnaire étymologique de la langue grecque.* Vol. 1–4 (= DELG). Paris: Klincksieck.

Chiarini, G. 1991. *Odisseo. Il labirinto marino.* Rome: Kepos Edizioni.

Clay, J. Strauss. 1972. "The Planktai and Moly: Divine Naming and Knowing in Homer." *Hermes* 100.127–31.

———. 1974. "Demas and Aude." *Hermes* 102.135–36.

———. 1976. "The Beginning of the *Odyssey.*" *AJP* 97.313–26.

———. 1980. "Goat Island: *Odyssey* 9.116–141." *CQ* 30.261–64.

Codino, F. 1965. *Introduzione a Omero.* Turin: Einaudi.

———. *Omero, Dolonia.* Bari: Adriatica Editrice.

Collins, Leslie. 1988. *Studies in Characterisation in the "Iliad."* Frankfurt am Main: Athenaeum.

Cook, E. 1992. "Ferrymen of Elysium and the Homeric Phaeacians." *Journal of Indo-European Studies* 20.239–64.

Crane, Gregory. 1988. *Calypso: Backgrounds and Conventions of the Odyssey.* Frankfurt am Main: Athenaeum.

Crotty, Kevin. 1994. *The Poetics of Supplication.* Ithaca: Cornell University Press.

Culler, Jonathan. 1981. *The Pursuit of Signs.* London: Routledge & K. Paul.

Davies, M. 1989. *The Epic Cycle.* Bristol Classical Press.

Decleva Caizzi, F. 1966. *Antisthenis fragmenta.* Milan: Istituto editoriale cisalpino.

de Jong, Irene J. F. 1985. "Iliad I 365–392: A Mirror Story." *Arethusa* 18. 5–22.

———. 1987. *Narrators and Focalizers. The Presentation of the Story in the "Iliad."* Amsterdam: B. R. Grüner.

———. 1992. "The Subjective Style in Odysseus' Wanderings." *Classical Quartely* 42.1–11.

de Jong, Irene J. F., J. M. Bremer, and J. Kalff. 1987. *Homer: Beyond Oral Poetry.* Amsterdam: B. R. Grüner.

De Man, Paul. 1979. *Allegories of Reading: Figural Language in Rousseau, Nietzsche, Rilke, and Proust.* New Haven: Yale University Press.

Derrida, J. 1967. *La voix et le phénomène.* Paris: PUF.

———. 1972. "La Differrence." In *Marges de la philosophie.* Paris: Éditions de Minuit.

———. 1972. "La Pharmacie de Platon." In *La Dissemination.* Paris: Editions de Seuil.

———. 1973. *Speech and Phenomena and Other Essays on Husserl's Theory of Signs.* Trans. David B. Allison. Evanston: Northwestern University Press.

———. 1977. "Limited Inc. abc . . ." *Glyph* 2.162–254.

———. 1980. *La carte postale.* Paris: Flammarion.

Detienne, Marcel. 1973. *Le maîtres de verité dans la Gréce archaique.* 2d ed. Paris: F. Maspéro.

Detienne, Marcel, and J.-P. Vernant. 1974. *Les ruses de l'intelligence: La μῆτις des Grecs.* Paris: Flammarion.

Detienne, Marcel, and Pietro Pucci. 1988. "Autour du Polytrope." *L'Infini* 23.57–71.

Diano, C. 1968. "La poetica dei Feaci." In *Saggezza e Poetiche degli Antichi.* Venezia. N. Pozza originally published in *Belfagor* 18.403–24.

Di Benedetto V. 1994. Nel laboratorio di Omero. Turin: Einaudi.

Dimock, G. E., Jr. 1963. "The Name of Odysseus." In *Essays on the Odyssey*, ed. C. H. Taylor. Bloomington: Indiana University Press.

Dodds, E. R. 1951. *The Greeks and the Irrational.* Berkeley and Los Angeles: University of California Press.

Dostoyevsky, F. *The Idiot.* Transl. David Magarshack. London: Penguin Books.

Drews, R. 1983. *Basileus: The Evidence for Kingship in Geometric Greece.* New Haven: Yale University Press.

Ducrot, O. 1980. "Presupposizione e allusione." In *Enciclopedia Einaudi*, vol. 10. Turin: Einaudi.

Durante, M. *Sulla preistoria della tradizione poetica Greca.* Vol. 1. Rome: Edizioni dell'Ateneo.

———. 1976. *Sulla preistoria della tradizione poetica Greca.* Vol. 11. Rome: Edizioni dell'Ateneo.

Easterling, P. 1989. "Agamemnon's *Skêptron* in the *Iliad.*" In *Images of Authority: Papers Presented to Joyce Reynolds,* ed. M. M. Mackenzie and Ch. Roueché. Cambridge: Cambridge Philological Society.

Ecker, Ute. 1990. *Grabmal und Epigram.* Palingenesia 29. Stuttgart: Franz Steiner.

234   The Song of the Sirens: Essays on Homer

Edmunds, Lowell. 1986. "Aristophanes' Socrates." In *Proceedings of the Boston Area Colloquium in Ancient Philosophy*, ed. John Cleary, vol. 1. Lanham: University Press of America.

Edmunds, Susan T. 1990. *Homeric Nêpios*. New York and London: Garland.

Edwards, A. 1985. *Odysseus against Achilles: The Role of Allusion in the Homeric Epic*. Beiträge zur Klassichen Philologie, vol. 171. Königstein: Hain.

Edwards, Mark W. 1980. "Convention and Individuality in *Iliad* I." *HSCPh* 84.13.

———. 1987. *Homer: Poet of the "Iliad."* Baltimore: Johns Hopkins University Press.

Eisenberger, H. 1973. *Studien zur "Odysee."* Wiesbaden: F. Steiner.

Erbse, H. 1972. *Beiträge zur Verständnis der "Odyssee."* Berlin: Walter de Gruyter.

Ernout-Meillet. 1932. *Dictionnaire étymologique de la langue latine*. Paris: Klincksieck.

Fagles, R. 1990. *Homer: the Iliad*. Translated by Robert Fagles. Introduction and Notes by B. Knox. New York: Viking.

———. 1996 *Homer: the Odyssey*. Translated by Robert Fagles. Introduction and Notes by B. Knox. New York: Viking.

Fenik, B. 1974. *Studies in the "Odyssey"* (= *Hermes Einzelschriften* 30). Wiesbaden: F. Steiner.

Fernandez-Galiano, M. 1986. *Omero, Odissea, Libri XXI–XXIV*. Milan: Fondazione Valla.

Finley, J. H., Jr. 1978. *Homer's "Odyssey."* New York: Viking Press.

Finsler, G. 1906. "Das Homerische Königtum." In *Neue Jahrbücher* 9.313–36, 393–412.

———. 1914. *Homer*. Vol. 1. Leipzig and Berlin: G. B. Tinbuer.

Focke, F. 1943. *Die "Odyssee."* Stuttgart and Berlin: W. Kohlhammer.

Foley, H. 1978. "Reverse Similes and Sex Roles in the *Odyssey*." *Arethusa* 11.

Ford, Andrew. 1992. *Homer: The Poetry of the Past*. Ithaca: Cornell University Press.

Frederick, R. 1982. "On the Compositional Use of Similes in the *Odyssey*" *American Journal of Philology*, 102.120–37.

Germain, G. 1954. *Genèse de l'Odyssée*. Paris: PUF.

Gernet, Louis. 1968. *Anthropologie de la Grèce antique*. Paris: Maspéro.

Gladstone, W. 1858. *Studies on Homer and Homeric Age*. Oxford: Oxford University Press.

Gnoli, G., and J.-P. Vernant. 1982. *La Mort, les morts dans les societes anciennes*. Cambridge: Cambridge University Press; Paris: Maison des Sciences de l'Homme.

Goldhill, Simon. 1991. *The Poet's Voice. Essay on Poetics and Greek Literature*. Cambridge: Cambridge University Press 1991.

Gourbeilloun, A. 1981. *Lions, heros, masques. Les representations de l'animal chez Homere*. Paris: Maspéro.

Gresseth, G. K. 1970. "The Homeric Sirens." *TAPA* 101.203–18.

Griffin, Jasper. 1980. *Homer on Life and Death*. Oxford: Clarendon Press.

Güntert, Hermann. 1921. *Von der Sprache der Götter und Geister: Bedeutungsgeschichtliche Untersuchungen zur Homerischen und Eddischen Göttersprache*. Halle: M. Niemeyer.

Hainsworth, Bryan. 1993. *The "Iliad." A Commentary*. Vol. 3. Cambridge: Cambridge University Press.

Hauser, Herzog. 1948. s.v. "Tyche" *RE* VII A2, col. 1651

Heidegger, Martin. 1976. "Hegel und die Griechen." *Wegmarken: Gesamtausgabe Band 9*. Frankfurt am Main: Klostermann.

Heidegger, M., and Fink E. 1993. *Heraclitus Seminar*. Trans. C. H. Seibert. Evanston: Northwestern University Press.

Heubeck, Alfred. 1983. *Omero Odissea*. Vol 3. Milan: Mondadori, Fondazione Valla.

Hoekstra, A. 1957. "Hésiode et la tradition orale." *Mnemosyne* 10.193–225.

Hogan, J. 1979. *A Guide to the "Iliad."* Garden City, NY: Doubleday.

Horkheimer, Max, and Theodor W. Adorno. *Dialectic of Enlightment*. Trans. Joyn Cumming. New York: Herder & Herder.

Humbach, H. 1967. "Indogermanische Dichtersprache?" *Münchener Studien z. Sprachwissenschaft* 21.21–31.

"Iliad" of Homer, The. 1951. Trans. Richard Lattimore. Chicago: University of Chicago Press.

Jacoby, F. 1945. "Athenian Epigrams from the Persian Wars." *Hesperia* 14.157–221.

Jaeger, W. 1960. *Scripta minora*. Rome: Edizioni di storia e letteratura.

Jahn, T. 1987. *Zum Wortfeld Seele-Geist in der Sprache Homers*. Zetemata 83. Munich.

Janko, Richard. 1992. *The "Iliad": A Commentary*. Vol. 4. Cambridge: Cambridge University Press.

Jörgensen, Ove. 1904. "Das Auftreten der Götter in den Büchern in der *Odyssee*." *Hermes* 39.

Kahn, L. 1978. *Hermès passe, ou les ambiguïtés de la communication*. Paris: F. Maspéro.

Kakrides, J. Th. 1949. *Homeric Researches*. Lund: C. W. K. Gleerup.

Katz, Marilyn A. 1994. "Homecoming and Hospitality: Recognition and Construction of Identity in the *Odyssey*." In *Essays on the Interpretation and History of a Genre*. Ed. Steven H. Oberhelman, Van Kelly, and Richard J. Golsan. Studies in Comparative Literature n.24.

Kennedy, George A. 1986. "Helen's Web Unraveled." *Arethusa* 19.5–14

Kirk, G. S. 1970. *Myth, Its Meaning and Function in Ancient and Other Cultures*. Cambridge: Cambridge University Press.

———. 1985. *The "Iliad": A Commentary*. 2 vols. Cambridge: Cambridge University Press.

Krapp, H. 1964. "Die akoustische Phänomene in der *Ilias*." Ph.D. diss., Munich.

Krarup, Per. 1948. "Verwendung von Abstracta in der direkten Rede bei Homer." *Classica et Mediaevalia* 10.1–17.

Lacoue-Labarthe, Philippe. 1975. "Typographie." In *Mimesis der Articulations*. Paris: Flammarion.

236   *The Song of the Sirens: Essays on Homer*

Latacz, J. 1966. *Zum Wortfeld "Freude" in der Sprache Homers.* Heidelberg: Carl Winter Universitätsverlag.

———. 1977. *Kampfparänese, Kampfdarstellung Kampfwirklichkeit in der "Ilias," bei Kallinos und Tyrtaios.* Munich: Zetemata.

Latte K. 1968. *Kleine Schriften.* Munich: Beck.

Leaf, Walter. 1960. *The "Iliad." Edited with Apparatus Criticus, Prolegomena, Notes, and Appendixes.* London, 1900–1902. Reprint, Amsterdam: Hakkert.

Lesky, A. 1947. *Thalatta.* Wien.

———. 1961. "Göttliche und menschliche Motivierung im homerischen Epos." *SHAW.* Abh. 4.1–52.

Leumann, M. 1950. *Homerische Wörter.* Basel: F. Reinhardt.

LFGE (= *Lexikon des frühgriechschen Epos*). 1979–. Göttingen: Vandenhoek und Ruprecht.

Lohmann, Dieter. 1970. *Die Komposition der Reden in der "Ilias."* Berlin: Walter de Gruyter.

———. 1988. *Die Andromache Szenen in der "Ilias."* Hildesheim: G. Olms.

Loraux, Nicole. 1981. *L'invention d'Athènes.* Paris: Mouton.

———. 1982. "Mourir devant Troie, tomber pour Athènes: de la gloire du heros à l'idée de la cité." In Gnoli and Vernant.

———. 1983. *L'Ecrits du Temps 2.*

———. 1985. *Facons tragiques de tuer une femme.* Paris: Hachette. Trans. Anthony Forster under the title *Tragic Ways of Killing a Woman.* Cambridge: Harvard University Press, 1987.

Lord, Albert B. 1960. *The Singer of Tales.* 1960. Reprint, New York: Atheneum, 1976.

Lowenstam, Steven. 1981. *The Death of Patroclos: A Study in Typology.* Königstein: Anton Hain.

Luppino, A. 1971. "Verbi Omerici." *SMEA* 15.73ff.

Luther, W. 1966. "Wahreit, Licht and Erkenntnis." *Archiv für Begriffsgeschichte* 10.9.

Lynn-George, Michael. 1988. *Epos: Word, Narrative and the "Iliad."* Atlantic Highlands, NJ: Humanity Press International.

MacCary, Thomas W. 1982. *Childlike Achilles. Ontogeny and Philogeny in the "Iliad."* New York: Columbia University Press

MacLachlan, B. 1993. *The Age of Grace. Charis in Early Greek Poetry.* Princeton: Princeton University Press.

Maehler, H. 1963. *Die Auffassung der Dichtersberufs in frühen Griechentum bis zur Zeit Pindars.* Göttingen: Vandenhoeck & Ruprecht.

Marcus, S. M. 1979. "A Person's Relation to *psuche* in Homer, Hesiod, and the Greek Lyric Poets." *Glotta* 57.30–39.

Marg, W. 1971. *Homer über Dichtung.* Münster

Marin, L. 1981. *Le portrait du roi.* Paris: Editions de Minuit.

Marót, K. 1960. *Die Anfänge der Griechischen Literatur.* Budapest: Verlag der Ungar. AK. der Wissenschaften.

Martin, Richard P. 1989. *The Language of Heroes: Speech and Performance in the "Iliad."* Ithaca: Cornell University Press.

——. 1993. "Telemachus and the Last Hero Song." *Colby Quarterly* XXIX. 222–40

Marzullo, Benedetto. 1952. *Il problema omerico.* Firenze: La nuova Italia. 1970 2d. ed. Milan: Ricciardi.

Mattes, W. 1958. *Odysseus bei den Phäaken.* Würzburg: Triltsch.

Mawet, F. 1979. *Le vocabulaire homérique de la douleur.* Bruxelles: Palais des Academies.

Meschonnic, H. 1982. *Langue Francaise* 56.6–23.

Meuli, Karl. 1975. "Herkunft und Wesen der Fabel." In *Gesammelte Schriften*, ed. Thomas Gelzer. 2 vols. Basel: Schwabl.

Monsacré, Hélène.1984. *Les larmes d'Achille.* Paris: Albin Michel.

Most, Glenn. 1989. "The Structure and the Function of Odysseus' *Apologoi*." *TAPA* 119.15–30.

Muellner, L. 1976. *The Meaning of Homeric* EYXOMAI. Innsbruck: Institut für Sprachwissenschaft.

Naas, Michael. 1995. *Turning: From Persuasion to Philosophy.* Atlantic Highlands, NJ: Humanities Press International.

Nagler, Michael N. 1974. *Spontaneity and Tradition.* Berkeley and Los Angeles: University of California Press.

——.1990. "Odysseus: the Proem and the Problem." *Classical Antiquity* 9 n.2: 335–56.

Nagy, Gregory. 1974. *Comparative Studies in Greek and Indic Meter.* Cambridge: Harvard University Press.

——. 1979. *The Best of the Achaeans.* Baltimore: Johns Hopkins University Press.

——. 1990. *Greek Mythology and Poetics.* Ithaca and London: Cornell University Press.

——. 1990. *Pindar's Homer: The Lyric Possession of an Epic Past.* Baltimore: Johns Hopkins University Press.

——. 1996. *Poetry as Performance: Homer and Beyond.* Cambridge: University Press.

Nancy, J-L. 1996. "Scene: An Exchange of Letters." in *Beyond Representation.* ed. by R. Eldridge. Cambridge: University Press.

Nitzsch, G. W. 1826–1840. *Erklärende Annerkungen zu Homer's Odyssee.* Hannover.

Oksenberg Rorty, A. 1990. "Persons and *Personae*" in Ch. Gill. ed. *The Person and the Human Mind.* Oxford: Clarendon Press 1990.

Page, D. L. 1955. *The Homeric "Odyssey."* Oxford: Clarendon Press.

Pagliaro, A. 1953. "Aedi e rapsodi." In *Saggi di critica semantica.* Messina: G. D'Anna.

——. 1956. *Nuovi saggi di critica semantica.* Messina: G. D'Anna.

Papadopoulou-Belmehdi, Ioanna. 1994. *Le chant de Pénélope.* Paris: Belin.

Parry, Adam. 1956. "The Language of Achilles." *TAPA.*

Pasquali, G. 1968. "Pagine meno stravaganti." Florence: Sansoni.

——. 1951. "Il proemio dell' *Odissea*" *Miscellanea G. Galbiati.* Milan: Hoepli.

Pazdernick, Ch. F. 1995. "Odysseus and his Audience: *Odyssey* 9.39–40 and its Formulaic Resonances." *AJP* 116.347–69.

Pedrick, Victoria. 1992. "The Muse Corrects: The Opening of the *Odyssey.*" *Yale Classical Studies* 29.39–62.

———. "Reading in the Middle Voice: The Homeric Intertextuality of Pietro Pucci and John Peradotto." *Helios* 21.75–96.

Pelliccia, Hayden. 1995. *Body, Mind, and Speech in Homer and Pindar.* Hypomnemata 107. Göttingen.

Peradotto, John. 1990. *Man in the Middle Voice: Name and Narration in the "Odyssey."* Martin Classical Lectures, new series 1. Princeton: Princeton University Press.

Pfister, Frederick. 1924. "Epiphanie." *RE* (Suppl.) 4. col. 282.

Pindarus. 1975. Ed. Bruno Snell and H. Maehler. Leipzig: Teubner.

Pisani, V. 1957. "Thrak. Zeirênê. Osk. Herentâs."*Rhein. Museum* 100.

———. 1968. *Paideia* 23.

Podlecki, A. J. 1961. "Guest-Gifts and Nobodies in *Odyssey* IX." *Phoenix* 15.128.

Postlethwaite, N. 1995. "Agamemnon Best of Spearmen" *Phoenix* 49. 95–103

Pucci, Pietro. 1977. *Hesiod and the Language of Poetry.* Baltimore: Johns Hopkins University Press.

———. 1979. "The Song of the Sirens." *Arethusa* 12.121–32.

———. 1980. "The Language of the Muses." In *Classical mythology in Twentieth-Century Thought and Literature,* ed. Wendell M. Aycock and Theodore Klein. Lubbock: Texas Tech Press.

———. 1984. "Decostruzione e intertestualità." *Nuova Corrente* 93–94.283–85.

———. 1985. "Epifanie testuali nell'*Iliade.*" *SIFC,* 3d ser. 3.170–83.

———. 1986. "Les 'figures' de la metis dans l'*Odyssée*" *Metis* 1.7–28.

———. 1987. *Odysseus Polutropos: Intertextual Readings in the "Odyssey" and in the "Iliad."* Ithaca: Cornell University Press.

———. 1988. "Banter and Banquets for Heroic Death." In *Post-Structuralist Classics,* ed. Andrew Benjamin. New York: Routledge.

———. 1988. "Strategia epifanica e intertestualità nel secondo libro dell'*Iliade.*" *SIFC* 3d ser. 6.5–24.

———. 1993. "Antiphonal Lament Between Achilles and Briseis." *Colby Quarterly* 29.258–72.

———. 1994. "Gods' Intervention and Epiphany in Sophocles." *AJP* 115.15–46.

Race, William, H. 1993. "First Appearances in the *Odyssey.*" *TAPA* 123.79–106.

Ramersdorfer, Hans. 1981. *Singuläre Iterata der "Ilias."* Königstein: Hain.

Redfield, James. 1975. *Nature and Culture in the "Iliad."* Chicago: Chicago University Press.

Reece, Steven. 1993. *The Stranger's Welcome.* Ann Arbor: University of Michigan Press.

Reinhardt, Karl. 1961. *Die Ilias und Ihr Dichter.* Göttingen: Vandenhoek and Ruprecht.

———. "Die Abenteuer of Odysseus." In 1948. *Von Wegen und Formen.* Godesberg 52–162 = 1960. *Tradition und Geist.* Göttingen 47–124.

Renehan, R. 1987. "The *Heldentod* in Homer: One Heroic Ideal." *Classical Philology* 92.99–116.

Reucher, Theo. 1989. *Der Unbekannte Odysseus. Eine Interpretation der Odyssee.* Bern und Stuttgart: Francke Verlage

Richardson, Nicholas. 1993. *The "Iliad": A Commentary.* Vol. 6. Cambridge: Cambridge University Press.

Richardson, S. 1990. *The Homeric Narrator.* Nashville: Vanderbilt University Press.

Ricoeur, Paul. 1990. *Soi même comme un autre.* Paris: Seuil. Trans. Kathleen Blamey under the title *Oneself as Other.* Chicago: University of Chicago Press, 1992.

Risch, E. 1947. "Namendeutungen und Wortererklärungen bei den ältesten griechischen Dichtern." *Eumusia, Festgabe für E. Howald.* Erlenbach: E. Rentsch.

———. 1974. *Wortbildung der Homerischen Sprache.* Berlin and New York: W. de Gruyter.

Rousseau, Philippe. 1992. "Remarques complémentaires sur la royauté de Ménélas." In *L'univers épique: Rencontres avec l'antiquité classique II,* ed. Michel Woronoff. Publication de Institut Félix Gaffiot, vol 9. Paris: Les belles lettres.

———. 1995. "Preface" to P. Pucci *Ulysse Polytropos.* Trans. J. Routier Pucci. Lille: Presses Universitaires du Septentrion.

———. 1995. Διὸς δ' ἐτελείετο βουλή. *Destin des héros et dessin de Zeus dans l'intrigue de l'Iliade.* Thèse de l'Université de Lille. Forthcoming.

Rubino, C., and C. Shelmerdine, eds. 1983. *Approaches to Homer.* Austin: University of Texas Press.

Ruijgh, C. J. 1971. *Autour de te epique.* Amsterdam: Hakkert.

Russo, Joseph. 1985. *Omero Odissea.* Vol. 5. Milan: Mondadori, Fondazione Valla.

Rüter, Klaus. 1969. *Odysseeinterpretationen.* Hypomnemata 19. Göttingen: Vandenhoeck U. Ruprecht.

Sale, W. H. 1994. "The Government of Troy: Politics in the *Iliad.*" *GRBS* 35.5–102.

Schein, S. 1970. "Odysseus and Polyphemus in the *Odyssey.*" *GRBS* 11.81–82.

———. 1980. "On Achilles' Speech to Odysseus: *Iliad* 9.308–429." *Eranos* 78.125–31.

———. 1984. *The Mortal Hero. An Introduction to the "Iliad."* Berkeley and Los Angeles: University of California Press.

Schmiel, R. 1987. "Achilles in Hades." *Classical Philology* 82.35–37.

Schmitt, Arbogast. 1990. *Selbständigkeit und Abhängigkeit menschlichen Handelns bei Homer.* Stuttgart: Franz Steiner.

Schwabl, H. 1978. "Religiöse Aspekte der *Odssee.*" *Wiener Studien* 91.9–10.

———. "Religiöse Aspekte der *Odysee.*" *Wiener Studien* 91.15–28.

Segal, Charles. 1962. "The Phaeacians and the Symbolism of Odysseus' Return." *Arion* 1.17–64.

————. 1968. "Circean Temptations." *TAPhA* xcix.419-42.
————. 1970. "Nestor and the Honor of Achilles." *Studi Micenei e Egeo-Anatolici* 13.90ff.
————. 1983. "Kleos and Its Ironies in the *Odyssey*." *Antiquité Classique* 52.22–47.
————. 1994. *Singers, Heroes, and Gods in the "Odyssey."* Ithaca: Cornell University Press.
Severyns, A. 1966. *Les dieux d'Homère.* Paris: Presses Universitaires de France.
Slatkin, L. M. 1991. *The Power of Thetis. Allusion and Interpretation in the Iliad.* Berkeley and Oxford: University of California Press.
Snell, Bruno. 1948. *Die Entdeckung des Geistes.* Hamburg: Trans. T. G. Rosenmeyer under the title *The Discovery of the Mind in Early Greek Philosophy and Literature.* Cambridge: Harvard University Press, 1953.
Solmsen, F. 1909. *Beiträge zu griechischen Wortforschung.* Strasbourg.
Stanford, W. B. 1950. "Homer's Use of Personal Poly-Compounds" *CP* 45.108–10.
————. 1959. *The "Odyssey" of Homer.* London: Macmillan.
Steinkopf, Gerhard. 1937. "Untersuchungen zur Geschichte des Ruhmes bei den Griechen." Inaugural dissertation, Martin Luther Universität, Halle.
Steinrück, Martin. 1994. "Die Fremde Stimme: der Erzähler und das Schweigen der Frauen im 11 Buch der *Odyssee*." *Kleos* 1.83–128.
————. "La pierre et la graisse." Forthcoming.
Stewart, Douglas J. 1976. *The Disguised Guest: Rank, Role, and Identity in the "Odyssey."* Lewisburg: Bucknell University Press; London: Associated University Press.
Sulzberger, M. 1926. "ONOMA E ONYMA." *Revue des études grecques.* 39.381–447.
Svenbro, Jesper. 1976. "La parole et le marbre: Aux origines de la poétique grecque." Ph. D. diss., Lund University.
————. 1992. *La parole et le marbre: Aux origines de la poétique grecque.* Lund: Studentlitteratur.
Taplin, Oliver. 1977. *The Stagecraft of Aeschylus.* Oxford: Clarendon Press.
————. 1992. *Homeric Soundings.* Oxford: Clarendon Press.
Thalmann, W.G. 1988. "Thersites: Comedy Scapegoats, and Heroic Ideology in the *Iliad*." *TAPA* 118.1–28.
Todorov, Tzvetan. 1977. *The Poetics of Prose.* Trans. Richard Howard. Ithaca: Cornell University Press.
Turolla, Enrico. 1949. *Saggio su la poesia di Omero.* Bari: Laterza.
Usener, Knut. 1990. *Beobachtungen zum Verhältnis der Odyssee zur Ilias.* Tübingen: Narr.
Valgimigli, M. 1964. "Il canto di Polifemo." In *Poeti e filosofi di Grecia,* vol. 2. Florence: Sansoni.
van Wees, Hans. 1992. *Status Warriors: War, Violence, and Society in Homer and History.* Amsterdam: J. C. Gieben.
Vermeule, E. 1979. *Aspects of Death in Early Greek Art and Poetry.* Berkeley and Los Angeles: University of California Press.

Vernant, J.-P. 1979. *"Panta Kala* d'Homère à Simonide." *Annali della Scuola Normale Superiore di Pisa,* 3d. ser. 3, 9.

———. 1980. "La belle Mort et le cadavre outragé." *Journal de la Psychologie Normale et Pathologique* 77: 209–41.

———. 1990. *Figures, idoles, masques.* Paris: Julliard.

Vidal-Naquet, P. 1984. Preface to Hélène Monascré's *Les Larmes d'Achille.* Paris: Albin Michel.

Vivante, P. 1956. "Sulle designazioni omeriche della realtà psichica." *Archivio Glottologico Italiano* 41.113–38.

von der Mühll, Peter. 1952. *Kritisches Hypomnema zur "Ilias."* Basel: Reinhardt.

von Wilamowitz-Moellendorff, U. 1920. *Die "Ilias" und Homer.* 2d ed. Berlin: Weidmann.

Warden, J. 1971. *"Psuche* in Homeric Death-Descriptions." *Phoenix* 25.95–103.

West, L. M. 1966. *Hesiod. Theogony.* Oxford: Clarendon Press.

———. 1978. *Hesiod. Works and Days.* Edited with Prolegomena and Commentary. Oxford: Clarendon Press.

Whitman, C. 1958. *Homer and the Heroic Tradition.* Cambridge: Harvard University Press.

Willcock, M. M. 1976. *A Companion to the "Iliad."* Chicago: Chicago University Press.

Wofford, Susanne Lindgren. 1992. *The Choice of Achilles. The Ideology of Figure in the Epic.* Stanford: Stanford University Press.

Wolff, C. 1979. "A Note on Lions and Sophocles' Philoctetes." In *Arktouros.* Berlin and New York: W. de Gruyter.

Wyatt, F. 1989. "The Intermezzo of *Odyssey* 11, and the Poets Homer and Odysseus." *SMEA* 27.235–53.

Zanker, G. 1994. *The Heart of Achilles.* Ann Arbor: University of Michigan Press.

Zumthor, P. 1983. *Introduction à la poesie orale.* Paris: Seuil.

Index

Achilles: and Agamemnon 2, 163–71, 180–214; and Athena 71–76, 82–95; and Briseis 97–112; and Odysseus 3, 12–19, 168–171; and Patroclus 17; 97–111, 220–21; and Thetis 199–203; short life of 49n2, 102, 180, 201–203; voice of 98–99, 182–193; heart 203, 214–24; heroic death 168–170, 219; marginality 109–112, 184–86, 193–99; perverse *kleos* of 221–24

Acquaro, Giovanna, 85n11, 195n48

Adorno, Theodor W., 127n23

Agamemnon: and Achilles 2, 163–71, 180–214; and Odysseus 53; discourse of 98n4, 188–91; *atê* 186, 201–202; power of 180–90, 205; voice of 187–193

Ainos, 2n2, 131–4

Alcinous, 114, 122–25, 137–38, 173

Allusion, 19–29, 84–85, 96, 134; referentiality of 16–17

Ameis, Karl, 7n10, 25n26, 71n4, 86n14, 122n13, 188n27, 209n84

Antisthenes, 25

Aristides, 31

Athena, 17, 24, 71–76, 82–95

Auerbach, Erich, 148–49

Austin, Norman, 12n9, 22, 204n66

Autoaffection, 45, 62–63, 67

Bader, F., 226n115

Barmeyer, Eike, 31n3, 33–34

Barrett, W. S., 82n4

Barthes, Roland, 85n8

Bataille, George, 60n35

Beck, Götz, 160n68

Behr, C. A., 31n3

Bekker, Immanuel, 11, 14n10, 28

Di Benedetto, V., 223n110

Benveniste, E., 45n21, 61, 188n29, 206n71, 206n73, 208n82

Bergren, Ann, 29, 48n24, 147

Besslich, Siegfried, 116, 117n7

Blanchot, M., 175n103

Blössner, Norbert, 219n104

Brandestein, W., 8n13

Burkert, W., 115n2, 120n12, 125n17, 126n21, 164n79, 221n108

Buschor, Ernst, 6

Calame, Claude, 115n1, 116, 119n9, 135

Calypso, 88, 140, 145, 161

Canfora, Luciano, 36n10

Carlier, P., 52n7, 56n22

Cauer, Paul, 25n26, 71n4
Chantraine, Pierre, 8n13, 25, 59n30, 62n42, 74n9, 99, 118, 128n25, 131n1, 206n71
Chiarini, G., 150
Cicones, 150–154
Circe, 6–8, 35n7, 143–45, 159–163
Clay, J. S., 12, 19n19, 37n12, 39n14, 86n14, 122n13, 123n15, 137n13
Codino, Fausto, 12n2, 12n3, 53n9, 86n15, 100n7, 228n119
Collins, Leslie, 181n8, 190n35, 208n79
Cook, E., 123n14
Crane, Gregory, 160n68, 163n74
Crotty, Kevin, 144n25, 148n30
Culler, Jonathan, 85n8
Cyclopes, 113–22, 125–30, 143–45

Death: see Life and Death
Decleva Caizzi, F., 25n26
de Jong, I. J. F., 97, 202
De Man, Paul, 63n46, 66n53, 119, 122, 135n8
Demodocus, 5, 7, 135, 168, 171–72
Derrida, J., 20, 27, 34, 41, 45, 59n31, 61n36, 62n43, 227
Detienne, Marcel, 40n17, 82n2, 141n22
Diano, Carlo, 6n8
Dimock, G. E., 128n25
Dodds, E. R., 77, 78n19, 155n51
Drews, R., 51n7
Ducrot, O., 85n8
Durante, M., 8n13, 37n11, 53n10

Easterling, P., 204n66
Ecker, Ute, 106n18
Edmunds, Lowell, 82n4, 151n37
Edwards, A., 54n14, 163n74, 166n88, 214n94
Edwards, M., 72, 195n46
Eisenberger, H., 115n1, 116n5, 117n8, 120n11, 125n19, 127n23
Epictetus, 50n4
Epiphany, 69–80, 81–96, 194
Erbse, H., 86n13
Ernout, A., 45
Ethics: atasthaliai 150–154; human responsibility 19n19

Eukhos, 60–62
Eustathius, 22n21

Fernandez-Galiano, M., 86n13
Finley, Moses, 19n20, 23n24, 25
Finsler, G., 56, 207n74
Focke, F., 115n1 and n2
Foley, Helene, 6n8, 22, 166n88
Ford, Andrew, 137n13, 199n57, 219n104
Formulaic Diction, 4–5, 13, 14–15, 17–18, 87–90, 200; and repetition 16, 20–29, 93n29, 100–112, 192
Frederick, R., 51n7
Frisk, Hjalmar, 8n13, 128n25
Führer, R., 206n71

Germain, G., 133, 159n61, 160n68
Gernet, Louis, 204n66
Gifts, 115, 117–18, 145–47
Gladstone, W. E., 50n4, 56n21
Glôssa, 2–3
Gnoli, G., 49n1, 79n20
Goats' Island, 154–59
Gods: divine banquets 35–36; divine interventions 71, 76, 82–95, 194–199
Goldhill, Simon,134n6, 137n12, 175n104, 214n94, 223n111
Gourbeilloun, A., 51n7
Grammar, 3, 4
Gresseth, G. K., 8n13
Griffin, Jasper, 50n5 and n6, 53n9, 56, 60n33 and n34, 67n55, 184n16, 185n20, 223n111
Güntert, Hermann, 39n14

Hades, 24, 163
Hadinos: of the Sirens 6n9; of Achilles 98–99
Hainsworth, Bryan, 180n5, 191n39, 210n85
Hauser, G. Herzog, 85n9
Heart: êtôr 203, 216, 225; heart and belly 54; kradiê 203, 216; powerhouse of Homeric psychology 106, 214–24; thumos 52, 105, 203, 216–17, 225
Heidegger, M., 78n18

Hentze, Carl, 7n10, 25n26, 71n4, 86n14, 122n13, 188n27, 209n84
Hermes, 27; *polutropos* 159n62
Heroic Race: see Heroic Tradition
Heroic Tradition: end of 142, 165–66, 171–75. See also *kleos*
Hesiod, 36, 75
Hesychius, 8n13
Heubeck, A., 132n2, 145, 152n42, 155n48, 156n53, 157n56, 158n59, 160n68, 162n71 and n73, 169n90
Hoekstra, A., 13n7, 133
Hogan, J., 51n6
Horkheimer, Max, 127n23
Homer: literary character of the *Iliad* and *Odyssey* 39; poetic voice 43–48
Hospitality, 114–18, 121, 123, 126, 145–47
Human Responsibility: see Ethics
Humbach, H., 26
Humnos, humnein: see Music
Hyperbole, 44, 47, 136–37

Iliad: Iliadic *kleos* 224–230; Iliadic themes 5, 9, 12, 17, 49, 87–90; intertextual relationship with the *Odyssey* 4–6, 11–13, 15–17, 84, 89–96, 134, 168; poetics 78–79, 84; writing and orality 63–68
Intentionality, 21–22
Intertextuality, 4–5, 13, 14, 81–96, 134
Iteration, 16
Iterability, 20–21, 23–24

Jacoby, F., 93n30
Jaeger, Werner, 19n20
Jahn, T., 216n98
Janko, Richard, 188n27, 191n39, 193n44, 195n47
Jörgensen, Ove, 149

Kahn, L., 26n29
Kakrides, J. Th., 221n107
Katz, Marilyn A., 165n81
Kennedy, George, 195n46
King: portrait of 51–54, 57–59, 63–68; privileges of 51, 56, 179, 181n8, 207

Kirk, G. S., 92, 94n32, 116, 117n8, 120n10, 136n11, 188n26, 190n35, 204n68, 224n112
Kleos (glory), 5, 6, 28, 34, 36–42, 45–48, 51, 166–68, 179–230; and the portrait of a king 52–60, 63–68, 181n8; *aphthiton* (imperishable) *kleos* 37, 49, 65, 208–214; consolation for heroic death 49–50, 170–71, 175
Krapp, H., 98n3
Kristeva, Julia, 85n8
Kudos, 203–207

Lacoue-Labarthe, Philippe, 42n18, 199
Laestrygonians, 153, 157
Lamentation, 97–112; *thrênos* and *kleos* 35
Latacz, J., 55n19, 184
Latte, K., 8n13
Leaf, Walter, 14n9, 18n16, 50n4, 98, 187n24, 188n26, 191n39
Lesky, Albin, 19n20, 150n34, 200n59
Leumann, M., 85n9
Life and Death: existential terms of the epic 15, 59–61, 64–65
Logos, 34–35; and *muthos* 42–43, 62
Lohmann, Dieter, 97, 102
Loraux, N., 49n1, 64n51, 74n11, 79n20, 93n30, 104n14
Lord, Albert B., 47
Lowenstam, Steven, 182n10
Luther, W., 36n10
Lynn-George, Michael, 204n66

MacLachlan, B., 137n14, 180n3
Maehler, H., 19n20
Marcus, S. M., 15n11
Marg, W., 173n102
Marin, L., 54n13, 64n49
Marót, K., 8n13
Martin, Richard P., 171n96, 181n6, 185n20, 188n26
Marzullo, Benedetto, 12n5, 46n22, 91n27, 163n74
Mattes, W., 22
Mawet, F., 152n43
McCary, W. Thomas, 60n32, 78n19

Meillet, A., 45
Meschonnic, H., 99
Metaphor, 70, 119, 121–22, 124–25, 220
Metonymy, 70, 118–19, 121, 125
Meuli, Karl, 2n2, 132n2
Mnêmê: and hypomnêsis 40-41. See also Muses: memory of
Monsacré, H., 79n20, 200, 201n61
Most, Glenn, 142n23, 145
Muellner, L., 62n42
Muses: historical interpretation of 47n23; memory of 40–45; Pindar's myth of 31–34, 46; song of 6–9, 33-40, 46–48, 67, 143–145. See also Sirens
Muthos: see Logos
Music, 34–35

Naas, Michael, 183, 184n14, 197n52
Nagler, Michael N., 17, 151n37, 221n108
Nagy, Gregory, 5n7, 14n9, 19n20, 28, 52n8, 92, 105n17, 111, 131n1, 132n2, 136n11, 137n14, 140, 166n88, 167, 173n101, 181, 204n68, 208n80, 210n86-87, 211n88, 214n94, 219n105, 222, 224
Nancy, J. L., 199, 214
Nausicaa, 145–47
Nestor, 151–52, 204–205
Nietzsche, F., 179
Nitzsch, G. W., 144n24

Odysseus: and Achilles 3, 12–19, 168–71; and Agamemnon 53, 164–68; and Athena 69–70, 82–95; anonymity of 22, 126–29; as a literary character 5–9; as a survivor 17–18, 142; doloi/tricks 24–25, 135–36; etymology of 14n9, 128–29; homo faber 120, 125–26, 155–59; name 126–29, 136; narrator/I-narrative 113–130, 131–177; polu-epithets 23–25; poluainos 2 and n2, 131–2; polutropos 11, 18–19, 23–29, 163; ptoliporthos 140; puns 26–

27; rhetoric 93n30, 152, 156–59, 192n41
Odyssey: intertextual relationship with the Iliad 4–6, 11–13, 15–17, 84, 89–96, 134, 168; mêtis 89-91; Odyssean themes 12, 17, 88; poetics 6, 8–9, 12, 82, 84, 133, 140–42; proem 11–29; subjectivity 12n5; thelgein and enchantment in 8, 138, 141, 175–77; writing and orality 5, 68
Orality: see Writing
Otto, W. F., 31n3, 33
Oksenberg Rorty, A., 217n100

Page, Denys, 120n12, 125n18
Pagliaro, Antonino, 12, 19n20
Paioni, Pino, 47n23
Papadopoulou-Belmehdi, Ioanna, 160n64 and n69, 166n88, 214n94
Parry, Adam, 210n85
Pasquali, Giorgio, 12n2, 19n20
Pazdernick, Ch. F., 136n10, 151n36 and n37, 218n102
Pedrick, Victoria, 138n17, 141n22, 144n25
Pelliccia, Hayden, 216n98
Peradotto, John, 128n25, 135n9, 163n74
Pfister, Frederick, 81n1, 83n6
Phaeacians, 113–115, 122–25, 134, 136, 145–47
Phemius, 168, 171–72, 175
Pisani, V., 8n13
Plato, 32, 56n22, 222–23
Pleasure: and the Odyssey's poetics 45, 141; of the Sirens 7
Podlecki, A., 115n1
Poetic Voice: see Homer: poetic voice, Iliad: poetics and Odyssey: poetics
Polyphemus, 6, 114–22, 125–29
Polysemy, 38
Polytropy, 23–29, 159n62, 163
Postlethwaite, N., 170n95, 208n80
Psykhê, 14–15
Pucci, Pietro, 2n2, 26n29, 36, 54n14 and n16, 66n54, 70n2, 82n2 and n4, 85n8, 90n25, 93n29, 101n10, 132n2, 135n9, 138n15,

140, 141n22, 144n25, 148n29, 168n89, 185, 214n94, 219n104, 225n113, 226n114 and n15
Puns, 26–27

Race, W. H., 154n47
Ramersdorfer, Hans, 94–95, 96n34, 152n42, 185n18 and n20
Reading Scenes, 134–35, 146–47, 176–77
Recognition Scenes, 73–74, 143–45
Redfield, J., 77n17, 185n21, 205
Reece, Steven, 120n12, 154n47
Reinhardt, Karl, 73n8, 82n2, 84, 92, 142, 154n47, 163n74 and n75, 188n27, 221n109
Renehan, R., 219
Repetition, 41, 45–48, 106–112, 188. See also Formulaic Diction
Reucher, Theo., 171n96
Rhetoric: Existential 61–62, 199–203. See also Allusion, Hyperbole, Intertextuality, Metaphor, Metonymy, Repetition, Simile
Richardson, S., 135n7, 154n46, 209n84
Ricoeur, Paul, 138n18
Risch, Ernst, 4n4, 26, 54n17
Rousseau, J.-J., 122
Rousseau, Philippe, 156n55, 207n77, 213n93
Ruijgh, C. J., 7n10, 204n68
Russo, Carlo Ferdinando, 63n45
Russo, Joseph, 128n25
Rüter, Klaus, 11n1, 12n2, 19n19, 19n20, 22, 135n9, 163n74

Sarpedon, 49–53, 55–62, 65–68; heroic death of 60–62, 229
Schein, Seth, 116n6, 120n12, 125n18, 126n22, 128n25, 185n20
Schmiel, R., 169n94
Schmitt, Arbogast, 190n35, 196n51, 199n57, 216n98
Schwabl, H., 19n20, 83n5
Segal, Charles, 6n9, 24n25, 120n12, 135n9, 136n11, 140n19, 160n67 and n69, 166n88, 176n105, 187n25, 214n94

Severyn, A., 86n14
Simile, 52, 119–20
Sirens: as Muses of Hades 6–7, 9; diction 2–9, 175–77; etymology 8; song of 1–9, 132, 175–77
Slatkin, L. M., 194n45, 213n92
Snell, Bruno, 31n3, 32n5, 77–78
Solmsen, F., 8n13
Stanford, W. B., 23n24, 25n26, 26, 122n13, 133, 158n59
Steinkopf, Gerhard, 206n71, 207, 209n83, 209n84, 210
Steinrück, M., 152n40, 163n74
Stewart, D. J., 12n5, 22, 142n23, 145
Stoma, 2–3
Subjectivity, 12, 44, 186–87
Sulzberger, M., 55n18
Supplementarity, 27, 34, 65–66
Svenbro, Jesper, 47n23, 199n57

Taplin, Oliver, 82n4, 188n26, 195n50
Terpsis: See Pleasure
Text: orality and writing 63–65, 109, 226n115; reading of itself 66–68
Thalmann, W.G., 191n37, 207n76
Theology: Homeric 31–36, 49, 65–66, 69–71, 76–80, 123; of the *Iliad* 19–20, 81–82, 198–99; of the *Odyssey* 17–19, 82, 153–54; theory of double motivation 150n34
Thrênos: see Lament
Thumos: see Heart
Timê (honor) 56–61, 77, 169, 179–230
Todorov, Tzvetan, 134n6
Tropos, 25–29
Turolla, Enrico, 219n104

Usener, Knut, 152n43, 155n50

Valgimigli, M., 119n9, 125n17 and n20
van Wees, Hans, 179n1, 181n8
Vermeule, E., 15n11
Vernant, J.-P., 49n1, 79n20, 82n2, 104n14
Vidal-Naquet, P., 49n1, 79n20
Vivante, P., 15n11

Voice: See Achilles, Homer
von der Mühll, Peter, 71n5, 85n10,
    94
von Wilamowitz-Moellendorf,
    Ulrich, 12

Warden, J., 15n11
West, M. L., 75n13, 210n87
West, Stephanie, 162n73
Whitman, C., 187n23
Wilcock, M. M., 51n6
Wisman, H., 73n8
Wofford, S. L., 216n97
Wolff, C., 51n7
Wood, R., 50n4
Writing, 5
Wyatt, W. F., 146

Zanker, G., 180n4, 181n6, 204n68
Zeus: boulê of 165–66; 171n96,
    172–75. See also Theology
Zumthor, Paul, 99

Ancient Sources

Antisthenes, 25
Apollonius of Rhodes, 98n5
Aristides, 31
Aristophanes, 82n4
Aristotle, 141n22
Artemidorus, 73n7

Choricus of Gaza, 31
Cypria, 197

Diogenes Laertius 82n4

Epictetus, 51
Euripides, 73n7, 156n51, 224
Eustathius, 12, 22n21

Heraclitus 208
Herodotus: 4.201, 26n28
Hesiod: Fr. 165.5 (MW), 71n4; Fr.
    204.96ff (MW), 171n96;
    Theogony: 22ff., 75; 27, 7;
    28, 7, 225; 31f., 37n12, 40;
    44, 37n12; 91, 64n48; 97ff., 6;
    98ff., 225; 272, 155n49; 406,
    103n12;

Works and Days: 1, 37n12;
    67, 26n29; 78, 26n29; 268,
    225; 358, 13n7; 416, 74
Homer:
—Iliad: I.2, 13; 3, 13, 15n12; 5,
    19, 166; 34ff., 199; 122, 208;
    135f., 186; 149ff., 53n10,
    182, 183; 156f., 184; 160,
    74n10; 161ff., 185; 164, 18;
    174f., 182; 185ff., 187;
    188ff., 76, 83, 85n11, 94n31,
    190, 194; 189ff., 71; 194, 92;
    194ff., 69, 72, 194; 195ff.,
    71, 76, 85; 197, 72; 198, 71,
    72, 73; 199ff., 69, 74; 200,
    74n11; 203ff., 195; 207, 196;
    208ff., 75; 218, 77; 249, 2;
    266, 17n15; 274ff., 204; 281,
    182; 287ff., 190n35; 345, 100;
    348ff., 199; 350, 200; 352ff.,
    187, 201; 365ff., 202, 203;
    396ff., 199; 417, 102; 479,
    149n31; 601ff., 35
    II.2ff., 76; 5, 76; 75, 90;
    80ff., 191; 111ff., 98n4; 133,
    18; 139ff., 98n4; 155ff., 85;
    165ff., 69, 71n5; 166ff., 86,
    87; 167, 89; 169, 89; 172,
    88n19; 173ff., 92; 182, 76n15,
    86; 182ff., 94, 95, 134; 183,
    71n5, 95, 96; 203ff., 190n36;
    250, 2, 43n19; 273ff., 91n26;
    278ff., 93n30; 404, 89;
    484ff, 6, 7, 22, 36, 37, 43, 44,
    46n22, 67, 224; 486, 6n9,
    37n12, 44; 488ff., 43, 45;
    489f., 2, 225; 492, 38; 576ff.,
    205n69; 595, 226; 636, 89,
    155n50; 667, 13n8; 721, 13n8;
    846f., 150n32
    III.66, 7; 165, 107; 129ff.,
    194; 132, 107; 214, 131n1;
    380ff., 71n4, 81n1; 398ff.,
    73n7
    IV.73ff., 70n1; 74, 87, 89;
    92, 88n19; 331, 4n5; 338ff.,
    53, 55n20; 341f., 55n20;
    350ff., 54; 353ff, 26; 354,
    55n19; 378, 17n15,
    18n17; 409, 19n19

V.3, 40n16; **23ff**., 81n1; **78**,
64n48; **127ff**., 83n7; **288f**.,
105n15; **442**, 155n49; **595**,
72n6; **654**, 62n40; **676**,
138n16; **668ff**., 198n66;
733ff., 74, 75; **792f**., 40n16;
864ff., 71n4; **874**, 3
VI.145ff., 39; **441ff**., 215;
446, 51n7
VII.19, 89; **20**, 17n15; **47**,
89; **53**, 2; **81ff**., 61; **100**,
62n41; **200ff**., 62n40; **203**, 61;
451ff., 211; **458ff**., 211
VIII.191, 136n12; **237f**.,
208; **471**, 152; **516**, 107
IX.10ff., 98n4; **18ff**., 98n4;
26ff., 98n4; **33**, 188; **100**,
188; **155**, 64n48; **189**, 37;
198, 37n12; **240**, 109; **297**,
64n48; **302**, 64n48; **318ff**.,
179; **321**, 13, 14, 15, 16; **322**,
14, 15; **323**, 220; **410ff**., 49n2,
212, 222; **413**, 37, 212n90,
219; **466ff**., 152; **630**, 74n10;
673, 2; **704**, 192; **X.9f**., 200;
33, 64n48; **49f**., 64n48;
382ff., 26n28; **503ff**., 76n16,
86n15, 198n66; **507f**., 87, 88;
512, 76n15, 86n12; **544**, 2
XI.58, 64n48; **137**, 2, 89;
195ff., 86n15; **200**, 89; **210**,
94n31; **290**, 62n40; **317**,
93n30; **404ff**., 49n2; **410**,
61n39; **430**, 2, 131, 136; **445**,
62n40; **466**, 203; **471**, 109;
473, 91n27; **550**, 15n12; **596**,
599, 221n108; 53n11; **608**, 99,
108; **670ff**., 152; **762ff**., 221
XII.34, 73; **35**, 53n11; **75**,
192; **238**, 74n10; **299ff**., 51,
61n39; **300**, 52; **301**, 52; **306**,
52, 61n39; **307ff**., 52; **309**, 51;
310ff., 50, 51, 53, 55, 55n19,
78, 207; **311**, 52; **312**, 64n48;
313, 66; **315**, 57; **315ff**, 52,
53n11, 55n20; **317**, 57n23;
318, 62n41; **318ff**., 57, 66;
319f., 58n27; **321**, 52; **322ff**.,
51, 58, 59, 64, 67; **324**, 52;
325, 61; **327**, 61; **328**, 60, 61,
62; **407**, 111; **445ff**., 120

XIII.60ff., 83n7; **71f**., 70n1;
218, 64n48; **330**, 53n11; **355**,
3; **458**, 76, 87; **668**, 53n11;
670, 13; **768**, 88n19; **813**, 111
XIV.56ff., 43n19; **83**, 26,
192; **85ff**., 165; **91**, 2, 43n19;
102, 100n8; **161**, 76; **205**,
64n48; **230**, 103n12; **258f**.,
64n48; **466**, 203
XV.39, 4; **41**, 3; **59ff**., 194;
71, 174; **173**, 88n19; **236ff**.,
83n7, 86n15; **243ff**., 71n4;
245ff., 94n31; **247**, 83n7;
254ff., 83n7; **288**, 111; **462**,
62n40; **468**, 149n31; **473**,
149n31; **489**, 149n31; **607f**.,
74n11; **694f**., 72
XVI.5, 221n108; **7ff**., 221;
11, 110; **55**, 13, 16; **65**, 62n40;
97ff., 17, 18n16; **99**, 18n16;
100, 18; **434**, 64n48; **461**,
210; **481**, 99; **605**, 64n48;
652, 76; **725**, 62n40; **788ff**.,
81n1; **791**, 72
XVII.12, 100n8; **73**, 150n32;
253, 53n11; **333f**., 71n4,
86n15; **546**, 138n16; **690**, 109
XVIII.37, 98; **61ff**., 14n9;
70, 217; **71**, 98; **78**, 217; **90**,
214; **90ff**., 216, 228; **95**, 102;
98ff., 78; **120ff**., 219, 221;
123ff., 223; **165ff**., 71n4, 83;
181ff., 94n31; **316**, 99n6;
366, 6n9; **396**, 3; **397**, 13;
458, 102; **533f**., 153
XIX.9, 3; **16f**., 74n11; **219**,
3; **250**, 137n13; **279**, 103n11;
282ff., 97; **283**, 99, 101; **284**,
98; **287ff**., 99; **288ff**., 100,
103; **289**, 102, 103; **290ff**.,
101, 109; **291**, 102; **293**, 102;
295ff., 102, 103; **297**, 102,
103n11; **299**, 103; **300**, 100,
103; **301ff**., 104; **303ff**., 104,
105n17; **306f**., 106; **308**,
93n30; **312f**., 105; **314**, 98;
315ff., 105, 107; **319**, 109;
319ff., 105n17, 106, 111n20;
320, 109; **321ff**., 109, 110;
322, 111; **324f**., 108; **328ff**.,

102, 106, 110; **338f.**, 104, 111; **409**, 101
XX.78, 105; **83ff.**, 58n28; **131**, 70, 71n4; **203ff.**, 39; **204**, 37n12, 63n47; **213f.**, 39; **318ff.**, 81n1; **359**, 105n16; **375ff.**, 86n15; **380**, 86n12; **502**, 208
XXI.70, 105n15; **98**, 2; **100**, 101n10; **106ff.**, 49n2, 61; **108**, 17n15; **118**, 208; **168**, 105n15; **173**, 160n63; **221**, 100n8; **297**, 62n40; **440**, 3
XXII.7ff., 71n4, 73n7, 83n5, 86n15; **98ff.**, 78; **99ff.**, 58n28; **187**, 89; **188**, 102; **202**, 101n10; **214ff.**, 71n4, 75, 94n31; **224ff.**, 94n31; **267**, 105; **304f.**, 62n41, 212; **346f.**, 105; **394**, 64n48, 209; **407ff.**, 98; **428**, 108; **430**, 6n9, 99n17; **433ff.**, 64n50, 206; **447**, 98; **485**, 108; **487**, 107
XXIII.17, 99n6; **225**, 99n6; **312**, 3n3
XXIV.7, 13, 14n9; **8**, 14n9; **43**, 52n8; **110f.**, 209; **121**, 89; **123**, 99n6; **169ff.**, 71n4, 83n7; **200**, 98; **525**, 164; **545**, 200; **703**, 98; **720**, 220; **725ff.**, 104; **727**, 108; **773**, 103n12
—*Odyssey*: **i.1**, 13, 22, 44n20, 46n22, 144; **2**, 16, 18; **3**, 13; **4–5**, 13, 14, 15, 16n13; **4**, 13; **5**, 14, 15, 16n13; **6ff.**, 143; **7ff**, 19; **10**, 138; **11**, 138n17; **11f.**, 141; **62**, 129; **68f.**, 143; **102ff.**, 88n22, 89; **241**, 62n41; **283**, 37n12; **298**, 37n12; **325ff.**, 66, 175; **326ff.**, 168, 171; **337**, 7n12, 45; **338f.**, 37n12; **351f.**, 175
ii.19f., 143; **217**, 37n12; **237**, 15n12; **346ff.**, 225; **361**, 98
iii.71ff., 117; **73**, 15; **83**, 37n12; **147**, 138n16; **218ff.**, 71n4
iv.259, 98; **260**, 138n16; **352**, 158; **358f.**, 158; **363**,

158; **510**, 200; **716**, 162; **721**, 6n9
v.13, 13n8; **36**, 64n48; **149ff.**, 87, 88; **203ff.**, 92; **306f.**, 184; **328ff.**, 83; **360**, 76; **423**, 54n17, 128
vi.2ff., 145; **120f.**, 114; **145**, 76
vii.15, 138; **19ff.**, 83; **32f.**, 122, 123; **71**, 64n48; **199ff.**, 123; **200ff.**, 123; **201**, 71n4; **201ff.**, 123; **208ff.**, 124; **214**, 3; **215ff.**, 54n15, 125
viii.63, 6; **73ff.**, 6, 37n12, 44n20; **74**, 136n11; **81f.**, 172; **99**, 35; **173**, 64n48; **193ff.**, 83, 93n30; **378**, 3; **461f.**, 146; **481**, 44n20; **488–91**, 6; **499ff.**, 5; **521ff.**, 5, 139, 140; **527**, 98; **537ff.**, 137; **557ff.**, 123; **575f.**, 114; **577ff.**, 173
ix.2ff., 137; **5**, 137; **11**, 137; **12ff.**, 138; **14**, 139; **19f.**, 24, 54, 135; **36**, 135; **37f.**, 139, 150; **39ff.**, 150, 151; **41f.**, 147; **43**, 152; **44**, 147; **45f.**, 152; **53**, 13n6, 147; **54f.**, 153; **116ff.**, 154; **118**, 158; **119ff.**, 155; **122f.**, 156; **125ff.**, 120, 155; **131ff.**, 155; **142ff.**, 156; **154ff.**, 156, 157; **165**, 18n18; **174f.**, 114; **187**, 120; **190ff.**, 117; **215**, 121; **224ff.**, 154; **240ff.**, 121; **252ff.**, 117; **254**, 15; **263ff.**, 17; **264**, 214; **273ff.**, 117, 127n24; **278**, 121; **279f.**, 127n24; **288ff.**, 119; **370**, 118; **383**, 120; **405f.**, 126; **410**, 26, 126; **413f.**, 126, 142; **415**, 26; **494**, 120; **507ff.**, 143, 145; **513ff.**, 127; **534f.**, 154n45
x.14f., 139; **40ff.**, 147; **53f.**, 148; **87ff.**, 153; **99**, 158; **135ff.**, 156n52; **141**, 157; **149f.**, 158; **155ff.**, 157; **198ff.**, 154; **210ff.**, 159; **213**, 8; **221**, 35n7; **234f.**, 161; **237**, 161; **241ff.**, 159; **254**, 98n3; **257**, 153n44; **281f.**, 153n44; **291**, 8; **294**, 160n63; **308**,

122; **317**, 122; **318ff.**, 8, 159, 160; **325ff.**, 143; **326**, 8, 160; **330**, 23, 27; **360ff.**, 162; **410ff.**, 162; **437**, 19n19; **457**, 13n6; **466ff.**, 163
xi.214, 139; **333f.**, 7n12, 138, 143; **353ff.**, 125; **355ff.**, 115; **360ff.**, 162; **363ff.**, 143; **369**, 139; **390ff.**, 164; **435ff.**, 174; **436ff.**, 165; **475ff.**, 170; **481ff.**, 169; **538ff.**, 169; **558ff.**, 165
xii.39ff., 7, 8n13; **52**, 2; **87**, 43n19; **158ff.**, 7, 8n13; **160**, 2; **169**, 157; **181ff.**, 8n13; **184ff.**, 1, 132, 175; **185**, 4; **186**, 4; **188**, 2; **189ff.**, 36; **189**, 7; **191**, 7; **397f.**, 148
xiii.2, 7n12; **90**, 13, 14n9; **201ff.**, 114; **221ff.**, 70, 71n4; **254f.**, 134n6; **267**, 13; **287ff.**, 54; **288f.**, 69, 70; **289**, 82; **291ff.**, 24, 25; **296ff.**, 90; **313**, 124; **388**, 17, 18, 19; **418**, 13n8
xiv.32, 13n6; **131f.**, 157; **371**, 62n41; **462ff.**, 133; **499ff.**, 94; **508f.**, 132
xv.1ff., 87, 88; **487**, 13
xvi.157, 82; **159**, 71n4; **161**, 71n4; **195**, 139; **241**, 37n12; **455ff.**, 86n16; **461**, 37
xvii.13, 13n8; **119**, 3; **126**, 37n12; **272**, 35; **284ff.**, 54n15; **360ff.**, 71n4, 86n16; **514ff.**, 45; **518ff.**, 7n12, 138n15; **519**, 45
xviii.69f., 86n16; **137**, 7; **379**, 55n19
xix.37ff., 71n4; **174f.**, 155; **203**, 134n6; **280**, 64n48; **364ff.**, 26n28; **365**, 4n5; **406**, 26n28; **406ff.**, 55n18, 128; **479**, 138n16; **516**, 99; **521**, 25; **541**, 98
xx.18ff., 126, 143; **30ff.**, 71n4
xxi.338, 122
xxii.7, 122; **55**, 73; **297**, 75n12, 86n16; **317**, 19n19; **401**, 91n27; **416**, 19n19

xxiii.45, 91n27; **67**, 19n19; **248ff.**, 143; **306ff.**, 143; **326**, 6n9, 7; **339**, 64n48
xxiv.60ff, 6, 35n7, 220; **93**, 28, 175; **191ff.**, 166; **266ff.**, 134; **282**, 19n19; **295**, 98; **317**, 6n9, 99n6; **368ff.**, 86n16; **448**, 71n4; **488**, 89; **528ff.**, 86; **535**, 86n13
—*Homeric Hymns: to Demeter* [2]: **75ff.**, 82n4; **275ff.**, 70, 71n4; *to Apollo* [3]: **519**, 7; *to Hermes* [4]: **13**, 23, 26n29; **277**, 37n12; **439**, 23, 26n29; *to Aphrodite* [5]: **81ff.**, 71n4, 82n4; **170ff.**, 70, 71n4, 82n4; *Hymn 7*: 2, 71n4; *Hymn 24*: **1f.**, 155n49; *Hymn 33*: **12**, 71n4

Ibykos, 37n12

Pindar: *Hymn to Zeus*, 31; *Nemean 8*, 209n84
Plato: *Apology*: **28c**, 223; *Hippias minor*: **365a–c**, 25; *Symposium*: **177c**, 32; **177e**, 32; **179d–e**, 223; **198d–199a**, 32; **208d**, 223

Sappho, 107
Sophocles, 209n84

Thucydides: **3.34.3**, 26n28

Virgil, 49

M